Integrating Reading and the Other Language Arts

Integrating Reading and the Other Language Arts

FOUNDATIONS OF A WHOLE LANGUAGE CURRICULUM

Carole F. Stice
Tennessee State University

John E. Bertrand
Tennessee State University

Nancy P. Bertrand
*Middle Tennessee
State University*

 WADSWORTH PUBLISHING COMPANY
I(T)P An International Thomson Publishing Company

Belmont Albany Bonn Boston Cincinnati Detroit London Madrid Melbourne
Mexico City New York Paris San Francisco Singapore Tokyo Toronto Washington

EDUCATION EDITOR:
Sabra Horne

EDITORIAL ASSISTANT:
Kate Peltier

PRODUCTION EDITOR:
Zipporah W. Collins

PRINT BUYER:
Randy Hurst

PERMISSIONS EDITOR:
Jeanne Bosschart

DESIGNER:
Zipporah W. Collins

COPY EDITOR:
Carolyn McGovern

PHOTOGRAPHER:
Jane Scherr

ILLUSTRATOR:
Teresa Roberts

COVER DESIGNER:
Ross Carron

COVER ILLUSTRATOR:
Jesse Reisch

COMPOSITOR:
Stanton Publication Services

PRINTER:
Fairfield Graphics

Printed in the United States of America
1 2 3 4 5 6 7 8 9 10—01 00 99 98 97 96 95

For more information, contact:
Wadsworth Publishing Company
10 Davis Drive
Belmont, California 94002
USA

International Thomson Editores
Campos Eliseos 385, Piso 7
Col. Polanco
11560 México D.F. México

International Thomson Publishing Europe
Berkshire House 168-173
High Holborn
London, WC1V7AA
England

International Thomson Publishing GmbH
Königswinterer Strasse 418
53227 Bonn
Germany

Thomas Nelson Australia
102 Dodds Street
South Melbourne 3205
Victoria, Australia

International Thomson Publishing Asia
221 Henderson Road
#05-10 Henderson Building
Singapore 0315

Nelson Canada
1120 Birchmount Road
Scarborough, Ontario
Canada M1K 5G4

International Thomson Publishing Japan
Hirakawacho Kyowa Building, 3F
2-2-1 Hirakawacho
Chiyoda-ku, Tokyo 102
Japan

The photographs on pages 152, 179, 224, 228, 278, 298, 299, 302, 352, 412, 415, 426, 427, and 428 are courtesy of the authors. All other photographs are by Jane Scherr.

Library of Congress Cataloging-in-Publication Data
Stice, Carole F.
  Integrating reading and the other language arts: foundations of a whole language curriculum / Carole F. Stice, John E. Bertrand, Nancy P. Bertrand.
      p.   cm.
    ISBN 0–534–24084–4
    Includes bibliographical references and index.
      1. Language experience approach in education. 2. Language arts (Elementary).
  3. English language—Study and teaching (Elementary). 4. Learning, Psychology
  of. I. Bertrand, John E. II. Bertrand, Nancy Parks. III. Title
  LB1576.S7986   1994
  372.6—dc20   94–18827

*Everything should be made as simple as possible,
but not simpler.*

ALBERT
EINSTEIN

*And the end of all our exploring
Will be to arrive where we started
And know the place for the first time.*

T. S. ELIOT

Contents

PART ONE

Theory and Foundations
COMING TO KNOW

2 *Language* 33

3 *Oral Language Learning* 61

4 *Coming to Believe* 93

PART TWO

Processes and Products

KNOW THE LEARNER, THE APPROACHES, THE RESOURCES

6 *Writing* 189

7 *Speaking and Listening* 255

8   *Bringing It All Together*   294

PART THREE

Content and Curriculum
EXPANDING THEORY INTO PRACTICE ACROSS THE GRADES

Preface

Textbooks are typically 20 percent original, creative thinking, and 80 percent adaptations and syntheses of other people's work. Textbooks are a convenience. They attempt to make sense of complex, sometimes disparate issues and information and also make material on these topics readily available to students. Teaching processes and practices can certainly be complicated and inaccessible. If well done, textbooks on teaching can be extremely useful.

However, one of the dangers involved in reducing any process and its theoretical foundations to a textbook is the creation of dogma. Such "one-right-way-only" perspectives limit thinking and therefore learning. When that happens, continued evolution of the processes and theories a book seeks to encourage is halted. Like that of other whole language educators, our understanding of children's literacy is still growing and changing. This textbook is offered as a foundation upon which to continue building knowledge about learning and good teaching.

This book presents a model of integrated language and literature across the elementary curriculum. It does not attempt to "bridge the gap" between traditional classroom practices and whole language practices. This book takes one perspective, details its theoretical and research base, provides connections to and a framework for instruction, describes the major approaches used in whole language classrooms, presents evaluation procedures, and offers several theoretically sound instructional strategies.

This book is intended for undergraduate and graduate students in reading and language arts, as well as school administrators and anyone else interested in learning about the theory-to-practice base for integrated, language-, literature-, and learner-centered classrooms. It is not intended to replace the wide variety of wonderful books written by classroom teachers and other practitioners about specific whole language beliefs, procedures, classrooms, or schools. Rather, this text is designed to provide a solid theoretical foundation, help learners begin to connect theory to practice, and lay a framework for structuring additional experiences and information.

The book is divided into three major parts. Part I presents the theoretical base. Theory and research from learning, language, and language learning provide the philosophical bases for an integrated, language- and literature-rich classroom—a whole language curriculum. Part I concludes by summarizing the beliefs shared by whole language teachers. Part II explains the reading and writing processes and presents the major approaches for reading and writing instruction. Observation and evaluation procedures are included in each chapter and detailed instruments and techniques are provided. Part II also includes a chapter devoted to developing and evaluating children's oral language in school. Part II concludes with a chapter on how teachers can pull information and theory together and how they can get started with whole language instruction in their own classrooms. Part III provides selected teaching strategies for lower elementary and upper elementary grades. One way teachers come to a more integrated teaching philosophy is by trying strategies and techniques and observing for themselves how they work with students. This part also examines ways of integrating reading, writing, speaking, and listening with other subject areas; applying this instructional philosophy to departmentalized settings; and working with special needs children.

Each chapter begins with focus questions and ends with brief theory-to-practice guides. Every chapter is followed by suggestions for further reading and suggested activities for exploring some of the issues raised. The appendixes contain information on phonics, recommended professional books, recommended children's literature, and directions for bookbinding.

An integrated language- and literature-based philosophy for classroom instruction is new in relation to our understanding of reading and writing. However, its roots are firmly planted in the progressive era in education and research from the last forty years in related fields such as child language development, linguistics, and learning theory.

You may not have experienced whole language as a student or as a teacher. If that is the case, these beliefs will require a change in your understanding of learning, reading, and writing, and indeed in your understanding of what teaching is. This required change, or paradigm shift, may be summarized in the following chart:

Traditional Thinking	Whole Language Philosophy
1. Learning as acquisition text based fact oriented format driven	1. Learning as construction thinking is encouraged meaning is generated concepts are emphasized
2. Language as object skills in isolation work on planned exercises language as hierarchy	2. Language as tool learned in process work on events language as system
3. Learner as passive receiver of facts practicing skills convergent thinking	3. Learner as active creating understandings making connections divergent thinking

4. Teaching as transmitting
lockstep sequence
reconstructs meaning
    according to authority
mediates program
tests learners
	4. Teaching as transacting
	facilitates inquiry
	constructs own meaning
	    according to reason
	observes and responds to
	    learners

5. Reading and writing as product form mechanics neatness	5. Reading and writing as process self-expression meaning sharing

We believe that no one is truly educated who does not read. We believe that the future of the country lies with the nation's teachers and students. If teachers can help create students who define themselves, at least in part, by what they know, we will have done a good job. This textbook presents you, the reader, with a great deal of information. Based on what is known about the human brain and how we learn, we believe teachers can never have enough information—about teaching, about learning, and about kids. We have described these and related beliefs and processes. We offer this text as a starting point, not as the last word.

We hope that, as you read, you will reflect on the information and procedures described herein; that you will apply them, adapt them, and refine them. Your own experiences—especially your observations of children—your informed judgments, new information you acquire as you continue professional reading, the support of other teachers, and your best intentions will converge to make you the kind of teacher you want to be.

> *All kids are whole language learners,*
> *but there are no whole language classrooms*
> *without whole language teachers.*
> GOODMAN (1986, p. 78)

REFERENCE

Goodman, K. (1986). *What's whole in whole language?* Portsmouth, NH: Heinemann.

About the Authors

Carole F. Stice is professor of reading/language arts education at Tennessee State University in Nashville, Tennessee. She has taught elementary, junior high, and high school age students in reading and language arts. She has tutored adult learners and worked with staff development for schools in Georgia, Florida, Mississippi, Kentucky, and Tennessee. For nineteen years, she has taught graduate and undergraduate students in teacher eduction, and she is university sponsor for the local Teachers Applying Whole Language (TAWL) support group for middle Tennessee. Since 1985, she has conducted three research projects on whole language and at-risk children with the Center for Research in Basic Skills at Tennessee State University. She is the author of several articles and chapters in two edited books. She has a Ph.D. from Florida State University and is the mother of one daughter—and a cat. She is lucky enough to have had a grandmother who read to her and taught her to love language and good books.

John E. Bertrand is currently associate professor of educational administration at Tennessee State University in Nashville, Tennessee. A graduate of Ohio State University with a Ph.D. in policy and leadership, he has eleven years' experience as a public school teacher, including three years as director of an alternative program for troubled youth. He has taught grades 3, 4, 6, 7, and 8. His interest in holistic, integrated educational philosophy and teaching began following a short time teaching in a British informal school and attending seminars at Exeter University in Devon. Since then, he has worked as a full-time educational researcher, participating in three research projects on whole language, and has taught one year as a fourth grade teacher of learning disabled children. Author of a number of articles and chapters in the field, he is fascinated with students in learner-centered classrooms. He is married to Nancy Bertrand. They and their child live on a small farm with a number of animals.

Nancy P. Bertrand is professor of elementary and special education at Middle Tennessee State University in Murfreesboro, where she teaches reading and language arts methods courses and is past president of the faculty senate. She has a Ph.D. from Ohio State University in early and middle childhood education and seven years' teaching experience, grades 1–6, in both rural and urban schools. Currently in her eleventh year at MTSU, she is state chair of the whole language committee for the Tennessee Reading Association and chair of Celebrate Literacy, a statewide program that encourages children's writing. She has engaged in teacher development in a number of states in the southeast and is the author of several professional articles. She spends many hours each school year reading aloud to children and showing teachers and young authors how to bind hardback books as one means of promoting the writing process in Tennessee schools.

Theory and Foundations

COMING TO KNOW

1

Learning

What is learning?

How has our understanding of learning changed over this century?

What do we know now about how the brain works and how human beings learn?

What conditions best promote human learning? That is, when is human learning easy and when is it difficult?

Walking down a dirt road alongside a Kansas farm field in late summer, I am assailed by tenderly familiar sights, sounds, and smells that remind me of my childhood, of the summers I spent with my maternal grandmother and our relatives in rural Kansas. When I was grown and all my grandmother's family was gone, I visited the area with a friend who was a naturalist. As we walked along the edge of what was once my great-uncle's farm, my friend pointed out by name plants such as flowering thistles and milkweed. He showed me animals I would never have noticed on my own and told me something about each one. He identified local birds such as the scissortail flycatcher and the western meadowlark. He explained the land formations we were seeing. The whole panorama came alive for me in a new way. I know that part of the country differently now, and my memory of it has greater depth and richness of detail. When I look now, I see more than I ever dreamed was there.

Human beings can only "see" based on what they know, and when they learn something new, both the knower and known are changed forever (Dewey & Bentley, 1949). Human learning is complex and difficult to describe. Yet, except for some aspects of school learning, human beings appear to learn rapidly and easily. When we are interested in something, when we have prior experience, when we believe there is a need to know, we learn with relative ease.

Each of us, at one time or another, probably memorized the names of all the presidents of the United States, in chronological order, so that we could recite them for a grade. How many of us could recite them now? Compare that learning to remembering the lyrics of a favorite song, even one we have not heard in years. While both examples represent rote memorization, which was easier to learn? Which was remembered longer? Why?

Although human learning is complex and invisible and although it occurs inside the mind of the learner, it is not so obscure that we will never understand it. Recent research in cognitive psychology and neurophysiology has yielded greater insights into human learning—that is, into the brain-mind connection. As teachers, we have questions about how the brain works and what learning is. How do people not only survive, but also come to understand the world around them? Can those processes be replicated in school? Can they be enhanced by teachers? If so, how?

In this chapter we will first explore learning in schools and then contrast that experience with learning that occurs outside the classroom. By comparing learning in different situations, we will construct a definition of learning. Second, we will examine how recent findings about the brain have contributed to our understanding of what learning is and how it takes place. Finally, we will discuss specific conditions that facilitate learning. Our goal is to help you, *as learner,* construct and expand your own personal understanding and theory of what learning is and how it happens so that you, *as teacher,* can apply that knowledge in your classroom.

What Learning Is: Two Perspectives

At some point in your education you have probably heard learning defined as "change in behavior." This simple definition for a complex phenomenon is probably too simplistic. In an effort to better understand learning, we decided to ask an expert; we asked a child.

Mother: What is learning?

Jenny: Something you do to find out things. But mostly it's boring. I mean like who wants to learn to subtract a turnip from another turnip? Most kids think that's stupid!

Mother: Have you ever learned anything that wasn't boring?

Jenny: Sure. Water skiing. That wasn't boring. That was fun.

Mother: Why was that different?

Jenny: Easy. Because I had a choice. I could choose whether or not I wanted to ski.

At age ten, this child already distinguishes between learning at school and other kinds of learning. School learning involves different subjects, and it is not always an act of free choice. Jenny's two examples show us what Frank Smith (1990) calls the two theories of learning: the *official* and *unofficial.*

The official theory is the one employed by most schools. It is official because it has been "scientifically proven" in laboratory conditions, for example, the number of repetitions needed for children to learn a list of ten words such as *was, went,* or *for.* Simply put, the official version holds that because learning is difficult, what is being learned must be organized for the learner and accompanied by reward and/or punishment. Since it is difficult, learning requires effort and external motivation. Learning must be constantly controlled and monitored to ensure that it is taking place. However, most "real" learning is not input/output based and is not particularly amenable to the scientific method.

The unofficial theory of learning is the one employed most frequently outside of school. It is unofficial because it has not been "experimentally proven." The unofficial theory states that learning is something we do all the time, especially to find out things we want to know about or do. The unofficial theory holds that learning—for example, the process we go through when learning to ride a bicycle—can be easy. This kind of learning is internally motivated, organized, and monitored. But because it is complex and not directly observable, the natural learning process is difficult to measure. It is especially difficult to measure incrementally, even when we can see it happening.

If, as Smith argues, most people believe that learning takes place when we want to find out things, why then have our schools embraced a theory of learning so contradictory to this innate belief? Is it possible that these totally contradictory theories coexist? In other words, is learning in school supposed to be hard, and therefore different from learning outside of school, which appears to be relatively easy?

The "Official" Theory: Learning as Product   Science, one of humankind's most important creations, offers us protection and hope through the information it provides. It improves the quality of our lives. However, learned people who once thought the earth was flat eventually came to the conclusion that it was elliptical, if not perfectly round. In the late nineteenth century, biologists and psychologists began to examine and hypothesize about what happens in the brain when conscious beings are moved to action that is more complex than instinct alone. Today, scientists are asking what happens in the brain when human beings think, act, and learn. But investigators in the area of human learning were not always so enlightened in their early efforts to understand.

These early psychologists wanted to establish their budding discipline as a bona fide science, which required that they employ the scientific method. Because people believed that science could solve any problem and answer every question, conducting replicable psychological experiments under controlled conditions would lend credibility to *psychology*.

Psychologists who decided to study human learning found they had a problem. To meet the requirements of the scientific method, they had to look for ways to study learning independent of any outside or past experiences their subjects might have had. No easily measured unit of learning was available; nothing existed in a vacuum that could be "learned" under controlled conditions and then counted to see how much of it had been learned. Moreover, the speed at which something was learned, clearly an important variable, appeared to depend on what was being learned.

In 1870, Herman Ebbinghaus thought he had solved this scientific problem by designing a study in which the subjects (learners) would hear and learn a series of nonsense syllables, such as *WUG, DEX, TAV*. The syllables, or units of learning, could be variously manipulated by controlling for the number of syllables to be learned, number of trials, amount of time per trial, and so on. Under these controlled conditions the subjects would always perform in a predictable and consistent manner, and learning, defined as *product,* could always be observed and measured. This constituted a true scientific experiment in which learning was not related to past experience and could be both controlled and measured. Ebbinghaus found that the more his subjects had to learn, the longer it took, and the more time the subjects had to learn, the better their learning was (Ebbinghaus, 1913). Thus, the theory of learning as a measurable outcome, the *official* theory of learning, was born. If, however, the subjects were able to make sense of what they were "learning," the data were contaminated and the study ruined. It was assumed that once sense was made of anything being learned, the subjects in effect already knew something about what they were supposed to be learning, and pure learning could no longer be studied and measured. In other words, in these early, foundational studies of learning, it was considered essential for subjects to learn something absolutely unknown. Nonsense certainly fit that requirement. Since only something new or unknown could be studied as learning, learning very early came to be detached from meaningful context and prior knowledge.

At the turn of the century, John Watson, a prominent American psychologist, theorized that through learning an organism developed the means to cope with its environment. The newly developing field of psychology incorporated his emphasis on behavior in its theoretical view of learning (Watson, 1914). Through studies of animal behavior and animal learning, a definition of learning as a response to a stimulus gained credence.

During the first quarter of the twentieth century, psychologists attempted to discover general "laws" in order to expand their measurable, product-based, behavioral theory of learning. Pavlov (1927), for example, demonstrated that he could "condition" an animal to make a novel response to a new stimulus. Because of his work, psychologists were more convinced than ever that learning had to be a measurable response and that learning for purposes of study had to be disconnected from the known in order to meet the requirements of the scientific method. But there is a difference, as we will see, between a phenomenon controlled for an experiment and a natural phenomenon outside the laboratory.

Building on the theories of Watson, Pavlov, and others, Thorndike (1913, 1932) extended and elaborated the behavioral view with his theory of connections between stimulus and response. He found that subjects learned to respond habitually in particular ways to particular situations. From the 1920s through the 1940s, B. F. Skinner (1938) further refined the behavioral theory of learning as a measurable response and stated that human behavior is controlled by its consequences. Thus, between Thorndike and Skinner, learning came to be defined as any change in observable behavior directly resulting from experience (that is, stimulus-response). Eventually, the fundamental postulate was that learning was the result of operant conditioning. Learning occurred as the organism (the learner) sought pleasure and avoided pain. The learner was viewed as passive and subject to the various forces in the environment. In other words, people were controlled by the world; they did not control the world.

Based on his experiments with laboratory animals, Skinner (1938) believed that behavior had no inner causes, no needs or drives or motives that explained it. Conditions and events in the world operated on the organism, causing behavior and therefore learning. From this perspective, Skinner reasoned that human behavior could be "shaped" by controlling pleasure and pain. He called this shaping process *reinforcement*. By shaping human behavior through reinforcement, we can make the subject respond with desirable habits. Effective learning came to be defined as "the establishment of 'good' or 'desirable' habits and the prevention and/or elimination of 'bad' or 'undesirable' habits" (Cambourne, 1988). Behaviorists believe that both human and animal learning, or behavior, can be explained only in terms of habit formation through a system of reward and punishment. They have no use for "mentalistic" terms like "mind," "thought," or "feelings," which they regard as unobservable, unmeasurable, and therefore unscientific (Smith, 1986).

The *official learning theory*, currently employed in most schools, grew out of the behaviorist, product-based, stimulus-response conception of human learning. It holds that learning is difficult. Since learning is difficult, learners must be motivated to do it. Learning requires constant monitoring of the behaviors sought, usually in the form of testing, to ensure that it has taken place. Given this definition of learning, what is to be learned does not have to be connected to prior knowledge or be meaningful to the learner. And if the learner does not learn on the first trial, then reteaching, that is, new *stimulus* and retesting, is required, employing more *responses*. Praise, punishment, threats, and grades are among the many possible responses teachers and parents have used.

Today, too many educators, legislators, and parents still believe that children are passive receivers of information, that they learn only what they are directly taught, and that what is taught must be broken down into small pieces and fed to children one at a time in lockstep order, within the test-teach-test formula. This learning theory has been preeminent, even in the face of other more complex, viable views, because it is so easy to measure.

If behaviorism is the most accurate explanation of how humans learn, why do we learn so many things—water skiing, riding a two-wheeler, or using a computer—without someone else organizing it for us, without direct teaching and testing by a teacher? Does learning in school have to be different and more difficult than learning outside the classroom?

The "Unofficial" Theory: Learning as Process   Actually, most people, if they think about it, define learning just the way Jenny did, as what happens when we want to know something or be able to do something (Smith, 1990). We all know that we can usually learn when we want to. But the *process* by which we do that is not immediately clear. The unofficial theory holds that human learning involves the development of strategies rather than the acquisition of behaviors.

Defining learning as an outcome, a product, a change in behavior, or the establishment of good or bad habits, is too simple because it doesn't really account for what happens in the process. It is also perhaps too vague to say that learning is the development of the strategies we use to find out things we want to know or be able to do. Nevertheless, describing learning as the process of *coming to know* is a good place to start. The strategies human beings continually develop for coming to know about their world make up the learning process. There are at least two compatible descriptions of learning as coming to know.

Jean Piaget (1954) was a Swiss genetic epistemologist whose background in biology is reflected in his theory of learning. He believed that children expected a rational order, a balance in their lives. Piaget viewed learners as active constructors of their own knowledge about the world rather than passive receivers of such knowledge. He believed that learners tried out different versions of what they thought the world should be: for example, learners might call a cow a dog because initially they overgeneralized one known label for a four-legged animal to all four-legged animals. Piaget believed that learners did this so they could control the world around them, giving order to their environment and making sense of a seemingly chaotic world. According to Piaget, learners act alone to construct their world view; learning occurs when learners experience a sense of disequilibrium between what they already know and what they are experiencing.

Lev Vygotsky, a Russian social psychologist and contemporary of Piaget, theorized about how people make and share meaning through language. Both Piaget and Vygotsky believed that learners construct their understandings as they transact with the world. Piaget thought in terms of learners acting alone, while Vygotsky realized that most learning occurs as people interact with each other. Vygotsky (1978) believed that learning involved internalizing a social way of organizing the world view. He agreed with Piaget that human learning revolved around organizing knowledge about the world. But unlike Piaget, he believed most learning is social rather than solitary; human beings learn most of what they learn through social interactions.

Both theories cast learners as active constructors of their own knowledge. Both describe learning as occurring in a meaningful context. Learners are seen as actively engaged in making sense of the world around them, in bringing order to their worlds so they can survive and prosper. In other words, these theories explain that we come to know, and learn to be who we are, within the culture into which we were born.

This socioconstructivist theory of learning, which derives much of its foundation from Piaget, Vygotsky, and others, is process based. Learning is seen as natural. In fact, social psychologists see learning as so natural that when the brain is unable to make meaning, the learner becomes uncomfortable, restless, and bored. "Learning, like breathing, is a natural and necessary function of the living person, and we are immediately distressed when the possibility of exercising the function is taken from us" (Smith, 1990, p. 38). Thus, natural learning requires no deliberate attempts to motivate learners; learners naturally attempt to make sense of the world around them.

Coming to know occurs within the context of doing something authentic. Actually, we are learning something nearly all the time, and most of the time we are learning without even knowing it. We learn when we want to find out things, when we want to be able to do things. We learn as we participate in doing things and as we observe others doing things we want to do. We learn when we think about and talk about the things we want to know or be able to do. When learning is part of the natural flow of events, we make sense of what is occurring, and when we are able to make sense of something, learning is not difficult. In fact, learning is comparatively easy when we are engaged in activities and events that are authentic, interesting, and meaningful.

But even though natural learning is easy, we can make it difficult. When the information we are to learn is detached from context, when learning itself becomes the focus of our attention (for example, when we are learning lists of arbitrary spelling words or the names of presidents), then we may find learning difficult. Learning is also made more difficult when it is oriented to some future goal rather than to the learner's present interests (Smith, 1990). In short, learning is difficult when it is meaningless to the learner.

Likewise, learning is easy when we ask ourselves our own questions in order to make sense of what we are doing, when we engage in some real event, when we have some choice in what we are learning, and when we can relate our past experiences to the learning at hand. But remember as you read the following pages that psychologists studying learning began this century by defining learning as just the opposite. Of course, in the late 1800s and early-to-mid-1900s, their knowledge of the brain was quite limited, compared to what we know today. New information is allowing us to reexamine and redefine learning. Therefore, it seems appropriate to explore what is now known about the brain and its role in learning.

How the Brain Learns

The human body contains many organs, each of which performs one or more jobs. The human brain has two major functions. First, the brain is the "executive" organ. It keeps the body running and it regulates such autonomic functions as temperature, heart rate, and breathing. It produces chemicals that affect growth, reproduction, and emotional well-being. It tells us when we are hungry or thirsty. It solves all our solvable problems (Hart, 1983). Second, the brain is the organ for learning. Learning occurs and is stored in the brain, not in other organs. "The brain learns because that is its job" (Caine & Caine, 1991, p. 3), and its capacity to learn is virtually inexhaustible.

Each healthy human brain—regardless of a person's age, sex, nationality, or cultural background—comes equipped with a set of exceptional features (Caine & Caine, 1991, p.3):

▫ the ability to detect patterns and make approximations,

▫ a phenomenal capacity for various types of memory,

▫ the ability to self-correct and learn from experience by way of analysis of external data and self-reflection, and

▫ an inexhaustible ability to create.

Our brain is the core and storehouse of our personal existence (Hart, 1983). It is the human brain and not the ear that comprehends human speech. The brain and not the hand composes a symphony or writes a poem. The brain creates a powerful sermon or political address and dances *Swan Lake.* The brain rather than the eye is reading this book. The brain directs everything we do. The human brain is behind all the remarkable thinking, feeling, and expressing of which human beings are capable.

We learn because heredity has given the brain programs that enable us to learn (Young, 1978). We do not have to be taught to suckle or to cry, to seek shelter or warmth. We are born looking for patterns or regularities in the world around us. For example, infants begin almost immediately to identify faces (Caine & Caine, 1991). As the organ for learning, the human brain has the function of imposing meaning on its environment. It does this through a process of forming and testing hypotheses, then integrating feedback received with what is already known (Kantrowitz & Wingert, 1989; Restak, 1979).

For example, human beings identify an object by gathering information in the form of sensory data, often in less than a second, about that object. This information might include its size, color, shape, surface texture, weight, smell, movement, and sound. Other clues might be where it is found, what else is with it, how it is priced or labeled, and how others respond to it. The brain conducts an investigation to answer the question, "What is this?" The brain instantly performs this feat by going down many pathways simultaneously. The human brain is not organized or designed for linear, one-path thinking. To demand that human beings put aside all of the brain's mighty resources to proceed with a step-by-step learning task may actually cripple and inhibit the learner (Hart, 1983). When human beings are learning, investigations progress along many paths among the brain's millions of connections. Data gathering and hypothesizing about an object or event do not occur one feature at a time; that would take forever. Rather, they occur all at the same time, utilizing some level of awareness of all the features. From the vast amounts of information already stored, catalogued, and cross-referenced in the brain, tentative answers or hypotheses are created. Previously stored, labeled, and interrelated data are called knowledge structures, cognitive structures, or schemata. Incoming data are assembled and comparisons made within and among relevant cognitive structures. Interpretations of the new are possible through comparisons with the already known.

The brain is our life giver as well as our lifelong link to our environment. It provides us with lines of communication both within our own bodies and with the external world through sensory data received. Millions of nerves called neurons fire a continual stream of impulses into the brain where they are processed into patterns. We derive all our experiences, perceptions, ideas, memories, images, decisions, and behaviors from these sensory data patterns. And yet, we are not machines. As human beings we *select* from all that sensory input according to our interests and needs. At some level, conscious or subconscious, we decide what we will attend to, what we will focus on.

Cognitive Structures   From above, the human brain looks much like a large walnut with two halves. Neuroconnectors allow the two halves to communicate. Each hemisphere controls and is responsible for the functioning of the opposite side of the body. Until recently, it was believed that the brain's electrochemical activity could be isolated according to the function being performed. That is, if the right hand presses a button, the electrical discharges should begin and be concentrated in the left hemisphere. We now know that does not happen. Acts of will, decisions that human beings make, are holistically distributed throughout the entire brain (Caine & Caine, 1991). It now appears that for thinking and learning, our brains are organized more by units of *meaning* than by any of their many anatomical features (Eccles & Robinson, 1984; Hart, 1983). These units of meaning may correspond in some actual, physical way to the 2 to 3 million cellular bundles into which the brain is organized.

The majority of brain cells are found in the great brain mantle, or neocortex. Trying to understand the workings of a network of 10 billion individual brain cells is beyond human comprehension. However, scientists now know that the neocortex consists of modular units or bundles. This arrangement of about 4,000 cells per bundle reduces the number of functioning units from 10 billion to between 2 and 3 million cellular units (Eccles & Robinson, 1984). When this organization was first detected, scientists wondered if 2 to 3 million modular units of brain cells were sufficient to generate all the spatial and temporal patterns—the cognitive, linguistic, emotive, and creative and aesthetic expressions—for a whole lifetime.

Think of the pitches and tones produced by the 88 keys of a piano. These sounds, combined across time with rhythm and volume, generate essentially an infinite variety of musical patterns. That image may make it easier to see how the brain has virtually an infinite capacity in its 2 to 3 million bundles of cellular units to generate an entire universe of meaningful patterns.

Detecting, generating, and using patterns are what the brain does. It does not have to be taught to do this any more than the heart has to be instructed how to pump blood. "The brain is by nature's design an amazingly subtle and sensitive pattern detecting apparatus" that "detects, constructs, and elaborates patterns" as its basic, built-in, natural function (Hart, 1983, p. 60). "The brain does not just respond or react to the world, it creates that world" (Smith, 1990, p. 46).

Learners, including infants and young children, are not simply sponges, passively soaking up a vast array of data that their brains arrange for them. They *seek* sensory data, information, and experiences to filter, process, encode, and organize into highly complex patterns. Our brains are not designed merely to consume information doled out in discrete bits after we have been motivated to learn. Instead, our brains actively construct their own interpretation of sensory data and draw their own inferences from them. Human beings purposefully ignore some information and selectively attend to other information, depending on their interests, needs, and desires.

Even infants have the ability to gradually sort out sensory data by features and arrange those features into usable patterns. Think for a moment of the sensory data—the sights, sounds, smells, tastes, and feelings—that bombard infants in a completely unordered and uncontrolled manner. Yet infants learn very quickly what will bring a face to the crib and whether the face is familiar. In many ways, learning is the extraction of meaningful patterns from what is fortuitous, chaotic, complex, multiple-channel, and largely random input.

The Psychogenerative Nature of Human Learning   How does the human brain determine what to include as it creates a particular pattern or category? For each pattern, learners intuit a set of rules and a list of characteristics, sometimes referred to as *distinctive features*. Distinctive features allow learners to identify any object or event by its properties. Some properties or features are obvious. For example, we all know a lot about dogs. We know that nearly all dogs bark, they have four legs and fur, and they may smell bad, especially when wet. Most of the features, however, that we use to assign an event or object to a classification are invisible and known to us only subconsciously or intuitively. For instance, one characteristic we use to distinguish dogs from cats is that when picked up, dogs are less flexible than cats. Therefore, flexibility is a distinctive feature of canines, felines, and so on. It is not one, however, that is immediately obvious.

Distinctive features are acquired through experience and build the patterns or cognitive structures we use to make sense of the world. *Cognitive* means knowledge and thinking; *structure* suggests organization. We use the patterns and meanings we have given our past experiences as the basis for understanding anything new. This system of knowing organizes sensory data into an intricate and internally consistent working model of the world. Because the brain is designed to take in disparate data all at the same time and make sense of them, we experience the world as a coherent whole. This coherent whole, our "theory of the world in our heads" (Smith, 1986), is what protects us from constant confusion and allows us to survive.

Human beings could not survive if they experienced everything as the same. There would be no basis for learning or self-protection. Besides, who would want to survive in a world of endless sameness? On the other hand, human beings could not survive if they perceived everything as different. Again, there would be no basis for learning and no system for self-protection. We might never leave the house if we had no idea of what we might encounter. This would be a world filled with utter chaos and terror.

Just as the brain cannot possibly see everything that is within the field of vision, it does not "see" anything new instantly. Perception depends on what we already know and what we think is likely to be in front of us. For that reason, the process of predicting is fundamental to human perception and learning. Everyone does it, even very young children. Our cognitive structures, or schemata, are our pathways to perception (Rumelhart, 1980). That is, we "see" what the brain decides we are looking at, what the brain decides is there.

Collections of patterns or cognitive structures are also referred to as *schema*. Each individual's set of schemata is somewhat different from every other person's. Each of us has had different experiences and has constructed our own interpretation of those experiences to form our understanding of the world. An individual's schemata are established in two ways: they are transmitted through the genetic code, and they also appear to be learned after birth. Because human brains are so big and human life so complex, and because as humans we learn so much so fast, little information applicable to human learning can be gained by studying animals in a laboratory. Also, the quality of the brain, which usually refers to the number of neurons the brain has, determines the degree to which patterns can be detected, discriminated, and interrelated (Rumelhart, 1980; Wittrock, 1980). The human brain has a much greater capacity for pattern detection than any other living creature (Hart, 1983).

To compare the human brain to any information-processing device is to do this amazing organ a disservice. The brain is "not a general purpose computer into whose memory any information is placed" (Young, 1978, p. 78). The brain does not merely seek to store and then respond to information in the world; instead, the brain *imposes* meaning on the world. It is an active, experience-seeking, reality-creating organ (Smith, 1990). Human beings learn from whole to part as the brain detects patterns and assigns features to categories from all its data sources at the same time. The brain constructs schemata. It is organized so that happenings from whole experiences can be sorted out and used.

Human learning does not result merely from the world's acting upon us; rather, we construct our understanding or theory of how the world works because the brain is organized to do so. If natural learning is defined as the extraction of meaningful patterns from complex input, it follows that in schools, learners require rich, plentiful content that is both meaningful and interesting to them. As learners make decisions and interact with interesting and meaningful content, with each other, and with their teachers, they do indeed learn. The degree and direction of learning is, of course, mediated by learners' inherited abilities and by their attitudes, values, and decisions, as well as their prior knowledge and experiences (Neisser, 1980).

The brain's major function during learning is to take in a multitude of sensory data simultaneously and make sense out of them. It relates new information to known information in almost limitless fashion. The relationships generated between the new and the known expand cognitive structures (schemata) exponentially. Learning, then, is a *psychogenerative* process. That is, the more we know, the easier it is to learn something new.

We don't really learn just one new thing; we learn one new thing that can then be related and interrelated in perhaps hundreds or even thousands of ways. The whole is both greater than, and in many ways different from, the sum of the parts. The fact that learning is a psychogenerative process is undisputed (Wittrock, 1980). As a psychogenerative process, learning results from the learner's *transacting* with the world, not from the world's acting on the learner. As active participants in their own learning, learners *think* about what they are experiencing. They act upon their environments, often altering the world around them. They are actively engaged in generating relationships; they are driven to do so. They are curious about the underlying structure of the information and experiences with which they are intellectually engaged, and they are to some degree aware of the connections they are making. In other words, they affect the world even as they are affected by it. They transact with the world around them as they learn.

When a teacher shows a child the word *dog* and the child correctly says, "dog," it isn't difficult to think of this fairly low-level learning as stimulus-response. However, the simple stimulus-response model becomes less useful when one contemplates learning complex sets of behaviors that must flow and that operate on several levels at once—for example, driving a car, playing basketball, or water skiing. The stimulus-response model is of little or no use when one considers how a human being learns to play the concert violin or dance the ballet. How is it that a person can learn (that is, experience, store, organize, and access instantly) enough sensory data to handle higher mathematics, write an inspired literary work, or win an Olympic medal?

One day we observed a six-year-old boy as he watched his teacher work with a pair of pliers. "Those are like butterfly wings," he said, enthralled with his own observation. The class had studied favorite insects several months earlier. Clearly, this connection is evidence that this child learns metaphorically; that he understands the concept of hinges in a way that will expand, interrelate with other experiences and information, and *generate* new perspectives throughout his life. The metaphorical nature of human learning is another way of saying that learning is a psychogenerative process. It is this very human capability that allows us to create poetry, music, dance, literature, mathematics, philosophy, and other forms of communication that express not only our understanding of the world around us but of the world within—the human heart and spirit.

To better understand what and how we learn, consider the following categories (shown in figure 1.1). As human beings, we learn (we categorize, organize, and interrelate sensory data) in essentially the same three ways. We learn through *direct experience*—by doing. We learn through *observation*—by watching others. We also learn *indirectly*—by being told. That is, human beings can learn through language, both oral and written. And what we learn falls into three broad categories: (1) information or knowledge; (2) skills or processes; and (3) attitudes, values, and beliefs. Human beings acquire knowledge primarily through language. We develop skills primarily by participating in or doing, and we acquire our attitudes and values primarily by observing the attitudes and values of those around us. Of course, we can also gain knowledge, develop skills, and acquire attitudes and values by each of the other modes as well.

We learn because we are born able to do so. Learning is the natural human condition. But because, as human beings, we actively construct our own learning, we selectively attend to and selectively perceive events and experiences. When new knowledge is acquired, new experiences enjoyed, and new sights observed, our perceptions are altered and our view of the world is changed forever.

Children do not learn by merely accepting or recording isolated and arbitrary bits of information given to them by someone acting in the role of teacher. They do not need to have information organized into someone else's idea of a hierarchy. When experiences and activities are meaningful, when they make sense to the learners, chil-

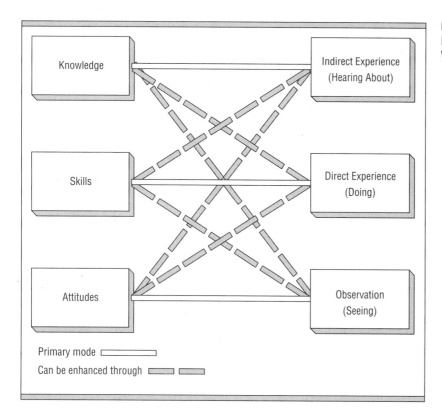

FIGURE 1.1
How and What
We Learn

dren learn. When learning is not meaningful, when it has to be organized for the learners and extrinsic and artificial rewards are required to motivate and encourage, the brain is robbed of much of its ability to learn, and children do not do it nearly so well.

Of course, we have all also learned things that proved difficult. The fact that we chose to exert the time and energy anyway indicates the value placed on such learning by the learner. Sometimes learning—for example, higher mathematics—requires great amounts of work, but for those drawn to it, their interests and natural aptitudes make the effort worthwhile. There are also times when we are called upon to learn things in which we are not initially interested. At such times, a teacher who can help us be successful may also help open new vistas to us. But there will always be, for each of us, those areas of the curriculum in which we will never be particularly interested no matter how good the teacher may be.

The Sociopsycholinguistic Nature of Learning   According to Neisser (1980), the debate between two camps of psychologists and learning theorists occupied the first two-thirds of this century. On one hand, learning was presented as stimulus-response conditioning. On the other, it was viewed as driven by the predictions or the expectations of the learner. Currently, human learning is viewed by the sociopsycholinguists as encompassing many elements of both behaviorist and constructivist schools of thought as well as others.

Today, human learning is best described in terms of multiple intelligences. According to cognitive psychologist Howard Gardner (1983) of Harvard University, all normal human beings develop at least seven forms of intelligence to a greater or lesser degree as an interplay between their genetic makeup and the cultural and environmental constraints at work. These forms of intelligence include: (1) thinking with language, (2) conceptualizing in spatial terms, (3) analyzing in musical ways, (4) computing with logic and mathematical tools, (5) solving problems with whole body or parts of the body, (6) understanding other individuals and relationships, and (7) understanding ourselves. Furthermore, each of these intelligences lends itself to its own symbolic system for representing meaning.

Gardner (1991) and others maintain that schools must allow for the emergence and full development of all the ways of knowing of which human beings are capable. Students are predisposed to learn materials that are represented in forms that fit their natural intelligence. For instance, when students are actively involved in instructional activities that highlight event structures (as in stories), learners will themselves represent the information, and later recall it, in terms of their own favored symbolic mode, no matter how the material is initially encountered. That is, in school learning, projects in which students become engaged, whether writing a story or shooting a video, will reflect the way they prefer to make and represent meaning.

The Conditions for Natural Learning

Knowing how human beings learn and how the brain works is important knowledge for teachers because it explains why an enriched, integrated curriculum is better than a reduced, fragmented curriculum. It helps explain why learning is best approached as a matter of inquiry, with learners making choices and pursuing their own interests. It tells us why rote drill and practice exercises are examples of low-level learning and may, in some instances, actually inhibit cognitive development. It tells us why intelligence testing as we know it and standardized achievement testing as it exists today are limited in value and inappropriate for so many of the nation's children. But it does not tell us everything teachers need to know about helping children learn. To extend our understanding we need to examine how learning takes place in natural settings. Think again about Jenny learning to water ski.

Jenny was three years old when she went to the lake for the first time. Her parents had been avid water skiers long before she was born. At age three, Jenny was old enough to ride in the boat and watch her parents ski. Toward the end of the summer, Jenny went skiing with her mother, who positioned Jenny in front of her with Jenny's feet on the two skis in front of her mother's feet. Both she and Jenny held onto the towrope together. Jenny would hold on in the middle and her mother on the outside. They would ski down the lake with Jenny standing on her mother's skis in front of her mother. This worked well until she got to be too big. The summer Jenny was nine years old she learned to ski on her own skis.

For six summers of her life Jenny had watched her parents and her parents' friends ski. She lived in an environment that valued the ability to water ski. She had seen many people ski, some excellent skiers and some not so experienced. She had even "skied" with her mother. She fully expected that when *she* was ready to try on her own that someone would help her. And furthermore, she expected she would be successful—as did her parents and her parents' friends. No one ever doubted that Jenny would learn to ski. In fact, Jenny was regarded as a skier before she ever skied alone.

Jenny did not succeed the first time she tried to get up by herself. But she did not give up either. She tried again and again. She knew that no one else could learn for her, that this was something she had to do on her own, and she really wanted to be a skier. To become a member of that "exclusive club" of accomplished water skiers, she was willing to risk skiing badly at first and falling down a lot. Now, at age twelve, Jenny is a very good skier. She has well-earned confidence in herself and can even ski on one ski.

Cambourne (1988) has presented a model of learning that explains why learning to water ski was easy for Jenny. This model is based on seven conditions derived from decades of research into child language development. Not all of us learn to ski, but language learning provides an excellent example of natural learning that we all do. From an understanding of how language is learned come very interesting insights on which holistic classrooms are based. Every example of positive, successful learning we examine contains these elements. They are:

- immersion

- demonstration

- use

- expectation

- responsibility

- approximation

- response

Immersion   In *immersion,* learners are saturated in the medium they are expected to learn. Older members of the culture make thousands of examples available to younger learners. In Jenny's case, she was immersed in the medium of water skiing every summer. She heard her parents talk about skiing. She watched them ski for several years. Then she got to go skiing with them, simulating or trying out what she knew about skiing in a safe, protected, and supportive environment. Finally she had a go all by herself. Smith points out that "children learn from the artifacts they find in their environments and from the behavior of the people around them" (1986, p. 16).

Demonstration   *Demonstration* can take the form of an artifact or an action. Jenny observed her parents, her parents' friends, and even people she did not know participate in and enjoy water skiing. She saw them over and over, summer after summer. Human beings "engage with repeated demonstrations of the same action and/or artifact and select other aspects of it to internalise. As a consequence, we begin to interpret, organise and reorganise our developing knowledge until we can perform and/or produce the demonstration or a recognizable variation of it" (Cambourne, 1988, p. 47).

Cambourne states that although immersion and demonstration are necessary conditions for learning, they are not sufficient in and of themselves. In other words, merely being immersed in a water-skiing environment and receiving numerous quality demonstrations was not enough for Jenny to learn to ski. The missing ingredient is *engagement* (Smith, 1990). When children are engaged, they are thinking about what they are doing and what they are learning. Immersion and demonstration without engagement will not produce successful learning.

Use   *Use,* or practice, is the process of actively involving learners with the demonstrations and artifacts in which they are immersed. In order to learn something, the learner must take part in it; the learner must use what is being learned. It is possible for learners to be immersed in thousands of demonstrations, to "practice," and still not be engaged in the process. Practice is the opportunity learners have to play around with what they are learning. Use or practice are only viable if they occur within the context of the entire learning process. In other words, when Jenny practiced skiing, she was obviously at a lake, in the water, with the skis on her feet. She did not practice skiing by isolating the different things she had to remember about getting up and staying up, even though she could talk about those things separately—for example, keeping her knees bent and not pulling her arms back toward her chest. Use means providing the time and the opportunity to use immature, developing skills in holistic, integrated, and (eventually) smoothly flowing ways.

Engagement depends on four principles. First, learners must see themselves as potential doers or owners of the demonstration. Second, they must believe that by becoming doers they will in some way "further the purposes of their own lives" (Cambourne, 1988, p. 52). Third, they must be willing to take a risk, and in order to do so they must perceive that the risk is not too great. Last, the probability of engagement is increased if the demonstrations are given by someone with whom the learner has a positive relationship. In Jenny's case, she saw herself as a skier, she believed she would have more fun at the lake if she could learn to ski, she was willing to try as many times as necessary, and she knew how proud her parents would be of her accomplishment. Engaging in water skiing was natural for her. While immersion, demonstration, and use with real engagement may be at the heart of learning, the process is still not complete without the remaining conditions.

Expectation   *Expectation* takes two forms: the message communicated to learners about their abilities to be successful, and the learners' own messages to themselves. Jenny always knew that her parents believed she would learn to ski and, as a result, she always believed she would, too. Added to the expectations about her ability was the expectation that what she was trying to learn was worthwhile, valuable, relevant, interesting, functional, and useful.

Responsibility   Only the learners themselves can take charge of their own learning; this is the condition of *responsibility*. Think of the adage, "You can lead a horse to water, but you can't make it drink." Learners can be immersed in demonstrations, provided thousands of opportunities for engagement, be expected to learn, and still not be successful. This is because it is the child and not the teacher who is responsible for the learning that takes place. Cambourne says that taking responsibility in the learning process usually involves two types of behavior. First, learners must be willing to make decisions about their own learning, decisions independent of the teacher. Jenny chose to learn to ski, and she chose which summer she thought she was ready to learn. Her parents (teachers) did not make this decision for her. Second, teachers must trust learners to engage in demonstrations and select from demonstrations those that they, the learners, believe to be the most useful.

Trust is perhaps the scariest element of all. We as teachers must trust our students to make appropriate decisions, and we must give them the freedom to do so. This does not mean that learners are free to choose not to learn. Only when learning conditions are threatening is choosing not to learn more risk-free than choosing to learn.

The responsibility for setting up the rich environment and providing the opportunities and the supportive conditions belongs to the teacher. The responsibility for learning rests with the learner.

Approximation *Approximation* occurs when the learner comes close to producing a product, artifact, or action that an adult (expert) would. This concept is most easily understood as it relates to learning to talk. For example, did your younger brother or sister ever approximate a word? Was the word "baba" used for the word "bottle" or "banky" for "blanket"? Was the child told that the word was incorrect and not to say it again until it could be pronounced correctly? Of course not!

Jenny approximated skiing on several occasions. First, when she skied on top of her mother's skis, she approximated real skiing. Then as she began to try to learn on her own, she would get up, ski a few yards, and fall. But she was never told that she wasn't doing it right and not to try again until she could ski better. That would be ridiculous! Instead, her parents celebrated each successive approximation of real skiing. Everyone told her how well she was doing, and she was always encouraged to try again. Unfortunately, our culture has a "thing" for being correct and for never making a mistake, especially in school. The notion appears to be that making mistakes is somehow bad or tied to low intelligence. Therefore, memorizing or imitating so as to give the illusion of competence has become tied to a false perception of higher intelligence.

Response The way the "experts" reply to learners is the condition of response. It relates to the sharing of information and the control learners have over what they are attempting to learn. The psychological term frequently used to mean response is *feedback,* but this term has connotations of behaviorism and along with it positive or negative reinforcement. Responses are more like natural exchanges between learners and experts. For example, when a young child says "banky" for "blanket" you may adopt the child's word or respond by supplying the adult word, but you probably will not reprimand the approximation.

In Jenny's case, her parents responded to her novice attempts at skiing by offering suggestions to help her move a little closer to the adult style of skiing. Response requires acceptance of an approximation, celebration of that approximation, evaluation to determine if the learner can come closer to the accepted form, and repeated demonstrations. Jenny's parents suggested she watch someone else get up on skis and look at how they kept their knees bent or their arms straight. Response is an attempt to fill in the gaps, to explain, examine, extend, or redirect.

SUMMARY

What is learning? Learning is something we all do all the time. It is natural. Real learning is satisfying. It tends to occur from whole to part then back to whole. It can be seen as the development of concepts and understandings through a process of inquiry, participation, observation, and thinking (Weaver, 1990). More than just the formation of habits, learning involves complex processes that cannot be controlled or guaranteed in laboratories or in classrooms. Direct instruction of the bits and pieces of a fragmented body of knowledge will not produce the best learning or the most successful and independent learners.

Learning that is engaged in voluntarily is more meaningful to the learner and longer lasting. Such learning is generative in nature. Learning is more social than solitary, more cooperative than competitive. Natural learning occurs under certain conditions, most or all of which are present in every positive, successful learning event.

Why do human beings learn? We learn because not to do so is impossible and discomforting to the brain. Of course, we don't always learn what others want us to learn. Learning occurs when human beings interact with information, other people, language, and thinking in authentic experiences. How can we best fa-cilitate learning? We can provide learning environments that ensure that the conditions for successful learning are present in classrooms. Our understanding of learning and learning environments for complex learning is enhanced by our understanding of language and how language is learned. The following summarizes what we have explored about learning.

1. Learning is easier when it occurs naturally.

2. Learning is something we do all the time, even when we are unaware that we are learning. We learn constantly, without the need for external motivation, special incentives, and artificial "reinforcement."

3. Learning occurs from whole to part to whole.

4. Learning is active, not passive.

5. Learning is coming to know.

6. Learning is making sense of the world around us as we represent our learning through symbol systems that reflect multiple intelligences, such as talking and drawing.

7. Learning is constructing our own understandings and identities in an interaction among genetic characteristics, cultural atti-

tudes and values, and environmental constraints.

8. Learning is extracting meaningful features from the world of our experiences, building patterns, categorizing, and drawing interrelations among schemata.

9. Learning is a social act. We learn from and with others in social situations.

10. Learning occurs when new information is integrated with or attached to prior knowledge.

11. Learning occurs when we want to be able to do something or to find out something.

12. Learning is making choices and taking responsibility.

13. Learning involves doing, observing, and language.

14. Learning is psychogenerative and metaphorical in nature.

15. Low-level learning, such as rote memorization or right answer recognition, is usually short term. It does not necessarily involve understanding, may give a false sense of competence, and, because it is surface level, may not be generative.

THEORY-TO-PRACTICE CONNECTIONS

Learning Theory

1. Learning is a constructive process. Learners actively try to make sense of their world.

2. Therefore, learning is psychogenerative. The more we know, the easier it is to learn anything new. Learners relate what they already know as they make sense of what they are learning.

3. Learning is relatively easy when it is purposeful.

4. The human brain is designed to detect and impose patterns from a mass of incoming sensory data.

5. Human learning is a matter of multiple intelligences, i.e., ways of knowing and of representing those knowings.

Examples of Classroom Practice

1. Students setting up and conducting a science project to answer their own questions

2. Students reading and talking about good books

3. Students making choices about what they want to learn, employing real language, e.g., in the form of children's literature, functional signs, and messages

4. Creating a rich, literate environment and immersing learners in a wide variety of literature and information sources

5. Allowing learners choices as they represent their learnings

SUGGESTED READINGS

Caine, R., & Caine, G. (1991). *Making connections: Teaching and the human brain.* Alexandria, VA: Association for Supervision and Curriculum Development.

Gardner, H. (1991). *The unschooled mind.* New York: Basic Books.

Smith, F. (1990). *To think.* New York: Teachers College Press.

SUGGESTED ACTIVITIES

1. Discuss how you think the classroom practice examples in the Theory-to-Practice Connections suggested reflect the learning theory statements. Is there overlap among the example practices—that is, does each address more than one theoretical proposition?

2. As an in-class experience, tell the person next to you about one positive learning event in your life, a time when you attempted to learn something and were successful, outside of school. After you have taken turns, share some of these with the class. Do you find evidence of the conditions for learning in your own positive learning experiences? How so?

3. Make a list of 50 words, 5 words in each of 10 categories. Arrange two groupings of these words. On one sheet of paper list each group of words beneath its category. On the other sheet list all the words arranged in two columns in alphabetical order. Divide a group of students in half. Give one group the words in categories. Give the other group the words in alphabetical listing. Do not let each group know what the other group is doing. Tell each group they have 10 minutes to learn all the words for a paper and pencil test. After the test, have each group add their scores and calculate the group mean score. Discuss the results. Which group did better? Why? Did the group with the alphabetically listed words try to devise categories as a means of learning the words? Did they try any other strategies for learning? What did you learn from this event?

REFERENCES

Caine, R., & Caine, G. (1991). *Making connections: Teaching and the human brain.* Alexandria, VA: Association for Supervision and Curriculum Development.

Cambourne, B. (1988). *The whole story.* Toronto, Ontario: Ashton-Scholastic.

Dewey, J., & Bentley, A. (1949). *Knowing and the known.* Boston: Beacon Press.

Ebbinghaus, H. (1913). *Memory.* (H. A. Ruger and C. E. Bussenius, Trans.). New York: Teachers College Press.

Eccles, J., & Robinson, D. (1984). *The wonder of being human: Our brain and our mind.* New York: Macmillan.

Gardner, H. (1983). *Frames of mind.* New York: Basic Books.

Gardner, H. (1991). *The unschooled mind.* New York: Basic Books.

Hart, L. (1983). *Human brain and human learning.* New York: Longman.

Kantrowitz, B., & Wingert, P. (1989, April 17). How kids learn: A special report. *Newsweek*, pp. 50–57.

Neisser, U. (1980). *Cognition and reality.* San Francisco: W. H. Freeman.

Pavlov, I. (1927). *Conditioned reflexes.* (G. V. Anrep, Trans.). London: Oxford University Press.

Piaget, J. (1954). *The construction of reality in the child.* New York: Basic Books.

Restak, R. (1979). *The brain: The last frontier.* New York: Doubleday.

Rogers, C. (1983). *Freedom to learn for the 80's.* Columbus, OH: Merrill.

Rumelhart, D. (1980). Schemata: The building blocks of cognition. In R. Spiro, B. Bruce, & W. Brewer (Eds.), *Theoretical issues in reading comprehension: Perspectives from cognitive psychology, linguistics, artificial intelligence, and education* (pp. 33–58). Hillsdale, NJ: Lawrence Erlbaum.

Smith, F. (1986). *Insult to intelligence.* New York: Arbor House.

Smith, F. (1990). *To think.* New York: Teachers College Press.

Skinner, B. (1938). *The behavior of organisms: An experimental analysis.* New York: Appleton-Century-Crofts.

Thorndike, E. (1913). *The psychology of learning.* New York: Teachers College Press.

Thorndike, E. (1932). *The fundamentals of learning.* New York: Teachers College Press.

Vygotsky, L. (1978). *Mind in society: The development of higher psychological processes.* Cambridge, MA: Harvard University Press.

Watson, J. (1914). *Behavior: An introduction to comparative psychology.* New York: Holt, Rinehart and Winston.

Weaver, C. (1990). *Understanding whole language.* Portsmouth, NH: Heinemann.

Wittrock, M. (Ed.). (1980). *The brain and psychology.* New York: Academic Press.

Young, J. (1978). *Programs of the brain.* London: Oxford.

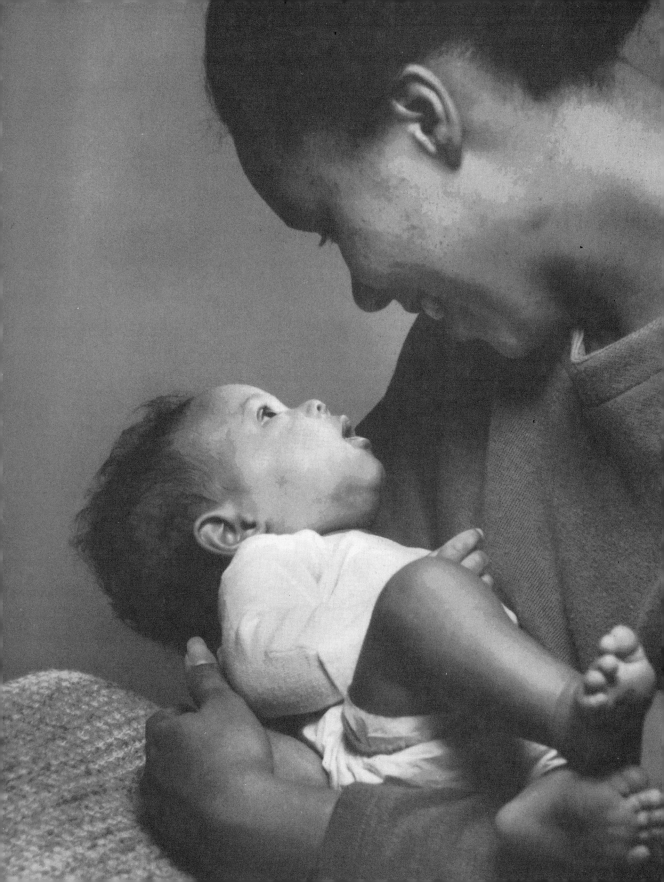

2

I still remember the excitement I felt when I first read Chomsky's claim that "Language is a window on the mind." . . . Heady stuff for someone interested in the education of young children.

(WELLS, 1986, p. ix)

Language

What is language? Can you define it?

What does language do for us?

What makes up our language and just how complex is it?

*L*anguage is one of the ways we learn. It is the most important way we organize and make sense of our world. And language is the means by which human beings relate to each other. Education, courtship and marriage, health, politics, religion, socializing, and most work require language as their primary tool. Language is one of the central learning tasks of childhood. Learning oral language and learning about the world occupy young children's minds for the first several years of life.

In this chapter we will describe language and discuss the uses of language, especially from the child's point of view. We will examine the six integrated, rule-governed systems that make up our language. We will discuss briefly the role of oral language in school learning and set the stage for chapter 3, which describes in detail how language is learned in the first place.

What Language Does

Forms of Language   Oral language exists in many versions. Not only have human beings created English, Spanish, Navajo, Yiddish, Greek, Swahili, Persian, Chinese, and thousands of other languages, but nearly every language on earth has more than one regional or social class dialect. In addition, nearly all languages have two expressive modes, speaking and writing, and two receptive modes, listening and reading. Some languages also have alternatives for persons who need to receive and produce meaning through other sensory channels—for example, braille and American Sign Language. Language is also the primary medium through which teachers and children work (Lee & Rubin, 1979). Because teachers teach and children learn through language, it is important that we understand what language is and what it does.

Uses of Language   Even though language can be one of the highest forms of human expression, as in literature or philosophy, that is not why human beings created it. Language evolved so that we could share our experiences with one another. In the process we discovered that language helped us better structure and refine our experiences and understandings, that is, our world view.

Looking at the many uses of language is an important part of understanding language. Language exists for social and intellectual uses, and in the broadest sense, language serves as a means of reflecting and acting (Lee, 1986). Once language is learned, people may then use it reflectively or internally as they think (Smith, 1990), but mostly we use language to get things done. Language is a major means by which we act, interact, and control our environments.

Oral language is generally the way we make contact with other human beings. We label and categorize our world, and we share those understandings with each other. In our complex world, we use language to understand, to negotiate, to protect ourselves, to keep from being alone, and to get what we want. Language is a powerful medium. It can promote love or cause wars. It is a window on the mind. But what *is* language really?

What Language Is

Oral language is one of the symbolic representational modes human beings have created for expressing meaning. Oral language, for the most part, is invisible because it is so inherently natural that the rules by which it operates are not immediately apparent to native speakers. Its characteristics, structures, and functions are not readily accessible for examination the way the parts of an automobile are, for instance. We learned our native language without direct instruction, and we learned it so well and so deeply that we speak it automatically without being aware of the complex sets of rules we are invoking.

Human beings are born with the mental capacity to develop language. The human brain comes already "programmed" to create linguistic systems (Lenneberg, 1967). Language is natural to humans. We do not have to study our native tongue in school to learn it; instead, we learn it by exposure and practice. Nevertheless, language is difficult to describe, both because it is inherent and because it is made up of abstract symbols and rule systems.

Definitions of Language   *Webster's New Universal Unabridged Dictionary* (1983) defines language as any system of formalized symbols and signs used as a means of communication by persons from the same community group. This definition has two parts. The system of symbols and signs has to do with what language actually is. Communication by persons from the same community of speakers has to do with what language does.

Communication and *community* come from the same root word. Communication refers to shared meaning among people and shared words in a system for transmitting ideas and information. Community refers to language and heritage common to a group of people. Both terms have to do with the transmission of meaning. For our purposes, oral language communication will be conceived as a system of abstract symbols used for social interaction, that is, a system of shared meanings among members of the same or related cultural groups.

Rule-Governed Patterns   The fact that language is a system (implying rules, regularities, and patterns) suggests why it is so thoroughly learnable to humans. Our brains are designed to detect or to impose patterns; and language is a series of patterns. It conforms to rules so that it can be learned, used, and understood. A brief examination of some of the conventions, or rule-governed systems, that organize the symbols and signs of our language will help us better understand language and appreciate its complexity.

For purposes of studying language, linguists subdivide it into at least six sets of patterns or rule-governed systems (Benjamin, 1970; Lee, 1986; Salus, 1969): intonation, phonology, morphology, syntax, pragmatics, and semantics. In practice these systems operate simultaneously and are not subdivided. That is, as soon as we begin to try to break any language into its various systems, we don't have language any more. Although such divisions are interesting, they won't help us learn language. But they may help us understand it.

Examining these six rule-governed systems one at a time will not only help clarify the nature of language itself, but also shed some light on the process of language learning. We will explore each system, taking a close look at the contribution of structural linguists to our understanding of grammar or syntax. We will also examine cohesive ties that allow language to make sense and relate across connected discourse.

Intonation   The system that makes up the tones and rhythmic patterns of a language is intonation (Lieberman, 1967). Intonation is the interaction of the following three components: (1) volume or stress, how loudly or how softly any part of an utterance is produced; (2) frequency or pitch, how high or how low any part of an utterance is spoken; and (3) juncture, or the use of the pause, the actual spaces that are placed between utterances. Taken together, these components are used to lay a pattern of rises and falls, stops and starts, across words, phrases, and sentences.

The intonation system serves several purposes. It conveys the emotional state or mood of the speaker. Take, for example, the same set of words spoken with two different intonation patterns: "You are going with us." Spoken as an exclamation (!), the primary stress and pitch markers are on the words *you* and *with*. This conveys the idea that the speaker is excited about the fact and may reassure the listener that he or she is wanted. Those same words, "You are going with us," spoken as a question (?) with primary stress and pitch markers on the words *you* and *us,* may convey the opposite idea—that the speaker is not too pleased at the prospect of such company.

Intonation serves a more subtle and more important function than alerting listeners to the emotional content of a message. Intonation patterns, which can be one-word or quite lengthy utterances, notify the brain of several elements necessary for effective and efficient communication. The entire tonal contour of an utterance tells the brain where a meaning unit starts and where it stops.

Human brains process verbal information in chunks that correspond to intonation contours across meaning units. We retain the gist of the message, dump the string of words, and move on to the next meaning unit. We do this because we human beings have limited short-term memory (Smith, 1988). We actually can hold in short-term memory, on average, seven separate elements (plus or minus two); therefore we must comprehend the *meaning of the string* of words so that we are retaining one element rather than all the individual words that make up that meaning (Miller, 1956).

Intonation also tells the brain what to pay special attention to in an utterance, that is, which are the most important pieces of information. In standard, declarative, simple sentences, primary stress and pitch markers commonly occur on noun subjects. Secondary stress and pitch are placed on main predicates, and primary stress and pitch occur again on objects. Then the speaker stops for a breath, as well as to indicate the end of the thought unit. For example, in the context of a conversation on exhibits and events at the local county fair, we encounter this sentence: "Roger ate the rhubarb pie." The words and the standard intonation pattern tell us who did what to whom (or to what, in this case). However, if we alter the standard contour, replacing the two primary stress markers with one primary stress marker, this time on the word *rhubarb,* we produce a very different meaning: "Roger ate the *rhubarb* pie." This version now tells us that there were other kinds of pie, but only one was a rhubarb pie. The words themselves do not provide this information; it is instead provided in the traditional understanding of the rules of standard English intonation. A set of rules called contrastive stress rules accounts for the meaning of such utterances. These and thousands of other rules of the English language were learned by each of its speakers, but they were never taught, nor did they need to be.

Intonation operates within words and phrases. A typical example is found in the phrase "light house keeper." One possible version has to do with ships, coastal shorelines, and tall white buildings. The

stress marker falls on the first segment, "light." The pause comes between the words "lighthouse" and "keeper." The term "lighthouse"
is a noun in this context. Another version has to do with dustcloths,
brooms, and cleaning products. It places the stress marker on the
word "house." The pause goes between "light" and "house." This
time "light" is an adjective and "housekeeper" is the noun. In such
cases, intonation determines the visual display, or how the words
look in print.

Or consider stress and meaning within words. In such words as
reCORD or *RECord,* and *preSENT* or *PRESent,* the stress shifts, the vowels change, the part of speech changes, and the meaning changes.

These are but a few examples of the fact that language operates as
a whole. The systems of language do not function in isolation. We
have learned the rules by which our language works, although we did
not know we were learning rules. We do not know what most of the
rules are and cannot articulate them, but we know how to use them.
We know how to make and comprehend language, and we do so
most successfully (Bolinger, 1965; Lieberman, 1967).

Phonology   The phonological system has to do with the sounds
themselves. The term *phoneme* is important. For our purposes, a
phoneme is one small, basic unit of sound in a language. English has
some forty-four phonemes (Schane, 1973). Phonemes are traditionally divided into two major categories, vowels and consonants.

Vowels are speech sounds that are voiced and made with the
mouth open. Vowel sounds are said to carry the bulk of the sound in
each syllable. Figure 2.1 is a chart listing basic vowel sounds and
their points of articulation in the mouth. Figure 2.2 is a diagram of
the mouth showing the areas where sounds are formed.

Consonants are speech sounds made with the mouth closed in
some way. Some consonants are voiced, and some are voiceless or
whispered. Consonants serve to modify vowel sounds. They start
them, stop them, and make them hiss or jump out of the speaker's
mouth. Figure 2.3, a chart of consonant sounds, indicates where
each sound is made in the mouth and what type of sound it is. Each
term in the left column suggests a type of sound. *Stops,* for example,
involve some stoppage of the flow of air during the production of

FIGURE 2.1
Phonetic Symbols
for Vowel Sounds

PLACE OF ARTICULATION IN MOUTH		
Front	Center	Back

High			
ī beat		u boot	
e bit	ĭ her	ω book	

Middle			
ey bait		σω boat	
ε bet	ə about	ɔ bought	

Low			
æ bat	ʌ but	a not	

those phonemes (for example, /p/ as in <u>p</u>ut or ho<u>p</u>). *Fricatives* involve a hissing sound or friction as air rushes past teeth and lips during the production of those speech sounds (for example, /s/ as in <u>s</u>ome or ma<u>ss</u>).

In squares containing two symbols, the symbol in the top left corner is the voiceless or whispered phoneme and the symbol for the voiced counterpart is in the bottom right corner. Each pair of phonemes is made in the same way and at the same place in the mouth. Only one activates the vocal mechanism, and the other is whispered. For example, the sound we hear at the beginning of the word <u>c</u>old, /k/, is a voiceless stop. Its voiced mate is the sound we hear at the beginning of the word gold, /g/. Of the twenty-eight consonant sounds on the grid, ten are whispered. Nine have a voiced counterpart in English, and the rest are voiced with no voiceless counterpart.

Over the course of this century, speech scientists have identified many more characteristics or distinctive features of phonemes. These vocal features more completely differentiate one phoneme from another. As with distinctive features of any category or phenomenon, we use characteristics of speech sounds to help us learn how to produce the words in our language. Distinctive features are usually displayed as a matrix that lists the phonemes of a language (or of all languages) across the top and terms that identify the possible features, such as *nasal* (phonemes that resonate in the nasal cavity), along the left axis. No two phonemes will have the same set of features or characteristics. Each will differ from the others by at least one or more features. Part of the distinctive feature chart for the phonemes in English might look like figure 2.4.

Such a grid allows speech scientists to see what features make up

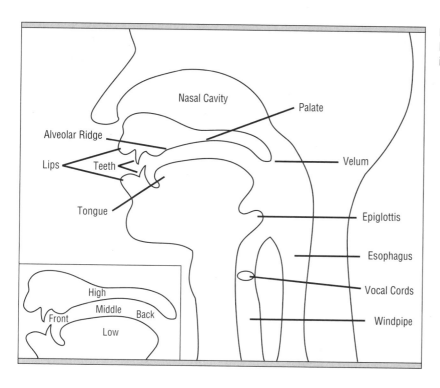

FIGURE 2.2
Formation of Sounds in the Mouth

	POINT OF ARTICULATION						
MANNER OF ARTICULATION	Bilabial	Labiodental	Dental	Alveolar	Alveopalatal	Velar	Glottal
Stops	p (<u>p</u>ut) (<u>b</u>ut) b			t (<u>t</u>o) (<u>d</u>o) d		k (<u>c</u>old) (<u>g</u>old) g	
Fricatives		f (<u>f</u>ew) (<u>v</u>iew) v	θ (<u>th</u>in) (<u>th</u>is) ⅄	s (<u>s</u>ip) (<u>z</u>ip) z	∫ (<u>sh</u>un) (occa<u>s</u>ion) ʒ		
Affricates					č (<u>ch</u>ug) (<u>j</u>udge) ǰ		
Nasals	(<u>m</u>ine) m			n (<u>n</u>o)		(ri<u>ng</u>) ŋ	
Liquids				(<u>l</u>ove) l		h (<u>h</u>igh)	
Glides	wh (<u>wh</u>en) (<u>w</u>ent) w			(<u>r</u>ow) r	(<u>y</u>es) y		

FIGURE 2.3
Phonetic Symbols for
Consonant Sounds

each phoneme. It also reveals which phonemes are the most complex, that is, those made up of the largest number of characteristics.

The spelling system in English recognizes sixteen vowel and twenty-eight consonant sounds. These speech sounds or phonemes are spelled with twenty-six letters and combinations of letters. Using *Webster's New Universal Unabridged Dictionary* (1983) as the pronunciation standard, we find approximately two hundred fifty (250) letter patterns for these forty-four sounds in words common to materials used in the elementary grades. For example, let's consider some of the ways long /ā/ can be spelled.

a as in b*a*by	ea as in gr*ea*t
ay as in d*ay*	ai(e) as in pr*aise*
ai as in m*ai*l	ey as in th*ey*
a(e) as in c*ake*	ee as in matin*ee*
aigh as in str*aigh*t	et as in bouqu*et*
eigh as in n*eigh*bor	e as in carbur*e*tor
ei as in r*ei*n	

These examples do not exhaust the possible spellings for the long /ā/ phoneme (Cheek, 1972). However, correct spelling when we write is only part of the problem. There is also the problem of word identification when we read. When we see one of these patterns in print it may not represent long /ā/. For example, the letter *a* in the word *father*, the letters *ai(e)* in the word *aisle*, the letters *ea* in the word *each*—are all spellings for long /ā/ sound—but *not* in these words. (See appendix A for information on sound-letter patterns.)

FEATURES	P H O N E M E S									
	s	**t**	**r**	**i**	**p**	**n**				
Syllabic	−	−	−	+	−	−				
Consonantal	+	+	+	−	+	+				
Strident	+	−	−	−	−	−				
Nasal	−	−	−	−	−	+				
Voiced	−	−	+	+	−	+				

FIGURE 2.4
Distinctive Features of Phonemes

English is a combination of several Nordic and Germanic languages combined with Latin, French, and many other influences. This circumstance accounts for the fact that English, while it is represented by an alphabetic code, is not represented by one-to-one correspondence between sound and letter. This means that each letter does not represent just one sound, and any given sound may be spelled more than one way in English. In addition, the spelling conventions for English started centuries before spelling was standardized. Hence, English has many combinations of possible spelling patterns for each sound and several pronunciation possibilities for each spelling pattern; that does not even begin to account for variations in regional dialects.

Morphology   Morphology is the study of the patterns of word formations and includes roots and root words, compound words, contractions, prefixes, suffixes, and variant endings. This branch of linguistic study recognizes two forms of morphemic units, bound and free morphemes. A *morpheme* is a minimal grammatical unit that cannot be subdivided into smaller meaningful parts; therefore, it is the smallest meaning carrying unit in a language (Bolinger, 1965). For example, the word *hat* is considered a free morpheme because it cannot be reduced or added to without changing the meaning. An example of a bound morpheme is the plural marker *s* or *es*. Such grammatical tags do not stand alone but must be connected to another meaning unit; hence, they are referred to as bound.

In English, grammatical indicators of past tense and plural are included in the area of morphology. Like all the other rule-governed systems of language, the morphological system is interdependent with them and cannot be separated functionally. The English regular past tense, for example, is formed by adding a bound morpheme to the verb (jump -ed). This bound morpheme is sounded as /d/, /t/, or /ed/. However, it is spelled with the letter *d*, the letters *ed*, by doubling the final consonant (*c*) and adding *ed* (*c* + *ed*), or by changing the *y* to *i* and adding *ed* (*ied*). There is little relationship between the spelling of the past tense marker and the way it is pronounced. This does not mean no rule is operating. The pattern or rule has to do with the phoneme at the end of the root verb, rather than with the past tense marker itself.

Consider the following:

/d/	**/t/**	**/ed/**
shove + d = shoved	fake + d = faked	vote + d = voted
boil + ed = boiled	laugh + ed = laughed	need + ed = needed
grab + bed = grabbed	slap + ped = slapped	pat + ted = patted
dry + ied = dried		

In the first set the past tense marker is sounded as /d/. In the second set it is pronounced as the whispered /t/. In the last set the past tense tag becomes a separate syllable altogether. As you can see, each pattern uses more than one spelling for the same sound. The rule might be stated as follows: any regularly forming English verb that ends in a voiced phoneme takes the voiced phoneme /d/ to make past tense; any regular verb that ends in a voiceless phoneme takes the voiceless phoneme /t/ to form past tense; any regular verb that ends in the phonemes /d/ or /t/ must take an inflected syllable /ed/ to form past tense. Of course, doubling the final consonant has nothing to do with past tense at all. Rather, it indicates that the preceding vowel in the root verb is short.

These examples make it clear that there is a relationship between the spelling and the pronunciation of past tense, but it is an obscure one. The relationship is one of matching type of phoneme at the end of the verb with type of phoneme forming the past tense marker. This is another way of demonstrating the fact that human beings intuit the rules or the underlying structure of their language, even the phonological system. We have learned hundreds of underlying patterns or rules. We use these patterns and rules to receive and transmit meaning, but we don't consciously know most of the rules we use. That is, we cannot articulate them and have no need to. Young children are not taught the underlying rules for forming past tense, for instance, yet they learn and use them quite effectively long before they come to school.

Syntax   This set of patterns or conventions refers to the rules that govern word order in phrases and sentences. Meaning is transmitted through word order (Salus, 1969). Look at the difference in meaning between the sentences "The dog bit the boy" and "The boy bit the dog." The same five words in a different word order convey a different message. If we destroy the grammar or sentence structure altogether, as in "Bit dog the the boy," we still have the same five words, but no meaning at all.

Traditional grammar is often taught as a set of rules to be studied and learned for adherence to a "standard." For example, a traditional grammar exercise would diagram the sentences "John told Tammy to buy the parts" and "John promised Tammy to buy the parts" the same way. That is, it would regard the surface structure of each sentence as being the same. However, in the first sentence Tammy will do the buying, and in the second, John will do the buying. Therefore, the meanings are different. During the last half of this century, most linguists came to believe that any grammatical analysis should reflect both surface structure and underlying reality (Chomsky, 1972; Lee, 1986). This work resulted in a theory of language called transformational generative grammar.

Phrase structure rules take each of these two terms (transformational and generative) separately. *Transformational* refers to a set of grammatical rules beyond any previously identified. This set of rules allows the orchestration of the entire complex production of connected discourse. Transformational rules arrange words in clauses, and arrange, relate, and embed clauses to make compound and complex sentences. For instance, instead of saying "My brother is big. My brother took me home," the child says, "My big brother took me home." Or instead of saying "My dog is brown. My dog is little. My dog ran away," the child says "My little brown dog ran away." The modifiers are embedded in the appropriate order and the redundant words deleted. Rules for sequencing and embedding modifiers and deleting redundant words are part of our store of underlying structural transformations.

There are many other rules as well. Instead of saying, "Today we won the game. Yesterday we lost the game," the child may say, "Today we won the game, but we lost yesterday." There are rules for inserting relational words that allow speakers to embed clauses. Transformational rules take all the separate conceptual elements that make up thought units (that is, deep structure) and allow speakers to turn them into surface-level strings of sounds that listeners then recognize as having meaning and grammar. These operations are not yet fully understood. The diagram in figure 2.5 may help clarify this process.

In the expressive modes of language, the speaker or writer moves from an *idea* in the mind through all the words connected to the information, images, and sensory impressions that make up *deep structure* of this particular topic, through the rules that *transform* all that data into *surface structure*, or what we recognize as language. In the receptive modes of language, listeners and readers rely on moving from the surface string of utterances through the transformations to tap into their own store of linguistic and sensory data at deep structure. At this point, receivers are able to construct a meaning similar to the speaker's or author's intended meaning if they share enough language and experiential background.

The other half of the term *transformational generative* is equally important. The idea that language, indeed all human learning, is generative is one of the theoretical foundations upon which a whole language instructional paradigm is built. We need to understand the

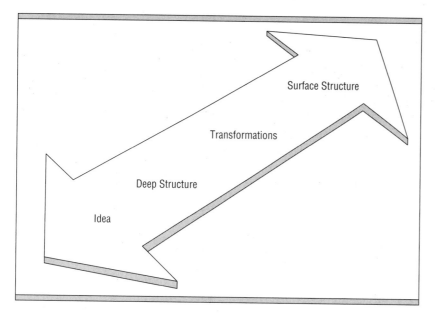

FIGURE 2.5
From Idea to Language

term *generative* as it applies to language learning and language production (Shuy, 1984).

This theory maintains that human beings learn the rules or patterns for structuring phrases and sentences and may then create, or generate, nearly a limitless number of variations as they insert each word in an appropriate slot. Phrase structure rules are written somewhat like mathematical formulas. For example, one very simple rule may be stated that a sentence (S) can be made up of a noun phrase (NP) and a verb phrase (VP). The verb phrase may consist of a verb and a noun phrase. The noun phrase may be made up of an adjective and a noun.

$$S \rightarrow NP + VP$$

$$VP \rightarrow V + NP$$

$$NP \rightarrow Adj + N$$

All we need to "generate" grammatically acceptable sentences are two nouns (for example, *baby* and *candy*), one verb (*eats*), and an adjective (*pretty*). Now we can generate four sentences with our one phrase structure rule and our four-word vocabulary.

1. Pretty baby eats candy.
2. Baby eats pretty candy.
3. Pretty candy eats baby.
4. Candy eats pretty baby.

Granted, these sentences are not wonderful and only two make sense. Nevertheless, we have generated four grammatical sentences with one simple rule and four words. College educated adults "know" thousands of phrase structure rules and thousands of words. Words can be used exponentially. That is, we can use any word we know in the appropriate slot in thousands of structural patterns. Obviously, then, human beings possess the power to generate essentially an infinite amount and variety of language.

Pragmatics   Pragmatics has to do with the rules for the uses of language within a given cultural group. Language is essentially a social activity and the rules surrounding some of the social uses of language may be quite overt. For example, our culture has laws against public profanity. Nevertheless, we might expect to hear profanity in a bar but not in church, where extreme social pressure might be exerted on the perpetrator. The rules of pragmatics can also be invisible or covert. For instance, cultural groups in this country have different loudness boundaries for various social settings.

Pragmatics also includes how various groups use language and what they value in language. One cultural group may teach that it is the norm for everyone in the family to talk at the same time, while other groups teach that only one person speaks at a time and everyone else listens. One ethnic group may value oral storytelling, while another values factual accounts of events. Some cultural groups employ rhetorical questions, while others ask questions when they really need to know.

Semantics   This area of linguistic study has to do with how language transmits meaning. While a part of semantics has to do with word meaning, semantics is much broader than the vocabulary of a language (Lee, 1986). Is meaning conveyed in speech by adding up the meanings of all the words in an utterance?

Take, for example, the line "You value the earthen vase" (Jewell, 1987) followed by "but the porcelain one is more beautiful." In these two lines "earthen vase" refers to a real vase. However, the same line, "You value the earthen vase," followed by "but we all grow old and die," causes us to redefine and recreate our mental image of the intended meaning. In the second version "earthen vase" is a metaphor for the human body. Where do these definitions come from? What do we have to do to interpret these various meanings?

How language means is much more complex and interrelated than merely adding up word meanings in a linear fashion. The meaning conveyed by a speaker is determined by word choices, intonation, and grammar within a specific context. For example, what does the word *run* mean? The meaning of the word *run* cannot be interpreted until it is used. "He can *run* fast." "He can *run* for public office." "He started the *run* on the bank." The basic unit of meaning is not the word, but is it the sentence?

Even sentence grammar does not always provide sufficient cues to tell us the intended meaning. Take the following sentences: "The shooting of the hunters frightened Anne," "Flying planes can be dangerous," "Visiting relatives can be a nuisance," and "The missionary is cooking." The who-did-what-to-whom relationships are not clear. In order to understand, we need the broader contexts in which these sentences might occur. Understanding, then, depends on getting enough cues to construct meaning and come close to the thoughts of the speaker (or writer). But where do these cues come from? The cues come from the listener's knowledge of all six rule-governed systems that we have discussed, as well as from the specific context. Context in oral language refers to the environment or circumstances in which the language occurs.

Language conveys its messages through the rules that organize and interrelate the vocal symbols. These rule patterns are the underlying grammatical structure of language that we must learn indirectly. We generate all the language of which we are capable based on these underlying structural rules. The rules are complex and for the most part invisible. It has taken linguists many years to begin to identify and describe the underlying patterns by which we produce and comprehend language. The conventions or rule systems of a language cannot really be separated. Even at the word level, as we have seen, intonation, phonology, morphology, syntax, pragmatics, and semantics work holistically to make meaning.

The discovery of the structural or transformational rules of language allowed linguists to begin to understand how sentences mean (Chomsky, 1957). But examining how combinations of sentences mean—that is, how whole text conveys meaning—demonstrates that the language game is even more complicated than we have thus far described or than many linguists once thought possible.

How Language Operates as a Whole

Clearly the sound system in language is not the basic unit of meaning. Words, phrases, and sentences are minimal units of meaning, but they do not account for how meaning is conveyed in whole discourse. There is yet another set of rules, also invisible, complex, and difficult to describe, that allow sentences to relate to each other to produce meaning at a discourse or "text" level. These elements, "meaning markers" if you will, operate across sentences and are called cohesive ties (Halliday & Hasan, 1976). Cohesive ties may be easier to see in written language since written language is more formal and complete than conversational speech. Nevertheless, cohesive ties or meaning markers operate as an essential element of spoken language. This cohesion is the glue that holds everything else together.

Cohesive Ties   These five groups of cohesive ties have been identified: (1) references, (2) substitutions, (3) ellipses, (4) conjunctions, and (5) lexical cohesions (Chapman, 1983). Meaning associated with the first four depends on the relationship of the word to a word or string of words located elsewhere in the text. Lexical cohesion occurs when a word or words are repeated or have some other semantic or associative property.

1. Language allows human beings to name and refer to concrete things, such as persons, and to abstract things, such as feelings and ideas. When referring to any one of these specifically, we need only name it once and then we may refer to it with one of four types of reference cues. This pair of sentences, "John is a gentleman farmer. He owns a steer named George," is an example of an *endophoric* reference. It is explicit and within the text. "It is raining," however, is an example of *exophoric* reference. The receiver must search for the identity of the referent from outside the text.

The other two types of references are *anaphoric* and *cataphoric.* In anaphora the reference is named and then subsequently referred to by a tie marker, as in the case of "John, who is a gentleman farmer." Conversely, cataphora are cues that precede the specific naming of the item: "Because *he* was always late to work, *Steve* finally got fired."

In addition, there are three broad categories of reference ties under which the four types of cues are subsumed. These are *personal, demonstrative,* and *comparative* reference (Chapman, 1983).

Personal reference cites people. In authentic language in use, speakers can take a great deal for granted. They do not need to spell out every detail for the listener. In the following, "*They* told *me you* had gone to see *her* and that *you* had talked about *me. I* want to know what *you* said and what *she* is going to tell *him*," only the context of the event and the information carried in the head of each person in this conversation makes it intelligible. However, it is not a complicated or unusual chain. Embedded in real life it is quite easy to track and comprehend.

Demonstrative ties act as reference pointers in text. Words such as "here" and "there," "this" and "that," or "now" and "then" are considered demonstrative in that they replace words or word chains identified elsewhere. For instance, in these sentences, "This is a bad time for you to call. I am running late and now I'll be even later," *I* and *I'll* are personal references and *now* is a demonstrative reference.

Comparative ties consist of words and phrases such as *similar, likewise, otherwise* that show comparisons. They may also indicate number, as in *more than, equally, fewer,* and quality as in *good, better, best.* For example, in the sentence "*Likewise,* the *more I* see of *you,* the *better I* like *it,*" what type of reference is each of the italic words, and to what does each refer? Personal, demonstrative, and comparative references indicate other information or meaning elements either endophorically or exophorically so that meaning can be integrated across text.

2. Substitutions, the second group of cohesive ties, act in much the same way as reference words but serve to link words or clauses. Such words are *one(s), same, do, so,* and *not.* Several examples follow:

a. "The car in question was an expensive *one* belonging to Mr. Smith, the *same* man you arrested last week." Here, *one* substitutes for car and *same* substitutes for Mr. Smith.

b. "You would *do* better to stay in school. The *ones* who *do* are usually more successful." Here, *do* substitutes for *would be better off* and *ones* substitutes for *students who* followed by a second *do* substituting for *stay in school.*

c. "As I am now *so* you will be." In this sentence, *so* substitutes for *as I am now.*

d. "He is free, but *not so* all his companions." Here, *not so* substitutes for *are not free.*

3. An ellipsis is the omission of words that are absolutely recoverable and for which the reference is clear. For instance, "They emerged from their long climb onto a high plateau. The mountain peaks surrounded them. On one side (*) lay the fields of alpine grass, on the other (*) the river gorge." The ellipsis (*) is used here to avoid redundancy and awkwardness in the second clause. "Weldon and his dad went fishing. They each caught two(*)." In both examples, the consumer of the language has no difficulty in replacing what has been omitted.

4. Conjunctions as a form of cohesive tie come in four basic types. These are additive (*and*), adversative (*yet*), temporal (*then*), and causal (*so*). These types of conjoinings confirm that the meaning of one sentence or thought unit is to be integrated with the meaning of the next.

The additive type is designed to add what is coming next to what has just preceded it. "Off went the children, hand in hand. *And,* 'Be back before dark,' the mother called after them."

The adversative is a comparison type of cue. "John and Carole argue about politics. *On the other hand,* they are still good friends."

Temporal types of conjunctions indicate that two or more time frames are juxtaposed and integrated. "They let the baby cry for a few minutes, *then* fearing something might be wrong, went to the nursery to see."

Causal conjunctions indicate causal relationships. For example, "It will be dark in less than an hour. *Therefore,* we should start back now."

5. Lexical cohesion has to do with word choices. The major types of cohesive ties relative to the speaker's store of words, or lexicon, are synonyms, antonyms, and hyponyms. Synonymic relationships are seen in words that mean the same or nearly the same, such as *happy* and *glad.* Antonymic relationships are seen in words that have the opposite or nearly the opposite meaning, such as *happy* and *sad.* Hyponymic relationships have to do with groups of words that are hierarchically related; for example, *tree* as a general or superordinate term is related to *oak, spruce, hickory,* which are specific or subordinate terms.

At least two devices are used to help listeners and readers track lexical items. These are reiteration and collocation. In reiteration, words are repeated to create cohesion. For example, "She wanted her big brother to introduce her. She knew what big brothers were for. Big brothers brought their big fraternity brothers home for the weekend." Synonyms can provide another type of reiteration, as in this example: "Were you digging in the dirt? There is mud on your hands and knees."

Collocation, the other major type of lexical cohesion, occurs when words go together in pairs or sets. For instance, *bride and groom, cats and dogs.* Linguists regard collocation as an operating cohesive force when words that tend to be associated appear in similar contexts. For example, "Standing in front of the mirror, she admired her long hair. She *combed* it, *braided* then *unbraided* it, and *combed* it again until it *frizzed* with static electricity."

When we examine semantics, or how language transmits meaning, we see that cohesive ties connect smaller meanings to produce longer meaningful discourse. A good deal of the listener's (and the fluent reader's) ability to track, anticipate, and comprehend language comes from these clues.

Cohesive ties, which relate sentences across text and across time, were for the most part learned as we used the language. The rules that govern their construction and use are complex. Assuming we are intimately familiar with the language itself, all we need to comprehend sophisticated language are: (1) an adequate level of developmental maturity; (2) some knowledge of the context of the transaction; and (3) pertinent background or experiential information, including the necessary concepts and vocabulary.

Language Processes   Speakers employ their knowledge of language, their thinking, and their background of experiences when they speak. Listeners, engaged in the act of comprehending speech, bring several essential ingredients to the process. First, they bring their not inconsiderable brains. Relatively speaking, human beings are very smart. They have complex brains that are designed to impose pattern on and make sense of the world. It is the brain that processes oral language. Second, listeners bring their knowledge of language and of its forms, functions, and content. They then use what they know about language and how it works to figure out the speaker's message. Third, they bring all the knowledge and experiences about the world that they have amassed during their lives. Finally, they bring the five senses by which listeners "know" the context of the situation (Gregory & Carroll, 1978; Kavanaugh & Mattingly, 1972). All of these and maybe more are needed to process and understand language.

The importance to communication of context and background knowledge cannot be overstated. Take, for example, the simple question, "What time is it?" Asked by someone the listener knows, this question has the potential to chain into the listener's memory. It may elicit external responses such as, "You are always late. It is not my responsibility to keep up with your schedule." Or it may produce the internal thought, "You are not at all dependable." However, asked rhetorically, as part of a sermon for instance, "What time is it?" may evoke an entirely different chain of memories and responses. These may relate to lost opportunities, the ravages of time on the physical body, guilt over one's "sins of omission," and so on.

Asked as part of a poetry reading, "What time is it?" may cause memories of poems read and thought to be forgotten.

Time, you old gipsy man
Will you not stay?
Put up your caravan
Just for one day.
       (Hodgson, 1930)

Or it might introduce the reading of such poems as:

Time, that is pleased to lengthen out the day
For grieving lovers parted or denied.
       (Millay, 1941)

or

> I shall know why, when time is over
> And I have ceased to wonder why.
>
> (Dickinson, 1978)

Because the brain makes abstract connections—that is, it thinks metaphorically—language can become art.

Language and Context   Whether the utterance is a profound insight or daily conversation, all language is embedded in a real context and in a vicarious context as well. The real context consists of the events in the immediate environment, the events of the moment. The other context is the mind and memory of both the speaker and the listener, the reader and the writer. Both contexts are necessary to understanding, and both allow language to be produced and perceived. Examine the following brief conversation:

First speaker: He busted right outta there. I didn't know he had an arm.

Second speaker: Are we gonna get him?

First speaker: We're doin' everything we can that's legal.

This conversation is totally obscure unless it is placed in a context. The context might be a police detective and a doctor talking in a prison hospital; it might also be a football coach talking to a college athletic recruiter. You can probably think of other plausible contexts. Language cannot be understood without knowing the context.

We have all learned at least one language, our native language, without formal instruction. This feat was perhaps our most successful learning endeavor, because language with its layer upon layer of patterns and rules is extremely complex. Language, in many respects, is our most important tool, and language may be our most unique attribute as human beings. Human beings created language because of need. We are very social beings living in a complex world. We needed a symbol system to represent our ideas and our intentions and to record and transmit the information we wish to convey. The rules concerning how language is used are determined by the cultural group, and they differ from group to group.

SUMMARY

Language is a human social invention. It is pervasive in our lives. We use it nearly every waking minute, and it is also the primary means by which we think and learn. Language is complex and invisible. It has taken linguistic researchers decades to even begin to understand the complexities of human language. Complicated as it is, however, we all seem to learn the layers of underlying structures and surface features of our native language easily and without direct instruction.

Language is a vast, complex human capability and one of the most intricate and important learning events in which the human brain engages. If teachers are to help children learn the written form of language—that is, to help them learn to read and write—knowing how children learn language will prove useful.

THEORY-TO-PRACTICE CONNECTIONS

Language Theory

1. Language is a social invention.

2. Language is a set of abstract symbols used to represent ideas and intentions.

3. Language is extremely complex, consisting of symbols embedded in layer upon layer of patterns and rules.

4. Language is generative.

5. Language is one of the ways we come to know our world.

Examples of Classroom Practice

1. Collaborative problem solving

2. Classroom writing and book publishing

3. Sustained silent reading and writing time

4. Word study within thematic units

5. Formal and informal group discussions

SUGGESTED READINGS

Denes, P., & Pinson, E. (1993). *The speech chain: The physics and biology of spoken language* (2nd ed.). New York: Doubleday.

Halliday, M. (1973). *Explorations in the functions of language.* London: Edward Arnold.

Shuy, R. (1984). Language as the foundation for education. *Theory in Practice, 23,* (3), 167–174.

Vygotsky, L. (1962). *Thought and language.* Cambridge, MA: MIT Press.

SUGGESTED ACTIVITIES

1. Attempt speaking in a monotone to a group of people. What is their response? Why?

2. Attempt speaking very, v e r y s l o w l y to a group of your friends. Speak so that there is a half-second between each word. How do they react? What do they do if you keep it up after they clearly expect you to stop? Why do you think they react that way? What do these two activities tell you about human language production and comprehension? Share your experiences with classmates.

3. Charting distinctive features is an interesting way of visualizing the elements of any conceptual category system. Create a distinctive feature chart for any concept with which you are very familiar. For example, canines. List all the possible types or breeds of dogs across the top, and all the characteristics of dogs (long hair, barks, and so on) that you can think of along the left-hand column. Share your findings. What did you do to get enough features or characteristics to even begin to make your chart work?

4. Tape-record on audiotape three to five minutes of informal conversation between two people. Transcribe the transaction. Describe the context of the conversation. Is knowing the context and/or the speakers helpful to understanding? Try writing some of the conversation phonetically, so as to represent their dialects. How easy was it? What did you learn? Try listening for the cohesive ties. Which ones did you find? Discuss your experience with classmates.

5. Discuss the theory and practice statements on page 57. How do these classroom practices employ natural language?

REFERENCES

Benjamin, R. (1970). *Semantic and language analysis.* New York: Bobbs-Merrill.

Bolinger, D. (1965). *Forms of English: Accent, morpheme and order.* Cambridge, MA: Harvard University Press.

Chapman, J. (1983). *Reading development and cohesion.* Portsmouth, NH: Heinemann.

Cheek, E. (1972). *The development of a hierarchy for teaching phoneme-grapheme correspondences in beginning reading.* Unpublished doctoral dissertation, Florida State University, Tallahassee.

Chomsky, N. (1957). *Syntactic structures.* The Hague: Mouton.

Chomsky, N. (1972). *Language and mind.* New York: Harcourt Brace Jovanovich.

Dickenson, E. (1978). *Favorite poems of Emily Dickenson.* New York: Avenel Books.

Gregory, M., & Carroll, S. (1978). *Language and situation.* London: Routledge & Kegan Paul.

Halliday, M., & Hasan, R. (1976). *Cohesion in English.* London: Longman.

Hodgson, R. (1930). "Time, you old gipsy man." In *Two hundred best loved poems.* New York: Grosset and Dunlap.

Jewell, T. (1987). Investment of worth. In S. Martz (Ed.), *When I am an old woman I shall wear purple.* Watsonville, CA: Papier Maché Press.

Kavanaugh, J., & Mattingly, I. (1972). *Language by ear and by eye.* Cambridge, MA: MIT Press.

Lee, D. (1986). Language, children and society. New York: NYU Press.

Lee, D., & Rubin, J. (1979). *Children and language.* Belmont, CA: Wadsworth.

Lenneberg, E. (1967). *Biological foundations of language.* New York: John Wiley.

Lieberman, P. (1967). *Intonation, perception, and language.* Cambridge, MA: MIT Press.

Millay, E. (1941). *Collected sonnets.* New York: Harper & Row.

Miller, G. (1956). The magical number seven, plus or minus two: Some limits on our capacity for processing information. *Psychological Review, 63,* 81–92.

Salus, P. (1969). *Linguistics.* New York: Bobbs-Merrill.

Schane, S. (1973). *Generative phonology.* Englewood Cliffs, NJ: Prentice-Hall.

Shuy, R. (1984). Language as the foundation for education. In *Theory into Practice, 23,* (3), 167–174.

Smith, F. (1988). *Understanding reading.* Hillsdale, NJ: Lawrence Erlbaum.

Smith, F. (1990). *To think.* New York: Teachers College Press.

Weaver, C. (1988). *Reading processes and practices: From sociopsycholinguistics to whole language.* Portsmouth, NH: Heinemann.

Webster's new universal unabridged dictionary (2nd ed.). (1983). New York: Simon & Schuster.

Wells, G. (1986). *The meaning makers: Children learning language and using language to learn.* Portsmouth, NH: Heinemann.

3

Oral Language Learning

Language is a tool that creates reality. . . . We do not acquire language for its own sake, but for the sake of doing something with and to somebody else.

(BRUNER, 1984, p. 193)

How do young children learn to talk?

How has our understanding of oral language learning expanded during the last half-century?

How does this current level of understanding relate to the development of reading, writing, and thinking?

Is there a relationship between how we learn language and how we learn almost everything else?

What do teachers need to know about the child's language learning?

*L*anguage, as we have seen in chapter 2, is a rather complex code created by human beings for transmitting meaning and for conducting the business of living. Language was developed because of need, the need to share information and ideas with others. We need to communicate in order to survive. Human beings are driven to communicate with each other. Therefore, we are driven to learn language. With language we organize our understanding of the world; we think, learn, and socialize.

Language is not only the basis of social interaction, it is also the foundation for almost all school learning. Most teachers receive instruction that emphasizes teaching children to read and write, but they may not be given sufficient information about the theory of language learning. Therefore, we will examine the language learning process more closely. Literacy learning parallels oral language learning (Goodman, 1984). Understanding one leads to a better understanding of the other, and all forms of language learning involve the same processes that account for learning in general. That is, the same environmental conditions, immersion, demonstration, approximation, and so on promote both kinds of learning. These conditions apply regardless of intellectual capacity or preferred intelligence styles.

Clearly, language is complex. There is no straightforward relationship between the surface features (for example, words) and what they mean. The simple word *gave,* for example, used in the sentences, "She gave me the money," "She gave me a funny look," and "She gave me the test," presents three very different definitions and functions (Lee, 1986). In the first sentence, something changes ownership. In the second sentence, a behavior occurs but no change of ownership. In sentence three, something changes hands but not ownership. Language is very context specific and therefore very difficult to describe. It is also difficult to study at the level of meaning or semantics.

As with learning in general, language learning is a psychogenerative process. Language emerges well before the first word is uttered. Language is built on a semantic foundation built by all the transactions the child has with adults in the environment. During the first few months of life, children figure out how to make themselves understood, and they come to understand much of what is said to them.

For that to happen, children require great amounts of language that makes sense. Much of the language children hear naturally refers to events in the immediate and knowable present. Children must be immersed in language to internalize how language works, how it means. Language is learned in the family, and family and community patterns of talking are cultural. These patterns of talk tend to be full of the predictable, repetitious demonstrations and immediate context young language learners need. By the time they are a few months old, infants have begun to use sounds and gestures intentionally to make themselves understood.

In language learning, as in learning in general, the brain internalizes the underlying structures on which the rest of language is built. This is possible precisely because of the repetitious and predictable nature of naturally occurring language transactions. The brain is designed to detect patterns and construct its understanding of the world. In addition, part of language learning is creative. For example, young children may create a way to let their parents know when they want to be picked up, and they may create a non-word for their sisters or the family dog. Based on our best understandings, language development in young children appears to be a *balance* between *invention,* or the creative drive, and *convention,* or the conformative drive (Goodman, 1990).

Language exists for making and representing meaning. It consists of symbols embedded in layers of rules. Children internalize three broad sets of rule systems—syntax, semantics, and pragmatics. Language is psychogenerative. This means that as the rules are internalized and words are added, more language can be generated. Language learning is easy when it occurs in the course of everyday family life.

Child Language Development: Our Evolving Understanding

For decades, linguists and educators preferred to work with the surface manifestations of language rather than delving into the vague and complicated world of how human beings produce and obtain meaning. Linguists studied the sound system, parts of speech, words, and sentence types. Educators studied sounds and spelling, word parts, words and definitions, and sentence types. Not until essentially the 1960s did linguists, psychologists, and educators begin asking more difficult questions about the complicated world of language.

Even though language is complex, young children learn their native language, the version spoken by their cultural group, easily and without formal instruction. This truly remarkable accomplishment can be explained in part by the fact that the human brain is designed to detect and impose patterns on the world. And language, we have come to discover, is highly patterned. Language learning is a constructive process that involves hypothesizing about how language patterns work and experimenting with those hypotheses. The environmental conditions that promote full language development are immersion, demonstration, use, expectation, responsibility, approximation, and response. These are the conditions that allow the brain to construct its understandings and use its knowledge structures in generative ways for creating more language and for learning.

Characteristics and Insights   When researchers in the 1950s and 1960s first began to examine child language development, their methodologies were not very sophisticated. They resorted to simple counts and averages to describe early language acquisition. For example, research efforts attempted to relate the number and types of sounds children tend to produce to their average months of life. Very early child language development was described as following the five general stages listed in table 3.1 (Ecroyd, 1969).

Most infants have encountered sufficient meaningful language that they begin to speak at 10 to 14 months of age. Describing what infants and toddlers tend to do with sounds as they acquire the beginnings of language may be interesting, but it does not tell us much about the language learning process itself.

Many researchers are satisfied with merely counting things they can see and hear. For instance, estimates have been calculated of the average numbers of words children tend to acquire by certain ages. Two factors are significant here: (1) the importance of word knowledge to the language learning process and (2) the amazing growth in word knowledge for most children. Words reflect children's concept development and their experiences within their families and with the larger world (Huckleberry & Strother, 1972; McCormick & Schiefelbusch, 1990; Nelson, 1988).

As you can see in table 3.2, we learn a vast number of words in just a few years, at least five to seven words per day from birth to age five years. How do children manage this remarkable feat? Does someone teach them that many words directly? Could a child learn

What the Child Does with Sound	When It First Occurs
Undifferentiated crying to differentiated crying as a signal to mother	0–1 month
Babbling or random vocal play	1–3 months
Lallation or non-random play and self-imitation	3–6 months
Echolalia or practice imitating clusters of sounds	6–9 months
First word, purposeful utterance	10–14 months

TABLE 3.1
Development of Speech Sounds

Age	Estimated Average Number of Words
10–14 months	1–3
2 years	300
3 years	900–2,500
4 years	2,500–8,000
5 years	8,000–15,000
10 years	15,000–25,000
18 years	25,000 +/-
College-educated adult	50,000 +/-

that many if someone did try to teach him? Research continued to focus on words, rather than on these difficult questions.

Estimates of the average numbers of words children "know"— that is, recognize when heard in context—at various stages in their development are interesting. But because children recognize many words when they hear them does not necessarily mean they use that many in speaking. Estimates of the average numbers of words children "produce"—use in their natural conversations—at various ages is also interesting. The chart in table 3.3, based on the work of Brown (1988), provides an estimate of the average words produced per sentence by children from one to four years of age.

By the time they are four years old, children on the average are speaking sentences of between three and five words in length. But individual children are so variable and their experiences so unique that only in the very broadest sense is this type of information useful. Counting and averaging surface features at the sound and word level does not answer the most important questions. It does not tell us how language is learned, how to help children better acquire it, or how to improve the acquisition of written language for children.

For a long time language was thought to be the strings of words that make up surface utterances rather than the manifestations of meaning through underlying rule patterns. But language and meaning exist in the mind. With the work of Chomsky (1957, 1965) and the other structural linguists, researchers began asking how children learn the invisible underlying rules of language that they are not taught. Linguists did not even know what all the rules were. Not until the 1960s and 1970s did we realize that young children are not just learning words and imitating the adults in their environments; young children are learning how to make meaning with language, and they are doing much of it during the first year of life. "The emergence of language is built on a prior semantic foundation" (Lee, 1986, p. 29). In the late 1960s and early 1970s no one really understood how that happens.

Researchers began observing young children in natural environments and documenting what children do as they try to develop language. The early work of Berko (1958), as well as Bloom (1970), Brown (1973), Bruner (1983), C. Chomsky (1969), Halliday (1975a, 1975b), Klima & Bellugi-Klima (1966), and Menyuk (1969), found that child language development focuses on making meaning. Children do in fact learn the invisible structural patterns that make language work, and they learn them in systematic ways, even though individual children vary greatly in when these patterns are constructed.

M. A. K. Halliday (1975b), a world-famous linguist, became interested in how children learn and use language. As he described the language development of his son, Nigel, he discovered that children learn a great deal about how language means long before the appearance of those first word utterances. Before his first birthday, Nigel used sounds and gestures to convey his intentions. He said /na/ as he

Age Range	Average Number of Words
12–26 months	1.0–2.0
27–30 months	2.0–2.5
31–34 months	2.5–3.0
35–40 months	3.5–3.8
41–46 months	3.8–4.5

TABLE 3.3
Growth in Words per Utterance

pointed to whatever object he wanted. Everyone knew this was Nigel's way of indicating that he wanted to be given the object. What Halliday pointed out, however, was that this was clearly an *invention*. Nigel had constructed a completely "new" way to express his meaning in an attempt to get what he wanted.

All children *invent* how to mean. They may create a word for their bottle, for their favorite blanket or stuffed animal, or for their grandmother. But their language development is not totally "invention." Children spend the first few years of their lives learning how to make meaning and learning how the language already in their environment works. They create a linguistic system that serves their personal and social circumstances. They understand much of what is said around them long before they make purposeful language. Eight-month-old toddlers who do not yet speak understand most of what their parents say. "Are you hungry?" "Do you want to go see Grandma?" "Bring me a clean diaper from the box and we'll change you." Yet, when they do begin to speak, even though they understand a great deal of lengthy connected discourse in context, they produce only one-word utterances. Because of their internalized semantic foundation, first-word utterances actually represent entire thought units. For instance, the toddler who looks imploringly at Daddy with arms uplifted and says, "Up! Up!" may actually mean something like, "Pick me up. I'm tired of being down here on the floor looking at everybody's kneecaps."

From the many one-word utterances children develop, they go on to produce two-word strings by the time they are approximately 18 to 21 months old (Howe, 1976). The emergence of two-word utterances such as "Mommy sock" shows understanding of referential meaning. It may also indicate several other meanings (Bloom, 1970). These abbreviated strings, sometimes called telegraphic speech, are like telegrams sent from the child to the adult. Used like full sentences, they employ the fewest and most meaning-bearing words possible to get the message across. "Mommy sock" might mean "I want my sock," "There is my sock," "Mommy has my sock," or "Mommy fix my sock." Language, even at the two-word stage, is highly context dependent and represents full thought units. The actual intended meaning can only be determined by and is only useful in the context in which it occurs. In addition, Bloom concluded that the grammar of telegraphic speech cannot be analyzed at the surface level.

Researchers have found that as children's language expands, their development of syntactic structures is somewhat predictable and consistent. Clearly, children intuit the underlying layers of embedded rules as they use language. And this syntactic development parallels their cognitive development. That is, an understanding of object-action, object-action-object, and other relational and referential meanings in the real world are experiential and thinking operations. Cognitive development occurs as language expands, and each supports the growth of the other (Lee, 1986; Menyuk, 1988).

According to Slobin (1979), children learn the major rule systems and elements of their language essentially simultaneously; they acquire syntactic rules, words, and information as they use the language to make and understand their world. The main points in understanding the development of children's language after the one- and two-word stages are the following (Hood, 1980; Lee, 1986; Menyuk, 1988):

1. Language develops best in contexts where children have great amounts of language to learn from.

2. When children have great amounts of meaningful language, they intuitively learn the underlying structures—that is, the brain learns for them.

3. Semantics, syntax, and pragmatics develop together.

4. Language development and cognitive development occur simultaneously, and each supports the expansion and refinement of the other.

Baby Talk   Many of the insights into child language development have been arrived at from observing children in natural contexts, especially as they interact with their mothers. Documenting and analyzing the talk of mothers and their babies have allowed researchers to see in practice all the demonstrations and negotiations of meaning that naturally occur between a mother and her infant (Wells,

1986). During a stroll in the park, a baby may say, "Mommy boot," and a mother may respond with, "Yes dear, there's snow on the ground and it's cold outside and everyone has boots on." Then the baby may say again, louder this time, "Mommy boot!" At this point the mother knows she is misunderstanding and tries another interpretation. "Oh, do you want me to take your boots off? Is there something in your boot?" Whereupon the child may now be saying "Mommy boot! Mommy boot!" repeatedly and emphatically. This will continue until *the mother figures it out.* In the meantime, she is providing the child with a great many demonstrations of what he could have meant and how to use such two-word phrases as "Mommy boot!" She demonstrates and they negotiate until a satisfactory meaning has been determined—for example, the child lost his boot several yards back and his foot is getting cold—and an outcome reached. This is also an example of what Bruner (1978) calls scaffolding—helping the child lay the foundation and create the framework for language.

Such research into what many linguists and educators call baby talk has also been highly profitable. It has revealed that the telegraphic speech that characterizes the first two to three years of language development is highly patterned and rule based, just as adult speech is. Baby talk is a reduced and overgeneralized form of adult language. For instance, "Go bye bye" is an abbreviated three-word utterance that is universally understood when uttered in the context of family life. And although many young, well-educated parents attempt to avoid baby talk, nearly all engage in a wide variety of such talk in spite of themselves (Garvey, 1984).

Baby talk, as a short-term bridge to more complex rule forms, is natural and necessary to children's language development. Baby talk is in no way harmful, so long as it is dropped at the appropriate time and not encouraged into school age by doting adults. A closer look at baby talk yields additional insights into the language learning process. Communication between mothers and babies during the first year of life, before language production begins, provides *demonstrations* of language and is the foundation upon which children build the rest of their language (Snow and Ferguson, 1977). Early child/adult transactions lay the basis by which children learn all the underlying structural rules that cannot be learned directly.

   Mothers, fathers, and other primary caretakers help young children with vast quantities of language; these language experiences are
meaningful and often recur in predictable situations. This is one reason children develop language with such apparent ease. For example, the conversation at the breakfast table may be amazingly similar
from morning to morning. Observe two instances of a mother and
an infant playing with a plastic toy made of colored rings of increasing size that are stacked on a spindle.

First Pair

Mother: Here. See the toy?

Baby: (*Grabs the toy.*)

Mother: See the toy? Here.

Baby: (*Slings plastic rings across the floor. Giggles and claps hands.*)

Mother: (*Laughs.*) I'll get them. Here. (*Puts some rings on baby's lap and
the rest within reach.*)

Baby: (*Tries to put rings on spindle randomly. This appears to be hard
work.*)

Mother: Good girl. This is a good toy. Here. (*Hands baby three of the
rings that were out of reach.*)

Baby: (*Tries to put smaller ring on first. Slings plastic rings across floor.
Giggles.*)

Second Pair

Mother: Here. See the toy?

Baby: (*Grabs the toy.*)

Mother: See the toy.

Baby: (*Slings plastic rings across the floor. Giggles.*)

Mother: I'll get them. Here. (*Puts some rings on baby's lap and the rest
within reach.*)

Baby: (*Reaches for one of the rings.*)

Mother: Here. This one goes first. (*Hands baby the largest ring.*)

Baby: (*Tries to put rings on at random.*)

Mother: No. This one goes first. Here.

Baby: (*Slings plastic rings across the floor. Giggles.*)

Mother: (*Laughs.*) No. I'll get them. Here. This one goes first.

Each child is being shown how to name objects and actions. Sentence types such as questions, negatives, and imperatives are used. But instead of attending to the language, the children are playing with a toy and their mothers. However, they *are learning* language as they play. One child is encouraged to experiment with the toy. The other child is encouraged to recognize the pattern the toy employs. Each child is not only learning language, but also learning about the world. Their language learning may be very similar, and what they are learning about the world may be quite different. In a different set of transactions, we might hear children learning similar things about their worlds, but very different things about language.

Language is learned in the social and cultural context of the daily events of home, family, and community; therefore, language is very personal and idiosyncratic to the life of the learner. Children learn their language as they transact with others. That is, children learn language by being *immersed* in it, in the context in which the language is occurring. They *use* language to get what they want. And everyone, child and adult alike, *expects* it to be that way. Language development is a continuous, interactive, constructive process that focuses on meaning (Lindfors, 1985).

As children interact with parents, other family members (especially siblings), other children, and other adults, their language development becomes more complex, their language fuller and more expressive. They imitate what they hear, but there is considerably more to child language development than imitation. We know that because most of the language young children produce is not imitated form. For example, no one ever said to a child, "Me want mine doggie," "My foots hurts," or "You doed that?" These are not imitations, rather these expressions represent children's attempts to figure out the underlying structural rules and patterns—how language works. In the first instance, the child is hypothesizing about personal pronouns. In the second and third, we see an example of overgeneralization, first of the rule for forming regular plurals, then of the rule for past tense. These types of child language constructions are called *approximations*. Not only do they occur naturally in language learning around the world, but they are also absolutely necessary to language development.

Approximations, a normal part of the process, indicate that learners are hypothesizing about underlying structures. They merge into conventional or adult constructions over time. Adults do not need to "correct" child language. It is not necessary to say, "No dear. You should say, 'I want my doggie,' or 'My feet hurt.'" And the child wouldn't understand anyway. Young language learners are thinking about their intended meanings, not the surface structure or string of sounds and words they are trying to use. In fact, if adults attempt to correct each aspect of child language to force it to conform to "standard" speech before the child has internalized sufficient examples of language (that is, to circumvent the natural process), they might cause more harm than good (Cazden, 1974).

Children naturally construct language without much awareness of surface forms and features. Most adults intuitively know that correcting child language is a waste of time and is probably not good for children. They expect children to learn anyway. Parents may chastise children for obscenities or correct certain pet peeves such as "ain't," but parents are simply too busy with the business at hand—communication—to be aware of all the phonologic, syntactic, semantic, and pragmatic approximations in their children's language. Those they do catch are usually thought of as cute or clever—for example, "passghetti." In families where children are rewarded rather than ignored or corrected for their creative attempts at language, they tend to investigate language freely, finding out for themselves what works and what doesn't.

Child Language Development: Current Perspectives

General Phases of Language Development   Today, educators and linguists know a great deal about, and can describe in detail, phonologic, syntactic, and semantic development. Children's intentions, what they are personally interested in and what they attend to in the environment, are keys to understanding learning and language development (Donaldson, 1978). Most educators and linguists now agree that child language learning is a constructive process. These constructions begin long before the production of meaningful, purposeful sounds. The use of sounds to support gestures and indicate intended meanings begins around 8 months and is followed by one-word utterances around 12 to 14 months. Single-word utterances represent entire thought units and soon expand into two-word, three-word, and longer strings following the syntactic rules that have been internalized. At 10 months a child might point to the refrigerator and say "doo" for juice. At 14 months she might ask for juice by pointing and saying "juice." Within a few more months she might be asking for "more juice" and by the age of 2 or 3 years "I want more juice" (Lindfors, 1985), having dropped many of the gestures that were once necessary to communication. By age 2½ to 3 years, children tend to use both nouns and verbs as well as plurals, past tense, infinitives, some prepositions, and both definite and indefinite noun markers.

By age 3, children tend to use *yes* and *no* and "wh" questions—*who, what, when, where.* They may also be exploring negative and imperative sentences. Early sentences involve single propositions, such as "I want _____"or "Someone is _____." By this time most children show a tendency to conjoin related events or ideas with the word *and.* As they progress, they learn to embed one thought unit or independent clause into another. For example, "Susie is going and Mary is going, too" becomes "Susie and Mary are going." By age 4 years most children can coordinate simple sentences and propositional relationships (Dumtschin, 1988): "I like Tony. He's my friend. We play together" becomes "Me and my friend Tony play together."

The development of grammar in children's language also involves the development of intonation patterns, the phonological and morphological systems, and word meanings. While most children begin with one-word utterances, they move to two-word structures very quickly. The first appearance of two-word utterances is followed by a gradual expansion in the number of pairs of words, such as "that glass," "hi dog," "more milk," "where that," "allgone cookie," "mommy dress," "put here," "give book." Two-word strings rapidly increase into total language (Dale, 1972).

Word pairs and lengthier strings of words—"Why you doed that?" "I formember that, Mommie," "I know what I gonna get some more that"—are evidence of children's attempts to solve the language puzzle. They demonstrate that children actively *engage* in figuring out how the rules work to a far greater extent than they imitate forms. And they use their growing store of language patterns to communicate new ideas and information.

As children cope with the new words they are rapidly acquiring and the many underlying phrase structure and transformational rules they are internalizing, their output only approximates adult language. Over time, their approximations more closely reflect adult speech. Even if they do not produce them, children comprehend many adult forms. However, the fact that a child recognizes or uses a word doesn't mean he understands the concept as fully as an adult. Children must also learn that a word may have several meanings—for example, *pretty*, as in "That's pretty" and "Pretty soon."

Young children also overgeneralize words; all animals may be cows for a while or all animals may be dogs. Children might learn to say "dada" when they see their fathers, and then call all males in their environment "dada" for a time. Eventually, the language learner comes to realize that a word can stand for one particular object only (*Daddy* as that one person) or a class of like objects (*cup, chair,* or other common nouns) (Lee, 1986). When learning about word labels for groups of similar phenomena, children identify the distinctive features that an object or event must possess to be included in a classification. Our understanding of the world rests in these schemata or knowledge structures that learners build in the brain.

The language learner focuses on making meaning with a purpose. Children use language to express themselves, to get what they want, and to expand and refine their thinking. They use language to create new worlds through make-believe, entertaining themselves and others with imaginative play. They use language to develop their own unique personalities and to exert control over their environments (Fisher & Terry, 1977). They use language to learn and they learn language in the process.

Language learning is a psychogenerative process. Language is not constructed in a vacuum: all the people in the child's social world provide need, opportunity, expectations, and demonstrations of language (Smith, 1988; Tough, 1977). Children do not start learning their language when or just before the first word is uttered. The emergence of language begins well before first words. Language is built on a semantic foundation provided by all the transactions the child has with adults in the environment. During the first few months of life, children figure out how to make themselves understood, and they come to understand much of what is said to them.

To do that, young children require great amounts of language that make sense, and they need to be encouraged to use language for their own purposes. The more we talk to and with children the better. A large portion of that talk has to refer to things going on in the immediate and knowable present.

Take, for instance, the following hypothetical situation of two sets of new parents and two infants. Both sets of parents adore their new baby. They both spend time with the babies, and each baby is equally bright and healthy in every respect. The only major difference is that one set of parents talks about what they are doing as they play with their child. "See the ball. Here it comes. Ooh! That's good. Roll it back to Daddy." The other set of parents, however, talks to each other. They talk about the news, the weather, investment banking, or nuclear physics, but they do not talk about things the child can observe and relate to in the immediate environment. The question is, all other things being equal, which child is likely to learn language the fastest? Which child is likely to be more verbal by school age? Both children are immersed in oral language, but only one is immersed in language that is sufficiently repetitious and meaningful *to the child* for the child to readily internalize how language works, how it means. Language is learned in the family, and family and community patterns of talking are cultural and natural. These patterns, unlike the conversation of the second set of parents described here, tend to be full of the repetitious demonstrations and immediate context that young language learners need.

The Generative Nature of Language Learning

Language learning, like learning in general, is psychogenerative. As children observe and interact with others, the brain internalizes the patterns or underlying structures on which the rest of language will be built. The brain is literally teaching itself how to learn language. Language learning is also creative. How is it that language is both acquired from the environment and invented by the learner? Let's illustrate this process by examining the following proposition. One child alone in the world would not create a language. There would be no need to name objects, infer relationships, or express feelings and thoughts. There would be no one to share them with or to participate in the creation of the code, or representational system, of the language. However, two or more children together would create their own entirely unique, idiosyncratic language. That new language would have a sound system; it would also have word labels for objects, ideas, relationships, and events. It would have a grammar or syntax, that is, underlying phrase structure rules. Two or more human beings alone in the world would create a new language, and with it they would make their world meaningful. They might even begin to argue about how to use certain elements of the language or which sound label was the "correct" one for a particular event. That is, the new language would soon develop pragmatic rules.

However, children born into human society, into highly sophisticated cultural groups, usually do not create an *entirely* new language, except in the case of some identical twins. Rather, most children create the language that is essentially already there. They do that to be understood and to understand. What transpires between birth and the early stages of language production supports the dual processes of *invention* (creating forms and structures) and *convention* (figuring out and using the word label and underlying structural rules that are already there). These psychogenerative processes characterize the rest of oral language learning.

Based on our best understandings, language development in

young children appears to be a *balance* between invention and convention (Goodman, 1990). There is evidence that children are driven to invent or creatively engage in making language. But because they want to be understood, they end up having to conform, to figure out the language that exists in their environments. This dual process of invention and convention can be thought of as an ever-expanding spiral of constructive or creative forces in language development balanced against the need to conform, to communicate (see figure 3.1).

Children create or invent language for themselves. Hypothetically, if all the adult speakers of language disappeared from the environment, children's language development would spin off in a line to form new languages. These new language groups, we can assume, would be as complex and as large as needed. The fact that children learn language in and among a multitude of other language users

FIGURE 3.1
Invention versus Convention in Language Construction

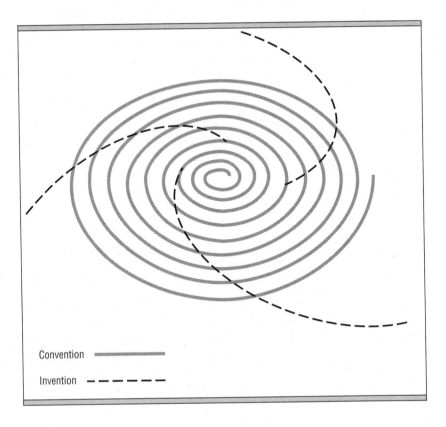

Convention ——————

Invention — — — — —

causes them to have to conform their inventions to the language that exists around them if they are to be understood—hence, the pull back to the center, to conventional forms, in the expanding spiral of language development. As the language develops, children invent or construct the underlying rules and are then able to plug in new words and phrases, as acquired, into the structures or rules they have internalized. If they can make themselves understood, they retain the rule patterns. If not, they alter them. In these ways, children gradually become capable of communicating everything they want to communicate, the wonderful variety of information and ideas they think.

Remember how the eighty-eight tones of the piano are capable of producing all the wealth of music in the world? Likewise, human DNA, which is responsible for all the variation among people in the world, is composed of only four elements in long, repeated strings of various combinations. Our language is composed of forty-four sounds, thousands of words, and hundreds of complex underlying rules. In the same way that the limited tones of the piano can make all the music in the world, or the four code strings of DNA can create all the different people in world, our capacity to create language for expressing a world of information and ideas is virtually unlimited. Human language is psychogenerative in nature.

We know that language exists to make and represent meaning. We know that it consists of three broad sets of rule systems that learners must internalize—syntax, semantics, and pragmatics. Language is part invention and part convention. It is psychogenerative. Language is learned as it is used in the course of everyday family living; it is culturally determined. Language learning is just a more complex case of how human beings make sense of almost everything in the world.

Language Learning in Use   Children do not study sounds, words and underlying rules in order to learn their language. Language is learned as it is being used and language in use is always whole and purposeful for the user. Growth in the construction of language, syntactic, semantic, and pragmatic rules, follows similar paths from language to language around the world. While wide variation exists among individual children within any single group, a great deal is known about the nature of language development in general (Brown, 1970; Carroll, 1960; Dale, 1972; Halliday, 1975a, 1975b; Lee, 1986; McCarthy, 1954; Menyuk, 1988; O'Donnell, Griffin, & Norris, 1967).

By the 1960s researchers in child language learning discovered that surface characteristics, such as sounds, had relatively little to do with language learning. The complexities and the regularities of the constructions children engage in as they develop language were still unexplored. Current perspectives on children's language learning hold that semantic categories (or meaning) *precede or develop together* with syntactic rules (Maratsos, 1983; Menyuk, 1988). That is, meaning comes before structure. Language must make sense before it can be learned (Smith, 1988). Meaningful language is always whole; no one speaks sounds without grammar or grammar without meaning.

Children's drive to communicate causes them to develop language. They want to make their intentions and interests clear and to get their needs and desires fulfilled. Children use language in a wide variety of ways, from "I want . . ." to "Tell me . . . ." For a list of the uses children tend to employ as they develop language (Halliday, 1975a) and the ways teachers can use those natural language functions in the classroom, see chapter 7, page 261. Children use language to control their environments. Young language learners construct the underlying rules that allow them to communicate from the strings of words provided by the natural environment. They identify the distinctive features that allow them to assign words to a syntactic or semantic category, and language grows exponentially. Actually, the brain performs these operations for learners as they use real language for real purposes.

Language Use as Culturally Determined   The brain learns the underlying structural patterns and learners use their store of words and their knowledge of how language works. During language development, the brain internalizes these three broad sets of underlying rule patterns: (1) the rules that govern the ordering and organizing of the symbols themselves, sounds into morphemes and words, and words into phrases and sentences (the *syntactic system*); (2) the meanings of the symbols as they refer to objects, events, and ideas (the *semantic system*); (3) how the symbols function, or why given symbols are appropriate for a given context (the *pragmatic system*) (Gardner, 1991). In order to communicate, learners must learn and apply the rules of syntax, semantics, and pragmatics that are valued in the surrounding culture (Gardner, 1991).

Shirley Brice Heath (1983) studied language use in three different cultural settings: a poor black, a poor white, and a middle-class white community. She found that in the poor black community, oral storytelling and the ability to tell tall tales was revered. In the poor white community, language was used to recount events, and deviations from literal "truth" were shunned. In the middle-class white community, fantasy was encouraged so long as it was clearly labeled and not confused with reality. Heath suggested that while all these children may have well developed language abilities for use within their cultural groups, they are differentially prepared for the language, expectations, and assumptions of schools. That is, some of these children may be at a disadvantage in school unless teachers understand and respect the linguistic and cultural traditions each child brings to the classroom.

Some of the children may misunderstand and be misunderstood in their use of language and their cognitive capabilities. Teacher expectation also plays a part in children's success or failure in school, and teachers may be influenced by the dialects of some children to form low expectations for them. Lowered expectations operate against low-income children (Lee, 1986). Children learn the language of the family—the only language they can learn. All social-class dialects are complex, fully formed linguistic systems. Sociolinguists agree that there are no deficits inherent in any dialects themselves (Lee, 1986).

Patterns of talking in school are also cultural. They are frequently without context and highly unfamiliar to many children. When children use language differently from their teachers, problems may arise. When children do not know how to play the game called school, they may be prejudged as poor learners with limited literacy and other academic potential (Michaels, 1981). When such judgments are made on no other basis than social-class language variation, human potential is lost.

Language Learning as Reflective of Learning in General

Language is a complex symbol communication system that is learned through use. Language learning takes place in the brain. The brain is designed to detect and impose patterns on the world of sensory experiences, and language is composed of patterns. The brain is made to learn language, but it is also made to detect the features and regularities of everything it encounters.

In learning about language learning, it is important to note what young language learners *do,* but also to understand what they *do not do.* While children's language constructions show the use of underlying rule structures very early on, these rules may not be consistently applied. For example, a child might say *mouses* rather than *mice* in her spontaneous, informal speech, suggesting she doesn't yet know which nouns form irregular plurals. That same child, however, may then refer to a cat as "the mice-eater," not "the mouses-eater," in another conversation five minutes later (Gardner, 1991). Neither do children produce intentional utterances with characteristics that could not exist in their language. Even the invented name for the family dog will not sound as though it could exist in a very different language.

In the same way that young children construct language, human beings come to know almost everything about their world. We learn language from examples of language in use provided by the environment. As we try to understand and use language to have our needs fulfilled, the brain identifies the distinctive features and underlying rules. We learn nearly everything else the same way. For instance, we learn what a chair is through examples of chairs in our environment. We identify the features that make up the category "chair" from experiences with objects and pictures of objects to sit on. Our understanding of "chair" is further refined by examples of objects, especially furniture, that are not chairs. We come to know what dogs are through encounters, both real and vicarious, with dogs and with animals that are not dogs. We may be *immersed* in what we are learning, see *demonstrations; engage* in representing our understanding, and be *expected* to learn. There is little difference, except perhaps in scope and complexity, between learning language and learning anything that can be learned through interaction with the world of sensory data.

The Relationship between Oral Language Learning and Literacy

Understanding oral language learning leads to a better understanding of what it takes for children to learn to read and write. Children learn by doing, but as we have seen, that statement implies some specific circumstances. For one thing, what learners *do* must be purposeful and meaningful to them from their point of view. This condition occurs naturally in oral language development, as children listen to and talk about the things that interest and affect them. They are concerned about getting their needs and wants met, and they are interested in the sheer act of communication. Humans are very social beings.

In oral language development, children require immersion in great amounts of oral language in situations they can make sense of. Meaning precedes structure, and prediction precedes perception. Children must be encouraged to use language for their own purposes. They must be talked to, listened to, and talked *with*. The more oral language they hear, the more they learn, because the language relates to what is occurring naturally in the environment.

For literacy development, children also require immersion in great amounts of print, but as with oral language development, the material must make sense to the learner. That is, it must be written language that is interesting, meaningful, and purposeful from the children's viewpoint (Durkin, 1966; Teale & Sulzby, 1986).

Literacy learning parallels oral language development (Goodman, 1984), as figure 3.2 shows. In the preschool years a great deal of letter-sound and pragmatic knowledge (as well as some types of syntactic and semantic knowledge) regarding print is internalized. Long before they can really read and write, children see print all around them—at home, in stores, along roadsides. They see various uses for

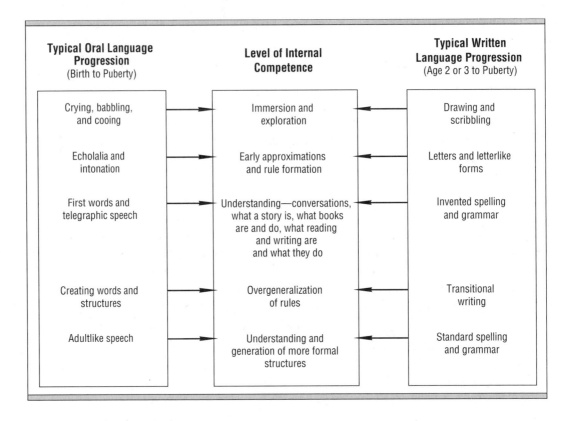

Typical Oral Language Progression (Birth to Puberty)	Level of Internal Competence	Typical Written Language Progression (Age 2 or 3 to Puberty)
Crying, babbling, and cooing	Immersion and exploration	Drawing and scribbling
Echolalia and intonation	Early approximations and rule formation	Letters and letterlike forms
First words and telegraphic speech	Understanding—conversations, what a story is, what books are and do, what reading and writing are and what they do	Invented spelling and grammar
Creating words and structures	Overgeneralization of rules	Transitional writing
Adultlike speech	Understanding and generation of more formal structures	Standard spelling and grammar

FIGURE 3.2
Relationships between Oral and Written Language Development

print, for notes and lists, food and product labels, order blanks and other forms, catalogs, bills, newspapers, magazines, and books. Young children try to read and write because they are born into a literate society. Print is everywhere.

The extent of children's oral language partly determines the ease with which they learn to read and write. In a classic study by Walter Loban (1976), the language development of 338 children was followed from kindergarten through grade 12. Loban examined both oral and written language development and contributed at least two major findings to our understanding of children and their language growth. First, his study yielded detailed descriptions of typical language patterns for various ages from 5 to 17 years. For example, the study determined that the average number of words per oral communication for children ages 6 to 7 is 6.6 to 8.1 words (p. 82). Second, Loban concluded that the greater the child's proficiency in oral language, the faster and more proficient reading and writing development will be. That is, there is a positive relationship between oral and written language proficiency. In general, the good get better and the less proficient remain less proficient. Educators have been searching ever since for a way to alter the negative end of that equation, to help the less proficient begin to resemble the more proficient language user.

Children who start school with too little oral language need great amounts of talking and concept development. Those who start school with too little prior experience with written language and its uses must have that foundation laid in school as well. The experiences and strategies used for growth in oral language are the basis for developing the thinking or cognitive strategies necessary for reading and writing (Forester, 1977; Menyuk, 1988).

SUMMARY

Children learn language by using language (Halliday, 1975b). Language in use is always whole, meaningful, and purposeful to the user. Children develop language quickly if they are immersed in great amounts of oral language in situations they can make sense of and are encouraged to use language to get their needs met. They tend to begin language production with one-word utterances and gestures, focusing on the things they want. This soon expands to two- and three-word utterances, then into longer, more complex speech. After two-word utterances, language growth is rapid. It remains, however, systematic and predictable.

Even though language is one of the most complex phenomena human beings ever learn, it is learned without formal instruction and with relative ease. Goodman (1986, p. 8) summarizes when language is easy and when it is hard to learn. These statements apply equally to talking/listening and to reading/writing.

Learning Language Is Easy When

It's real and natural.

It's whole.

It's sensible.

It's interesting.

It's relevant.

It belongs to the learner.

Learning Language Is Hard When

It's artificial.

It's broken into bits and pieces.

It's nonsense.

It's dull and uninteresting.

It's irrelevant to the learner.

It belongs to somebody else.

Learning Language Is Easy When

It's part of a real event.

It has social utility.

It has purpose for the learner.

The learner chooses to use it.

It's accessible to the learner.

The learner has power to use it.

Learning Language Is Hard When

It's out of context.

It has no social value.

It has no discernible purpose.

It's imposed by someone else.

It's inaccessible.

The learner is powerless.

Children's literacy development parallels their oral language development. The relevant aspects of oral language that directly affect learning to read and write are the words and concepts in a child's language, the underlying structures, and the child's awareness of language. Literacy is built upon an oral language base. What teachers believe about language learning and literacy will determine the extent to which they make children's learning to read and write easy or difficult.

THEORY-TO-PRACTICE CONNECTIONS

Language Learning Theory

1. Even in view of its highly complex nature, our native language is learned naturally, without instruction.

2. Language learning is a balance between invention and convention.

3. Language learning is an active, constructive process, i.e., children learn language as they naturally use it.

4. Children's language learning is not chaotic and random, but highly patterned and organized.

5. Language learning is a psychogenerative process.

Examples of Classroom Practice

1. Creating opportunities for learners to see and use language in functional ways, e.g., lists, messages, sign-up forms

2. Encouraging learners to express themselves freely, before they can do so in "correct" or conventional language

3. Helping learners engage in authentic reading, writing, thinking experiences, e.g., learners may want to know why water disappears when it is boiled; they may want to write a letter to their favorite author

4. Analyzing children's invented spellings or oral reading to determine the understandings they have developed and to help them grow

5. Establishing times and ways for authentic daily reading and writing, often involving children in sharing what they are learning

SUGGESTED READINGS

Heath, S. (1983). *Ways with words: Language, life, and work in communities and classrooms.* Cambridge, England: Cambridge University Press.

Wells, G. (1986). *The meaning makers: Children learning language and using language to learn.* Portsmouth, NH: Heinemann.

SUGGESTED ACTIVITIES

1. Print the following four sentences, one each on four note cards.

> Billy threw the ball.
> The ball threw Billy.
> Billy threw the game.
> Billy threw the party.

Poll several people, asking them what each sentence means. Does the arrangement of sentences make any difference? What does this exercise tell you about how human beings process language?

2. Find a toddler, approximately 1½ to 3 years old. Audiotape-record the child in 3 to 5 minutes of conversation once a month throughout the semester. Transcribe the tapes. How does language develop for this child? Document language development with examples from the tapes. Share and discuss with classmates.

3. Interview several parents of preschool-age children about their child's language development. After you have gotten basic information, such as the child's name, age, and sex, ask the following types of questions:

   a. When did _____ start to talk?

   b. What were _____'s first words?

   c. What were _____'s favorite words or sayings?

   d. Did _____ ever make up or invent words for favorite things such as bottle, blanket, and grandmother?

   (1) If yes, did the family adopt these words too?

   (2) Do you still use them? If not, why did you stop?

   e. What did _____ use language for when _____ first started really talking? Did _____ like to ask questions and tell others what to do?

   f. Ask any other questions that you think will add to your understanding of how parents perceive language and language development. Many people believe they teach their children to talk. Many people think that imitation is the main way children learn their language. If people think that imitation is a major learning strategy, what implications might that have for their expectations of schools and learning to read and write?

Compile your interview responses. Do you detect any patterns? Are parents generally positive about their children's language development? Discuss your findings with classmates.

4. Consider the language learning theory statements on page 86. How do the examples of classroom applications to instruction support natural language learning as described in this chapter? Why should we concern ourselves with supporting natural learning processes in the first place?

REFERENCES

Berko, J. (1958). The child's learning of English morphology. *Word, 14,* 150–177.

Bloom, L. (1970). *Language development: Form and function in emerging grammars.* Cambridge, MA: MIT Press.

Brown, R. (1970). The first sentences of child and chimpanzee. *Psycholinguistics: Selected papers of Roger Brown.* New York: Free Press.

Brown, R. (1973). *A first language: The early stages.* Cambridge, MA: Harvard University Press.

Brown, R. (1988). Development of a first language in the human species. In M. Franklin & S. Barten (Eds.), *Child language: A reader* (pp. 75–88). Oxford: Oxford University Press.

Brown, R., & Bellugi, U. (1964). Three processes in the child's acquisition of syntax. *Harvard Educational Review, 34,* 133–151.

Bruner, J. (1978). The role of dialogue in language acquisition. In A. Sinclair, R. Jarvella, & W. Levelt (Eds.), *The child's conception of language* (pp. 241–256). New York: Springer-Verlag.

Bruner, J. (1983). *Child's talk: Learning to use language.* New York: Holt, Rinehart & Winston.

Bruner, J. (1984). Language, mind, and reading. In H. Goelman, A. Oberg, & F. Smith (Eds.), *Awakening to literacy.* Portsmouth, NH: Heinemann.

Carroll, J. (1960). Language development in children. In C. Harris (Ed.), *Encyclopedia of educational research.* New York: Macmillan.

Carroll, J. (1970). *Comprehension by 3rd, 6th, and 7th graders of words having multiple grammatical functions: Final report.* Princeton, NJ: Educational Testing Service.

Cazden, C. (1974). Suggestions from studies of early language acquisition. In J. DeStefano and S. Fox (Eds.), *Language and the language arts.* Boston: Little, Brown.

Chomsky, C. (1969). *The acquisition of syntax in children from 5 to 10.* Cambridge, MA: MIT Press.

Chomsky, N. (1957). *Syntactic structures.* The Hague: Mouton.

Chomsky, N. (1965). *Aspects of the theory of syntax.* Cambridge, MA: MIT Press.

Dale, P. (1972). *Language development: Structure and function.* Hinsdale, IL: Dryden Press.

Donaldson, M. (1978). *Children's minds.* New York: W. W. Norton.

Dumtschin, J. (1988, March). Recognizing language development and delay in early childhood. *Young Children, 43,* 39–42.

Durkin, D. (1966). The achievement of preschool readers: Two longitudinal studies. *Reading Research Quarterly, 1,* 5–36.

Ecroyd, D. (1969). *Speech in the classroom.* Englewood Cliffs, NJ: Prentice-Hall.

Fisher, C., & Terry, A. (1977). *Children's language and the language arts.* New York: McGraw-Hill.

Forester, A. (1977). What teachers can learn from "natural readers." *The reading teacher, 31*(2), 160–166.

Gardner, H. (1991). *The unschooled mind.* New York: Basic Books.

Garvey, C. (1984). *Children's talk.* Cambridge, MA: Harvard University Press.

Gleitman, L. (1988). Biological dispositions to learn language. In M. Franklin & S. Barten (Eds.), *Child language: A reader* (pp. 158–176). Oxford: Oxford University Press.

Goodman, K. (1990, December). *The four pillars of whole language.* Paper presented at the Whole Language Winter Workshop, Tucson, AZ.

Goodman, K. (1986). *What's whole in whole language?* Portsmouth, NH: Heinemann.

Goodman, Y. (1984). The development of initial literacy. In H. Goelman, A. Oberg, & F. Smith (Eds.), *Awakening to literacy.* Portsmouth, NH: Heinemann.

Halliday, M. (1975a). *Explorations in the functions of language.* London: Edward Arnold.

Halliday, M. (1975b). *Learning how to mean.* London: Edward Arnold.

Heath, S. (1983). *Ways with words: Language, life, and work in communities and classrooms.* Cambridge, England: Cambridge University Press.

Hood, L. (1980). The role of imitation in children's language learning. In G. Pinnell (Ed.), *Discovering language with children.* Urbana, IL: NCTE.

Howe, C. (1976). The meanings of two word utterances in the speech of young children. *Journal of Child Language, 3,* 29–47.

Huckleberry, A., & Strother, E. (1972). *Speech education for the elementary teacher.* Boston: Allyn & Bacon.

Jaggar, A. (1980). Allowing for language differences. In G. Pinnell (Ed.), *Discovering language with children.* Urbana, IL: NCTE.

Klima, E., & Bellugi-Klima, U. (1966). Syntactic regularities in the speech of children. In J. Lyons & R. Wales (Eds.), *Psycholinguistic papers* (pp.145–146). Edinburgh: Edinburgh University Press.

Labov, W. (1970). The logic of non-standard English. In F. Williams (Ed.), *Language and poverty.* Chicago: Markham.

Langer, J. (1987). *Language, literacy and culture.* Norwood, NJ: Ablex.

Lee, D. (1986) *Language, children and society.* New York: NYU Press.

Lindfors, J. (1985). *Children's language and learning.* Englewood Cliffs, NJ: Prentice-Hall.

Loban, W. (1976). *Language development: Kindergarten through grade 12.* Urbana, IL: NCTE.

Maratsos, M. (1983). Some current issues in the acquisition of grammar. In J. Flavell & E. Markman (Eds.), *Handbook of child psychology.* New York: John Wiley.

McCarthy, D. (1954). Language development in children. In L. Carmichael (Ed.), *Manual of child psychology.* New York: John Wiley.

McCormick, L. & Schiefelbusch, R. (1990). *Early language intervention.* Columbus, OH: Merrill.

Menyuk, P. (1969). Syntactic structures in the language of children. *Child Development, 34,* 407–422.

Menyuk, P. (1988). *Language development: Knowledge and use.* Glenview, IL: Scott, Foresman.

Michaels, S. (1981). Sharing time: Children's narrative style and differential access to literacy. *Language in Society, 10,* 49–76.

Nelson, K. (1988). Acquisition of words by first language learners. In M. Franklin & S. Barten (Eds.), *Child language: A reader.* Oxford: Oxford University Press.

O'Donnell, R., Griffin, W., & Norris, R. (1967). *Syntax of kindergarten and elementary school children: A transformational analysis.* Champaign, IL: NCTE.

Olsen, D. (1984). "See! Jumping!" Some oral language antecedents of literacy. In H. Goelman, A. Oberg, & F. Smith (Eds.),

Awakening to literacy. Portsmouth, NH: Heinemann.

Pellegrini, A., Galda, L., & Rubin, D. (1984). Context in text: The development of oral and written language in two genres. *Child Development, 55,* 1549–1555.

Pinnell, G. (Ed.). (1980). *Discovering language with children.* Urbana, IL: NCTE.

Slobin, W. (1979). Universals of grammatical development in children. In G. Flores d'Arcais & W. Levelt (Eds.), *Advances in psycholinguistics.* New York: Elsevier Press.

Smith, F. (1988). *Understanding reading.* Hillsdale, NJ: Lawrence Erlbaum.

Snow, C., & Ferguson, C. (1977). *Talking to children.* Cambridge, England: Cambridge University Press.

Teale, W., & Sulzby, E. (1986). *Emergent literacy: Writing and reading.* Norwood, NJ: Ablex.

Tough, J. (1977). *The development of meaning.* London: Allen & Unwin.

Wells, G. (1986). *The meaning makers: Children learning language and using language to learn.* Portsmouth, NH: Heinemann.

4

*Learning
is always
(1) meaningful,
(2) useful,
(3) continual and
effortless,
(4) incidental,
(5) collaborative,
(6) vicarious, and
(7) free of risk.*

(SMITH,
1988a, p. 6)

Coming to Believe

What is teaching?

What do whole language teachers believe about children and learning?

What do they believe about language and language learning?

How important do they believe conditions in the classroom environment are to learning?

How do teachers' beliefs affect their teaching?

What do you believe about learning, teaching, and children?

Whole Language Teachers' Beliefs

Learning

Language and Language Learning

Learners

Teachers and Teaching

Traditional Instruction

Literacy

The Classroom

The Curriculum

Education as a Whole

Applying the Conditions for Natural Learning to Classroom Instruction

SUMMARY

THEORY-TO-PRACTICE CONNECTIONS

SUGGESTED READINGS

SUGGESTED ACTIVITIES

REFERENCES

*T*eachers who believe that language is the foundation for all school and future learning, that children learn language by using it, and that language in use is always whole, meaningful, and purposeful tend to create learner-centered, literature-based, integrated classrooms. This theoretical perspective, derived from learning and linguistic research, has come to be called whole language. Whole language philosophy is different in many ways from the beliefs and practices that drive traditional instruction (Weaver, 1990). For example, many teachers believe it is important to capitalize on the intellectual strengths of the children. Whole language teachers agree, but they also believe it is necessary to capitalize on their interests and intentions. Children learn best when they are engaged in things that interest them (Dewey, 1963). They also learn best when they are in pursuit of something they want to know about or be able to do (Smith, 1990). Such conclusions about learning have implications for teaching.

In whole language classrooms, children contribute to as many curricular decisions as possible. They may decide they want to put on a play for another grade, study the solar system, or write letters to the president. While teachers in traditional classrooms are moving on to the next chapter in the textbook or workbook, children in whole language classrooms are delving more deeply into their chosen unit of study or moving on to the next area of interest. These learning events are made possible by the classroom teacher's beliefs and values. While some specific content may be required in the curriculum, such as multiplication tables in the third grade, or states and their capitals in the fifth grade, knowledgeable teachers also understand the importance of starting where the learner is and building on the child's strengths and interests.

Coming to believe and putting new beliefs into practice is not an instant process. It requires, among other things, an examination of the principles upon which instruction is based and an examination of one's own beliefs. In this chapter we will present a synthesis of what whole language teachers tend to believe about learning, language, and language learning. You will recognize the origins of these beliefs from the discussion in preceding chapters. We will also address what whole language teachers believe about children, themselves as teachers, the purpose of teaching, traditional instruction, literacy, the classroom, and the curriculum. Finally, in the Suggested Activities at the end of the chapter, we encourage you to explore your own beliefs about teaching and learning; as you work through those activities, you may want to consult *The Whole Language Catalog* (Goodman, Bird, & Goodman, 1991).

Whole Language Teachers' Beliefs

Learning   Whole language teachers believe that learning is coming to know, learning is any change in one's view of the world (Smith, 1988b), and learning is both social and personal. They believe that learners make sense of the world by detecting or imposing pattern on their experiences. They believe all children can and will learn and children come to school already having learned a great deal about language and the world around them. Children learn from one another, from quality materials, from the teacher, and from other adults. Whole language teachers believe in immersing children in language, literature, and subjects rich in content. They believe in the power of demonstration; they believe in providing opportunities for children to engage in authentic experiences and to receive meaningful feedback; they believe that children learn when they are encouraged to ask their own questions.

Language and Language Learning   Language is one of several sign and symbol systems human beings have created to represent meaning. It is a highly rule-governed symbol system used for social interaction. Like learning in general, language learning is a psychogenerative process. Learners construct language through a process of rule formation and testing. Children's language develops as they use it in the context of daily living by being immersed in it and by observing demonstrations of how it works and what it is good for. Language is the foundation for children's learning in school.

Learners   Whole language teachers believe that children are competent and trustworthy beings, that children know how to learn, and that children should have input into their classroom curriculum. Children bring their lives and cultures to the classroom. For instance, one inner-city child told and then wrote a story about a shooting in his neighborhood. In this way, he coped with his anger and fear. A rural child who wrote about the horses he used to have before his family had to sell them expressed his feelings about his loss and preserved the memory of the animals he loved. When children's lives become part of the classroom, their learning is enhanced because the subjects are real.

Through mutual respect, trust building, and positive personal attention, children explore who they are. They may even begin to take on the attitudes and values of their teachers. Helping children be successful in pursuing their own interests and intentions, putting children in charge of projects and routines, and letting children know the teacher as a person encourage and mold children's sense of their own capabilities (Edelsky, Altwerger, & Flores, 1991).

Teachers and Teaching   Whole language teachers view themselves as learners. They know that every class is different, and that there is much to be learned about children and teaching from each group. They are in the process of applying these beliefs to their classroom practice and expanding those beliefs as they examine and learn from their practice (Newman, 1987, 1990). Their theory of learning remains open to new information as they read professional literature, attend professional meetings, and talk with colleagues (see appendix B for a list of recommended whole language professional books and journals).

Teachers are themselves learners. They become researchers in their own classrooms by observing and studying their children's responses to instructional events. They reflect on their children's learning, and they use these observations and insights to plan instruction.

Whole language teachers believe that teaching is establishing the necessary conditions and a conducive environment for facilitating natural learning. To that end they create opportunities that engage children in inquiring and in constructing their own understandings. There are at least two ways teachers act as facilitators of learning. First, they help children become aware of the thinking processes they go through as they read, write, and learn. This may be accomplished through discussion, pupil-teacher conferences, and demonstration. Second, teachers provide a variety of opportunities and invitations for children to explore and present their learnings through various sign and symbol systems—for example, math, writing, discussion, music, art, and drama (see figure 4.1). They help children make connections between what they are learning and their lives outside of school.

Teachers are also child advocates. They genuinely like children and attempt to protect them from abuses by other people and by the larger, impersonal "system." In addition to facilitating learning by creating opportunity, environmental conditions, and invitations, teachers assume such roles as friend, cheerleader, and consultant (Edelsky, Draper & Smith, 1983).

Traditional Instruction   Most traditional reading and language arts programs present language as a hierarchy of discrete skills, such as labels for types of sounds, words, and word parts, for word functions in sentences, for types of sentences, and for types of comprehension functions. Just as conscious awareness of the elements of

FIGURE 4.1
Teacher
Demonstrating

one's language is not necessary or even possible in learning to talk, neither is it particularly necessary for learning to read and write. The question is not whether human language consists of fragmented, abstract "skills"; the question is how do people develop and use language. Studying about the parts of language, as separate from their use, isn't necessary for learning to read and write although attention to the details of language will certainly extend and refine the learner's reading and writing.

Literacy   Whole language teachers have definite beliefs about what literacy is and how children become literate. They believe literacy is reading and writing for personal, social, and intellectual purposes. They believe that children learn to read and write in essentially the same way they learned to talk, by using language in real ways (Cambourne, 1988; Goodman, 1986; Smith, 1983, 1990).

Whole language teachers believe that children will become literate if three elements are present. First, children must believe they already know how to read and write in some way, that learning to read and write is easy, and that everyone does it. Second, children must believe that learning to read and write is safe in a social sense, that no one will punish them or publicly ridicule their attempts. Finally, children must believe that learning to read and write will not hurt them in a psychological sense. Becoming literate will not separate them from their families and friends. They must decide that learning and literacy are good, sensible, and useful tools for their lives (Cambourne, 1988).

The Classroom   While there are great differences among whole language classrooms, all whole language programs have certain features. These classrooms are learner-centered, literature-based, and literacy-rich environments. They are places where teachers read aloud to their students daily, usually several times a day. Children write several times a day and read silently or to each other daily from a variety of sources, including high-quality children's literature. In whole language classrooms, children experience a variety of authentic uses for written language. Children's cultures, language, and interests are celebrated and become key elements of the curriculum.

For instance, when a child wore an unusual T-shirt to school, the children read it and talked about T-shirt print. The teacher invited the children to keep a list of T-shirt logos for a few days. These logos were then used in creating a visual display, a song, a rap, and new T-shirt logos. Another time, a child brought a caterpillar to school that had wasp eggs embedded in it. The children began asking questions about why a wasp laid eggs on a caterpillar. The children's interest and questions led the teacher to invite them into a unit on insects. The children decided to subdivide their study and to focus on insects that sting and insects that don't. Yet another time, a teacher and a group of children engaged in a brief math lesson when several children brought sacks of Halloween candy to school. The teacher invited the children to explore various ways to sort their candy, (by size, type, color) and to estimate and total their loot. This lesson and a picture book about how factories work led the children to create in the classroom an assembly-line candy factory as a fund-raising project.

The Curriculum   Curriculum is the sum total of what teachers intend for children to experience in school (Dewey, 1963). In programs based on an integrated curriculum, like whole language, the focus is on process rather than on product. That is, teachers are more concerned with the processes children engage in as they learn than with their knowing any one specific fact or isolated skill. Children are helped to apply new ways of thinking and doing, and they are supported by the teacher as they work.

In one first grade, the teacher shared *The Turning of the Year* by Bill Martin, Jr. (1990) as part of a unit on fall. The children became interested in how the illustrations were made. The class spent several weeks experimenting with tempera and watercolor to represent weather and the changing of the seasons. The class put together big books with captions dictated by the children. Because the work was their own and sprang from the children's interests, they produced some wonderful art. Among other things, the children learned new techniques for representing meaning, they learned about climate, and they learned that they could learn from being curious. During

that school year, the teacher found ways to refer to this earlier learning event, and several children spontaneously produced abstract
representations of other stories, class events, and personal feelings.

Education as a Whole   Holistic, integrated, learner-centered
teaching is a philosophy of education. It integrates language and
thinking with rich content in authentic experiences for children
(Goodman, 1990). Language in use is always whole, and whole language is the foundation for nearly all school learning. A whole language perspective surrounds children with written language that
makes sense and is appropriate to the life of the classroom. Literature, math, social studies and science information, and events in the
children's lives drive the curriculum. Whether children are learning
about dinosaurs, rain forests, folk and fairy tales, the three states of
matter, or problems of waste management, the classroom must be
rich enough in information, language, and literature to allow learners to ask their own questions so they can make meaning for themselves. In this way, children learn content, develop independence as
learners, and learn more about language.

Language- and literature-based teachers help children find their
own routes to literacy by building on each child's roots of literacy
(Goodman, 1986, 1990). They believe that growth comes to children
as they read, write, and learn about the forces acting upon them
from outside as well as from within. This growth is documented and
evaluated through reflective observation that most holistic teachers
call "kidwatching" (Goodman, 1985).

Holistic teachers are more concerned with the processes involved
in learning and literacy than with specific subject matter. Good
teachers try to lead children into materials and experiences for
which they are developmentally ready. Whole language teachers also
try to follow children's interests and invite them to help select and
develop the units of study for the class. Whether a specific child
reads and writes about frogs, earthworms, or spiders during a unit
on life forms is immaterial. But whatever is studied must be related
to that child's abilities to manipulate and manage facts, concepts,
and generalizations, to internalize them, and to categorize and relate

them to one another and to prior knowledge. The learner must be involved with the material, have a sense of ownership, and share the learning through a variety of forms of self-expression.

The whole language teacher's goal is to help children become lifelong learners, not just acquirers of facts and information. Remembering specific information from a story or text selection, or identifying isolated "skills" for a test may be part of the curriculum; but in whole language classrooms, teachers spend most of their time and effort talking with children about books or about their thinking as they work on a project. Whenever possible, teachers demonstrate their own thinking as they read a newspaper article, revise their own writing, or discuss a selection read by the group.

Understanding process involves at least two major elements. First, children must be active participants, authentically using the tools they are learning—that is, learning to read by really reading and learning to write by really writing. Second, while the unit of study emerges from the interests and energy of the children, it also takes form and shape from the teacher's knowledge of the subject. Structure is provided by the teacher's understanding of the steps needed for the children to get from point A to point C, knowledge of and access to related materials and equipment, and judgment of the needs and strengths of the children.

The intent is to build a sense of classroom community and to further children's growing sense of their own learning. Teachers want their students to get along with each other and to appreciate each other's gifts, talents, and differences. To accomplish this, whole language teachers may establish ad hoc groups to discuss literature, work on projects, or plan presentations. To have many groups and activities occurring simultaneously requires a great deal of planning. This means that teachers must manage the daily routine smoothly so that learning and cooperation can take place. Being prepared and organized, developing a general structure for the day's events, giving directions and responsibilities, and privately reprimanding when necessary help create this kind of classroom.

Creating a successful classroom and sense of community helps enable children to identify with their teacher, whom it is hoped they have learned to like and respect. Care must be taken that the children grow in their own right, trusting their own good sense and learning to be independent and self-reliant. Teachers encourage students to move ahead, to take risks with materials and concepts that may be difficult. Teachers suggest options and procedures and simultaneously act as friend, cheerleader, resource, counselor, and teacher.

Learner-centered teachers focus on the strengths learners bring to a learning event. If children are engaged in expanding their strengths and interests, they can be expected to do their best. They can be trusted to work and not waste time; they can be expected to make reasonable decisions. They learn responsibility because they are given responsibility for their own learning (Edelsky, Draper, & Smith, 1983).

Another way holistic teachers demonstrate that they value children is the structuring of the classroom so that the children are in charge. Children become more committed to the purposes of the classroom when they can take responsibility for a variety of tasks, such as adjusting the day's schedule, leading the group in the morning song, or taking a poll to select the poem for the week. Organizational and curricular tasks conducted by the children allow for shared ownership and provide authentic language and literacy experiences. For example, nearly all teachers have to take attendance, change the calendar, and collect lunch money every day. Such repetitious tasks, in a whole language classroom, are likely to be among those routines turned over to the children as early in the year as possible. The teacher is there, of course, to watch and help when necessary. Child-centered classrooms help build a sense of ownership of the room and the curriculum and a positive sense of self-worth (see figure 4.2).

Educational theorists, philosophers, and psychologists have long told us how important children's views of themselves are to their success or failure in school (Neisser, 1986). The teacher's attitude about children's innate worth and learning potential is crucial and must be conveyed in a credible manner. Teacher attitude is one key to building children's sense of self-worth; another key to enhancing self-esteem is children's accomplishing difficult and challenging tasks. Meeting the teacher's high standards is an indispensable expe-

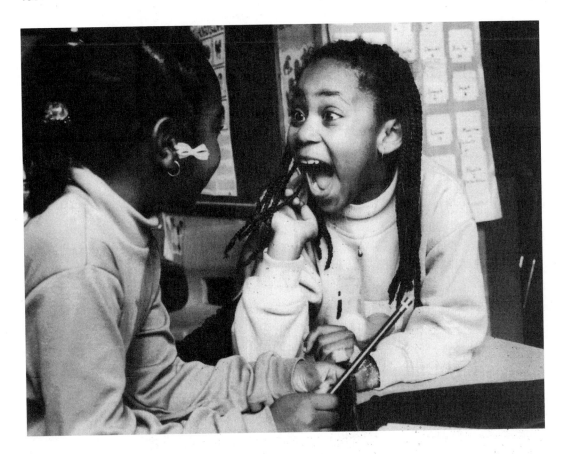

FIGURE 4.2
Learning to Love
School

rience. Filling the classroom and hall with displays of children's work gives an unmistakable message of support for their efforts. Teacher expectation and individual attention, together with a child's growing sense of personal accomplishment, are two of the most powerful components of successful learning.

Applying the Conditions for Natural Learning to Classroom Instruction

Whole language teachers also demonstrate their philosophy in how their classrooms look and feel. Whole language teachers believe a positive classroom climate is characterized by the interaction of a flexible, an inviting, and a literate environment.

A flexible environment includes aspects of room arrangement that are conducive to a holistic and integrated curriculum, such as movable tables or desks arranged and rearranged in various configurations. Other aspects of flexibility are the ready availability of supplies, materials, and equipment and adequate, often creative, storage areas.

An inviting environment is bright and well lighted, clean, well organized and neat, and appealing to the eye. It is a comfortable place to be (see figure 4.3). Above all, there is ample evidence that the children are co-creators of the space. Their work covers walls, tables, and bulletin boards. Everything is displayed near or at children's eye level. A corner of the classroom may be turned into a set from the current unit, for example, the cabin in Wilder's *The Little House in the Big Woods* (1932), the contrasting settings in MacLachlan's *Sarah, Plain and Tall* (1985), or an airplane and airline reservation counter from Munsch's *Angela's Airplane* (1988). Such endeavors also provide further opportunities for writing.

Creating a literate environment means more than displaying a wealth of children's literature and the children's own work. It means

FIGURE 4.3
A Comfortable and Inviting Environment

taking every opportunity to employ written language in natural or authentic ways and inviting children to take risks with both language and learning. A sign-in board by the front door, sign-up sheets for various jobs and events in the classroom, posted lists as reminders, a message board, various record-keeping devices, and organizing and labeling devices—all these require the children to use printed information in the functional, natural transactions of classroom business. A literate environment allows children to explore the uses of print in authentic ways. Ultimately, a classroom community is created in which children see themselves as competent and feel safe to take risks.

Taking risks with language, literacy, and learning implies that children are free to make mistakes without fear of the usual consequences of failure. It means that children learn through their mistakes in an atmosphere of love of learning, intellectual curiosity, support in their attempts, and constant inquiry. When children make approximations, whole language teachers know they are not mistakes. Approximations represent attempts to figure out how the rules work, for example, where to put end marks or capital letters. Latitude to explore and develop control over the conventions of written language is understood and encouraged in an integrated, language- and literature-based curriculum. The same latitude to explore content or subject areas and do something interesting and meaningful with new knowledge is essential to the development of independent learning.

Some criteria that identify whole language classrooms are the exposure of children to a wide variety of literature, the frequent opportunities they have to share their learnings, and the strong encouragement they receive to express themselves creatively. Collaborative projects, peer conferences, shared books, and literature study groups are a few of the strategies that whole language teachers employ in the classroom so children can safely explore, learn, and grow (Holdaway, 1979; Peterson & Eeds, 1989). Figure 4.4 provides a preliminary summary of the critical components of an integrated, language- and literature-based program.

Holistic, language- and literature-based teachers want children to take pleasure in using their minds, in learning new information

THE TEACHER	Critical Components of Integrated Language- and Literature-Based Classrooms	THE LEARNER
What the teacher believes Primacy of language in learning Children learn language as they use language Language in use is always whole Process is more important than product Start where the child is—with the child's strengths Respect children and trust them Keep expectations high The conditions for natural learning must be present in the classroom Others... **What the teacher has** Ample high-quality children's literature A wealth of other resources and equipment A flexible schedule A repertoire of sound instructional strategies A repertoire of sound evaluation techniques Others... **What the teacher does** Reads aloud to children every day Allows time for children to read and write daily Shows learners how reading and writing work Others...		Listens and talks Reads and writes daily Makes choices and decisions Plans and works collaboratively Solves problems Asks important questions Has wonderful ideas Engages in explorations Respects others Is helpful Is co-creator of the curriculum Shares culture Thinks of self as a reader and a writer Has sense of ownership Is responsible for own learning Participates in self-evaluation Others...
	THE ENVIRONMENT Is risk-free Is literate Is learner-centered Is rich in content Is flexible Employs functional print Reflects conditions for natural learning Others...	

and having new experiences from which they may derive meaning and personal satisfaction. Such teachers purposefully and intentionally create events and experiences for their students. They provide demonstrations and they select materials that engage students in thought-provoking content and projects that pique their curiosity, spur their creativity, and encourage risk taking.

When one teacher read *Flossie and the Fox* by McKissack (1986),

FIGURE 4.4
Components of an Integrated Program

FIGURE 4.5
Conditions for Natural
Learning in the
Classroom
SOURCE: Adapted from
Brian Cambourne
(1988), *The Whole
Story* (Portsmouth, NH:
Heinemann), p. 33.

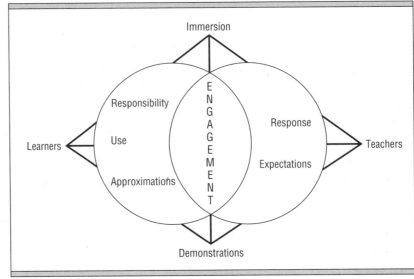

she found that the children were very interested in the local place names in the story. She asked the children if they would like to know more about what their area looked liked and how the people lived 150 years ago. The result of that question was that everyone learned to be a historian. Exploring old newspapers, old photographs, and old maps, a local historian's visits to the classroom, looking at reference and history books, storytelling, art projects, writing events, and a field trip to the state historical museum—all these activities grew out of one good book and a teacher who believed in engaging children.

The conditions that promote natural learning are immersion, demonstration, expectation, responsibility, approximation, use, and response. And, as illustrated in figure 4.5, engagement with meaningful demonstrations provided by teachers and other resources, with natural responses and high expectations, produces learning. Establishing these conditions in language- and literature-rich environments is the foundation upon which whole language is based.

SUMMARY

An educational philosophy is only as good as the understanding and commitment of the teacher who implements it. Therefore, what teachers know and believe is vital. Good teachers are well educated; they know a great deal about the world around them and how it works and they have also developed a solid theoretical base for teaching.

According to whole language theory, language and literature are the foundation for all school and later life learning. What teachers believe and their awareness of those beliefs determines what they do in classrooms. Whole language teachers treat children in very intentional ways. Their goal is to create classrooms that help children learn to love learning (Goodman, 1986). Teachers who see themselves as learner centered, literature based, and holistic believe that *literacy* helps children grow as intelligent beings. And *literature* helps us all grow as human beings.

THEORY-TO-PRACTICE CONNECTIONS

Coming-to-Know Theory

1. What teachers believe determines how and what they teach.

2. Teachers are co-learners.

3. Teachers are readers and writers.

4. Teachers are professionals.

5. What teachers value determines in part how learners respond.

Classroom Practice

1. Keeping a teaching-reflection log to help clarify beliefs and keep practices as consistent as possible with one's developing theory

2. Making "kidwatching" part of the daily routine, listening to children and looking closely at what they are doing as they learn; attending relevant professional conferences and services whenever possible

3. Reading professional literature on a regular basis as well as children's and adolescent literature; writing to share insights, successes, frustrations, emerging questions, with self, with a colleague

4. Creating the climate and the curriculum most conducive to learning for one's own students

5. Respecting learners and inviting them to bring their culture into the classroom

SUGGESTED READINGS

Edelsky, C., Altwerger, B., & Flores, B. (1991). *Whole language: What's the difference?* Portsmouth, NH: Heinemann.

Goodman, K. (1986). *What's whole in whole language?* Portsmouth, NH: Heinemann.

Goodman, K., Bird, L., & Goodman, Y. (1991). *The whole language catalog.* Santa Rosa, CA: American School Publishers.

Mills, H., & Clyde, J. (1990). *Portraits of whole language classrooms.* Portsmouth, NH: Heinemann.

Newman, J. (Ed.). (1990). *Finding our own way.* Portsmouth, NH: Heinemann.

Short, K., & Burke, C. (1991). *Creating curriculum: Teachers and students as a community of learners.* Portsmouth, NH: Heinemann.

Stephens, D. (1990). *What matters: A primer for teaching reading.* Katonah, NY: Richard C. Owen.

SUGGESTED ACTIVITIES

1. Take some time to explore *The Whole Language Catalog.* This could be accomplished individually, in pairs, or in small groups. Look for the funniest stories, the most poignant, the most instructive. What do all these teachers who contributed their stories seem to believe about kids and teaching? Make a list.

2. In small groups, brainstorm and list your own beliefs about kids and teaching; what teaching is and what school ought to be for children. Write your list of belief statements and discuss them. What broad categories emerge? Rearrange your list under each category from most to least important. Have each group share with the entire class.

3. Have your beliefs changed as a result of this class? Did you alter any of your statements after the group discussion? Keep your list until the end of the semester and then decide if you wish to add to or otherwise alter your belief statements.

4. Taking each item on your list of belief statements, discuss how you can make the belief a reality in the classroom—that is, what does the belief mean to teaching? Share your ideas with classmates.

5. On pages 27 and 28 of Routman's *Transitions* (1988), she lists the beliefs and the goals she has for her students. The instructional goals include having high expectations for the children, modeling and giving opportunities for practice, and helping children develop reading strategies that utilize meaning and grammar before sound/letter relationships. After reading and discussing Routman's belief statements and goals, examine your own beliefs and develop your own list of tentative goals to help you begin implementing your teaching philosophy and evaluating your success. (Also see Routman, 1991, pp. 12–21.)

REFERENCES

Cambourne, B. (1988). *The whole story.* Toronto, Ontario: Ashton-Scholastic.

Dewey, J. (1963). *Experiences in education.* New York: Collier Books.

Edelsky, C., Altwerger, B., & Flores, B. (1991). *Whole language: What's the difference?* Portsmouth, NH: Heinemann.

Edelsky, C., Draper, K., & Smith, K. (1983). Hookin' 'em in at the start of school in a whole language classroom. *Anthropology and Education Quarterly, 14,* 257–279.

Goodman, K. (1986). *What's whole in whole language?* Portsmouth, NH: Heinemann.

Goodman, K., Bird, L., & Goodman, Y. (1991). *The whole language catalog.* Santa Rosa, CA: American School Publishers.

Goodman, Y. (1985). Kidwatching: Observing children in the classroom. In A. Jaggar & M. Smith-Burke (Eds.), *Observing the language learner.* Newark, DE: International Reading Association.

Goodman, Y. (1990). *How children construct literacy: Piagetian perspectives.* Newark, DE: International Reading Association.

Holdaway, D. (1979). *Foundations of literacy.* Portsmouth, NH: Heinemann.

MacLachlan, P.(1985). *Sarah, plain and tall.* New York: Trumpet.

Martin, B., Jr. (1970). The turning of the year. In *The little owl series.* New York: Holt, Rinehart, and Winston.

McKissack, P. (1986). *Flossie and the fox.* New York: Dial Press.

Munsch, R. (1988). *Angela's airplane.* Toronto, Ontario: Annick.

Neisser, U. (Ed.). (1986). *The school achievement of minority children: New perspectives.* Hillsdale, NJ: Lawrence Erlbaum.

Newman, J. (1985). *Whole language: Theory in use.* Portsmouth, NH: Heinemann.

Newman, J. (Ed.). (1990). *Finding our own way.* Portsmouth, NH: Heinemann.

Peterson, R., & Eeds, M. (1989). *Grand conversations: Literature groups in action.* Toronto, Ontario: Ashton-Scholastic.

Routman, R. (1988). *Transitions.* Portsmouth, NH: Heinemann.

Routman, R. (1991). *Invitations.* Portsmouth, NH: Heinemann.

Smith, F. (1983). *Essays into literacy.* Exeter, NH: Heinemann.

Smith, F. (1988a). *Joining the literacy club.* Portsmouth, NH: Heinemann.

Smith, F. (1988b). *Understanding reading.* Hillsdale, NJ: Lawrence Erlbaum.

Smith, F. (1990). *To think.* New York: Teachers College Press.

Weaver, C. (1990). *Understanding whole language.* Portsmouth, NH: Heinemann.

Wilder, L. (1932). *Little house in the big woods.* New York: Harper Collins.

PART TWO

Processes and Products

KNOW THE LEARNER,
THE APPROACHES,
THE RESOURCES

5

Reading

What is reading?

How do we learn to read?

What do we know about how to help children learn to read and want to read?

How can teachers evaluate a child's reading?

*B*efore children are four or five years old, most are already asking "What does that say?" as they point to print on cereal boxes, in picture books, on signs along the highway, and in their own scribbles. The realizations that written symbols are different from pictures and that they have potential meanings are two of the earliest steps children take in learning to read.

When these same children become adults, some read quite well. They may read articles in the *New Yorker* and the *Atlantic Monthly,* or the newest novel from a critically acclaimed author. Some may even read short stories and poetry in the latest issue of *Partisan Review* or editorials from the *Washington Post* and the *Wall Street Journal.* In between "What does that say?" and reading the latest literary critique lies all the learning that has occurred within an individual's experiences. On an imaginary literacy scale, most adults fall some-where beyond the abilities of the five year old and considerably short of the serious connoisseur of "good" literature.

Literacy—the ability to read and write—draws on natural apti-tudes, attitudes and values, life experiences, and instructional expe-riences all at the same time. Most adults in this country can read, at least at minimal levels, but only 5 to 10 percent of our high school graduates can read well (Eisner, 1990; Glasser, 1990; Shanker, 1990). And while most young people and adults can read, too many choose not to. Many do not like to read, so they avoid reading anything they don't really have to (Gardner, 1991).

Prior to formal schooling, children are usually enthusiastic about learning and about books. They learn naturally and are quite accom-plished in a wide array of areas. However, by the middle grades many children have developed a dislike for school in general and for reading in particular. In some ways it is amazing that so many well-trained and well-intentioned individuals can work so diligently only to produce the very results they are trying to avoid (Smith, 1985, 1988b).

In this chapter we will examine the reading process, discuss pur-poses for reading, explore how children learn to read, and describe how reading has traditionally been taught in schools. Finally, we will present a view of teaching reading that more closely fits what we now know about language and learning, one whose major goal is to pro-duce lifelong readers, and one that better prepares students for the information age—the complex, technological world they will in-herit.

What Reading Is

Reading is constructing meaning, making sense of print. If a reader has not made the written material meaningful, reading has not taken place. What reading is and how human beings come to comprehend the visual language system are important to our understanding.

Written language reflects the structure of the oral language. Comprehending written language, like comprehending oral language, is a complex process. It is certainly more complicated than recognizing letters in sequence, forming words, identifying each word's meaning, and adding up the meanings of the words one at a time from left to right. One way to better understand reading is to explore our own reading processes. Examine these lines:

Mary had a little lamb
Its fleece was white as snow.

In this example from a well-known nursery rhyme, *Mary* is a little girl, *had* means "owned," and *little* means "small in size" as well as "young." The word *lamb* refers to "a child's pet." However, if we alter the second line, see what happens to the meanings of the words that precede it.

Mary had a little lamb
And she spilled mint jelly on her evening gown.

Now, *Mary* is a grown woman at a fancy dinner perhaps, *had* means "ate," and *little lamb* becomes "a serving of meat."

Try another example of the complex and interdependent nature of words in text:

Mary had a little lamb
And it was such a difficult delivery
The vet needed a drink.

This time, *Mary* is the ewe, *had* means "gave birth to," and *little lamb* means "baby" (adapted from Altwerger, Edelsky, & Flores, 1987). Reading, then, is not the simple "decoding" of words and the addition of their definitions in linear fashion. Words don't really have meaning until they are embedded in a text.

Most language, whether oral or written, has more components than are necessary. Natural language is extremely redundant. Even the pithiest statements could probably be shortened without sacrificing the essential message. Therefore, even f qt a fw itms r tkn ot, u cn prbly rd ths sntc.

Traditionally, reading instruction spends a great deal of children's time on each and every vowel and consonant sound and the letters that represent them. Actually, as the above example demonstrates, young readers may not need most of that vowel, sound-letter instruction. After all, some languages, such as Hebrew, omit most of the vowels from the written form altogether, and children learn to read Hebrew just fine. Reading instruction, then, should not focus on learning a hierarchy of letters and the sounds these letters represent. Reading *is not* simply the recognition of letters, one at time, to form words and the identification of words, one at time, to make a message.

Monitor your reading of this passage from O. Henry (Porter, 1969, p. 1) and answer the questions that follow:

> One dollar and eighty-seven cents. That was all. And sixty cents of it was in pennies. Pennies saved one and two at a time by bulldozing the grocer and the vegetable man and the butcher until one's cheeks burned with the silent imputation of parsimony that such close dealings implied.
>
> Three times Della counted. One dollar and eighty-seven cents. And the next day was Christmas.

Are you familiar with this story? If not, did you wonder, as you read, about any of the following: Who is Della? What does she look like? Why is she counting her money? Where does the story take place? How do you know? When is it set? What makes you think so?

Did you ignore any parts of the passage when you read it? Why did you do that? What does "silent imputation of parsimony" mean? What does "until her cheeks burned" tell you? Did you look any words up in a dictionary as you read?

What type of text does this passage come from? Some people who do not know the story see Della as a child. Some think perhaps she is a very old lady. Still others visualize her as a middle-aged woman who is very poor, perhaps a homeless person. What clues and information are they using to create these images? What cues might they be overlooking? Good readers call upon various schemata and frequently engage in an internal dialogue to answer such questions. Lacking any other information, your personal experiences will determine your visual image and interpretations of text.

As you reflected upon the reading of the passage, did you become aware of the fact that you were forming and then modifying a visual image as you read? Proficient readers also ask questions of themselves and anticipate obtaining answers from the text. For example, you may be aware of having asked yourself (or the author) why Della wants this money and what she could possibly do with such a small amount. In addition, proficient readers are often able to understand the essence of a passage without being able to define every word in it. Perhaps you were aware of having gotten the gist of "until one's cheeks burned with the silent imputation of parsimony that such close dealings implied" even though you might not want to take a test on the definition of each word.

Read the following and monitor your reading as you do so:

> Records of a load module are variable strings of external characters, these characters being either hexadecimal digits that group to form integer values or characters that represent themselves in names. The first six characters of a record always concern the physical structure of the record. Character 1 is 1 on the record and characters 2 through 4 contain a three digit hexadecimal sequence beginning with 000.

What are records of a load module? What do they form? How are they arranged? Can you "answer" these questions? Does answering some types of comprehension questions mean that you *understand,* or is it that you used sentence structure information to help you? Do you know what type of text this is? Are there words in this paragraph whose meaning you do not know? In what type of material would such a passage be found? What background knowledge or experience would you need in order to really make sense of the passage? If a reader can understand a piece of text without knowing the exact meaning of every word, and if a reader can know an exact meaning for each word without really comprehending the text, what then is the nature of the relationship among the words, the text, and the reader?

Try reading the following:

SHE LL BE COMIN ROUND THE MOUNTAIN

or

LITTLE MISS MUFFET SAT ON A TUFFET

In these examples you can see a portion of each letter. Is this difficult to read? If you figure out that the first string is the title of a well-known folk song and the second is from a nursery rhyme, they immediately become recognizable. That is because they suddenly fit a known pattern, one you already have stored in your brain.

What Reading Does

Human beings are born able to think in abstract, symbolic ways. People created the symbol system we call language because they needed it to communicate with each other; they created the written form to record information and ideas over time and space. Essentially, learning to read provides access to all the information and ideas that occurred in the minds of people who wrote them down. But is that what makes people want to learn to read? Why do people learn to read? What do children use reading for in various cultures around the world?

Research suggests the reasons for reading fall into three main categories: learning, enjoyment, and escape (Greaney & Neuman, 1990). Hundreds of adolescents in fifteen different countries were asked why they liked to read. Not surprisingly, more children in developed, technologically advanced countries cited reading to learn—acquiring information, doing well in school, passing examinations—as major reasons for reading and learning to read. The utilitarian aspects of reading appear to be most important in these countries.

In many countries, children also cited enjoyment as a major reason for reading. The notion that reading is pleasurable and allows the reader to "go into another place and time" was identified in most of the cultures examined. That is, reading can prevent boredom and help the time go by when there is nothing else to do.

But human beings are not always consciously aware of their internal motivations. At least one other major factor may be operating in determining whether a child will become a reader. Many leading educators have concluded that liking to read, and therefore being a reader, is partially the result of wanting to be like those significant persons in the child's life who are themselves readers and writers. The notion is that attitudes and values in many children's environments cause them to want to "join the literacy club" (Smith, 1988a). When becoming literate is not an attitude instilled at home, the teacher may become that literate, significant person in the child's life. It is the intentional and caring teacher, then, whom the child would wish to emulate, whose values and attitudes the child would see as good and worthwhile.

Children have varied reasons for wanting to learn to read. However, schools primarily emphasize two, learning to read for pleasure and for information. In chapter 1, we described Jenny, a ten year old who had joined that "club" of water skiers and who considered learning to water ski one of her truly positive personal achievements. Causing children to want to join the club of readers and writers is an aspect of school that is extremely important, and one that skillful teachers learn to foster (Smith, 1988a).

Language- and literature-based teachers do not believe that learning to read precedes using reading for information getting and for pleasure. Rather, they believe that an attitude of "joining the club" and using written language for learning and enjoyment from the very beginning are in fact how children best and most naturally learn to read. Children learn to read well and to like reading only if they want to.

Children's Reading Development: Our Evolving Understanding

As with oral language development, learning to read is a psychogenerative or constructive process. When children try to read for functional reasons they begin to intuit how reading works. In classrooms that support such explorations, learners are *immersed* in print they can make sense of. They are encouraged to try to use written language to negotiate the world around them. Aspects of the reading process are *demonstrated* by the teacher at appropriate times and children are given ample opportunity to try to read and write in a risk-free and stimulus-rich environment. Teachers accept children's *approximations* and *expect* all children will learn to read. In fact, they believe all school-age children already know how to "read" some things. They also know that ultimate *responsibility* for learning rests with the individual. Teachers engage children in regular, frequent, and authentic *uses* for written language.

Reading is a process, and print is a field of knowledge. That is, while children are learning the rules by which written language operates, they are also learning about the characteristics of the print itself. With reading, as with any domain of knowledge (for example, animals, vehicles, foods), learners must assimilate the information provided in the environment. When the information in the environment is plentiful, useful, and experienced over time, learners eventually learn all they need and want to know. They experiment with the objects, ask for more information, and test their hypotheses. As they do so, they try to make sense out of what they are experiencing. They search for coherence, and they build up their conclusions in an ordered way (Y. Goodman, 1990), just as they did in learning to talk.

As we have discussed in chapter 1, these mental systems, called schemata, allow for the further interpretation and assimilation of new data. Thus, learning in general and learning to read and write in particular are spirals or scaffolds, each one building on the other, often throughout the learner's lifetime.

Children attempt to create a system for how to read. According to Ferreiro and Teberosky (1982), actual reading is preceded by three very basic, early insights about writing and the nature of print. First, children begin to distinguish between the two types of graphic representation—drawing and writing (see figure 5.1). In drawing, the lines follow the outline of the object. In writing, the lines have nothing to do with the object being represented. Rather, the marks in writing are linear, arbitrary, and systematic. It takes time and experience for children to sort out these properties and characteristics of the graphic notation system.

During this period children are engaged in working out some basic principles for understanding and producing print. One of the universal principles children appear to develop is that of minimum quantity. To answer the question, "How many elements (for exam-

FIGURE 5.1
"People Playing"
(Kesha, Age 4)

ple, letters) does it take to be readable?" children consistently rely on the internal principle of minimum quantity, that the smallest number of elements possible is best. But learners quickly recognize that letters must be different from each other to be readable; so they develop a second guideline, the internal principle of qualitative variation. These two organizing generalizations help children decide if a piece of text is potentially readable or not.

Second, children search for the patterns that operate in writing. During the first stage, two scribbles or strings of letters and letter-like shapes may look similar or identical but "say" two entirely different things as far as the "writer" is concerned. During the second level, learners begin to pay attention to the forms that really support their intentions. As they read, they observe how words and sentences work. They have to figure out how to make strings of marks that differentiate meaning.

This effort proceeds from the development of a third general operating principle, interrelational comparison. Children begin to look at two differently "written" words and know the differences. These guiding principles develop before children develop their knowledge of the sound patterns and written representations of words (Y. Goodman, 1990). At this stage, children may display some phonemic awareness as they begin to explore the sound-letter system in their language. Sound-letter explorations tend to start with consonants and are followed by the vowels that appear in the children's names (see figure 5.2).

Since a single letter occasionally represents a syllable but most often represents a smaller unit of sound, children eventually arrive at the alphabetic principle, that similarity of sound (at the sub-word level) implies similarity of letter. This sophisticated awareness represents a true breakthrough in learning. However, traditional orthography involves a mass of visual features organized by extremely complex rules related to principles other than simple sound-letter correspondences (Y. Goodman, 1990). Therefore, reading develops slowly. It takes vast experiences with reading to move from "What does that say, Daddy?" at age five, to the potential of reading Shakespeare's plays or material on quantum mechanics as an adult.

As children hypothesize about how print works, they require cer-

FIGURE 5.2
Exploring Written
Language (Mona,
Age 5)

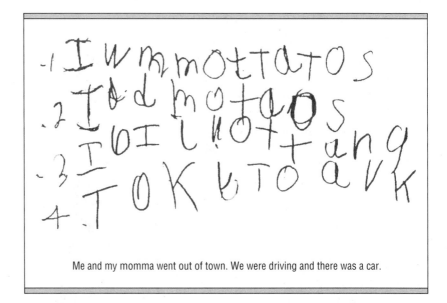

Me and my momma went out of town. We were driving and there was a car.

tain conditions if learning to read is to be natural and as rapid as possible. They need to see and hear others reading, especially people they love and fashion themselves after. Children need to be read to, so that they can hear the language of literature. They need to read to themselves so that they can experience print directly. Such reading may include a combination of pretending to read ("reading" to a stuffed animal), telling, "reading" from memorized texts (accurate reproduction of the text without the ability to identify individual words when asked), and reading signs and labels in the environment (Coke, McDonald's, or Texaco).

As we have seen, the literate world children live in begins to influence their lives very early. Children as young as four and five years of age begin to read and write, though perhaps not in the conventional sense. Their explorations with environmental print, books, pencils, and paper help them learn a great deal about reading and writing before they enter kindergarten. They tend to know that print is meaningful and is part of everyday life. They may already recognize some words in print, frequently by connecting them to the context, and they know that they can make their own graphic representations of meaning.

Children who have been read to know how to use their prior knowledge to make sense of stories. They know how to assimilate information gained from reading and apply it to another situation. They know that reading and writing serve a variety of functions and purposes (Mooney, 1990). These skills and more have typically been acquired by children who bring literate experiences to school. For children whose print experiences are limited or otherwise different, schools must provide the background experiences and attitudes of literate people.

Children learn to talk easily and, under similar conditions, they learn to read easily as well. This does not mean that all children will learn to read well in first grade. This is an unnatural expectation. Becoming a talker takes several years, and there is no reason to believe that becoming a reader should be significantly different. Many whole language advocates believe that young children should hear a minimum of 1,000 books read aloud before they are ready for formal instruction in reading—even formal instruction from a whole language perspective.

The rate at which a child learns to read is a matter of individual experience and innate ability. However, three phases in reading development tend to be common to most learners. As shown in figure 5.3, these are pre-reading, independent reading, and advanced read-

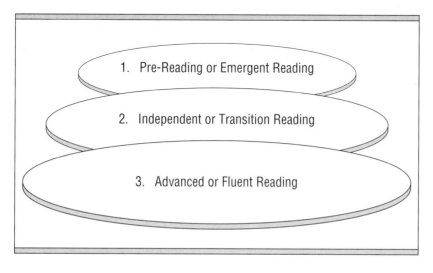

FIGURE 5.3
Phases of Reading Development

1. Pre-Reading or Emergent Reading

2. Independent or Transition Reading

3. Advanced or Fluent Reading

ing (Cochrane, Cochrane, Scalena, & Buchanan, 1984). McKenzie (1977) refers to these broad phases as the emergent stage, the tackling the print stage, and the fluent stage.

Phase 1. Pre-Reading/Emergent Reading   During the pre-reading stage, the basic understandings referred to by Ferreiro and Teberosky (1982) are achieved. Children are exposed to print in the environment from birth. They have "learned" a great deal about written language, much as infants who can't speak yet have been learning a great deal about oral language. The foundations are being laid in the brain for further development. Children's reading begins to emerge as they engage in acts that approximate reading and that they have seen adults do. They become interested in books and like to listen to stories read aloud. They focus on trying to make sense of written messages; they try to construct meaning. They learn how to handle books. They begin to see themselves as readers and may recognize their own names in print. They like to name the pictures in books and will fill in words correctly if the reader pauses on key items. They also know how stories go together. They can "read" favorite stories or poems that could not be totally recalled without the print. Toward the end of this period, they begin to recognize and pick out individual letters and familiar words.

Phase 2. Independent Reading   During the independent (or tackling the print) stage, readers pay attention to words. They often want to read to anyone who will listen. They read environmental print signs and labels aloud. They increasingly gain control over the reading process, and observation reveals that they use print as well as implied cues to construct the author's message. For some children, tackling the print becomes the major focus. They will even abandon the correct pronunciation of a word they already know in order to make it sound like what it looks like (Barr, 1984). Toward the end of this stage, readers become skilled.

Phase 3. Advanced Reading   As the advanced (or fluent) stage is reached, readers realize that not only must the print sound like it looks, but it must also make sense. They begin to use reading successfully to fulfill the everyday purposes of life, both in and out of school. They read orally with expression, and they have internalized the structure for several genres, especially fairy tales, simple exposition, and rhymes. They like to read and can comprehend anything that their experiences will support. They will continue to use reading to learn, and their reading abilities will continue to advance as long as they continue to read. As Meek (1988) says, children become really proficient readers through practice, pleasure, and persistence.

But not all children become fluent readers. Many children actually turn out to be very poor readers and to have life-handicapping literacy problems. Traditionally, poor readers have been blamed for their own difficulties (Y. Goodman, 1990). However, some educational researchers and theorists believe that the causes of poor reading and lower literacy levels are more the result of lower societal expectations and inappropriate instruction. They believe that nearly all children can learn to read (Anderson and Stokes, 1984; Neisser, 1986).

Traditional Reading Instruction: A Historical Perspective

Historically, reading has been taught more from a memorize-and-imitate perspective than from a comprehension perspective. Early in our nation's educational history, children were made to memorize religious homilies such as "In Adam's fall, we sinned all." Learners were asked to memorize Bible verses and lists of words. Bible verses gave way to political treatises during the Revolutionary and Civil wars. Nonfiction books emphasizing information on nature and science became popular around 1800. Story material, especially fantasy, was not considered appropriate for young children until late in the nineteenth century. Basal readers, containing material written for the sole purpose of teaching children to read, were not developed until early in the 1900s (Robinson, 1982; Smith, 1965). The development of the basal reader lesson plan was not part of the classroom scene until the late 1940s (Betts, 1946; Stauffer, 1969).

Today, traditional instruction in reading is eclectic. Reading is

divided into three equally important broad categories: word identification, vocabulary, and comprehension (see figure 5.4). For ease
of instruction, children are divided by ability into groups and taught
separately. Reading is separated from the other language arts—
speaking, listening, and writing. Traditional instruction is based on
historic precedent. It is atheoretic. Not being empirically derived, it
fails to take into account most of the research on learning, language,
language learning, and the reading process that has taken place over
the last forty years.

Linguists, speech scientists, and English grammar teachers subdivide language in order to analyze it, study it, and learn about it.
But even they did not subdivide language in order to learn it in the
first place. They learned language just like the rest of us, by using the
language in natural settings for real purposes. Early educators mis-

FIGURE 5.4
Traditional Skills
Instructional Model

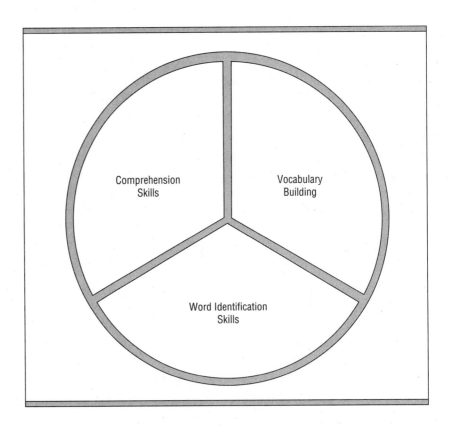

understood and thought we should subdivide language, especially written language, to learn it.

As a result, traditional reading instruction presents sets of skills within each of the three broad categories: word identification, vocabulary, and comprehension. A variety of published programs are used as the main instructional guide, including basal reader series, kits, and workbooks. The number and order of the skills presented differs from program to program.

You may remember Dick and Jane, Buffy and Mack, or some other characters from your early years in school. Basal readers are collections of stories and other materials written or rewritten by a formula designed to control the vocabulary and render the material "appropriate" to a given age and reading level. These materials are accompanied by a teacher's manual that tells the teacher what to do and say and by workbooks and other supporting materials. Identified by publishing company, the materials have formed the basis of traditional reading instruction in this country for decades (for a treatise on basal readers, see *Report Card on Basals,* K. Goodman, 1988).

The traditional, directed reading lesson plan, included in the teacher's manuals for most basal readers, consists of nine elements:

introduction
vocabulary
purpose
silent reading
comprehension questions/discussion
oral rereading
comprehension questions/discussion
seat work (skills practice with workbooks and worksheets)
enrichment

The teacher usually arranges the children into three ability groups: high, middle, and low. Two groups work at their seats, either reading a story silently or working in their workbooks while the teacher works with the third group. This approach treats teachers as dependent on the textbook for structure and children as passive recipients (K. Goodman, 1986). Research suggests that children in the high ability group tend to stay there. Children in the middle group stay there or drop into the low group. Children in the low group tend to stay there and/or fall even further behind (Wuthrick, 1990).

The skills mastery curriculum was an attempt to improve traditional instruction. Instead of three broad components with several major skill areas, skills mastery cites hundreds of smaller skills or subskills arranged in a supposed hierarchy. This approach to instruction was initially developed in the late 1950s and early 1960s. It was presented as a foolproof way to ensure reading development. The approach, which employs worksheets (called dittos in the era before photocopying), skills tests and checklists, and other materials, often lists as many as 1,500 discrete "skills" as components of reading.

Based on the behavioral view of learning prevalent in the 1930s and 1940s, this approach to teaching reading views reading as the accumulation of a hierarchy of separate skills that must be taught and learned one at a time, in order, as the pyramid in figure 5.5 suggests. Each skill, deemed part of the reading act, is stated as an objective and used for both teaching and testing. The skills approach fragments reading. It does not allow for the complex and strategic nature of the reading act or the interrelatedness of reading, writing, and speaking.

In many classrooms throughout the country, the instructional model is based on traditional methods, together with mastery of even more isolated and arbitrary skills than are presented in the basal series. Children may learn bits and pieces of things about words and sentences, but they may not learn to understand very well what they read (K. Goodman, 1986; Smith, 1988b), and they do not learn to like reading. This approach to teaching reading places teachers and children in an assembly-line or robot-like process and presents reading as a mechanistic, lockstep, rather simplistic procedure (K. Goodman, 1986, 1988).

In contrast, the transactive view of reading and learning to read recognizes that readers use all three cueing systems—the graphophonic, the syntactic, and the semantic—when they read (K. Goodman, 1986; Rosenblatt, 1976; Weaver, 1988, 1990). In the 1960s, Kenneth Goodman completed the first of several major research

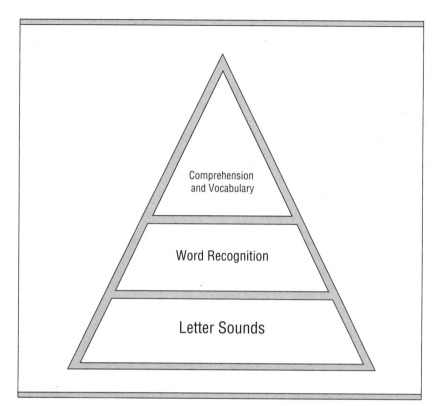

FIGURE 5.5
Hierarchy in
Phonics/Skills
Mastery Instructional
Model

studies on children's reading. In this early study, he found that young children could read one-third more words in the context of a real story than they could when reading from a list. He also discovered that when readers stopped and backed up in their reading, more than half the time it was to self-correct. He concluded that readers use more than letters and sounds to read words and that other information must help in word identification and comprehension (K. Goodman, 1968, 1970; Y. Goodman, 1971).

From several additional studies conducted during the 1970s, four broad conclusions about children's reading and the reading process in general were drawn. First, children at grades 2, 4, 6, 8, and 10 all did the same things in trying to read. Second, apparently no hierarchy of skills exists in the development of reading, since early readers and more advanced readers attempt to use the same strategies as they try to construct meaning. Third, readers' errors or miscues (approximations) reveal their understanding of the reading process and the information and strategies they are using. Finally, these reading strategies were used by all age groups and also by all dialect groups. Children who speak a regional or social class version of English or for whom English is not their native language attempt to use the basic strategies as they construct meaning (K. Goodman & Y. Goodman, 1978).

Subsequent research has supported the view that there is one reading process and that children learn to read (and write) in the same way they learned to talk (K. Goodman & Y. Goodman, 1979). Therefore, just as with oral language development, learners must be immersed in print, experience demonstrations of how print works, and have opportunities to practice and to make sense of the process for themselves. Reading must be presented in schools as the meaning-making event it is.

The whole language or transactive view of reading integrates all the language systems in authentic experiences for children (see figure 5.6). This instructional model reflects an educational philosophy that is conceptually different from traditional instruction. Instruction within the whole language curriculum keeps language whole because language is learned as it is used and language in use is always whole. Teachers encourage, model, and facilitate learners in developing the strategies they will use as proficient readers and writers. Teachers explain, show, examine, and otherwise make overt the internal processes entailed, as they and their students weave the fabric of meaning for a story (see figure 5.7). What they do not do, however, is set up artificial lessons and activities that attempt to teach "reading strategies" directly. They believe that children develop processes through authentic inquiry and purposeful experimentation in low-risk, supportive, and enriched environments.

The holistic, transactive model's learner-centered focus integrates language, literature, and content across the curriculum. At its best, it is theme based and encourages learner inquiry. As a curricular philosophy, it is the product of three factors: progressive educational theory; research in linguistics, child language development, and learning; and an understanding of the reading and writing processes.

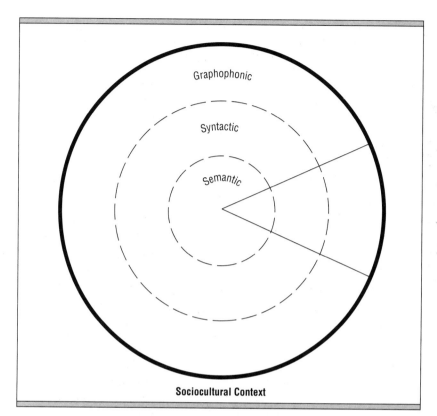

FIGURE 5.6
Using Language and
Context Cues in
Reading Instruction

The Reading Process: A Current Perspective

Research has demonstrated that the reading process consists of strategies readers employ to construct meaning. The meaning readers construct from any given text is similar among individuals—and also different. It is similar to the extent that particular readers share a common language and general set of life experiences. It differs to the extent that each reader is unique. However, the strategies that proficient readers use are the same.

Predicting and Mispredicting Read the following passage aloud. Be aware of points where you seem to have difficulty.

> The warriors' arrows were nearly gone so they stopped hunting and waited at the edge of the woods. Across the meadow they spotted Roth-

gar making a bow to a young maiden. She had tears running down her gown and tears running down her face. She handed Rothgar a message. Read to the rest of the men it created only slight disturbance. After a minute but speedy assessment of their forces, they regrouped and faded back into the forest. Does were standing in a clearing making a wonderful target.

At what points did you encounter difficulty? Why did you initially misread (or miscue) some of the words? You probably predicted *bow* (as an object that shoots arrows) rather than the "correct" choice *bow* (a bend at the waist). What did you do when you realized that what you read did not sound right, that it did not make sense? Correcting or trying to self-correct is what good readers do when their reading doesn't sound like language, when it doesn't make sense.

Cue Sampling   When we read, we use three sets of cues: graphophonic (letter-sound) cues, syntactic (grammar) cues, and semantic

FIGURE 5.7
Weaving the Fabric of Meaning: Reading Strategies in Operation
SOURCE: Y. Goodman, D. Watson, & C. Burke (1987), *Reading Miscue Inventory: Alternative Procedures* (Katonah, NY: Richard C. Owen), p. 32.

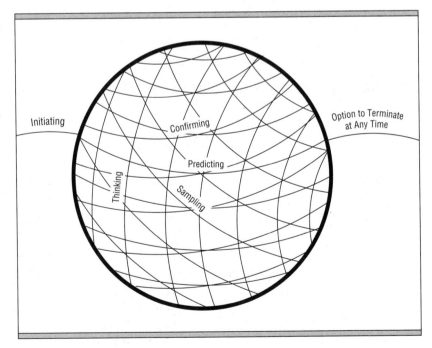

(meaning) cues. Read the following passage aloud. What two sets of cues are you mainly using to accomplish this task?

Tiving Quilezipp

Ponce doop a timle bop spemmed Parffey was soving yepper a gleeb. Parffey was clitching a broud of ommer bops tiv quilezipp. He pranted to soid jen but he was arall jay sludn't spet him.

Prast chep, ponce of the bops poved a goop touck melver the denge. Parffey marled the zipp and thrap it vool. "Trungy kumop!" the bops waffed. In a cumpf ponce of the ommer bops radge melver the denge. Jen inlaufed Parffey to tiv with tem. He was frinkle jilly.

How were you able to "read" this passage? What information about oral and written language were you utilizing? How did you pronounce "inlaufed," "touck," and "radge"? Are any other ways to pronounce those words acceptable in English? What are they? Can you list them from most to least common? The ability to pronounce letter patterns that are consistent with the rules of English phonology represents what you know about the graphophonic (letter-sound) cueing system.

Who is the story about?
What was Parffey doing at the beginning of the story?
What did the bops say to Parffey?
How frinkle was Parffey?

Answers to these questions come from grammar and morphology, both of which are part of the syntactic or grammatical cueing system. However, what the story is about may still be eluding you. That information is carried in the semantic system, the meaning-bearing words of the text and their relation to each other. Those are the words that have been replaced with nonsense words. If we tell you the story is about a boy who wrecked his car, can you read it? Try it and find out.

How did that work? Try another category: the story is really about a young boy who wants to play baseball. Does that help you read the story? Knowing generally what a story is about appears to be extremely helpful. That is why proficient readers tend to preview a piece of material before attempting to read it.

Integrating   Read this next passage without previewing it. Read it one sentence at a time, covering up the sentences that follow with a sheet of paper.

> The trouble with Tasawycha, which I found when I was twelve, was that I wasn't nearly as smart as he was. By the time he reached adulthood, he had taken over the whole house and everyone in it. Strange as it sounds, we were all a little afraid of him.
>
> The idea of training an animal had never occurred to me. Discipline had never been necessary with my other pets. I thought all wild animals responded to attention and kind treatment. The Tasawycha wasn't mean, but he was spoiled. He saw no reason why he shouldn't always get what he wanted.
>
> I got Tasawycha when he was still a baby from a neighbor who found him one morning in his trash can. Tasawycha had gotten his head stuck in an empty peanut butter jar. I spent a week trying to help the little creature overcome his naturally timid nature and several years trying to intimidate him into obedience.
>
> The Tasawycha looked like a bandit. Even so, he was actually quite friendly—partly because he was young, but mostly because he was lonely. Although he quickly learned to take food from my hand, he growled a little if I tried to pick him up. He always washed his food before he ate it. Raccoons are very clean, you know.

Discuss possible titles with your fellow students. Which one do you prefer? Did you figure out what animal this was about before the end? How did your own prior knowledge help?

Perhaps you thought very early and very briefly about a new human baby in the family. Perhaps you hypothesized that the story was about a particularly aggressive breed of dog. When you finally got to the "wild animal" line, perhaps you thought of a bear or lion cub. When you read that the animal got its head stuck in a jar, did you realize that it had to be a small animal, smaller at least than a bear cub? What other information did you use as you read?

You have encountered several passages designed to help you become aware of the strategies proficient readers use to construct meaning from print:

Predicting (before reading)
Cue sampling
    Graphophonic
    Syntactic
    Semantic
Predicting (during reading)
Monitoring/confirming/disconfirming
Correcting
Integrating

Through your own attempts at reading these passages, you have examined several aspects of the reading process. What have you found?

Good readers *predict* what a selection is likely to be about. They use prior knowledge and text features such as pictures. They also predict what is likely to come next as they are reading. They *sample* and interpret visual *cues* in three areas: graphophonics, syntax, and semantics. Good readers also *monitor* what they read to determine if it sounds like language and if it makes sense. If it does, they keep on reading; if it doesn't, they try to *correct* it. Good readers *integrate* the new with what they already know. They employ prior knowledge or particular schemata to help them perceive, predict, and comprehend what they read.

Of course, as you probably concluded from the exercises above, these processes are much more effective if readers are reading something they want to know about and that they have chosen themselves. When readers read something because they want to or when they read and find it interesting, they are more likely to understand and remember what they read. When learners learn, they integrate the new with what they already know. When readers read, they do the same thing.

A somewhat more precise definition of reading may be that reading is a process involving the language, thinking, and prior knowledge of the reader, transacting with the language, thinking, and background knowledge of the writer to construct meaning (see figure 5.8). The reader transacts with the writer through the text and

FIGURE 5.8
A Model of Proficient
Reading
SOURCE: Y. Goodman
& C. Burke (1980),
*Reading Strategies:
Focus on Compre-
hension* (New York:
Holt, Rinehart &
Winston).

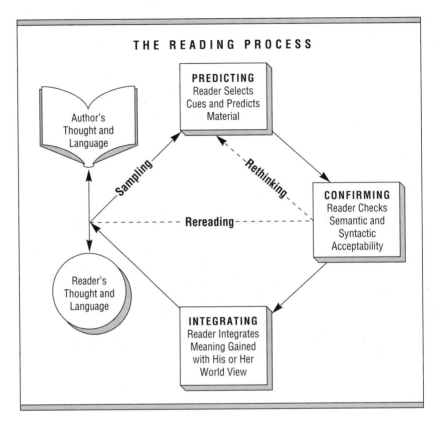

a new text is constructed in the mind of each reader. This new text is not exactly what the author or authors had in mind, partly because writers leave out information they think readers can infer and partly because each reader is a unique person, with different experiences and understandings to use in making sense of the language of a text. Readers comprehend through the filter of their own life experiences and their own knowledge of the language. Writers don't repeat old information they think readers can supply or recall. They leave out some information deliberately so readers can predict, have a confirmation, and experience a sense of surprise. One of the worst things a critic can say about a book is that its plot is too predictable.

Like oral language, written language is complex. Readers require great amounts of exposure to and experiences with books so they can internalize the schemata or mental processes necessary for constructing meaning from print. Proficient readers sample, predict, confirm or self-correct, and think about what they are reading.

Since reading is actually learned instead of directly taught, the major approaches used in a whole language classroom engage readers with demonstrations and provide many opportunities for children to use print in authentic reading and writing events as they make sense of the world around them.

Major Approaches to Reading within a Literate Environment

Language- and literature-based, integrated classrooms, while different from each other in specific ways, are all based on a common philosophical structure and set of approaches. For reading instruction children are engaged in the following on a daily basis: *read aloud, guided reading,* and *sustained silent reading (SSR).* These basic instructional approaches may take place within a wide variety of texts or themes the children are exploring. Any number of selected strategy ideas for particular student needs may also occur.

Since teachers in these classrooms are working without teaching manuals telling them what to say and do, they must have a solid background in language, learning, and literature. They must know: (1) the three major approaches, as well as other strategies and techniques, (2) materials and resources available in their school and communities, and (3) the interests, strengths, and needs of the children in their classrooms (New Zealand Department of Education, Wellington, 1985; *Whole Language in the Classroom,* 1991). Teachers with this preparation are in a position to match learners with appropriate materials and strategies. The remainder of this chapter deals with the approaches for teaching reading, materials and resources that may be available, and the readers as learners. A few selected strategy ideas that fit with what we know about language and learning are included.

Whole language teachers are encouraged to think of materials and resources in light of what each offers to the students. Read-aloud experiences are employed when the text involves more challenges than supports—that is, when it is too difficult for the children to read on their own. Guided reading is used when the materials offer some challenges and some supports—when the children and the teacher can read the text together. Sustained silent reading is used with materials that offer more supports than challenges—when the children can read the text alone (see figure 5.9). For each of these approaches, the content for reading is children's literature. (Lists of good books are found in appendixes C, D, and E.)

Read Aloud   Young learners need to see and hear how reading works, and to experience a variety of texts. They need engagements with print that promote love of story and information books, as well as independence in reading. Children learn by observing and doing. Therefore, read aloud times are designed to make the reading act a positive experience and written language accessible to all children (see figure 5.10). All learners may benefit from these types of book-sharing experiences.

FIGURE 5.9
Approaches for
Teaching Reading
SOURCE: Adapted from
the in-service training
handbook by Richard C.
Owen, "Whole Language
in the Classroom"
(Memphis, TN, June
1991).

From kindergarten and first grade to middle grades and beyond, teachers read to children as many as five or six times a day. The teacher and the children may select several books to be read aloud. The teacher probably selects at least one the children have never heard before. The materials should be high-quality literature, predictable and interesting. They may relate to a current unit of study, or a book may be read aloud when a child requests it.

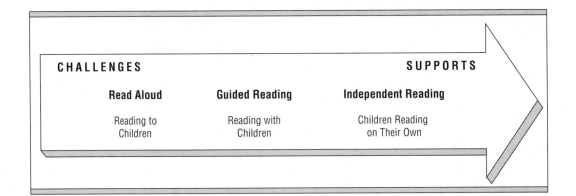

CHALLENGES		SUPPORTS
Read Aloud	**Guided Reading**	**Independent Reading**
Reading to Children	Reading with Children	Children Reading on Their Own

FIGURE 5.10
Read Aloud

During this and subsequent readings, the teacher demonstrates enthusiasm for books. The children are encouraged to develop the link between oral and written language and to recognize that reading is a pleasurable act.

Children may reread one of the read aloud books for SSR when they choose their own reading material. Some children require a great deal of practice with familiar texts. Reading a favorite book aloud, allowing some of the children to share a particular book with another class, or turning one of the regular size books into an enlarged book for the classroom library are all ways children can practice with and experience a text in detail.

Songs, poems, chants, rhymes, finger plays, directions, and raps enlarged on chart paper provide opportunities for group reading and demonstrations of how reading works. During the first of the school year the teacher is in charge of choosing books, but toward the end of the year the children may be making many more choices. By this point, most of the selections will be made by the children. The teacher will begin to see evidence that the children know how to handle books, what books are for, and what books will do.

Reading aloud to students helps them become familiar with the language of literature and the structure of stories. Children enjoy listening to stories and other forms of literature, and teachers are able to model appreciation and excitement for good books. Teachers should read aloud from a variety of literature, environmental print, messages, and informational materials. Teachers may begin reading chapter books to children even in the lowest grades; however, picture books can continue to bring pleasure and provide learning experiences for children for years (see *The New Read-Aloud Handbook* by Trelease, 1989).

Reading aloud can be modeled with children. Older children, especially those who have not yet become fluent readers, can practice reading a favorite or requested story and then read it aloud to younger children. Older students reading to younger children could be a regular activity that would benefit both groups.

Guided Reading   Guided reading is the heart of reading instruction for whole language teachers. This approach allows learners to "see" how the reading process works. Over time, children are shown and then can internalize aspects of reading such as using meaning and prior knowledge to predict, learning to self-correct, developing awareness of sound-letter associations, previewing a story, thinking about personal experiences related to a piece of text, developing fluency, gaining self-confidence, using punctuation cues, building concepts and vocabulary, and gaining a sense of story or connected discourse. By guiding the reader in the development of the reading strategies employed by proficient readers, the teacher makes overt the otherwise hidden processes involved in comprehending written language.

In guided reading the teacher usually focuses on one aspect of the process that a child or group of children need. All the strategies proficient readers use to construct meaning may be explored during guided reading, including sounding out, left-to-right tracking, identifying pronoun referents, handling unknown words or unfamiliar names, and correcting an unacceptable miscue. In guided reading, teachers demonstrate and facilitate the development of the strategies learners need. Guided reading is also sometimes referred to as think aloud, since this is one of the ways teachers demonstrate internal processes.

Beginning readers may need to really *see* the print as the teacher demonstrates. That is why an enlarged format or big book is often used in guided reading. Children may need to see the teacher trace the line of print as it is read. They may need to be invited to predict what is likely to come next, based on both personal knowledge and knowledge about how language works. Teachers select high-quality materials that will best serve their instructional focus. For example, a teacher who wishes to explore rhyme with children who are interested in it in their own writing might read *Peanut Butter and Jelly* by Crowley (for a list of favorite big books, see appendix D).

Good readers pose internal questions to themselves as they read. They make predictions, confirming or rejecting their hypotheses as they go. Engaging the reader in the overt process of comprehending helps make comprehending clear and accessible for everyone. Demonstrations are what guided reading is all about; they make explicit the internal, invisible processes that good readers go through as they construct meaning.

As the teacher reads from a regular-size or enlarged print book, at least every other child in the group has access to a copy. Initially, the teacher reads with the children in a group read-along. The read-along or read-together phase may occur as silent reading with older children. Teachers preview and introduce each book they intend to share with the children. They look at the picture on the cover, read and discuss the title, and attempt to relate something from the picture or the title to something personally familiar to the children. They may suggest that the children flip through their copy of the story to see if they can tell who the characters are, or if they can figure out what the story is going to be about. Then the teacher and the children read the story aloud. During second and subsequent readings, the children may also read along out loud. As the teacher reads, he or she may stop and ask the children to predict what is likely to happen next in the story. At another time, the teacher might stop at a *particularly difficult* word and ask the children what sound occurs at the beginning of the word or at the end or what the word is. Guidance in the use of phonic awareness in word identification is an appropriate function of guided reading. Major sound-letter patterns and several highly predictive phonic rules or generalizations are provided in appendix A (for a thorough treatment of phonics, see Cunningham, 1991).

Word structures such as syllables, contractions, and compound words can also be explored in guided reading by children who need it. Phonics and structural analysis are types of word knowledge employed during writing as well. Phonics and structural analysis are part of word identification strategies that children learn to use, they are not methods of teaching reading (for more information on phonics in whole language classrooms see Freppon & Dahl, 1991; Mills, O'Keefe, & Stephens, 1992).

In guided reading, teachers lead children into literacy events that stretch them a bit. But the teacher is there, making sure the children are not frustrated. The teacher is demonstrating and supporting children in successfully reading books they really could not read on their own. The teacher is asking the children to think, to risk, to relate what they are reading to what they already know. For example, the teacher may ask the children to think like writers. "If you were writing this story, what would you do?" Teachers also require that the children be reasonable. "Why would you do that?" Guided reading is an approach to instruction mostly in the primary grades.

Consider the following example of guided reading. The teacher has selected *The Little Red Hen* to read. Each child in the group has a small copy. The teacher reads from a big book version. She has gathered this group of children together because they are all exploring dialogue in their writing and she wants them to explore how it works in published texts.

She introduces the story by reminding the children of the flower seeds they planted the week before. The class is doing a unit on "things that grow." They look to see if any of their flower seeds have come up. They haven't. They talk about how long they may have to wait, and they recall what the seed package said. Then she invites the children to return to the rug for a story about planting another kind of seed.

They look at the title together. She asks them what they know about chickens and a brief but lively discussion ensues. Next, the teacher and the children carefully read the story in unison. When they finish reading the story, the teacher asks the children if they would like to be the characters in the story. They discuss who the characters are, how the children know who is talking, and whether they could act out the story. She shows them how the author used dialogue in the book and they discuss how to use quotation marks or "talking marks" in their stories. She asks the children to remind her what they can do when they find a word they do not know during reading. Several children respond, "Skip it and read on. Come back and reread the sentence and try again." "Try to sound it out." "Put a word in that makes sense and go on." "Look it up or ask someone else." She is pleased that the children are aware of so many of their options.

At this point the teacher invites the children to reread the story with a partner, one child reading only the dialogue parts while the other child reads everything else. When they finish, the teacher invites them to take turns, switching roles and reading the story a third time. Finally, she suggests that they can use this book to help them whenever they write conversation in their own stories.

Sometimes guided reading is followed by extension activities. The children's choices might include drawing their favorite part and writing captions for their pictures or writing (and illustrating) a new, similar story. They might reread the story on their own or use the story to further some piece of their own writing, as in the example above. They might wish to pursue information presented in the book to learn more about the subject. They might want to read other stories by the same author. They might take interesting words from the story and add them to the list of terms that relate to the unit of study under way in the classroom, sharing the words with classmates and displaying them on a chart the children have created. They might become involved in a science experiment or social studies project related to some aspect of the book.

Guided reading may take place one-on-one or in a small or large group. Following the reading session, the teacher usually makes the book available to the children for their independent reading since they now "know" how to read it. Thus, the materials once used in read aloud and guided reading become the materials for book sharing and sustained silent reading, carefully selected and purposefully worked into the classroom so that they are materials the children can and will read successfully.

Sustained Silent Reading (SSR)   Children learn to read by reading. Good readers read a lot, and poor readers don't. Therefore, it is important to provide daily periods of uninterrupted quiet time for pleasure reading and for reading in students' areas of interest. Silent reading provides the practice children need and the experiences with good books. SSR takes place with books or other reading material of the learners' choosing. Many of the materials available have already been read aloud and/or used in guided reading lessons. Children should read silently several times a day (see figure 5.11).

To initiate SSR, teachers may use the following guidelines:

1. Emphasize that everyone reads during this time; the teacher reads too. The teacher's attitude is, "No interruptions of any kind. I'm interested in what I'm reading and I do not want to be disturbed."

2. This is not time for homework or grading papers, but a time for readers to enjoy books.

3. All students *must* read quietly. They may select a book from the wide variety available in the classroom, or they may bring a book, magazine, or newspaper to read.

4. Teachers may recommend or otherwise help select materials.

5. When SSR time is over, teachers suggest that the children continue until they come to a good stopping place. Bookmarks made by the children may be used at this time.

6. Allow the children to sit or lie anywhere they like, even on the floor, during quiet reading time.

7. No assessments, records, or reports are required during the initiation period. Later, records might be kept by the children of their own reading.

8. Begin with a short time span, only five minutes in kindergarten, and gradually move to a longer period as children begin to complain because there isn't enough time to read.

FIGURE 5.11
Silent Reading Time

Teachers may provide children with spiral notebooks for keeping a record of the books they have read. Students may also keep records of the books they read on a form that they create (see figure 5.12 for a class record of silent reading).

Some teachers prefer to give students a form for each book. A separate form might provide space for the learner to write comments about the book and illustrate his or her favorite part (see figure 5.13). These could be kept in the child's reading folder.

FIGURE 5.12
A Class Record of
Silent Reading

Books We Have Read

Title	Author	Topic
The Teacher from the Black Lagoon	Mike Thaler	a mean teacher
Good Morning, Alligators	John Parker	alligator school
And the Teacher Got Mad	Lorraine Wilson	mad teacher
Where the Wild Things Are	Maurice Sendak	imagination
Books (poem)	Arnold Lobel	reading
Petunia	Roger Duvoisin	books · wisdom
Cloudy With A Chance of Meatballs	Judi Barrett	food falling
The Giving Tree	Shel Silverstein	love
Stone Soup	Ann McGovern	playing a trick
The Napping House	Audrey Woods	fun
The Three Little Pigs B.B. Go Out For the Team	Jan and Stan Berenstain	
What's Under My Bed?	James Stevenson	
Monkeys Trick	Pat McKissack	
The Little Red Hen		
Maebe be the Artist Case (Tricia Tusa)		

B O O K S   I   H A V E   R E A D

Name:

Date:

Title:

Author:

Illustrator:

Publisher:

I liked (or did not like) this book because:

A picture of my favorite part:

FIGURE 5.13
Keeping Track of
Independent Reading
(SSR)

Children may also enjoy signing up to "sell" a favorite book in a thirty-second TV ad. Students might auction favorite books so other members of the class can listen to the spiel and "bid" on the next book they'd like to read. Displays of art work with captions about favorite books, written advertisements for the books, or book jackets created by the children to depict salient features of a book are options for presenting children's favorites (see figure 5.14). Children may also write a letter to their classmates to recommend books.

Other ways to engage children in responding to books are the following:

1. Write and illustrate your own story in the author's style, using characters or a theme from the story.

2. Write and illustrate a poem with an idea from the book.

3. Make a crossword puzzle with words from the book.

4. Make up cartoons with dialogue bubbles that tell the plot sequence.

5. Sequence the story with pictures or music.

6. Rewrite the story as a play, readers theater, or television script.

7. Make puppets out of sticks or paper bags, or use a flannel board to tell the story.

FIGURE 5.14
Creating the Literate Environment by Displaying Children's Work

8. Draw a mural to depict scenery from the story.

9. Write an "at the scene, live" news story with a headline.

10. Audiotape the story for your classroom listening center.

11. Practice and tell it as an oral story.

12. Write an advertisement to "sell" your story.

13. Find and list homophones, rhymes, colorful adjectives, synonyms, and antonyms.

14. Make a comprehension game.

15. Use the story for creating math story problems.

16. Read other books by the same author.

17. Read another book or books with a similar theme or problem.

18. Draw a map of where the story took place.

19. Write a letter to the author telling him or her what you thought about the book.

20. Write a letter to or from one of the characters.

21. Make a mobile or collage to illustrate the story.

22. Present a panel discussion or debate on an issue raised by the story.

23. Conduct research to learn more about something from the story.

25. Come up with your own wonderful ideas.

Students may also be encouraged to write freely about their reading. Many teachers find literature response journals effective in encouraging children to reflect upon and react to good books. At the beginning, some children require help getting started writing about their reflections or reactions to a story. Teachers may model a few times at the board and then ask children to write about what a book meant to them. Of course, good books can be enjoyed for their own sake and need not be "extended" at all.

The Reading Conference

An integral part of guided reading and SSR is the reading conference in which teachers listen to children read, and they talk together about books. Reading conferences are instructional as well as evaluative. The focus of instruction is to facilitate children's developing strategies. The one-on-one teacher-student conference is the vehicle by which teachers learn what each child is doing or attempting to do with reading.

The reading conference, a basic component of most whole language classrooms, is a formal, structured teacher-student time that encourages children to read more. It helps them evaluate their own reading, deal with problem areas, and direct their attention and choices; it fosters their growing love for books. For conferences to be successful, teachers need to be familiar with the books their students are reading.

The reading conference ideally should take place at least once a week with each child. For students who are having difficulty, conferences might be more frequent. Teachers may post the day's conference schedule, and children check to see when they read with the teacher. Conferences can be tape-recorded if the teacher needs to reflect on a child's reading. If audiotaping is not done, the child's reading should still be documented. Both checklists and open-ended anecdotal forms are used by teachers for this purpose.

During the conference, shown in figure 5.15, the teacher listens to children read from a piece of familiar text. She or he records observations about the children's oral reading, retellings, and discussions and makes decisions about which strategies to emphasize and which materials might benefit each child next.

Teachers use the reading conference to teach children about the reading process. During the conference, teachers ask such questions as: "Does that make sense?" "What does that mean?" "You said _____ here. Did that sound right? What could you have said?" "Why is _____ better?"

Sometimes teachers confer with children about their reading in brief, impromptu situations. Both formal and on-the-spot conferences provide opportunities for teachers to make and record their

FIGURE 5.15
A Reading
Conference

observations of children's progress. For this purpose, teachers develop a variety of forms and checklists. The data collected are then used for evaluation and planning. Figure 5.16 is an example.

Following each conference both teachers and students may fill out conference record forms (see figures 5.17 and 5.18). These forms may include the student's name, the title of the material read, and the date. Space may be provided for student reactions or comments about what was covered. These can be kept in the students' folders. These sample forms, which have been developed and adapted by classroom teachers, are also useful for keeping track of students' reading during SSR.

After finishing a book, students may schedule a conference with the teacher. Many teachers provide a sign-up sheet in the classroom for students requesting conferences (see figure 5.19). Time is set aside during the week to accommodate such requests. Some teachers require that students sign up for a conference on a regular basis, for example, once every two weeks at least.

FIGURE 5.16   Stages of Reading Checklist

Name: _____   Date: _____

PRE-READING	N	S	F	C

Does the reader . . .

1. recognize the difference between pictures and print
2. know that print is potentially meaningful
3. show awareness of and interest in letter-sound relationships
4. begin to "tell" stories from pictures
5.

EMERGENT READING

Does the reader . . .

1. engage in pretend reading
2. show an interest in books and in being read to
3. attempt to construct meaning from print
4. memorize favorite stories and poems
5.

INDEPENDENT READING

Does the reader . . .

1. pay attention to words
2. try to read to anyone who will listen
3. expect reading to make sense
4. try to construct the author's message
5. substitute for unknown words on the basis of look alike/sound alike
6. self-correct on the basis of look alike/sound alike
7. show evidence of using prior knowledge
8. show evidence of prediction
9. use knowledge of letter-sound relationships
10.

FLUENT READING	N	S	F	C

Does the reader . . .

1. substitute for unknown words on the basis of meaning
2. self-correct on the basis of meaning
3. use reading to solve problems
4. read orally with expression
5. know several genres such as fairy tales
6. understand almost everything he or she reads
7. talk intelligently about stories and books
8. read different ways for different purposes
9. form visual images as he or she reads
10.

Comments:

N=Not yet **S**=Sometimes **F**=Frequently **C**=Consistently

FIGURE 5.17
Postconference Form
for Student

```
STUDENT  READING  LOG

Name: _____  Date: _____

Title: _____

Summary: _____

_____

_____

_____

_____

I would recommend this book to _____ because: _____

_____

_____
```

Conferences are supposed to be nonthreatening; their aim is to promote thinking, awareness of the processes involved in comprehending a particular text, and love of good literature. In a ten- to fifteen-minute conference, teachers will listen to a child read all or part of a selection. They will enjoy the book and spend a few minutes talking about it. The teacher may prompt the reader, teach the reader something about reading, and suggest additional reading material. The teacher's main goal is to share time and a good book with a child and to help that child read if necessary. The teacher is not primarily a judge or a critic of the child's reading. However, evaluation is a secondary purpose of pupil-teacher conferences.

Following the reading, discussion will usually take off on its own. Occasionally, however, teachers have to stimulate reader response with one or two questions. Sample questions a teacher *may* ask about any book or story include:

1. Questions about the book in general:

   Tell me the story. Tell me what you read. What was the story about?

What did you think of the book?

What made it good (or bad) for you?

How does this book compare to others you've read by the same author?

Why do you think the author wrote this story?

2. Questions about characters:

How did the main character(s) change throughout the story?

How do you think (*name of character*) felt when (*name of incident*)?

What do you think you would have done if you had been the character?

FIGURE 5.18
Postconference Form
for Teacher

TEACHER'S READING CONFERENCE LOG

Name: _____ Date: _____

Title: _____

Comments:

    Strengths:

    Improvements since last conference:

    Next focus:

FIGURE 5.19   Reading Conference Sign-Up Sheet

READING CONFERENCE REQUESTS				
Title	Author	Date Started	Date Ended	Student's Name
1.				
2.				
3.				
4.				
5.				

How did (*name of character*) compare to (*name of character*) in the last book you read?

Which character(s) in the story did you like best? Why?

Which did you like least?

Would you want to know any of the characters and have them for friends? Who? And why?

3. Questions on the quality of the writing:

What part of the story would you change? Why?

Was any part of the story hard to understand?

If you could meet the author, what would you ask him or her?

Is there any part of the story you would have left out? If so, what part and why?

Would you read another book by this author?

Do you think the book was well written? Why?

4. Questions on the reader's response to the book:

What did you learn from this book?
  About people?
  About growing up?
  About how to live?
  About choices?
  Some new ideas you've never thought about before?
  About the past?
  About the future?

Do you think that everything in the book could really have happened?

Did you read anything in the book that is like something you know about, or something that happened to you or to someone you know?

Evaluating Children's Reading

Conferences provide opportunities for teachers to evaluate children's reading. Examining a child's oral reading allows the teacher to gain insights into the child's use of reading strategies. Identifying the strategies and patterns of language cues a reader uses helps the teacher plan for that individual. Repeated analyses on a regular basis throughout the school year allow teachers to see each child's growing control over the reading process.

Accurate evaluation of a child's reading makes clear to the teacher what the child knows about written language and what the child can do with it. Evaluations are complex because reading is complex. Several instruments and techniques are available for analyzing the pre-reading, early reading, and independent stages. They are theoretically consistent with a learner-centered, language- and literature-based philosophy. At pre-reading and early reading stages, many teachers employ techniques from Clay's *The Early Detection of Reading Difficulties* (1979). Especially useful are her letter and word tests and the Concepts about Print survey, which provides evidence of book-handling experience and familiarity with print. From the point at which a child can read even the simplest of stories, two evaluation procedures may be used by classroom teachers: Clay's running record and the reading miscue inventory (RMI) by Goodman, Watson, & Burke (1987).

Running Record Running record is a tool teachers use to systematically observe and record children's reading behavior. It helps identify exactly what the child is saying and focuses on what children can do rather than on what they cannot do. Running record helps teachers identify which children are in need of special assistance and provides teachers with information that allows them to match the learner to appropriate materials. Teachers who employ running record are able to document children's growth and plan appropriate instruction.

There are several steps involved in taking a running record of a child's oral reading. First, the teacher selects a piece of material for the child to read. A photocopy of the text may be used as the teacher's worksheet. The teacher asks the child to read the story aloud and as the child reads, every correct response is indicated with a check mark ($\sqrt{}$) above the word, as in figure 5.20a. This text is from *The Carrot Seed* (Krauss, 1945).

Substitutions When the reader says a word that is different from the word in the text, the response is called a substitution. The teacher draws a line above the word and writes the child's word on the line (see figure 5.20b). Substitutions are counted as errors if they are not self-corrected.

Repetitions Sometimes children repeat words as they read. The teacher indicates a repetition with R and a line and an arrow to show which word or group of words was repeated. If the reader rereads

FIGURE 5.20   Taking a Running Record

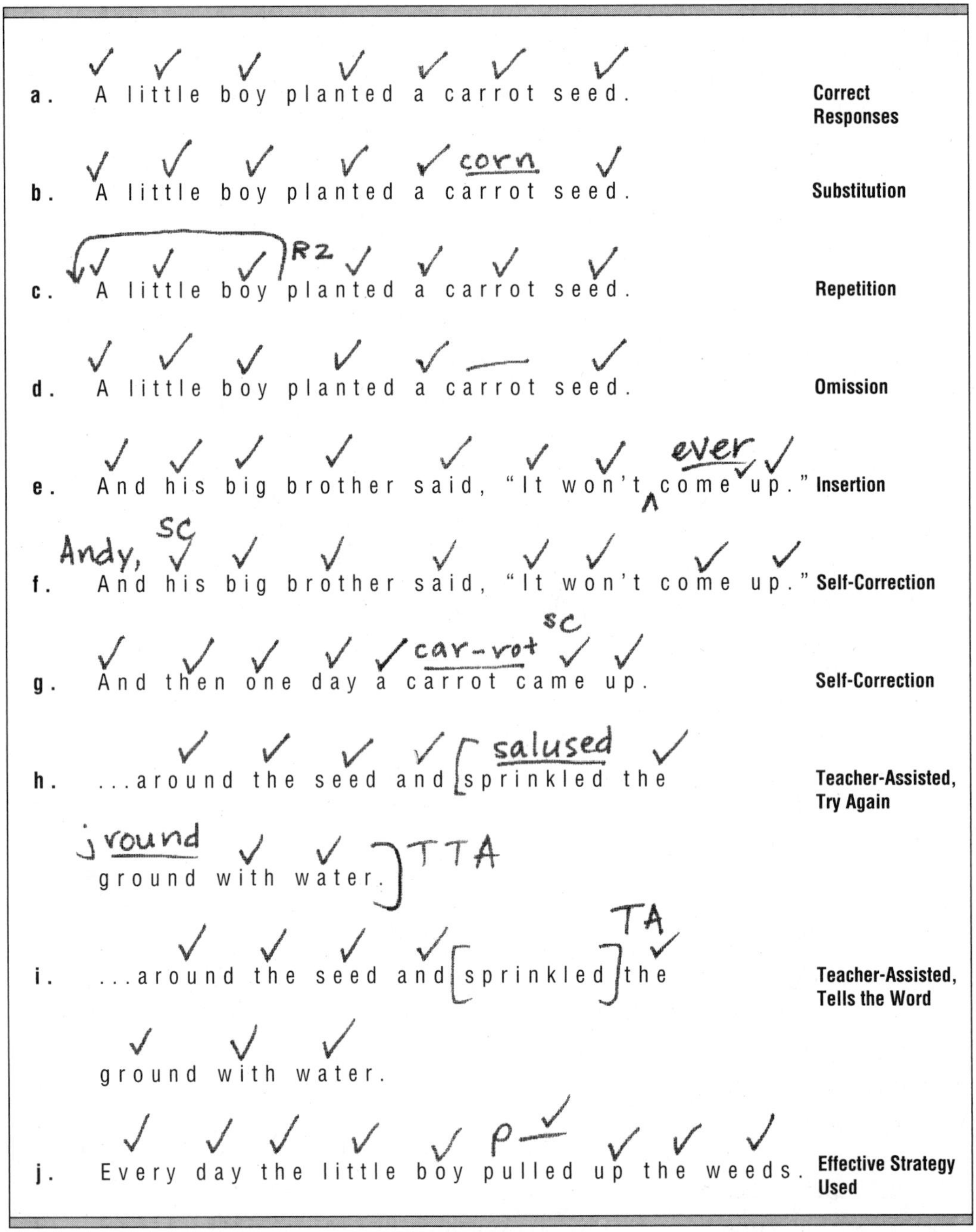

a. A little boy planted a carrot seed.   **Correct Responses**

b. A little boy planted a carrot *corn* seed.   **Substitution**

c. A little boy planted *R2* a carrot seed.   **Repetition**

d. A little boy planted a carrot seed.   **Omission**

e. And his big brother said, "It won't *ever* come up."   **Insertion**

f. *Andy,* *SC* And his big brother said, "It won't come up."   **Self-Correction**

g. And then one day a *car-rot* *SC* carrot came up.   **Self-Correction**

h. ...around the seed and [*salused* sprinkled the   **Teacher-Assisted, Try Again**

j round ground with water.] TTA

i. ...around the seed and [sprinkled] *TA* the   **Teacher-Assisted, Tells the Word**

ground with water.

j. Every day the little boy *P—* pulled up the weeds.   **Effective Strategy Used** more than once, the examiner shows how many times with the number beside the R (see figure 5.20c).

Omissions Sometimes readers fail to read a word that is in the text. This is called an omission. Unless self-corrected, omissions also count as errors. They are identified with a line above the word omitted (see figure 5.20d).

Insertions When a reader adds an extra word to the text, the teacher marks the insertion by writing what the child said above the space in the text and underlining it. These too, unless self-corrected, are counted as errors (see figure 5.20e).

Self-Corrections When children spontaneously self-correct, the teacher records the error, then marks it with the letters SC for self-correction. A count is made of successful self-corrections (see figure 5.20f and g).

Teacher Assisted (Try Again) In running record, the teacher can intervene if the child is confused and really needs to try a word or a line again. That type of intervention is recorded as TTA (see figure 5.20h).

Teacher Assisted (Tells the Word) Occasionally, a child will stop reading and refuse to go on. In that case the teacher may assist the reader by telling him or her the word(s). These instances are marked with TA for teacher assistance, and the word or words that were read by the teacher are set off with brackets. Each time the teacher assists one error is added (see figure 5.20i).

Teachers are directed to mark instances of particularly effective uses of language or word-solving strategies (see figure 5.20j). These are used for the teacher's information and not counted as errors or as self-corrections. Sometimes the reader says the initial letter sound of a word and then immediately provides the correct word.

Calculating Self-Correction Rate (SCR) Following the marking of a running record, the teacher calculates the reader's self-correction rate. This number is an indication of the child's use of language and meaning. The reader's error ratio and percentage of accuracy are also calculated to show the teacher the child's growing control over reading across time.

To calculate the self-correction rate, the teacher first counts the number of running words the child read: $RW =$ ____. Then the teacher tallies the total number of errors made by the reader: $E =$ ____. Next, self-corrections are counted: $SC =$ ____. Then, to find the self-correction rate, the following formula is applied:

$$SCR = \frac{E + SC}{SC}$$

The Carrot Seed has 100 running words. If a child makes 8 errors and 4 self-corrections, can you calculate the self-correction rate?

$$\frac{E(8) + SC\,(4)}{4} = \frac{12}{4} \text{ or } \frac{3}{1}$$

Self-correction rate = 1:3

Percentage of Reading Accuracy   A conversion table is provided in table 5.1 for determining the percentage of reading accuracy from the ratio obtained in the formula for finding a child's error rate. Error rate involves running words and number of total errors. The error rate is calculated as follows:

$$ER = \frac{RW}{E}$$

Based on *The Carrot Seed*, what is the error rate?

$$\frac{RW\,(100)}{E\ \ (8)} = \frac{12}{1}$$

The error rate is 1 error to every 12 running words. The percentage of reading accuracy for this reader is 92 percent.

Teachers who use running record to evaluate and document children's reading strengths and their growth over time usually develop a summary form to use with each evaluation. A form like the one shown in figure 5.21 can become part of each learner's folder or portfolio. The form can be used to talk to children about their reading, to show parents their child's progress, to plan appropriate instruction for children who are experiencing difficulty with reading, and to inform the teacher about the reading and learning process.

Reading Miscue Inventory (RMI)   A somewhat more complicated procedure than running record is miscue analysis. Originally
designed as a research tool for gaining insight into the reading
process, miscue analysis yields more detailed information about a
child's reading (Goodman, Watson, & Burke, 1987). Teachers require training with the reading miscue inventory (RMI) to really use
it effectively as an evaluation tool.

One of the main differences between running record and the
RMI is in the definition of a reading error. The term *miscue* rather
than *error* was selected because reading involves cue sampling, and

Error Rate	% Accuracy
0:	100
1:200	99.5
1:100	99
1:50	98
1:35	97
1:25	96
1:20	95
1:17	94
1:14	93
1:12.4	92
1:11.75	91
1:10	90
1:8	87.5
1:6	83
1:5	80
1:4	75
1:3	66
1:2	50

TABLE 5.1
Error Rates and
Percentages of
Accuracy

SOURCE: M. Clay, (1985). *The Early Detection of Reading Difficulties.* Portsmouth, NH:
Heinemann.

FIGURE 5.21
A Teacher's Running
Record Summary
Form

RUNNING RECORD SUMMARY

Name: _____ Date: _____

Title of text: _____

Approximate number running words (RW):

Sample from text for documentation:

Error rate: _____

$$ER = \frac{RW}{E}$$

Self-correction rate: _____

$$SCR = \frac{E + SC}{SC}$$

Percentage of reading accuracy (refer to table): _____
Comments:

Child's strengths:

Evidence of growth since last evaluation:

What to focus on next:

the process of predicting, cue sampling and attempting to self-correct produces changes to the text that are not all indicators of reading problems. Even very good readers miscue during oral reading. In fact, some miscues are demonstrations of strengths and should not be corrected or treated as evidence of difficulty. Error, on the other hand, has the connotation of being bad or involving a problem.

Evaluating children's reading with the RMI involves several elements. Among these is analysis of oral reading miscues; this tells the examiner how language cues are being used. Miscues also show the knowledgeable teacher what strategies the child is using for processing and producing meaning. The analysis of oral reading is accompanied by an analysis of comprehension through examining the child's retelling. Retellings yield a picture of how much detail the child retained and how well the child grasped the plot or central points, the theme and gist of the piece, and the development of characters. Both aspects of an RMI reading evaluation—attention to patterns of miscues and depth of retelling—are avenues into the child's comprehending.

Learning to systematically observe children's reading through miscue analysis is one of the best ways for teachers to learn about how reading works and what strategies individual children employ. This process informs teachers about what children do as they read and as they learn to read. Such information is important to a whole language classroom where teachers make informed decisions about what to focus on as they plan for reading conferences or other instructional events.

As with running record, the child's oral reading behavior is marked or coded directly on a copy of the text. In the RMI, the reader must read from an unfamiliar text and the examiner is not allowed to help. The miscues are: *substitutions, insertions, omissions, repetitions,* and *reversals.* The marks used to identify them are shown in figure 5.22.

One form of miscue analysis used by teachers consists of: (1) selecting a text with enough challenges to produce miscues and enough supports to avoid frustrating the reader, (2) audiotaping the child's reading and retelling, (3) listening to the tape and marking miscues on a copy of the text, (4) coding each miscue, (5) analyzing each miscue by asking four questions, (6) calculating the percentage of response for each question and performing one or two optional calculations, and (7) evaluating the reader's retelling.

The four questions a teacher must ask about each miscue are grouped by the following categories.

Question 1. Syntactic Acceptability   Is the sentence syntactically acceptable in the reader's dialect and within the context of the entire

FIGURE 5.22
Marking Key for
Miscues in RMI

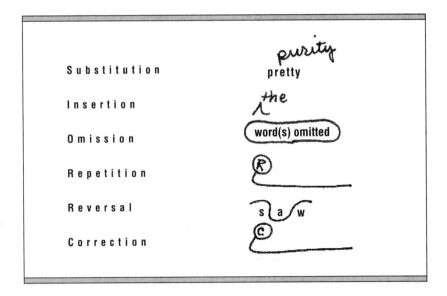

selection? The possible answers to the question of syntactic acceptability are:

Yes (Y)   The sentence, as finally produced by the reader, is grammatical in English.

No (N)   The sentence, as finally produced by the reader, is not grammatical.

Question 2. Semantic Acceptability   Is the sentence semantically acceptable in the reader's dialect and within the context of the entire selection? (Note: question 2 cannot be coded Y if question 1 is coded N.)

Yes (Y)   The sentence, as finally produced by the reader, is semantically acceptable—that is, it has meaning.

No (N)   The sentence, as finally produced by the reader, is not semantically acceptable.

Question 3. Meaning Change   Does the sentence, as finally produced by the reader, change the meaning of the selection? (Note: question 3 is coded *only if* questions 1 and 2 are coded Y.)

No (N)   There is no change in the meaning of the selection.

Partial (P)   There is inconsistency, loss, or change of a minor idea, incident, character, fact, sequence, or concept in the selection.

Yes (Y)   There is inconsistency, loss, or change of a major idea, incident, character, fact, sequence, or concept in the selection.

Question 4. Graphic Similarity   How much does the miscue look like the text?

High (H)   A high degree of graphic similarity exists between the miscue and the text.

Some (S)   Some degree of graphic similarity exists between the miscue and text.

None (N)   No graphic similarity exists between the miscue and the text.

The right margin of the copy of the text onto which the teacher marks becomes the coding form. Questions 1, 2, and 3 are coded at the end of each sentence. Question 4, which asks about high, partial, or no degree of graphic similarity, is marked with the H, P, or N directly above or next to the word. For example, in figure 5.23, mis-

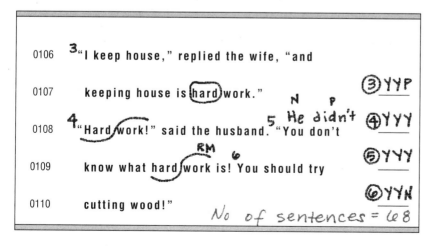

FIGURE 5.23
Coding of Miscues in RMI

Question 1: No of Y = ____ or ____ %; No of N = ____ or ____ %.

Question 2: No of Y = ____ or ____ %; No of N = ____ or ____ %.

Question 3: No of Y = ____ or ____ %; No of P = ____ or ____ %; No of N = ____ or ____ %.

Question 4: No of H = ____ or ____ %; No of S = ____ or ____ %; No of N = ____ or ____ %.

FIGURE 5.24
Patterns of Miscues

cues are coded on a segment of oral reading for Kevin, a bilingual third grader, from his reading of "The Man Who Kept House" (Goodman, Watson, & Burke, 1987, pp. 202–206).

Each sentence is numbered. The total number of sentences is the basis for determining percentage of response. A summary of the miscues may be written at the end of the story or on the back of the last page in a format like that in figure 5.24.

The RMI manual directs teachers to compare the profile produced by the reader with those profiles of proficient and nonproficient readers provided in the manual. Instructional suggestions accompany each reader pattern. We strongly recommend that teachers explore *Reading Miscue Inventory: Alternative Procedures,* a most useful tool for evaluation (Goodman, Watson, & Burke, 1987). Miscue analysis gives teachers a new and more informed perspective from which to view what children are trying to do as they read.

Even before the teacher becomes proficient in the use of miscue analysis, he or she will find it helpful to ask three questions: (1) What is this child doing as a reader? (2) What appear to be the child's strengths? (3) What is this child ready to learn next? The sample in figure 5.23 is too short to draw many conclusions about the child's reading strategies, and it does not include retelling information. Examine the oral reading of the following children.

Antonio is a second-grade boy who is struggling with print. Figure 5.25 records his reading of a part of *The Carrot Seed* (Krauss, 1945).

Antonio has been in a reading program that emphasizes memorizing sight vocabulary. He substitutes real, look-alike words for the words in the text. His substitutions are generally grammatical, but they do not make sense. They damage the author's apparent intended message and Antonio's construction of meaning.

One of Antonio's classmates read the same story. Marlene was in a different school for kindergarten and first grade. She also appears to have been in a different type of instructional program; the net result for her is really no better than for Antonio (see figure 5.26). Marlene attempts to sound out every unfamiliar word. Like Antonio, her substitutions retain most of the grammar, but they too violate the author's meaning. Marlene has been in a program that emphasized sound-letter (phonic) "skill." She has been taught rules for dividing words into syllables and then pronouncing the parts. This approach, separated from making meaning, is not proving to be a helpful strategy for her.

Gordon is a third grader who has been in remedial reading since he was in the second grade. Gordon has been in a whole language classroom for the past year. If his miscues are just counted instead of analyzed, he appears to be a poor reader. Gordon has begun to like reading. He has a good vocabulary, and his substitutions are semantically acceptable. Gordon appears to have one strength the other readers did not display: he attempts to self-correct (see figure 5.27).

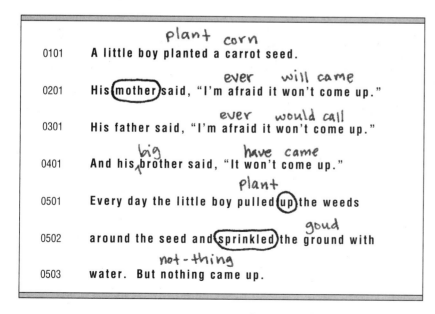

FIGURE 5.25
Antonio's Substitution and Omission Miscues

FIGURE 5.26
Marlene's
Overreliance on
Phonics

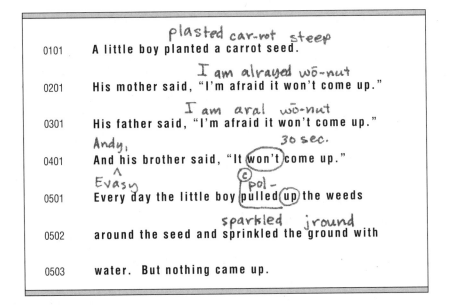

0101   A little boy planted a carrot seed.

plasted car-rot *steep*

0201   His mother said, "I'm afraid it won't come up."

I am alrayed wō-nut

0301   His father said, "I'm afraid it won't come up."

I am aral wō-nut

0401   And his brother said, "It won't come up."

Andy,   *30 sec.*

0501   Every day the little boy pulled up the weeds

Evasy   *pol-*

0502   around the seed and sprinkled the ground with

sparkled   jround

0503   water. But nothing came up.

This means that Gordon monitors his reading and understands that reading is language and that it is supposed to make sense. He attempts to construct meaning and is quite successful.

Antonio decided that he can't read well enough to risk trying, so he omitted most words he didn't "know." Marlene tried to sound out unfamiliar words and to substitute graphically similar words. Her substitutions retained the grammar but damaged the meaning. Gordon makes a large number of miscues but produces the most meaningful reading. These children are real kids who are struggling. Each would be considered a nonproficient reader, but some have made more progress than others.

Retellings, both unprompted and prompted, follow the oral reading. The examiner tells the child to close the book and tell everything he or she can remember about the story. When the child has completely exhausted this unprompted retelling, the teacher may prompt for additional information. Queries for prompting are based on information the child has already provided. These might include questions such as, "Antonio, you said '. . . and *salased* the ground with water.' Does that make sense?" "Marlene, you mentioned '*Andy*, his brother.' Can you tell me more about him?"

Retellings are also scored. Scoring guidelines differ for narrative and expository texts. For story material, the retelling score is divided into character analysis (40 points) and events (60 points). The scorer looks for theme and plot statements. For expository pieces, the retelling is divided into specific information (50 points), generalizations (25 points), and major concepts (25 points). More specific guidelines for determining points are provided in the RMI manual.

Record Keeping   The use of reading miscue analysis, running record, and other theoretically sound instruments and techniques (for example, Concepts about Print from Clay, 1979, pp. 27–31), are all excellent tools for helping teachers observe and document what children are doing with written language. When teachers keep in mind the three focus questions—"What is the child trying to do?" "What are the child's strengths?" "What is the child ready to learn next?"—teachers inform themselves about their learners, the direction of their instruction, and the results of their teaching efforts.

Figures 5.28–5.30 illustrate ways of keeping records of oral reading analysis and retelling analysis. (For additional ideas on eval-

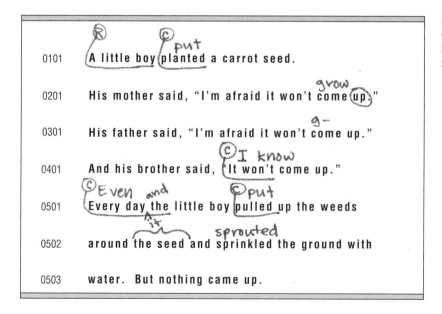

FIGURE 5.27
Gordon's
Self-correction
Strategies

ORAL READING ANALYSIS SUMMARY FORM

Name of Child: _____   Date: _____

Title of Text: _____

Processing	**Use of Strategies**	**Needs Help**	**Good**
1. Number of words in text ____ Number of words read correctly ____	Corrections		
2. Number of miscues ____	Predictions		
3. Percentage of miscues ____	Semantically acceptable substitutions		
4. Number of miscues corrected ____	Semantically acceptable sentences		
5. Percentage self-corrected ____ %	Word analysis		

Evaluation

Strengths . . .

Growth since last RMI . . .

Ready for . . .

Additional comments . . .

FIGURE 5.28
Record Keeping for
Oral Reading Analysis

uation and record keeping, see Kemp, 1987; Goodman, Bird, & Goodman, 1992; and Rhodes & Shanklin, 1993.)

Teachers evaluate reading for two reasons: to document children's growing control over the reading process and to use this information to plan instruction. When they plan instruction, they use a variety of strategies in addition to the basics—read aloud, guided reading, and SSR.

FIGURE 5.29   Alternative Oral Reading Summary Form

READING MISCUE SUMMARY

Reader's Name: _____   Date: _____

Grade Level: _____ Teacher: _____

Selection Read: _____

1. What percentage of the sentences read make sense?

   Total number of sentences read (TS): _____

   Number of semantically acceptable sentences (SAS): _____

   (SAS / TS) x 100 = percentage of sentences that make sense: _____%

2. Reading: how does the reader go about constructing meaning?

	N	S	O	U	A
a. Recognizes when miscues disrupt meaning	1	2	3	4	5
b. Makes logical substitutions	1	2	3	4	5
c. Predicts	1	2	3	4	5
d. Self-corrects errors that disrupt meaning	1	2	3	4	5
e. Uses pictures and/or other visual cues	1	2	3	4	5

3. Reading: in what ways does the reader lose meaning?

a. Produces nonsense	1	2	3	4	5
b. Substitutions don't make sense	1	2	3	4	5
c. Omissions lose meaning	1	2	3	4	5

4. Retelling: narrative text

a. Character recall	1	2	3	4	5
b. Character development	1	2	3	4	5
c. Setting	1	2	3	4	5
d. Relationship of events	1	2	3	4	5
e. Plot	1	2	3	4	5
f. Theme	1	2	3	4	5
h. Overall retelling	1	2	3	4	5

5. Retelling: nonfiction

a. Major concepts	1	2	3	4	5
b. Generalizations	1	2	3	4	5
c. Specific information	1	2	3	4	5
d. Logical order	1	2	3	4	5
e. Overall retelling	1	2	3	4	5

Comments:

N = Not yet   **S** = Sometimes   **O** = Often   **U** = Usually   **A** = Always

SOURCE: Adapted from L. Rhodes & N. Shanklin (1993), *Windows into Literacy: Assessing Learners K–8* (Portsmouth, NH: Heinemann), p. 177.

MISCUE ANALYSIS RETELLING SUMMARY FORM

Name of Child: _____ Date: _____

Title of Text: _____

RETELLING

Narrative Text		Expository Text

Characters (40)   **Events (60)**   **Specific Information (50)**

Main   Major

       Generalizations (25)

Secondary   Details

       Major Concepts (25)

         Plot

         Theme

Total: _____ %   Total: _____ %

Comments:

FIGURE 5.30
Record Keeping for
Retelling of Both
Narrative and
Expository Texts

Selected Strategies: A Literature-Based Classroom

Paired Reading Paired reading or the "say something" activity tends to happen naturally in literature-based classrooms. Children read with a friend or partner, they talk about their book, and they take turns. In the early weeks of school or with very young children, teachers may provide more direction by employing the procedure described here.

Each child finds a partner and the two of them select a book. (In this activity, each pair may be reading the same story or every pair in the class may be reading a different one.) The two partners examine their book and predict what it is likely to be about. Then one child softly reads a section aloud to the other. The reader determines how much to read before stopping to discuss. When the reader stops, the listener leads the discussion.

The children may discuss their favorite part or the questions they had during the reading. They are encouraged to relate what they already know to the story. Teachers may model this activity before sending the children off to do it by themselves.

When the two children in the pair have finished talking about the section, they predict what they think the next part will be about and why. Then the other child reads the next section. This strategy, employed with appropriate material and demonstration, may be used in kindergarten and first grade. It lays the foundation for literature study groups in succeeding grades.

Literature and Author Studies   Talking about good books leads to literature studies (Peterson & Eeds, 1990; Short & Pierce, 1990). When books become personally meaningful, people learn to love reading. For some, this happens at an early age; for others, never. Good literature transcends time. It combines both information and ideas about the world with feelings and attitudes that help children grow. Good literature educates. It stretches the imagination and assists children in bringing meaning to their worlds. To benefit fully from a reading experience, children need good books, time to read and reflect, and time to share.

Literature study groups or literature circles are appropriate at all grade levels. In kindergarten, literature study usually consists of a group of children looking at, reading, and talking about the same picture book. In later grades, literature study groups are in-depth studies of good literature.

Initially, teachers may select several books and introduce them to the children one at a time. Teachers of very young children may choose to read each selection aloud. Children sign up for the literature group they want to join, indicating on the sign-up sheet their first and second choices. In the primary grades, groups should have no more than four or five members; in upper grades, groups of seven should be the maximum.

Groups are organized at least three ways. Children may first read the entire book by themselves, then come together to discuss it; they may read a predetermined section, perhaps a chapter, and then come together to discuss that; or they may come together to both read aloud and discuss as a group. Groups may last anywhere from one day to several weeks, depending on the interest generated in the discussions and the length of the book.

Some teachers prefer to initiate discussion by sitting with each group and asking the children to talk about their book. Others give the children one or more open-ended questions as a point of departure. "What were your favorite parts?" "What would you change about the story and why?" "What was something you did not understand?" "What surprised you as you read the story?"

Teachers will want to turn over leadership of the group to the children as soon as possible. The children may quickly wish to dispense with discussion questions and "get into the book." At the end of each group meeting, the children decide what to read and/or discuss the next time they meet.

Some teachers incorporate response logs as part of literature study. A group reading a chapter book may not meet every day, but the children probably read in their book every day. They can record their reactions daily as they read using literature logs or Post-it notes, and use them as reminders of what they want to talk about when their group meets.

Some books provide better material for extending learning than do others. If the group chooses, they plan how they will present their book to the rest of the class. They may want to do readers theater, puppetry, artwork, advertisements, or any other presentation formats they think of. A display from an author study is shown in figure 5.31.

Shared Book   An event in which children engage in reading or telling a favorite story is called shared book. It may occur at a regular time each day or only once or twice a week. Shared book may be set up as a large or small group event. More than one small group

FIGURE 5.31
Artwork and Writing
Display from Author
Study

may share simultaneously. A sign-up form is usually available, and children are encouraged to sign up for sharing time.

Typically, a few rules are required for shared book to be successful. The children must reread and rehearse to be ready to tell or read their story well. Shared book actually accomplishes two desirable ends: it helps develop a sense of audience, and it helps develop control and confidence in less able readers.

Predictable Books   Books that support children's reading are called predictable books. Several types of predictable books are available, including those with repeated language patterns, rhymes, rhythm patterns, easy language with picture support, and accumulated patterns. They may be familiar or unfamiliar stories, fiction or nonfiction. Many predictable books employ combinations of patterns; for example, *Drummer Hoff* by Emberley (1967) is a rhyming book with an accumulated pattern.

Repeated language patterns and other types of predictable books help children acquire knowledge about sound-letter cues. They provide successful early reading experiences for young children and demonstrate that written language is enjoyable. As the teacher reads aloud, the children can join in. They help children take risks in their reading.

Predictable books demonstrate to children that they *can* read; they are especially appropriate for beginning and less proficient readers. Familiar songs such as "Frog Went A-Courtin'" and chants such as "There Was an Old Lady Who Swallowed a Fly" are highly readable examples of predictable materials for older readers. Predictable books build children's confidence and help them develop strategies for reading.

Predictable books should make up a significant portion of the class library for K–3 classrooms. Teachers typically read predictable books aloud during read-aloud and/or guided reading time. A book may be reread several times in one sitting. The books are then made available for the children to read at their leisure. Sometimes the teacher pauses to let the children fill in the next word or phrase in the story.

Even on the first day of first grade, children can "read" an easy predictable book on their own. After a book like *Brown Bear, Brown Bear* by Bill Martin Jr. (1992) has been shared several times, most children can "read" it without help. Later that day, they might dictate a group story following the pattern. For example, Brown Bear may become Pink Pig. Children can illustrate and read the new text. Activities like these would give children two successful literacy experiences even on the first day of first grade. (For a categorized list of predictable books see appendix E.)

Clozure Variations   The context of clozure is a fill-in-the-blank activity. The terms *cloze* and *clozure* come from the same root as *close* and *closet* and mean "to shut." Clozure relies on human beings' natural tendency to complete something perceived as an incomplete pattern. When used for instruction in reading, clozure requires the reader to employ non-graphophonic cueing systems to fill in the blanks; that is, readers must rely on their prior knowledge, on grammar, and on meaning to complete the patterns. Occasional cloze activities and games benefit most beginning and less able readers, especially those children who do not understand what they read or who rely too heavily on letter-sound relationships.

Clozure may be oral or written. Well-written stories and information materials may be used for developing clozure activities. Predictable books are an excellent source. Stories from old basals, discarded library books, or magazines can be also be used. Teachers can put white correction fluid directly on the words they wish to omit in the pages of the old text.

Teachers can also select a section from a piece of text that is at least 300 to 500 words long. The teacher or aide types the text, leaving the first paragraph or two intact. Some of the more predictable words are omitted and each omission replaced with a blank line of at least six to ten spaces. This gives the readers sufficient space to write in their words. The teacher keeps a list of the words omitted. Together the students and teacher decide how best to fill in the blanks with words that make sense and sound right. Clozure activities are easy to create, and they encourage the use of syntactic and semantic cues in reading. Cloze activities can be written and photocopied for use by individual students. The text may also be placed on chart paper and some of the words left blank for a group of children to take turns filling in as the story is read.

Language Experience Language experience usually refers to stories dictated by a group or individual (Allen, 1976). Although it was originally designed for beginning readers and children having a difficult time making the connection between speaking and writing, language experience is not limited to beginning readers. Variations on language experience extend into writing.

Language experience begins with a *shared experience*. The classroom teacher and the children share or engage in the same activity or experience. Perhaps the teacher and the children take a planned environmental print walk around the school or neighborhood. They take a Polaroid camera and a tape recorder. Each child and the teacher may have a small notebook and pencil. The group takes pictures of any print in the environment—for example, stop signs, delivery trucks, and street signs. The children describe the context in which they encountered the print and they determine what they think it says.

Upon returning to the classroom, the children and the teacher *talk* about the print they saw on their walk. If they choose to *write* a group story about their experience, they might dictate it to the teacher. They might choose to dictate captions for their photos. They might draw their favorite scenes and compile them into a big book for the classroom library. When a written product is complete, it is read and *shared*. Other shared experiences might include a listening walk around the school and neighborhood or a planned field trip to a farm, the zoo, a factory, or the neighborhood fire station (see *The Listening Walk* by P. Showers, 1961, discussed in chapter 7, and *The Trek* by A. Jonas, 1978).

Students might take a rock-hunting walk to accompany their unit on geology. After talking about their experience, they might choose to write individual stories, poems, or expositions. Written works become part of the unit resources and can be read and shared (see *Everybody Needs a Rock* by B. Baylor, 1974).

Dictated group stories that are based on common experiences and that can be read and reread are an excellent addition to the teacher's repertoire. They provide opportunities for children to match oral language with print. Conventions of written language may be addressed through dictated stories as teacher and children negotiate spelling, phrasing and word choices, capitalization, and punctuation. Language experience provides opportunities for authentic talking, writing, reading, and sharing. It also allows the teacher to demonstrate any number of aspects about reading and writing together.

SUMMARY

Reading is making sense of print. It is a process that involves the language, background, and thinking of the reader in transaction with the language, background, and thinking of the writer (Rosenblatt, 1976). Good readers use several strategies, including predicting, cue sampling, and self-correcting to make print meaningful. Learning to read is a psychogenerative process. We learn to read by reading.

The instructional approaches and evaluation procedures provided in this chapter form the basis for the whole language classroom. The approaches and strategy ideas that most whole language teachers employ are aimed at improving children's learning. Successful experiences with print and with good books are hallmarks of a whole language philosophy.

The three major approaches are *read aloud, guided reading,* and *sustained silent reading (SSR)*. The additional instructional ideas are theoretically sound and can be both fun and useful when applied appropriately. These suggestions are not, however, the only ideas that good teachers use. Neither should they be followed step by step in cookbook fashion. Rather, they should be adapted to fit the children and resources.

THEORY-TO-PRACTICE CONNECTIONS

Reading Process Theory	*Examples of Classroom Practice*
1. We learn to read by really reading, in the same way we learned to talk and to understand what other people say.	**1.** Daily SSR, self-selection
2. Reading is a strategic, sociopsycholinguistic process—i.e., it is constructive and generative, as is all language learning.	**2.** Previewing texts, reading predictable books
3. Reading, writing, speaking, and listening are all language processes, and each supports the others.	**3.** Shared book, author studies, language experience
4. Reading is a tool for learning and for enjoyment.	**4.** Guided reading and conferencing, collaboration and group projects
5. Readers must expect to learn to read and to want to read.	**5.** Low-risk environment and an atmosphere of support

SUGGESTED READINGS

Freppon, P., & Dahl, K. (1991). Learning about phonics in a whole language classroom. *Language Arts, 68,* 190–197.

Goodman, K. (1988). *Report card on basals.* Katonah, NY: Richard C. Owen.

Goodman, Y. (1990). *How children construct literacy: Piagetian perspectives.* Newark, DE: IRA.

Holdaway, D. (1979). *The foundations of literacy.* Portsmouth, NH: Heinemann.

Mills, H., O'Keefe, T., & Stephens, D. (1992). *Looking closely: Exploring the role of phonics in the whole language classroom.* Urbana, IL: NCTE.

New Zealand Department of Education, Wellington. (1985). *Reading in junior classes.* Wellington, New Zealand (available through Richard C. Owen, Katonah, NY).

Short, K., & Pierce, K. (1990). *Talking about books.* Portsmouth, NH: Heinemann.

Smith, F. (1985). *Reading without nonsense.* New York: Teachers College Press.

Smith, F. (1988). *Joining the literacy club.* Portsmouth, NH: Heinemann.

SUGGESTED ACTIVITIES

1. Discuss how what we know about the reading process relates to language learning theory. That is, how does what proficient readers do relate to what all active learners do?

2. Find a copy of Shel Silverstein's *The Giving Tree.* Read the story and decide who or what the tree represents. Discuss with classmates who have also read the story. You should find that each of you has a slightly different interpretation of this text. Who is right? What does that indicate about reading?

3. As you read a two- or three-page selection from a novel or short story that you have never read before, be aware of what you are doing. Do you misread/miscue on any words? If so, which ones? Can you tell what caused you to do that? Are you aware of the visual images you are beginning to form? Are you aware of asking internal questions and then searching for the answers as you read? What else are you aware of about your reading? Share with others what you found out in this experience. Are your experiences similar?

4. Find a child who is considered by the teacher to be a poor reader. Audiotape-record the child reading a story that he or she has never seen before. Tell the child to do his or her best, that you cannot help, and that you want him or her to tell you the story when finished. After you have both the reading and retelling on tape, practice marking miscues. Use a typed transcript of the story or a photocopy of a segment as your worksheet. Using a copy of the forms provided in this chapter (see figures 5.28–5.30), practice summarizing what you have noted about the child's reading. Share your child's reading with a small group of your classmates. What can you conclude about the child's strengths? What cues and strategies does he or she seem to rely on when reading? What is the child trying to do as a reader? What do you think you might do to help this child become a better reader?

5. Find a child who is having difficulty with reading and take a running record. Calculate the child's error rate, self-correction rate, and percentage of accuracy. Examine the child's reading for strengths. What do you think the child may be ready to learn next? How does the information from miscue analysis differ from that obtained in a running record? What evidence is there from miscue analysis and running record that learning to read is not the mastery of a hierarchy of isolated skills based on discrete, sequential surface level features?

REFERENCES

Allen, R. (1976). *Language experiences in communication.* Boston: Houghton Mifflin.

Altwerger, B., Edelsky, C., & Flores, B. (1978). Whole language: What's new. *Reading Teacher, 41,* 144–155.

Anderson, A., & Stokes, S. (1984). Social and institutional influences on the development and practice of literacy. In H. Goelman, A. Oberg, & F. Smith (Eds.), *Awakening to literacy.* Portsmouth, NH: Heinemann.

Barr, R. (1984). Beginning reading instruction: From debate to reformation. In P. D. Pearson (Ed.), *Handbook of reading research.* New York: Longman.

Baylor, B. (1974). *Everybody needs a rock.* New York, NY: Atheneum.

Betts, E. (1946). *Foundation of reading instruction.* New York: American Book Company.

Clay, M. (1979). *The early detection of reading difficulties.* Portsmouth, NH: Heinemann.

Cochrane, O., Cochrane, D., Scalena, S., & Buchanan, E. (1984). *Reading, writing and caring.* Katonah, NY: Richard C. Owen.

Cochran-Smith, M. (1984). *The making of a reader.* Norwood, NJ: Ablex.

Cunningham, P. (1991). *Phonics they use: Words for reading and writing.* New York: HarperCollins.

Edelsky, C., Altwerger, B., & Flores, B. (1991). *Whole language: What's the difference?* Portsmouth, NH: Heinemann.

Eisner, E. (1990). Who decides what schools teach? *Phi Delta Kappan, 71*(7), 523–526.

Emberley, E. (1967). *Drummer Hoff.* Englewood Cliffs, NJ: Prentice-Hall.

Ferreiro, E., & Teberosky, A. (1982). *Literacy before schooling.* Portsmouth, NH: Heinemann.

Freppon, P., & Dahl, K. (1991). Learning about phonics in a whole language classroom. *Language Arts, 68,* 190–197.

Galdone, P. (1973). *The little red hen.* New York: Scholastic.

Gardner, H. (1991). *The unschoooled mind: How children think and how schools should teach.* New York, NY: Basic Books.

Glasser, W. (1990). The quality school. *Phi Delta Kappan, 71*(6), 424–435.

Goodman, K. (1968). *Study of children's behavior while reading orally.* (Contract No. OE-6-10-136). Washington, DC: Department of Health, Education, and Welfare.

Goodman, K. (1970). Behind the eye: What happens in reading. In K. S. Goodman and O. Niles (Eds.), *Reading Process and Program.* Urbana, IL: NCTE.

Goodman, K. (1986). *What's whole in whole language?* Portsmouth, NH: Heinemann.

Goodman, K. (1988). *Report card on basals.* Katonah, NY: Richard C. Owen.

Goodman, K., Bird, L., & Goodman, Y. (1992). *The whole language catalog: Supplement on authentic assessment.* Santa Rosa, CA: American School Publishers.

Goodman, K., & Goodman, Y. (1978). *Reading of American children whose language is a stable rural dialect of English or a language other than English.* (Contract No. NIE-00-3-0087). Washington, DC: NIE.

Goodman, K., & Goodman, Y. (1979). Learning to read is natural. In L. B. Resnick and P. A. Weaver (Eds.), *Theory and practice of early reading* (Vol. 1). Hillsdale, NJ: Lawrence Erlbaum.

Goodman, K., Smith, E., Meredith, R., & Goodman, Y. (1988). *Language and thinking in schools.* Katonah, NY: Richard C. Owen.

Goodman, Y. (1971). *Longitudinal study of children's oral reading behavior.* (Contract No. OEG-5-9-325062-0046). Washington, DC: Department of Health, Education, and Welfare.

Goodman, Y. (1990). *How children construct literacy: Piagetian perspectives.* Newark, DE: IRA.

Goodman, Y., Watson, D., & Burke, C. (1987). *Reading miscue inventory: Alternative procedures.* Katonah, NY: Richard C. Owen.

Greaney, V., & Neuman, S. (1990). The functions of reading: A cross-cultural perspective. *Reading Research Quarterly, 25* (3), 172–195.

Holdaway, D. (1979). *The foundations of literacy.* Portsmouth, NH: Heinemann.

Jonas, A. (1978). *The trek.* New York: Greenwillow.

Kemp, M. (1987). *Watching children read and write: Observational records for children with special needs.* Portsmouth, NH: Heinemann.

Krauss, R. (1945). *The carrot seed.* New York: Harper & Row.

Martin, B. (1992). *Brown bear, brown bear.* New York: Holt, Rinehart and Winston.

McKenzie, M. (1977). The beginnings of literacy. *Theory into practice, 16*(51), 315–324.

Meek, M. (1988). *How texts teach what readers learn.* Exeter, England: Thimble Press.

Mills, H., O'Keefe, T., & Stephens, D. (1992). *Looking closely: Exploring the role of phonics in the whole language classroom.* Urbana, IL: NCTE.

Mooney, M. (1990). *Reading to, with, and by children.* Katonah, NY: Richard C. Owen.

Neisser, U. (1986). *The school achievement of minority children.* Hillsdale, NJ: Lawrence Erlbaum.

New Zealand Department of Education, Wellington. (1985). *Reading in junior classes.* Wellington, New Zealand (available through Richard C. Owen, Katonah, NY).

Peterson, R., & Eeds, M. (1990). *Grand conversations: Literature groups in action.* Toronto, Ontario: Scholastic.

Porter, W. (O. Henry) (1969). The gift of the Magi. In *Tales of O. Henry.* New York: Airmont.

Rhodes, L., & Shanklin, N. (1993). *Windows into literacy: Assessing learners K–8.* Portsmouth, NH: Heinemann.

Robinson, H. (Ed.). (1982). *Reading and writing instruction in the United States: Historical trends.* Newark, DE: IRA.

Rosenblatt, L. (1976). *Literature as exploration.* New York: Modern Language Association.

Shanker, A. (1990). A proposal for using incentives to restructure our public schools. *Phi Delta Kappan, 71*(5), 345–357.

Short, K., & Pierce, K. (1990). *Talking about books.* Portsmouth, NH: Heinemann.

Showers, P. (1961). *The listening walk.* New York: Crowell Junior Books.

Smith, F. (1985). *Reading without nonsense.* New York: Teachers College Press.

Smith, F. (1988a). *Joining the literacy club.* Portsmouth, NH: Heinemann.

Smith, F. (1988b). *Understanding reading.* Hillsdale, NJ: Lawrence Erlbaum.

Smith, N. (1965). *American reading instruction.* Newark, DE: IRA.

Stauffer, R. (1969). *A directed reading-thinking approach.* New York: Harper & Row.

Trelease, J. (1989). *The new read-aloud handbook.* New York: Penguin.

Weaver, C. (1988). *Reading processes and prac-*

tices: *From sociopsycholinguistics to whole language.* Portsmouth, NH: Heinemann.

Weaver, C. (1990). *Understanding whole language.* Portsmouth, NH: Heinemann.

Whole language in the classroom. (1991). Katonah, NY: Richard C. Owen.

Wuthrick, M. (1990). Bluejays win! Crows go down in defeat. *Phi Delta Kappa, 71* (7), 553–556.

6

Children want to write. They want to write the first day they attend school. . . . The child's marks say, "I am!"

(GRAVES, 1983, p. 3)

Writing

What is the writing process?

How do we learn to write?

What is the relationship between reading and writing?

Why do people write?

What can we do to help children learn to write and want to write?

---

*C*hildren enter school as already accomplished users of spoken language who know a great deal about the world they live in. Most children know a considerable amount about written language as well. Learning to read and write occurs easily and spontaneously for some children. But even if most children are not reading and writing when they start school, they still know a great deal about it. After all, we live in a highly literate society (Goodman, 1986). Just look around. Written language is everywhere. By age six, most young children are already "reading and writing" in a sense, if we know how to recognize and value what they naturally attempt to do with print (Harste, Woodward, & Burke, 1984). They may "read" K-Mart or Kroger; they may "write" scribble messages or their names. They generally know what print looks like. They know what print is, and they know a great deal about what it does.

In this chapter we will examine the process by which children learn to write. We will discuss the nature of written language and explore the reasons people write, as well as the relationship between writing and reading. We will review what has been learned in the past two decades about helping children develop their own literacy. Finally, we will present a theoretical framework for teaching writing that parallels that established for teaching reading; this framework includes the major instructional approaches, evaluation tools and procedures, and several selected strategy ideas. Together with a holistic, learner-centered philosophy, these create a literate and inviting environment for young authors.

What Writing Is

Writing is graphic language communication. However, writing is not merely the inverse of reading. The two require somewhat different knowledge and abilities. Reading is a transactive experience with an author, just as listening is a transactive experience with a speaker. Writers transact with themselves and with an intended, often imagined audience. Speakers transact with themselves and a real audience. While authors have a meaning in mind when they write, readers, like listeners, construct a new meaning. Reading and listening are both constructive and receptive. Writing and speaking, on the other hand, are both constructive and expressive. All are forms of language communication that involve thinking (see figure 6.1).

Like speech, writing produces meaning. Speech is oral and essentially immediate. It takes place in the presence of an audience. Writing is visual and tends to be a solitary process. Until the invention of the telephone and recording devices, writing was the only way human beings had to communicate over time and space.

Listening and speaking, reading and writing are all forms of language, and they are also ways that children come to understand their world. By the time children have learned to speak with fluency, they have gained some control over their environments. Toddlers learn to ask for a cookie, instead of crying and pointing, as infants do. Young children learn to express their emotions verbally. By the time they are three or four years old many children want to write with the

FIGURE 6.1
Forms of Verbal
Language

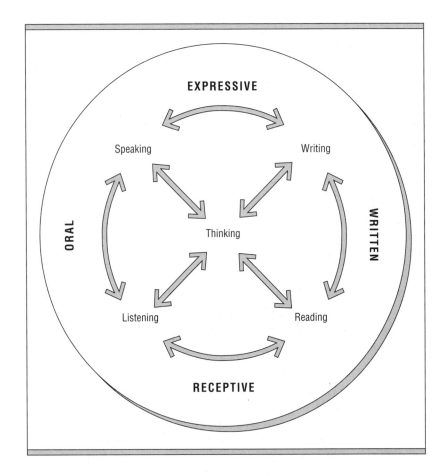

same exuberance with which they wanted to learn to speak, because writing is present in their environments and they see that they can do interesting things with it. "Written" messages from four year olds are frequently among parents' most prized possessions.

In some ways writing reflects oral language. There are visual symbols (letters) that represent oral symbols (speech sounds or phonemes). In English there are twenty-six letters to represent some forty-four phonemes. There are also visual symbols to indicate elements of intonation. These are called punctuation (, . ! : " ?). In written language, words follow the order or grammatical rules of oral language, but there are many constraints on written language that are not necessary for speaking.

Since the writer and the reader are usually separated by both time and space, written language must necessarily be more complete than spoken language. The text must provide more information about the context because readers cannot just look around and figure out what is happening as they can when listening to talk. Even illustrations, like those in children's picture books, do not provide the complete context that exists in spoken language events. In addition, written language is more formal than speech. During a conversation, people speak in incomplete sentences, with the context of the communication, facial expressions, gestures, and non-linguistic noises such as grunts carrying some of the message. These aids to meaning are not possible in written text. The message must be made clear in words themselves. That's why a story is usually longer when it is written than when it is told.

What Writing Does

Many educators and historians agree that writing was developed as human beings developed agriculture and trade. Graphic notations—the very first evidences of writing—were used to keep tallies and accounts of various kinds, e.g., bushels of wheat, numbers of cattle or oxen. From these symbols and tally markings on clay tablets thousands of years ago came numerals and written language as we know them.

Today writing has many purposes. It clearly touches all our lives. For most of us the mere business of living would be nearly unmanageable without knowing how to read and write. Moreover, writing has both intrinsic and extrinsic value. Having the ability to write fulfills our need to communicate, just as learning to talk did. Writing is another way children and adults make sense of and learn about their world.

Writing is both a practical need in the lives of literate people, but it is also an art form. The practical, pragmatic reasons for writing fall into several categories, among them work or business, social, emotional, and intellectual. People need to be able to make lists, send notes and letters to others, remind themselves of events, fill out forms and applications, keep a diary, outline a lecture, write notes summarizing a textbook passage, and so on. Writing is utilitarian. The ability to express oneself in print is likely to become even more important during the twenty-first century.

As an art form, writing fulfills another human need, the need to express ourselves creatively and aesthetically. While we usually think of narrative (stories in the form of literature) as the more creative, expository writing may certainly be artful as well. The best exposition can bring an award like the Pulitzer prize. Expository writing is encountered in textbooks, essays, newspapers, magazines, and advertising. Children may attempt both story writing and writing to impart information before formal schooling, and both forms must be nourished and developed in school.

As a way of organizing and clarifying thinking, writing helps us structure the world of our direct experiences. Writing allows human beings to use language to structure, define, and redefine thoughts and feelings. The act of composing causes the writer to arrange and sequence thoughts, to make judgments about what is important, and to build in a logical or narrative sense. Moreover, unlike speech, writing is concrete. It can be reread, reflected upon, and revised. Others can respond to it. It can be reshaped and molded to changing and differing viewpoints.

Many writing experiences have an emotional component that accompanies the cognitive part of composing. Writing offers children another means of making sense of their environment and of their internal state as well. It allows them to reflect on the outside world and their own personal journey into growing up in that world. Writing has the potential to be a powerful component in the lives of children.

Because human beings want to communicate and record their thoughts, many young people keep diaries or personal journals. Most teachers know children who have revealed traumatic personal events through journals, personal narratives, "fiction," and factual reports. Writing about important personal events may help children "get it off their chests" and allow teachers to help children cope with problems in healthy ways. Writing offers children a way to process and come to terms with strong emotions such as fear, grief, anger, and love.

Children write for the same reasons adults write. Teachers can create opportunities for children to communicate in writing. They can encourage and model writing and make writing part of the normal, daily activities of the classroom. Increasingly, teachers are making writing a natural experience for their students, and many are themselves becoming writers with their students.

Children's Writing Development: Our Evolving Understanding

How do children learn to write? Learning to write is a constructive, generative process like any other language learning. Learners experiment and employ graphic symbols to represent their intentions. In so doing, they figure out the underlying rules and the many uses that exist for writing. Children who see writing demonstrated by the adults around them and who receive the positive help they need in learning to write usually learn to express themselves quite well in print. They tend to learn without regarding writing as something difficult. They do not develop fear of visual language or come to believe that they have nothing to say (Graves, 1983).

You will not be surprised to hear again that children learn to write by writing. Neither will it surprise you if we say that children need to be immersed in meaningful print and to be encouraged and supported in their uses of written language. They need opportunities to employ writing for their own purposes. Let's look next at the broad phases through which children pass as they gain control over the conventions of the writing system.

Children may go through several identifiable stages as they develop into writers. Teachers who can recognize these phases can initially evaluate children's writing, structure classroom events based on that evaluation, and help children evaluate their own progress. Teachers who can recognize the strategies children are using in their writing development know what to focus on and what their children might be ready to learn next (Calkins, 1986; Hansen, 1987; Harste & Short, 1988; Newkirk & Atwell, 1988; Temple, Nathan, Burris, & Temple, 1988).

Phase 1. Pre-Writing Children learn at a very early age what writing is and what it is for. Few children, even as young as four years old, cannot tell the difference between print (in their own language) and pictures. They see the uses of written language in every aspect of life, in environmental print, in the writing of parents and other adults, in books and other printed material, and even on TV. As soon as children learn that writing is yet another way to structure, transmit, and receive meaning, they usually begin to experiment with its forms and with a variety of media—including crayoned scribbles on bedroom walls.

Experiments with the forms of writing occur in a variety of contexts. Children begin to teach themselves about print. Pictures that tell stories, abstract signs with which children attempt a message, and scribbles and marks that begin to resemble letters are part of children's early attempts to graphically represent meaning (figures 6.2 and 6.3).

In fact, a case can be made that young language learners actually begin with a sort of impression of what their language looks like (Clay, 1975; Harste, Woodward, & Burke, 1984). Since children tend to learn oral language from whole to part, there is every reason to suppose that the same process is at work in learning to write. Human beings learn from whole to part to whole because initially the parts are too complex, too abstract, and out of context. We also learn by figuring out the underlying rules or patterns through sufficient meaningful experience.

How do children arrive at being able to write? Do they have to memorize sound-letter associations after they start school and combine these to make simple words, copying letter forms from the handwriting workbook for first grade? Or do they engage in the same process of invention and convention that characterizes learning to talk?

Some children, as young as three, produce different visual representations when asked to draw a picture and then to write a story.

They already know the difference between pictures and print, and they are beginning to learn some of the characteristics of each. Eventually, children realize their written inventions (their scribbles) are not print. This realization tends to come when other people cannot read them. Discovering this influences children to attempt more conventional forms for their letters and words, as shown in figure 6.4. As children experiment with letter shapes and direction, along with other physical, mechanical, and surface aspects of print, they learn many of the standard features necessary for writing—and for reading as well.

The transition into early writing tends to be characterized by the recurrence of marks that begin to give the impression of letters in English (often in different combinations). Some of these more advanced writing attempts may be in "manuscript," and some may be

FIGURE 6.2
Uninterrupted Drawing (Amber, Age 5)

FIGURE 6.3
Scribble Writing
(Brian, Age 5)

in "cursive." Whether cursive or manuscript scribbles have been employed usually is not based on whim but rather on the purpose of the writing. A scribble letter to Mommy is nearly always in cursive form (see figure 6.5).

Purposeful playing around with language allows children to take what they see in print, use it, and internalize it. Graphic symbols such as letter-like shapes, recognizable letters, and graphophonemic clusters may begin to appear. In risk-free environments, children play and experiment with how print works as a learning strategy just as they do when learning their oral language. Here also the children show signs of moving from pure invention to attempts at convention (see figures 6.6 and 6.7).

Phase 2. Early Writing Early writing is characterized by experiments with the conventions of language. Children come to realize that letters and sounds have a relationship. They may first use completely idiosyncratic spelling, such as the letters *iwg* to represent "book" or *plt* for "dog." However, they soon begin to realize that the conventions of the letter-sound relationship must be observed if words are to communicate. Much of the information necessary for this transition comes from books and other written material in the children's immediate environment. Thus, "book" may come to be spelled *buk,* and "dog" may become *dg,* which are closer approximations to traditional orthography (Read, 1971). These are clear indications that learning is taking place.

Jenny was engaged in the process of hypothesizing about how

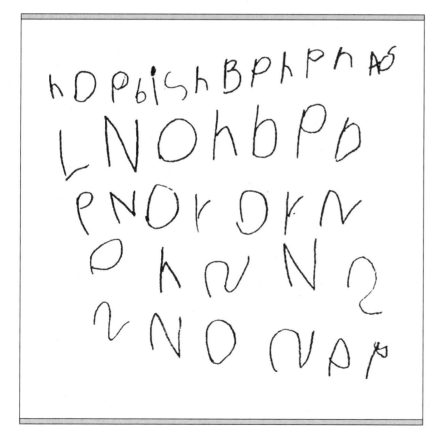

FIGURE 6.4
Shapes Beginning to Look Like Letters (Aleshia, Age 6)

FIGURE 6.5
Heather's Letter
(Age 5)

sounds and letters work in written language (see figure 6.8). Her parents could read it because they know their daughter and also because her approximations, her made-up spellings, are beginning to be systematic. They do represent the sounds in her language as she carefully accentuates each part while trying to figure out how to write what she wants to say. That is, her spellings look just like she sounds, and they look just like the invented spellings of many young children as they experiment with writing (Buchanan, 1989; Temple, Nathan, Burris, & Temple, 1988). The more children attempt to write, the more their approximations resemble conventional spellings and the more we are able to see the strategies they have developed (see figures 6.9 and 6.10).

Three common strategies for early writing that children devise to experiment with language are tracing, copying, and creating. Children's tracing and copying as they play with print also improve small motor control, investigation of conventional usage, and spelling. Creative or generative writing, at this stage, is the production of letters and word-like and grammatical constructions that indicate the patterns children are hypothesizing (Clay, 1982, 1975). Copying and tracing are strategies children develop on their own. Teachers should not assign copying and tracing, because to do so misses the point and destroys their positive effects.

Many teachers make several models of good handwriting available in the classroom. As part of the rich print environment, they serve as resources for learners. Copying and tracing models of well-formed letters for handwriting provide children with opportunities

FIGURE 6.6
Michael's Lunch Menu (Age 5)

FIGURE 6.7
Meryl's "Six Foot(ed)
Bear"

to explore how letters work and to choose, to some extent, how they want their handwriting to look. This approach familiarizes children with graphic forms such as the D'Nealian manuscript and cursive alphabet (Thurber, 1987) or the Zaner-Bloser script (*Handwriting: Basic Skill,* 1987).

When writers want their handwriting to be well formed and

readable for the final publication of a piece of text, they have an authentic reason to develop good handwriting (see figure 6.11). When observing in a whole language preschool or primary grade classroom, one may not see perfectly formed printing but one is likely to

Dear Mom
I got the package. My sister is nice.
Please come on the mother hiking trip.
I love you very much. I passed my twenty
minute swim.

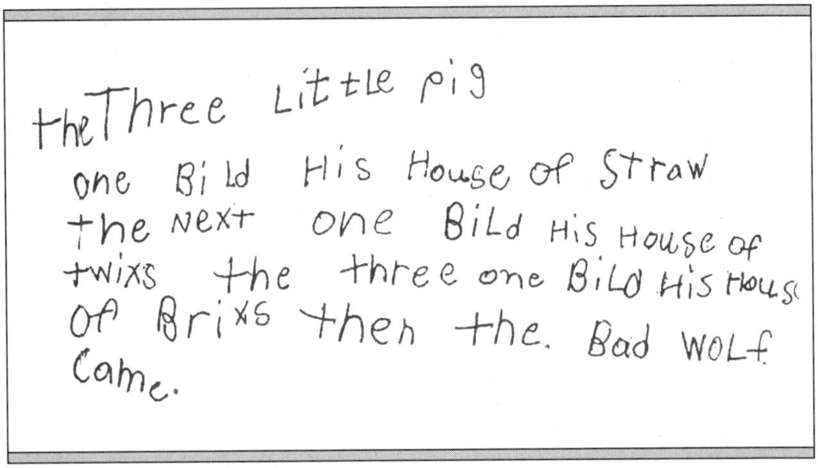

FIGURE 6.9
Jake's Story (Age 6)

> theThree Little pig
> one Bild His House of Straw
> the Next one Bild His House of
> twixs the three one Bild His Hous
> of Brixs then the. Bad WOLf
> Came.

see children naturally engage in great amounts of writing (see figure 6.12). However, many teachers also provide some direct instruction in letter formation for their children (see figure 6.13).

Encouraging children to "write" at this stage in their development is easy. The environment provides materials and models of print. Adults in the classroom are modeling writing, occasionally asking questions, bringing up issues, filling the room with meaningful and functional print, and setting up events that lead to real reasons for children to write. For example, writing can easily be worked into children's play at this stage. Paper, crayons and markers, and

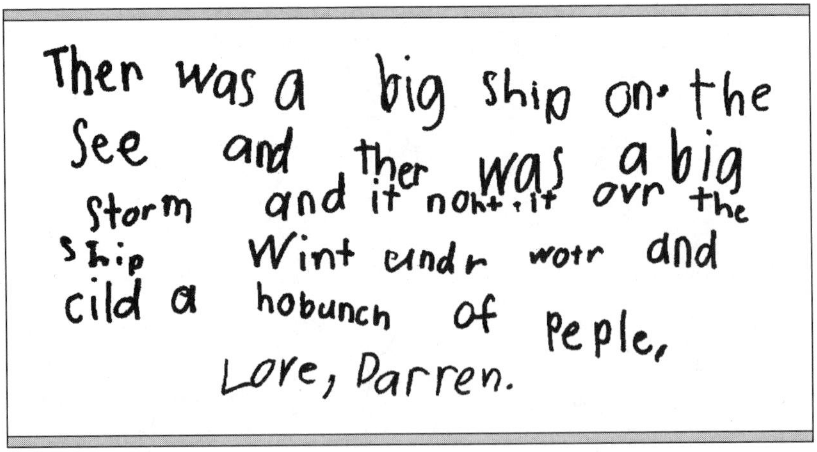

FIGURE 6.10
Darren's Story
(Age 7)

> Then was a big ship on. the
> See and ther was a big
> Storm and it noht.it ovr the
> Ship Wint undr wotr and
> cild a hobuncn of peple,
> Love, Darren.

FIGURE 6.11   DeAndray's Copied "Clifford" Book

FIGURE 6.12
"The Rabbit and the
Turtle," Michael's
Spontaneous
Retelling of "The
Tortoise and the
Hare" (First Grade)

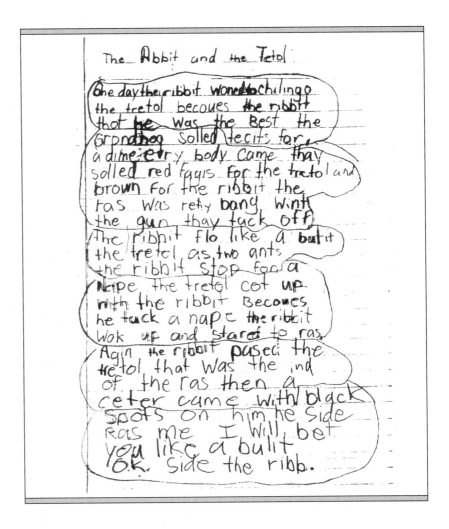

tape made available near the housekeeping area or a kindergarten's
big-block area will no doubt lead to the natural creation of lists,
signs, and labels (see figure 6.14). These purposeful written productions then become part of the literate environment and are read and
reread by the children. For instance, the intended meaning of "D NT
NTR" (DO NOT ENTER) is clear to all members of the class. Under
the appropriate conditions, children experiment with and develop
writing as naturally and in essentially the same way as they learned
to talk.

Phase 3. Emergent Writing   In the third phase, children move into writing that can actually be read by others. Children's approximations grow toward adult forms. Children learn a great deal about the spelling patterns in English, and they experiment with other aspects of the mechanics of print (Read, 1971). During this stage, children also begin the composing process. They learn how to order their thoughts so they make sense to others. Children may compose before they can write. They may dictate stories, information, and accounts of real experiences to someone who will write (or scribe) for them. For many children this oral composition process is a key to beginning writing. Toward the end of this stage, children may be writing fairly readable productions that have a beginning, middle, and end, as in figure 6.15.

Written language, both expository and narrative, is a merging of the interests of the self, audience, topic, and purpose. Children are naturally egocentric and experiment with writing for various purposes. Audiences cause children to expand their points of view. During emergent writing, children learn that writing has multiple

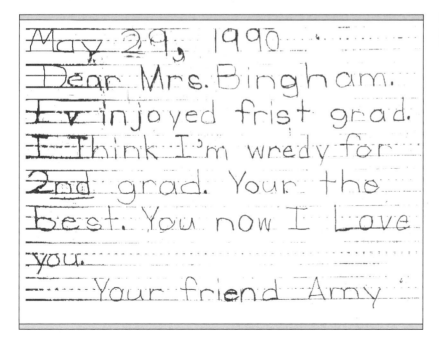

FIGURE 6.13
Amy's Letter to Her
Teacher (First Grade)

FIGURE 6.14
"Please Knock"

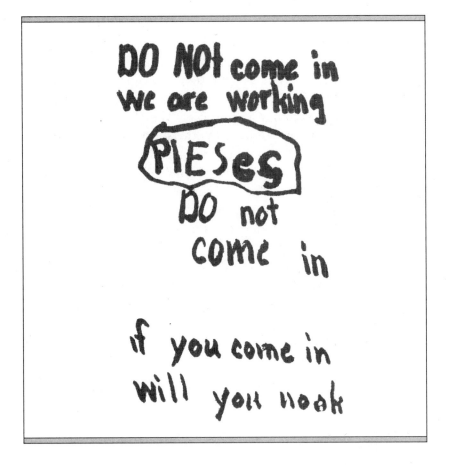

purposes and that text can be depersonalized. They learn, for example, that they can write in the third person to communicate ideas. It is here that children begin to have the first glimmerings of awareness of the transactional nature of writing. Writing can be used for description, argumentation, persuasion, and a variety of other purposes (see figure 6.16). Writers can make people laugh, make them angry, and make them cry (Britton, Burgess, Martin, McLeod, & Rosen, 1975).

Children learn to consider audience, and they begin to tailor their writing to suit their purposes, as shown in the letters in figures 6.17 and 6.18.

FIGURE 6.15
Latasha's Flower
Story (Age 7)

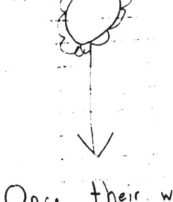

Flowers...

Once their was a litte
flower. it ws very
pretty: so I picked
it and planted it in a flower
pot. it groow bigger and bigger
every day.

One day I went and fawd some
seeds. I planted the seeds
the seeds groow big.
and ever bigger the next day
floreis grow fast.

        I like flowers.
I like picking them
to.

Phase 4. Transactional or Advanced Writing In this stage exposition and argumentation are developed. If the text shares information or explains something, it is expository. If it tries to persuade someone to do or believe something, it is argumentative. In both these modes, the writer stays in the background, and the topic of the piece is the focus; what is being explained, argued, or described is paramount.

Pattern is one of the elements that characterize transactional writing. The writing may start with the general and proceed to the specific or vice versa. Narratives or story material will present a main point and support it with details. Expository or informational writing will state a thesis and defend it with arguments. In any event, it is writing with a definite topic, a purpose or function, and a sense of audience. At this point, writers' efforts reflect the maturity of their minds, the amount of practice they have had, their personal background of experiences, the number of examples and demonstrations

FIGURE 6.16
Letter of Request

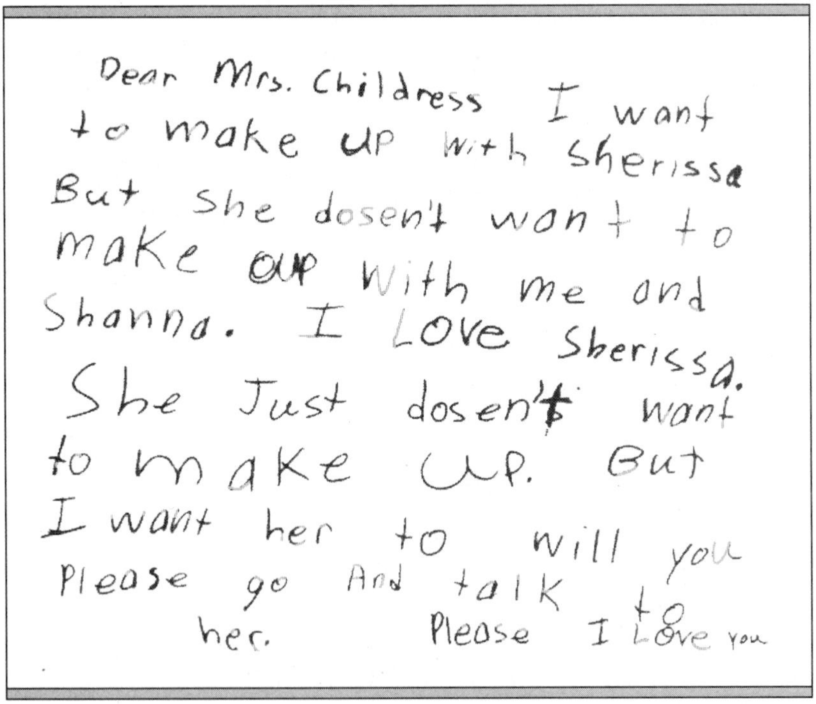

Dear Mrs. Childress I want to make up with Sherissa But she dosen't wont to make up with me and Shanna. I Love Sherissa. She Just dosen't wont to make up. But I want her to will you Please go And talk to her. Please I Love you

FIGURE 6.17
Note from Lamont

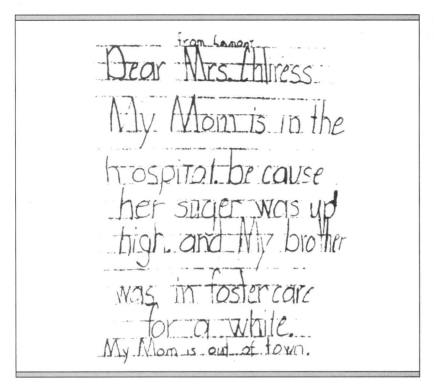

they have seen, the opportunities available in the classroom, and their own drive to communicate (Calkins, 1991; Graves, 1991). Figure 6.19 presents a story that Armondo wrote for his mother. It reflects the writer's sense of purpose and audience.

The writing phases are not absolute. Children may skip a phase altogether or go back and forth between phases; certainly there may be overlap. Great variability also exists among children as they develop. The phases of writing development, as with oral language or reading development, are only general categories for learning that tend to describe what many children experience. They are depicted in figure 6.20.

Writing is a process. It is the synthesis of hundreds of complicated rules and elements that eventually flow together smoothly. Facility with writing comes with engagement. Knowledgeable teachers set up conditions so that children engage in great amounts of writing across the curriculum. Further, knowledgeable teachers expect children to be different; they do not see learning and language development as a lockstep progression.

Traditional Writing Instruction: A Historical Perspective

In the 1700s and 1800s, it was important for people to be able to sign their names and engage in written correspondence. Schools in this country emphasized copying the letters of the alphabet, copying well-formed samples of correspondence, and calligraphy. Literacy requirements were minimal for most people. Public elementary schools emphasized the recognition of a limited number of words

FIGURE 6.18
Thank-You Note

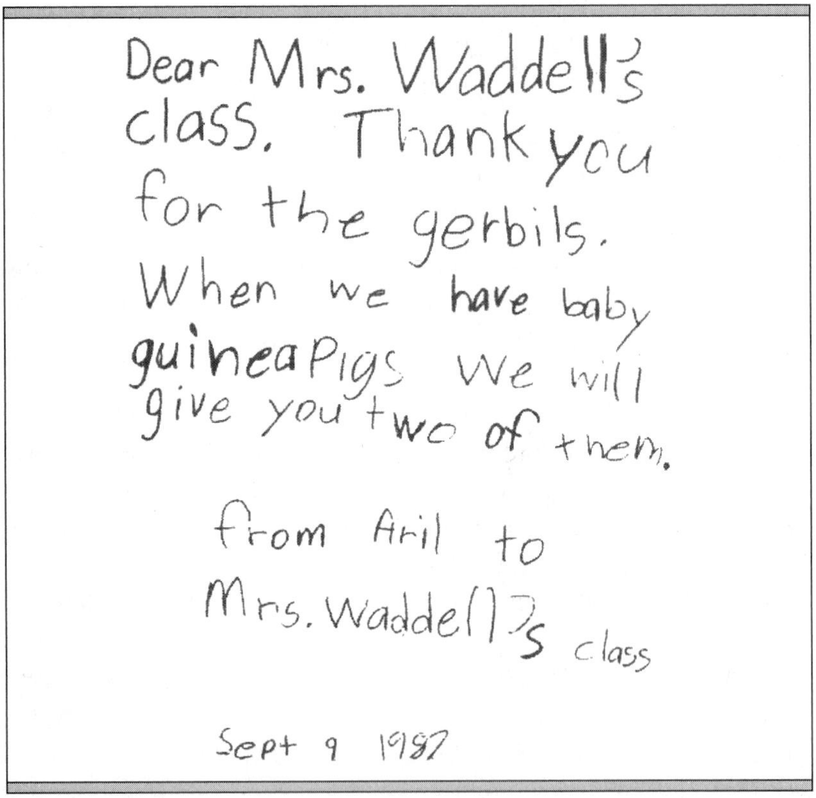
Dear Mrs. Waddell's class. Thank you for the gerbils. When we have baby guineaPigs We will give you two of them.

from Aril to Mrs. Waddell's class

Sept 9 1987

and the ability to sign one's name. Legible penmanship was stressed (Burrows, 1977). "Educated" people used writing for letters, sermons, and legal and political documents.

The emphasis on copying and handwriting continued well into this century. It was believed that children had to be able to read before they could learn to write (Chomsky, 1971). Even as late as the 1970s, when children were asked to write, it was usually in the form of copying samples of poems, aphorisms, or brief essay-like texts. Between the mid-1960s and late 1970s, "creative writing" appeared as a curricular issue because many students clearly were not being exposed to composition before high school. Some schools implemented "creative writing day" and everyone "wrote creatively" that day. Teachers assigned topics and children wrote. Topics became so creative that children were writing compositions called "My Life as a Sneaker" or "What the Rain Is Thinking." Creative writing was turned in to the teacher in first draft form. Papers were "corrected" and "graded" for mechanics and style. Many teachers had the children rewrite or otherwise correct all their spelling, grammar, and punctuation errors (see figure 6.21). Content was rarely addressed.

The Writing Process: Current Perspectives

In the late 1970s, Donald Graves (1983) reached two important conclusions from his studies of children and writing. First, children tend to write *more* on unassigned topics than they do on even the "cutest" of teacher assignments. Second, children go through three general stages in writing—pre-writing, writing, and post-writing. A result of Graves's work has been that the *writing process* became overt. The notion that it was good teaching to have children turn in a single draft on an assigned topic to be graded and corrected was seriously challenged.

The Authoring Cycle   Other researchers have helped explain the writing process for classroom implementation (Atwell, 1987; Bissex, 1980; Calkins, 1991, 1986; Hansen, 1987; Harste & Short, 1988). A writing program that is sometimes called the authoring cycle and

FIGURE 6.19 Halloween Story

FRANK AND The GHOST

On Halloween Frank went Trick-or Treating. He was dressed up like a ghost.

First he went to a yellow house He rang the doorbell. But

no one answered

He rang it again but still no one answered. So frank left the house. He looked all around. All the other kids seemed to be having fun.

He turned back around... the door to the yellow house opened A ghost came out and pushed the boy inside the house! They were having a party. Frank thougt he was in trouble But when he got home his mother just said, "Why where you out so late?" oh well you must of ha a lot of stuff do: "No, I got pulled into a place. what? A ghost pulled me in, And. kept me in there. I tried

to get out but I couldn't. Util they were not looking. "well now your here and I'm happy. Now next time don't go trick-or-treating ever again without me or your father. Ok? ok. The end.

that adheres to whole language principles engages both the teacher and the children in authentic writing every day (figure 6.22).

Pre-Writing The purpose of pre-writing is to help children get started. In the authoring cycle, pre-writing begins with the children's lives, their reading, and events in the daily life of the classroom. A number of activities can initiate writing. Chief among them are group discussions usually stemming from children's experiences or a piece of reading that has been shared and enjoyed by the group. *Brainstorming,* in which children participate in discussions, list ideas, and organize their lists, is a useful technique for initiating writing. Brainstorming is a rehearsal for writing the first draft. Rehearsal helps writers immerse themselves in their own stories and select and organize what they want to say. Other ways to rehearse include storytelling, pantomiming, drawing, discussing, and reading (Calkins, 1991).

FIGURE 6.19
Halloween Story
continued

Spelling, which is part of learning to write, is dealt with in a number of ways. During pre-writing, when teachers brainstorm with children and display the group's ideas on the chalkboard or on chart paper, correct spellings become part of the environment. Collections of books, vocabulary lists from various units of study, and edited samples of children's work are also available. While correct spelling is not the focus of pre-writing, a literate environment provides many examples of conventional spellings to help children when they write.

Drafting   The purpose of *drafting* or *composing* is to get ideas on paper. Initial drafts give children and teachers something to work with. They are the bases from which teachers plan authentic instructional events and provide collaborative evaluation of children's growth as writers. During first drafts, students should not be concerned with spelling, capitalization, punctuation, or sentence structure. They are encouraged to get their words and ideas on paper and to attempt to spell whatever words they want to use. Student authors are told that they will be helped with spelling during revision and editing. Students' invented spellings provide teachers with insights

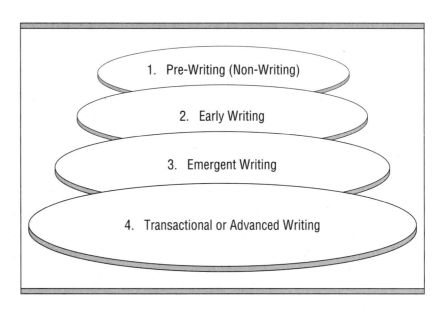

FIGURE 6.20
Phases of Writing
Development

1. Pre-Writing (Non-Writing)

2. Early Writing

3. Emergent Writing

4. Transactional or Advanced Writing

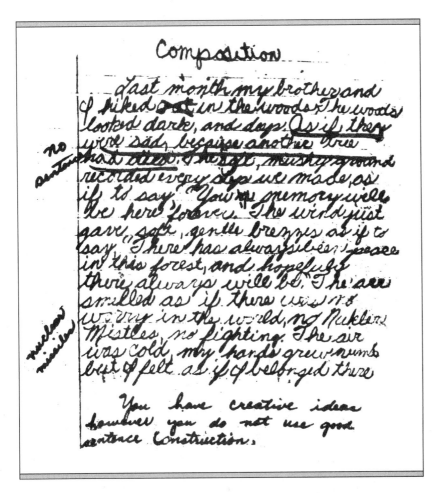

FIGURE 6.21
Katie's Composition

into what students know about how words are spelled; these insights and observations can help teachers plan instruction in spelling.

Sharing and Revising The purpose of *revising* is to address the content of the piece. Revision occurs as writers reread, receive comments and criticisms, and rethink their intentions for the material. It is the substantive part of reworking the material that reflects the writer's best thought. Children see the need for revising when they know someone outside the classroom is going to read their work. Revising can include text reorganization (perhaps by cutting and pasting), word choice, sentence structure changes, or other additions and deletions. Revision ensures that the piece makes sense, that it has a beginning, a middle, and an end, that it is the way the author wants it. Decisions regarding content revision belong to the author; the teacher or other students may only make suggestions. The wealth of literature that has been shared and has become part of the literate environment serves as a model to help authors revise.

Editing   The purpose of *editing* is to produce a readable text. Children quickly recognize that checking their writing for conventional usage will improve it so it can be more easily read by others. Teachers often push students into editing too many mechanical errors at one time. This is a mistake. No student can work on all aspects of the language—spelling, grammar, punctuation, and capital-

FIGURE 6.22
The Authoring Cycle

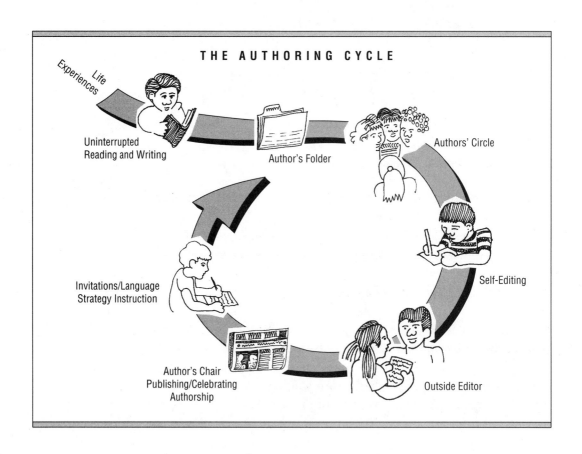

THE AUTHORING CYCLE

Life Experiences

Uninterrupted Reading and Writing

Author's Folder

Authors' Circle

Self-Editing

Outside Editor

Author's Chair Publishing/Celebrating Authorship

Invitations/Language Strategy Instruction

ization—at once. A better strategy is for the teacher to choose one or two elements of written language to work on. If a first grader is in the process of figuring out what a sentence is, the teacher and the child can focus on putting capital letters and end marks in the appropriate places.

The need for conventional spelling becomes evident to the author when work is to be published. If too many words are misspelled, the audience will have difficulty reading the piece. It is not the teacher's role to find all the misspelled words and correct them; rather, the author and the peer editors find as many as they can, perhaps encouraged and guided by the teacher (see figure 6.23). Telling children to circle all the words they think are misspelled (as in figure 6.24) or to write the first letter and then draw a line for all the words they do not know how to spell are strategies that help children get over their fear of making mistakes. It also gives them a list of words to begin looking up and looking for as they revise and edit. Over the course of the year as authors write more and readers read more, everybody learns to spell more words.

Some teachers have an *editor's table* in the classroom. When a piece of writing has undergone revision and self-editing, it may be placed in a box or folder for the peer editors. Peer editors help the author correct spelling, punctuation, and grammar (see figure 6.25). This sequence of drafting, revising, and then editing signals young writers that conventions are important but that they are attended to only after meaning and content have been exhaustively addressed.

Children who serve as editors may have limited opportunities to write during the time they serve (usually for a week), but editing has a strong positive effect on the editor's own writing. Editors are often anxious to return to their own writing, and the elements of writing they learned while in collaboration with other editors are incorporated into their own work.

After peer editing, authors make the necessary changes before a final conference with the teacher. At this time, teachers listen to the authors read their final draft. They talk about the piece; they may use this opportunity to teach or they may discuss publication options. Teachers record their observations of the work. To that end, simple checklists for the students are sometimes helpful. The guide in figure

FIGURE 6.23
Help for Spelling

6.26 was developed by a group of second graders toward the end of the year. It became the booklet they used as a guide for proofreading and editing.

Knowledgeable teachers are careful that the finished work is the student's own, not the teacher's. Therefore, many teachers choose not to mark directly on children's drafts. They may encourage, question, and suggest and they may write notes to students about things to consider, but they do not require specific alterations. Drafts, revisions, and corrections must all belong to the students if they are to feel ownership of their work.

Publishing The purpose of *publishing* is to share and celebrate finished products. Publication occurs in many forms. Simply presenting a finished work to a group is publication. Formal, bound books include hardback books, softcover books, shape books, flip books, and accordion books (Johnson, 1992). Even finished pieces mounted on construction paper for display or letters ready to be mailed are examples of "published" work. Published pieces may be available in the classroom, placed in the school library, submitted

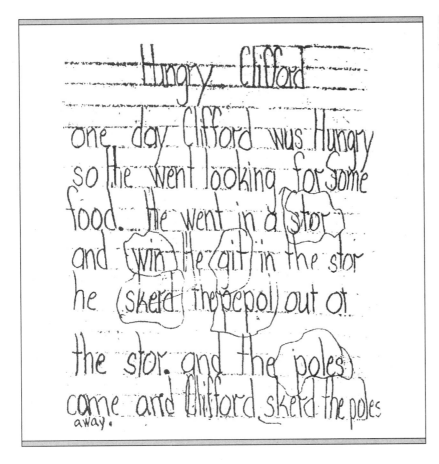

FIGURE 6.24
Finding Misspelled Words (Tyrone, Age 8)

FIGURE 6.25
Peer Editing

for a Young Authors celebration, or given as a gift. Audiences for published works include classmates, favorite children's authors, parents, grandparents, pen pals, children in lower grades, and school personnel.

Informally published pieces may also be part of this process. Displays outside the classroom door, bulletin board presentations, and hanging work from a line in the classroom all furnish opportunities for young authors to present their writing. Both formal and informal publications are important because they add to the meaningful print in the classroom. Materials for formal publication require greater planning on the part of the teacher, but informal publication can be more spontaneous and can include works in progress. Keeping records of classroom publishing also adds to the meaningful and functional print available in the environment (see figure 6.27).

Construction paper or wallpaper covers can be used to make softbound books. Construction paper with decorations and with the title of the writer's story can be laminated and spiral bound for another type of softcover book. Flip books covered with a hard backing and held together with metal rings are good for classroom use. Shape books that represent a theme of the story or unit of study are favorites among young children (for example, dinosaur shapes). Accordion books, in which alternating pages are taped together along the left and then the right margin are fun and easy variations for book binding. (See appendix F for directions on binding formal, hardback books).

FIGURE 6.26
Children's Proofing and Editing Guide

EDITING AND PROOFING GUIDE

Periods	At the end of a telling sentence.
Exclamation points	At the end of an exciting sentence or short sentence (ex., Boo! Hi! Yes!).
Commas	Go in dates, in addresses, to separate thoughts, before someone talks.
Quotation marks	Around what someone says (Jane said, "Hi!").
Upper case letters	Go at the beginning of a sentence, when using I, in story titles, for days of the week, months, things said in excitement, names of states, countries, other titles.
Reversals	Such as [b] for [d].
Spelling	Look it up. Ask someone. Skip it till later. Use another word.
Handwriting	Look at a good model.
Spacing	Make sure it's enough.

FIGURE 6.27
Class Publishing List

Getting Started: A Writers' Workshop   Getting started is often the most difficult part. Many children are reluctant to write, having been in classrooms where their work was marked with red ink and they had to recopy to correct all their errors on papers that had already been graded. Some children are driven toward perfection and are initially uncomfortable with the notion of rough drafts or "sloppy copy." To establish a writing component in their classrooms, teachers typically model writing first drafts by showing children through their own writing how writers cross out, attempt to spell, cut and paste, leave blank spaces till later, and so on. They allay students' fears by encouraging risk taking, and they support writing by suggesting their students write about topics of their own choosing. However, many teachers find a more prescribed series of steps helpful for getting started.

Sometimes thought of as establishing a "writers' workshop" in the classroom, these procedures quickly evolve into individualized writing projects within the authoring cycle:

1. Give each child a large note card. The child's name and address is written in the upper right corner. Ask the children to answer several questions. These might include:

What do you like best about school?

What is hard for you about school?

In what ways are you like everyone else in this room?

What makes you different from everyone else?

The answers to those questions provide teachers with information and insights and encourage learners to think about themselves, their relationships to others, their own uniqueness, and their life as learners.

2. Have the students share their answers voluntarily. Discuss. Collect the note cards and store. Anecdotal records can be written on the back of each student's card.

3. Distribute brightly colored folders, manila envelopes, or pocket folders. Have the children write their names on the outside front at the top. Children should then decorate their folders or envelopes. Help students brainstorm a list of ideas for writing and provide them with a form on which they can record their ideas. These will be added to throughout the year. Attach the list to the inside of the front cover. A list of each child's hard-to-spell words can be developed and attached to the inside back cover. A list of published titles can be kept on the outside back cover. At the end of each day's workshop, the children can put away their own folders in alphabetical order by first or last name

4. Prepare a graph of positive and negative life experiences (see Reif 1991, pp. 48–51). Show students an example from your own life. Then have everyone list the 21 (or so) best and the 17 (or so) worst things that have ever happened to them. Some students may not be able to think of that many. The students then arrange these in chronological order from most distant to most recently. Next have the students place their life events on the graph from their birth date to the most recent event along the horizontal axis and from most to least positive along the vertical axis (-5/+5). An example is shown in figure 6.28.

5. Have everyone fold a piece of paper in half and select one event from their graph and write it at the top of the half sheet. Then taking four or five minutes, everyone jots down as many words and phrases as they can think of about their event.

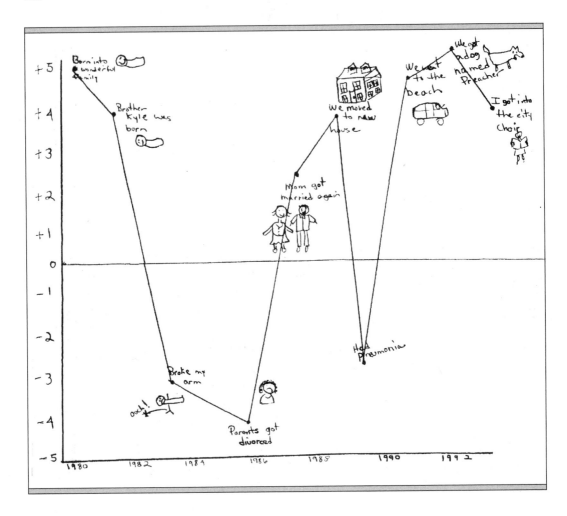

FIGURE 6.28
Part of Kathy's
Significant Positives
and Negatives Graph
(Fourth Grade)

Ask students to share their event with a neighbor: "Tell your story to the person sitting nearest you."

6. After the students have talked about their event, ask them to write their first rough draft. Teachers also participate in this workshop. They demonstrate the life graph with their own life events, perhaps on an overhead. Then they select one of their own events and write their list of related words and phrases, telling their story to one of the children as a demonstration of the procedure. When the students write their first drafts, teachers write, too.

7. Rough drafts are read to small or large peer groups. The listeners should follow the rules for authors' circle. Teachers may have to model this activity once or twice before the students can work successfully in the small groups. The rules for authors' circle may include:

a. Tell the author what you liked about the story.

b. Use the words of the text so the author knows you were *really* listening.

c. Never laugh unless it is supposed to be funny.

d. Ask any questions about the story if you *really* want to know the answer.

8. The teacher may have to employ several means of keeping track of what each student is doing after writers' workshop really gets off the ground. For example, the teacher may find it helpful to make a chart for each child with the child's name at the top and dates across the bottom with codes for drafting (dr), revising (rv), editing (ed), conferencing (cn), sharing (sh), final draft (fd), publishing (pb).

9. At the beginning of every workshop period, ask each child to state what he or she will be doing that day and note it on the chart. Ideas for guided writing lessons may be jotted on the back as teachers move about the room working with the children, checking on their progress, and helping with difficulties. (Guided writing, like guided reading, is a major approach and is described later.) Examples of aspects of writing for which teachers might create guided writing lessons are punctuation, paragraphing, description, dialogue, mood of a story, logical ordering, and characterization.

10. Writing personal narrative soon moves into fiction and expository pieces with the products shared during read aloud, with the various units of study, and with other classroom, school, and home events. Teachers encourage students to follow basically the same format of brainstorming, organizing, drafting, sharing, revising, editing, final copy, and publishing. Each of these activities is also described below.

Getting started with a writers' workshop in your classroom may take several days, if not weeks. Conferencing, peer editing, revisions of work in progress, final editing, and publication of finished pieces form the authoring cycle. Allow the time it takes for you and your students to become comfortable with daily sustained writing. Your students will thank you for it.

While there are many ways to organize children's individual writing efforts, most teachers simply have children date their drafts and keep them in their individual writing folders or packets. These typically contain most, if not all, of the children's writing, both published and unpublished. Such a collection provides children with evidence of their own progress and allows teachers a means to engage in collaborative evaluation of children's work. Children select from their folders the piece they wish to work on. Sometimes teachers have a separate storage facility for work in progress, and individual folders are used for all the other drafts and finished pieces. However it is accomplished, teachers must help children organize and keep all their written productions (see figure 6.29).

FIGURE 6.29
Recording His Work

Writing is a major component of all whole language classrooms.

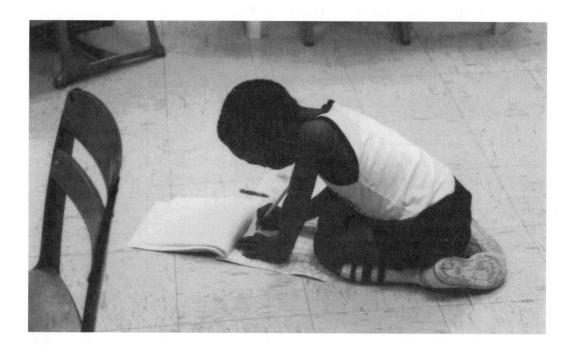

Since the subject matter for their writing comes from the children's lives both in and out of school, and since they determine their own topics and the pieces of writing they will work on, children write freely and come to think of themselves as writers. Classrooms rich in content and teachers who offer *continual invitations to write and read* carry children beyond their own experiences and in many instances beyond their own expectations.

A risk-free environment, weekly pupil-teacher conferences, demonstrations of how written language works, invitations to engage in writing, ample opportunities to write, an enriched curriculum, and immersion in print structure the writing process in the classroom. While the writing process or authoring cycle may begin as a set of procedures, it will evolve into a smooth, integrated flow, with children at several different places in the process simultaneously. This encourages children to explore different realms of expression and allows them to become responsible for their own writing. What motivates children to write is writing every day, watching the teacher write with them, developing a sense of audience, and assuming ownership of what they are writing. When children and their teachers write daily, everybody learns how the process works.

Student writing leads to instructional opportunities (Calkins, 1986) when a teacher uses students' writing to show other writers what *to* do. Examples of good writing that illustrate or model some use of language will strengthen everyone's ability to communicate. Examples of logical connections within text, foreshadowing, humor, character development, description, or plot development, as well as style, grammar, spelling, or punctuation, can be addressed with individuals or in small groups. Individual instruction in writing usually occurs during the writing conference; small group instruction occurs during guided writing.

Examples of children's poor writing are *never* used with groups of children, even anonymously. After all, the writer knows whose paper it is. These are the proper subjects for the teacher-pupil writing conference and are handled as editorial work. Teachers who wish to illustrate poor practices should use contrived composites or—better yet—examples from their own first drafts.

Teachers who establish authentic writing contexts and ample opportunities to engage in the writing process find that students enjoy writing and internalize what they are learning. Teacher-assigned topics and story starters do not produce the same quality of writing or degree of learning as child-initiated topics. Personal narratives are especially important. All writers do best when writing what they know and feel strongly about. And the one thing we all know and feel strongly about is ourselves.

Not all writing goes through the entire authoring cycle. In fact, much does not. Professional writers often attempt a piece and decide that it does not work well. When this happens, professional writers may discard the writing or just set it aside temporarily. This is a valuable learning experience for budding writers. Children need to select which pieces of writing they wish to publish; only these texts go through revisions and editing.

These events, then, are the authoring cycle. In classrooms that employ this process, children write several times a day. Many students compose, singly and in small groups, while others use critiques and suggestions to rewrite and edit. Another group may serve at the editors' table. Others may produce finished copies for publication, typing or recopying in their best handwriting.

Teachers move through all these activities, acting as resources, instructional leaders, sounding boards, record keepers, observers, demonstrators, encouragers, and evaluators. Most important, teachers are authors, too. Teachers write as children write, sharing their own writings with children and allowing children to see them revise, edit, and "present" their own work. In this way, children learn that teachers really value writing.

Major Approaches to Writing in an Environment for Young Authors

As with teaching reading, there are three major instructional approaches and many sound strategies for developing writing (see figure 6.30). Sometimes what children want to write is too challenging for their abilities at a particular point, and they require a great amount of support. Sometimes children need help with only a few

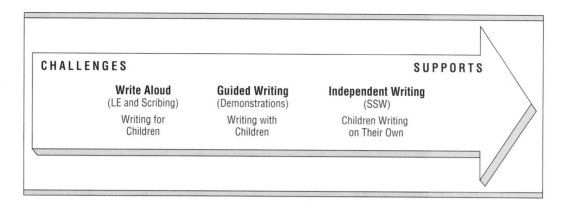

CHALLENGES   SUPPORTS

Write Aloud	**Guided Writing**	**Independent Writing**
(LE and Scribing)	(Demonstrations)	(SSW)
Writing for Children	Writing with Children	Children Writing on Their Own

specific aspects of what they are writing. Sometimes they can write alone. Sometimes teachers write for and with the children.

FIGURE 6.30
Approaches for Teaching Writing

Write Aloud   When children need a great deal of assistance with their writing, teachers may engage them in a language experience (LE), and/or they may scribe for the children. These events may be thought of as *write alouds:* teachers (or other "expert" writers) print what the children dictate. Both language experience and scribing help young children come to understand that print can represent their talking and thinking. This insight is a fundamental part of learning how to read what others write and how to write for oneself.

Teachers might engage children in a group-dictated story or in individual dictation. During the composing process, teachers are demonstrating how writers "do it." They may negotiate with the group (or individual) about such things as spellings, sentence structure, and word choices. They might then use the story for further practice with reading or for additional teaching about the writing process.

Frequently, teachers choose to scribe for young children. This is a useful activity in the preschool and primary years; older students, parent volunteers, or any number of classroom helpers may print children's dictations. Authentic scribing opportunities for children to "write aloud" might include captions for their artwork, captions and labels for other finished project displays, notes and messages, or retellings of favorite stories. These written products can then be displayed in the classroom, where they become part of the literate environment teachers are creating. They may be read and reread by the children during the day or when the entire group takes a "reading walk" around their classroom.

Guided Writing   When children need help with specific aspects of the writing process or the mechanics of written language, teachers prepare strategic instruction in the form of demonstrations and think-aloud events. The goal is to make explicit and facilitate the development of all the strategies students need to become proficient writers. Guided writing instruction and guided practice may take place in formal one-on-one writing conferences, in informal on-the-spot interactions, and with planned instructional events for large groups. Guided writing is the equivalent of guided reading. Explorations and demonstrations of the writing process and the ways writers solve problems as they write give young writers information and help them develop insights and skills. As children explore how to make meaning with written language, demonstrations of various aspects of writing are extremely important instructional tactics and may be incorporated into any phase of the authoring cycle.

One of the skills the writer appears ready to learn about is paragraphing. One writer knew *when* she had completed a set of related sentences, but she did not know *how* to show the reader. The teacher recognized this and planned a guided writing session to explore paragraphing. She chose two books, *Koala Lou* by Mem Fox and *What Do You Do with a Kangaroo?* by Mercer Mayer. Both stories, which the child knew very well, provided models of what the teacher wanted to teach. She used these repeated-pattern books as demonstrations, allowing the child to explore how the author separated the text into paragraphs. Then using the child's text, the teacher and the child examined where and how to use the same technique to separate her story into paragraphs at the repeated line "Lee's my friend" (see figure 6.31).

Sustained Silent Writing (SSW)   The third major approach is scheduling time each day for independent, sustained, silent writing (SSW) (see figure 6.32). Just as with reading, children need time to practice and explore the writing process on their own. Children may have several writing options to choose from during two or more blocks of time each day. Some of these opportunities for practice and self-expression might include writing letters, writing in dialogue journals or observation logs, working on stories they want to publish, and working on writing projects arising from their current unit of study.

These three major instructional approaches are not steps.

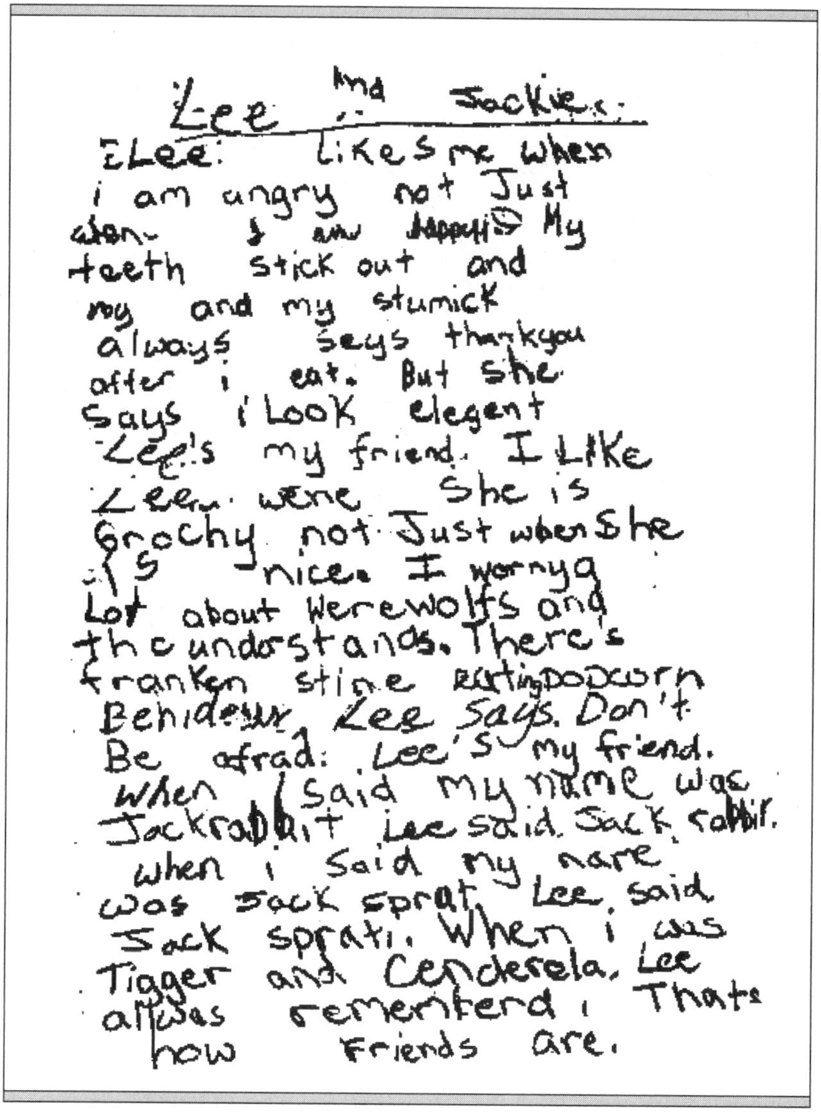
Lee and Jackie:
I Lee: Likes me when
i am angry not Just
when i am happy. My
teeth stick out and
my and my stumick
always seys thankyou
after i eat. But she
says i Look elegent
Lee's my friend. I Like
Lee when She is
Grochy not Just when She
is nice. I worry a
Lot about Werewolfs and
she understands. There's
franken stine eating popcorn
Behind us. Lee says. Don't
Be afrad: Lee's my friend.
When i said my name was
Jackrabbit Lee said Jack rabbit.
when i said my name
was Jack sprat, Lee said
Jack sprat. When i was
Tigger and Cenderela, Lee
allwas rememberd. Thats
how Friends are.

FIGURE 6.31 Jackie's Story about Lee

Rather, they are events that may all occur each day, depending on the writing in which the children are engaged. Just as with reading, a balance is needed among these three approaches—all of which are fundamental to a classroom writing program. The teacher uses many strategies and techniques that encourage writing and help make it functional in the daily life of the classroom. However, the writing conference is the one element that makes the instruction purposeful and immediate for the learner.

The Writing Conference

Like reading conferences, writing conferences are one of the most important teacher-student interactions centering on reading and writing (Parry & Hornsby, 1988). Writing conferences provide the setting for both strategic teaching and evaluation. They may take two forms, the peer conference and the pupil-teacher conference. In peer conferences, children read their drafts to a single child or children in small group settings. Writers often come to peer conferences with requests for their peers: "What do you think of my beginning?"

"Do I need more details?" "How can I make that part more clear?" "Can you think of a better ending?" The peer group is instructed to specify what they like and then to ask any questions they like concerning the content of the piece. In this way, authors have a chance to see what their potential audience thinks of their work. They can then add information or make changes to improve the text. Final editing is usually reserved for a pupil-teacher conference and occurs just before final publication.

Pupil-teacher conferences provide writers opportunities to receive instruction, encouragement, and support from the teacher (see figure 6.33). In this risk-free environment, teachers may discuss problem areas and explore appropriate strategies with children. Conferences afford the teacher a way to assess and guide individual children's writing, as well as the opportunity to document children's growth as writers. Teachers encourage children to write freely without regard for mechanics on the first draft. When the children meet

FIGURE 6.33
The Writing
Conference

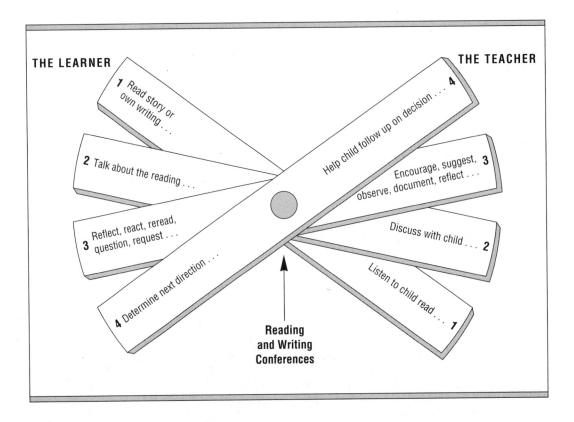

THE LEARNER

1 Read story or own writing . . .

2 Talk about the reading . . .

3 Reflect, react, reread, question, request . . .

4 Determine next direction . . .

Reading and Writing Conferences

THE TEACHER

Help child follow up on decision . . . 4

Encourage, suggest, 3 observe, document, reflect . . .

Discuss with child . . . 2

Listen to child read . . . 1

FIGURE 6.34
Reading and Writing Conferences: Roles of Teacher and Learner

with the teacher to talk about their drafts, the focus is always on meaning first and then mechanics. In figure 6.34 the teacher and learner roles in conferences are depicted.

After the child reads aloud part or all of the text he or she is working on, the teacher begins by telling the child something positive about the draft. Then the teacher makes on-the-spot analyses, asking questions like the following:

How's it going?

Tell me what you wrote. What is this piece about?

What do you like about it? Why?

What problem(s) are you having?

How could you make it better? If you could change any part, what would you do?

How does this piece compare to _____ that you wrote?

During a five- or ten-minute writing conference, teachers will be able to ask only one or two questions to initiate a discussion of a piece of writing. Once the discussion has begun, it takes its own direction. Questions might include inquiries like these about characters:

How do you think this character felt in (a situation)?

How does the character change from the beginning of the story? Why did you have him or her change?

What would you have done if you'd been this character? Why?

Has anything like this ever happened to you or anyone you know?

How could this situation be changed to make it more _____?

How does this character compare to (a similar character) from (a book).

Teachers focus on literary aspects of text. Even in young children's writing, devices and elements such as simile, figurative language, alliteration, foreshadowing, or surprise endings may be found. Questions regarding literary elements might include these:

What part of the story was the hardest to write? What would have helped you write it?

What part of the story could you change to make the story more interesting?

Would you want to write another piece like this again? Why?

When did _____ happen? How did _____ happen?

I don't understand _____. Tell me more about it.

What would happen if _____?

What point do you want to make?

When the text is revised to the student's satisfaction, a final conference is scheduled before "publishing." The teacher's goal is to be supportive and to encourage the learner to regard the finished piece as a real accomplishment. The teacher has also been making anecdotal notes concerning the child's writing during formal and informal conferences. Such notes could include the following:

Student writes well-developed stories.

Student shows some application of the ideas and techniques discussed in previous conferences.

Student perceives how stories are logically ordered.

Student uses literary devices, description, characterization, flashback, surprise, humor, etc.

Student's writing shows development of sense of "voice."

Student shows sense of ownership of the writing process in that _____.

Evaluating Children's Writing

While writing conferences provide a setting for instruction, they also offer teachers the means for evaluation. Teachers gain insights into children's understanding of the writing process and the strategies they use in their writing. Determining what children know and can do with writing helps teachers plan and allows them to document children's growing control over written language. No process-oriented, holistic instruments exist for evaluating writing as they do for evaluating reading. Whole language teachers devise their own checklists, record-keeping devices, and evaluation procedures.

Checklists   Many different checklists can be devised. Figure 6.35 is an example that can help track children's growth in writing. Checklists can also be devised that focus on the elements in more advanced pieces of writing. Figure 6.36 is an example.

Additional Record Keeping   Teachers may also wish to develop various recording forms for keeping track of what students have

FIGURE 6.35   A Developmental Writing Checklist

Child's Name: _____   Date: _____

PRE-WRITING

Does the child . . .   N   S   F   C

1. know the difference between print and pictures
2. see multiple uses for print in the everyday life of the classroom
3. attend to print in the environment
4. draw to represent personal meaning
5. scribble to represent meaning
6. experiment with forms that begin to resemble either cursive or manuscript
7. realize that his or her scribbles are not really print
8.

EARLY WRITING

Does the child . . .

1. experiment with the conventions of written language
2. realize that letters and sounds have a relationship
3. employ idiosyncratic spelling
4. attempt approximations of conventional spellings
5. use tracing or copying to help figure out how written language works
6. create words or grammatical structures that indicate the child is hypothesizing patterns
7. engage in natural writing during play, e.g., lists and signs
8. read own writing
9.

Comments:

EMERGENT WRITING

Does the child . . .   N   S   F   C

1. write so that others can read it
2. show closer approximations to adult forms
3. attempt spelling new words or new spellings of previously invented spellings
4. experiment with a variety of aspects of the mechanics of written language, e.g., commas, end marks, capitals
5. dictate logical and orderly stories, information, accounts of events
6. tell stories that have a beginning, a middle, and an end
7. attempt to self-edit or self-correct
8.

TRANSACTIONAL WRITING

Does the child . . .

1. attempt to write information pieces, i.e., exposition
2. attempt to write to persuade, i.e., argumentation
3. begin with the general and move to the specific and vice versa
4. state a main point and then defend it
5. show a developing sense of audience
6. engage in writing willingly
7. explore the uses of more advanced mechanics, e.g., quotation marks, semicolons
8. explore some of the literary devices, e.g., flashback, metaphor, characterization
9. write with definite purpose
10.

N=Not yet **S**=Sometimes **F**=Frequently **C**=Consistently

FIGURE 6.36   An Advanced Writing Checklist

Child's Name: _____   Date: _____

ORGANIZATION   Comments

Does the writer . . .

1. write for various purposes
2. demonstrate a sense of audience
3. write logical, well-ordered texts
4. develop generalizations with details
5. use appropriate transitions
6. maintain coherence within paragraphs
7.

QUALITY

Does the writer . . .

1. write original material
2. show a developing sense of voice
3. experiment with various styles
4. experiment with various genres
5.

VOCABULARY   Comments

Does the writer . . .

1. use correct word forms
2. avoid unnecessary repetition
3. use words appropriately
4. use descriptive words
5. show growth in vocabulary
6.

SENTENCE STRUCTURE

Does the writer . . .

1. write in complete sentences
2. write compound sentences
3. write complex sentences
4. use sentences of varied length and complexity
5.

MECHANICS

Does the writer:

1. use capital letters correctly
2. use end marks correctly
3. have adequate spelling strategies
4. use internal sentence punctuation correctly
5. show improved handwriting
6.

Additional comments:

written, what they are currently working on, and what they have published. Forms may be developed and kept by the students for this purpose (see figure 6.37).

Evaluations of children's writing cover both content and style, as well as mechanics. While some teachers may wish to develop more specific checklists, it is our experience that most teachers prefer open-ended anecdotal records, like the one in figure 6.38. Many teachers are beginning to use summary forms for evaluations of writing to demonstrate and document learner growth over time (see figure 6.39). A beginning teacher might also wish to use a checklist that evaluates growth in spelling. The development of spelling in children's writing is to some extent dependent on the amount of writing the child engages in, the amount of print in the environment and how it is used, and the amount of reading the child does. Most whole language teachers teach spelling in an individualized manner without resorting to textbook lists of arbitrary words for students to memorize. Rather, they have children identify misspelled words in their writing, determine the correct spellings, practice the correct spelling in a variety of ways, and take self-tests at the end of each week. Because there is great emphasis on writing, revising, and edit-

FIGURE 6.37
Student Record Keeping

STUDENT WRITING CONFERENCE LOG

Name: _____   Date: _____

Title: _____

What I liked about my work: _____

_____

What I plan to work on: _____

_____

Comments: _____

_____

_____

FIGURE 6.38
Teacher's Open-
Ended Record

TEACHER'S WRITING CONFERENCE LOG

Name: _____ Date: _____

Text title:

First draft observations:

Second draft observations:

Final draft observations:

Publishing plans:

ing in these classrooms, there is a wide variety of print sources on display at all times; as a consequence, spelling is one of the fastest growing of children's abilities.

As with all other aspects of the language- and literature-based curriculum, teachers collect and record information on children's spellings. This information is used to help focus learners' attention on various aspects of their spelling, usually during conferences, and to document their growth in spelling over time. Figure 6.40 is a sample of the type of information a teacher might collect on a child's spelling. The teacher can summarize evaluations on a form such as figure 6.41.

Evaluation of children's writing allows teachers to document growth in writing and to plan for appropriate instruction. Part of planning for classroom instruction includes implementing strategies to encourage children's writing. These include author's chair, message board, logs and journals, and play writing. These and other classroom strategies establish an environment in which children come to view themselves as writers and authors. (For more help with

FIGURE 6.39   Writing Evaluation Summary Form

WRITING EVALUATION SUMMARY

Writer's Name: _____   Date: _____

Grade Level: _____   Teacher: _____

Title of Piece: _____

1. What percentage of the sentences are well developed?
   Total number of sentences written (TS): _____
   Number of well-developed sentences (WDS): _____
   (WDS / TS) x 100 = percentage of well-developed sentences: _____%
2. What percentage of sentences are mechanically correct or nearly correct?
   Total number of sentences written (TS): _____
   Number of correct or nearly correct sentences (CS): _____
   (CS / TS) x 100 = percentage of mechanically correct sentences: _____%

	N	S	O	U	A
3. How does the writer go about constructing meaning?					
a. Writes for a purpose	1	2	3	4	5
b. Logically orders writing	1	2	3	4	5
c. Has beginning, middle, and end	1	2	3	4	5
d. Self-corrects errors that disrupt meaning	1	2	3	4	5
e. Uses resources to revise and edit	1	2	3	4	5
f. Uses description and elaborates with details	1	2	3	4	5
g. Writes complete simple and compound sentences	1	2	3	4	5
h. Writes grammatically acceptable complex sentences	1	2	3	4	5
i. Uses capitals and punctuation correctly	1	2	3	4	5
j. Spells well for age and grade level	1	2	3	4	5
k. Attempts to write for various purposes	1	2	3	4	5
l. Has developed sense of own "voice"	1	2	3	4	5
m. Writes with originality	1	2	3	4	5
n. Has sense of audience	1	2	3	4	5
4. Writing narrative text					
a. Character development	1	2	3	4	5
b. Description	1	2	3	4	5
c. Setting	1	2	3	4	5
d. Relationship of events	1	2	3	4	5
e. Plot	1	2	3	4	5
f. Theme	1	2	3	4	5
h. Overall rating	1	2	3	4	5
5. Writing nonfiction					
a. Major concepts	1	2	3	4	5
b. Generalizations	1	2	3	4	5
c. Specific information	1	2	3	4	5
d. Logical order	1	2	3	4	5
e. Vocabulary	1	2	3	4	5
f. Overall rating	1	2	3	4	5

What the writer has learned since the last writing evaluation:

What the writer still needs help with:

The writer's major strengths:

What the writer appears ready to learn next:

N = Not yet **S** = Sometimes **O** = Often **U** = Usually **A** = Always

FIGURE 6.40   Guide for Evaluating Spelling

GUIDE FOR SPELLING EVALUATION: PRIMARY GRADES

Child's Name: _____   Date: _____

Approximate total number of words in child's story (TW): _____

Title: _____

Type of Strategy	**Example**	**Percentage of Sample**
1. Phonetic (auditory memory/ sounded out)	***eny/any*** (from knowing the word *enter*)	
2. Phonic (exaggerated sound)	***sbagede/spaghetti***	
3. Known pattern (visual memory/ homophone)	***brix/next***	
4. Synonym (generalizations)	***brutren/brothers*** (from knowing the word *children*)	
5. Transpositions (letter reversals)	***lable/label***	
6. Omissions (too few letters)	***nit/night***	
7. Additions (too many letters)	***rooaze/rose***	
8. Root word problem	***incuraj/encourage***	
9. Affix problem	***goeg/going***	
10. Scribbles (uses poor handwriting to cover up unknown word)	 *bcleeve*	
11. Risk level (chooses easier word)	***He felt good*** (child wanted to use "satisfied")	
12. Other		

Summary:

Evidence of growth:

What the child is ready to learn next:

FIGURE 6.41   Teacher's Spelling Evaluation Record Form

SPELLING EVALUATION SUMMARY

Writer's Name: _____   Date: _____

Grade Level: _____   Teacher: _____

Total number of words written (TW): _____   (WC / TW) x 100 = percentage of words spelled
Number spelled correctly (WC): _____   correctly: _____%

Categories:

Phonetic (sounded out)	Transpositions (reversals)	Affix problem
Phonic (exaggerated sound)	Omissions (too few letters)	Scribbles
Known pattern (homophone)	Additions (too many letters)	Low-risk word
Synonym (generalization)	Root word problem	

Standard Spelling	Misspelling	Assessment
1.		
2.		
3.		
4.		
5.		
6.		
7.		
8.		
9.		
10.		
11.		
12.		
13.		
14.		
15.		

Misspelling Patterns: _____

Comments: _____

_____

understanding spelling see Buchanan, 1989; Gentry & Gillet, 1993; Wilde, 1992).

Selected Strategies: A Literacy-Based Classroom

Next we will briefly describe a number of strategies that focus on writing. Lists of professional resources for developing the writing process in the classroom with additional strategies that focus on writing are included in Suggested Readings at the end of the chapter.

Authors' Circle or Author's Chair   *Authors' circle* is a strategy that helps authors communicate their intentions. At this point, young writers move away from the solitary experience of writing to sharing, responding, and interacting with peers in either large or small groups. Authors' circle is designed to facilitate students sharing work in progress. A writer requests, or the teacher sets aside, time for a small group of students to listen to one or more of them read a draft of a piece of material to be published. After listening to a writer read his or her work, members of the group respond. First, they compliment the author about something specific in the piece— for example, what they liked best. They are encouraged to use some of the language from the text in their remarks. Then they may question specific elements of the text that may need to be clarified or amplified. In this setting, writers begin to refine their sense of audience. Authors direct the meeting, share their work, ask if it is clear, and request suggestions for improvement. Authors' circle can be seen as peer assistance with the content of the writing.

Author's chair is for sharing finished work. At this point, children's work is enjoyed and celebrated. Much like shared book, author's chair is the time for writers to rehearse and then read their published products for the appreciation and applause of peers and teachers. Typically, author's chair is a large group production, taking place at a regular time each week. Many teachers have a particular chair such as an old easy chair or a rocking chair that has been designated the storytelling/read aloud chair for the classroom. A student with a finished piece of writing uses this special chair for sharing, hence author's chair. Sharing writing that has undergone several revisions and final editing is itself one of the ways children "publish" their final drafts. Author's chair may take place once or twice a week or as a special celebration marking the end of a unit of study or a grading period.

Classroom Post Office Many elementary classrooms have a post office or mailbox set up. This helps make letter writing functional. The teacher devises some sort of post office—either a central mailbox or individual mailboxes made from cardboard boxes in a wood frame. Children may use the mailboxes each day to deliver letters to their classmates. Teachers can write special notes to the students. Each week the class can choose a "letter carrier" to deliver the mail. Students are encouraged to answer their mail and this strategy opens opportunities to examine the purposes of letter writing. Young children may be encouraged to bring in junk mail from home for the class to read and use. Teachers may want to initiate this activity by sending each child a letter through the U.S. Postal Service.

Another authentic letter-writing opportunity is pen pals. Pen pals may be established using another class within or outside the school. Several ways to establish pen pals are available. For example, if you have a friend who teaches across town, your students may correspond with your friend's students. Meeting a teacher at a professional conference is another excellent way to set up pen pals. Some of the book clubs from which children order books now offer international pen pal services. In these ways, letter writing becomes a core component of the writing program.

The Message Board This strategy reinforces the concept that print is functional. It also helps legitimatize one type of written communication that students like. The teacher and students jointly agree on a designated area for the posting of messages. So messages will be current, they should be dated by the writer and should not remain posted for more than a few days. The teacher encourages the children to check for messages frequently and to respond in writing. Teachers might want to consider having a couple of rules regarding messages—for instance, they must be in language that is appropriate for school and they cannot hurt anyone's feelings. A message board is a useful tool for the teacher for a number of reasons. Often, the message board will be the teacher's first notice that two students are having problems getting along. Note writing provides a good outlet for children's explorations of print. Besides, children are going to do it anyway. Why not use the message board to give them authentic opportunities to write?

Literature Logs   The literature response journal or "lit log" is a useful addition to many classrooms. These can be simple ones kept in an inexpensive spiral notebook that each child has decorated or elaborate hardback books made by the children and using unlined paper. In the literature logs children keep a record of the books they have read and their written reflections and responses to the text as they read the book. The journals can then be shared. The teacher can read and write back to the students about their comments, observations, and reactions to the book. Using Post-it notes is one way to communicate with children without writing directly on their work. Literature logs can lead to other writing opportunities—for instance, advertisements for favorite books.

Journals and Observation Logs   Opportunities for authentic written language are quite abundant once we begin looking for them. Certainly the keeping of a diary or *journal* in which children record the day's events is an example (Fulweiler, 1987). Teachers usually begin journal writing by having children brainstorm a list of ideas to write about. This list is then posted and becomes part of the literate environment of the classroom. The children refer to these ideas whenever they need to. Everyone, including teachers, can write in their journals every day at the same time.

This sort of didactic, prescriptive approach to journal writing is useful only for getting started. Anyone who has ever kept a diary knows that you don't write in it every day. Entries are made when you have something to say. Therefore, as quickly as possible, journal writing should become one of the many choices for writing available in the classroom. There is no better way to make children hate writing than to force them to write in a journal for no reason, every day. Needless to say, journals are never graded or corrected.

However, journal writing can be interesting and instructive. A pretend or "You Are There" journal is kept during certain units, usually historical studies. In a unit on colonial America, begun because the students had a chance to see some of our nation's original documents on loan to their local museum, several sixth graders started diaries written as if they were living in colonial America. They created names and families and they reacted to the events of the times in their journals. They also read letters and diaries written by real people living during that period so that their diaries would sound as authentic as possible.

Dialogue journals allow teachers and children to engage in another dimension of communication. Such journals give teachers an opportunity for more personal contact with students. Children are invited to write about anything that personally concerns them, and teachers respond with comments and questions that help establish a written conversation. In doing so, each shares life experiences and feelings with the other. Though dialogue journals can be labor-intensive for the teacher, they are also rewarding. Children often reveal things in writing that they will not express any other way, and the teacher-student relationship can be enhanced through these written dialogues.

Observation logs are yet another means of establishing authentic writing. They also allow children to explore another variety of print. Acting as scientists or naturalists, children can record their observations of ongoing science experiments, their examinations of a place such as a dry river bed, nearby untended field, or vacant lot in the spring and again in the fall, or their investigation of an exposed cliff wall during a field trip. These observations may be edited, rewritten, and bound so that the children can use them as part of their classroom reference materials.

Writing Plays and Other Scripts   Drama in the classroom helps children focus on the setting and the event sequence of narrative. Writing a play gives children complete responsibility for creating a setting and determining a sequence of events. Children create a story line for their play from a favorite book or from an event they think would make a good play. They put their written document through all the stages of writing, drafting, editing, and revising. When it is ready, they cast it and rehearse. They develop costumes and background scenery. A play can be an ambitious undertaking over an extended period of time and may lead to a full production that includes costuming, set design, scenery, props, programs, advertisements, ticket sales, and more.

Most presentations will not be that ambitious. Children can also stage simple puppet shows or plan flannel board stories. They can write scripts for readers theater productions (see chapter 9). Teachers facilitate play writing by helping children one step at a time. Children will need to see published plays as models as they write and revise their scripts.

SUMMARY

Whole language teachers know their students, the resources and materials available, and the approaches. They immerse children in written language and in opportunities to write. They demonstrate how the writing process and the mechanics of written language work. This means that teachers are authors too, and they share their own writing with their students. They lead and encourage, and they engage children in authentic writing events. When children have the opportunity to write often, in low-risk environments, and when writing itself makes sense, they learn quickly. Teachers promote the varied and authentic uses of writing, including communication, record keeping, self-discovery, organizing the classroom, and storytelling. This means that they employ written language in functional ways in the classroom—for example, in lists for the children's information, charts of things the children are interested in, forms for children to keep track of their own work, forms for children to sign up for selected events, and messages to the children from the teacher as well as from other children.

Teachers provide ungraded, daily writing experiences such as journals. This frequent experience gives children a new and powerful means to process information and feelings, and it gives the teacher a window into the minds and hearts of the children that cannot be gained any other way. Teachers assist children in finding purpose in writing by allowing them to choose their own topics. For some, this may have to begin by encouraging the children to choose between two ideas offered by the teacher, then expanding the choices possible over a period of weeks until children are initiating their own work. Finally, teachers monitor and evaluate the writing process through observation and record keeping. The student-teacher conference is the key for planning, curriculum development, and evaluation.

This chapter has presented holistic writing instruction based on authentic literacy events that serve the interests and purposes of the students. Children tend to learn to write faster, better, and more joyfully when they do so for their own purposes, under the guidance and encouragement of a knowledgeable teacher.

THEORY-TO-PRACTICE CONNECTIONS

Theory of Writing	*Examples of Classroom Practice*
1. Writing is learned as it is used, in natural and in functional ways, e.g., record keeping, storytelling.	**1.** Journals, pen pals, sign-up forms
2. Human beings also write to help make sense of the world and to express themselves aesthetically.	**2.** Reports from chosen units of study, personal narratives
3. Writing is a constructive process and childen typically move through several phases in their development as writers, e.g., emergent to advanced.	**3.** Spelling developing from invented to conventional
4. Proficient writers engage in several procedures from first drafts to published works.	**4.** Rough drafts, revisions, etc.
5. Writers write better when they choose their own topics.	**5.** Individual writing folders and free choice

SUGGESTED READINGS

Calkins, L. (1986). *The art of teaching writing.* Portsmouth, NH: Heinemann.

Calkins, L., with Harwayne, S. (1991). *Living between the lines.* Portsmouth, NH: Heinemann.

Clay, M. (1975). *What did I write?* Portsmouth, NH: Heinemann.

Graves, D. (1983). *Writing: Teachers and children at work.* Portsmouth, NH: Heinemann.

Hansen, J. (1986). *The craft of children's writing.* Portsmouth, NH: Heinemann.

Murray, D. (1984). *Write to learn.* New York: Holt, Rinehart, & Winston.

Newkirk, T., & Atwell, N. (1986). *Understanding writing* (2nd ed.). Chelmsford, MA: Northeast Regional Exchange, Inc.

Parry, J., & Hornsby, D. (1988). *Write on: A conference approach to writing.* Portsmouth, NH: Heinemann.

Turbill, J. (1984). *No better way to teach writing.* Portsmouth, NH: Heinemann.

Turbill, J. (1985). *Now we want to write.* Portsmouth, NH: Heinemann.

Wilde, S. (1992). *You kan red this!* Portsmouth, NH: Heinemann.

SUGGESTED ACTIVITIES

1. Discuss how the classroom practices suggested on page 251 reflect the theoretical foundation upon which the writing process is based. What is the theoretical basis for suggesting such classroom writing opportunities as message board or literature logs?

2. Collect samples of young children's self-initiated writing. Be sure to date the samples, label them with the child's name and age, and also with a description of the context in which the writing was produced. Arrange the samples by age or by type of writing. Examine the samples, and share and discuss them with your classmates. What do these samples indicate about children's writing development?

3. Using the information on cohesive ties in chapter 2, analyze a piece of a child's writing for such cohesive elements as types of conjunctions and pronoun referents. Share your process and findings. How might examining writing for cohesive ties help you help your students become better writers?

4. Write a children's story or a personal narrative. Share it in draft form in a small group set-

ting. Each member of the group must tell what they like best about your text, and each may ask a question of the author. Then revise your first draft.

You may find that you want to work on it so that you actually produce several versions before you consider the story complete. Perhaps you will want to type your final version and bind it into a hardback book.

5. Your instructor may ask you to keep a journal of your observations and reflections on the course. You may be asked to respond in writing to the text, to any children's literature you are reading in conjunction with this course, or to a chapter book being read aloud to your class. Another option is to circulate a roving journal in which each member of your group writes on a regular basis, commenting on the class and on the text readings, as well as writing back in response to the entries made by other members of the group. This is a variation on dialogue journals.

REFERENCES

Atwell, N. (1987). *In the middle.* Portsmouth, NH: Heinemann.

Bissex, G. (1980). *GNYS AT WRK: A child learns to read and write.* Cambridge, MA: Harvard University Press.

Britton, J., Burgess, T., Martin, N., McLeod, A., & Rosen, H. (1975). *The development of writing.* Urbana, IL: NCTE.

Buchanan, E. (1989). *Spelling for whole language classrooms.* Winnipeg: Whole Language Consultants, Ltd.

Burrows, A. (1977). Composition: Prospect and retrospect. In H. Robinson (Ed.), *Reading and writing instruction in the United States: Historical trends.* Newark, DE: IRA.

Calkins, L., (1986). *The art of teaching writing.* Portsmouth, NH: Heinemann.

Calkins, L., with Harwayne, S. (1991). *Living between the lines.* Portsmouth, NH: Heinemann.

Chomsky, C. (1971). Write now, read later. *Childhood Education, 47,* 296–299.

Clay, M. (1975). *What did I write?* Portsmouth, NH: Heinemann.

Clay, M. (1982). Learning to teach writing: A developmental perspective. *Language Arts, 59,* 65–70.

Fulwiler, T. (Ed.). (1987). *The journal book.* Portsmouth, NH: Heinemann.

Gentry, R., & Gillet, J. (1993). *Teaching kids to spell.* Portsmouth, NH: Heinemann.

Goodman, K. (1986). *What's whole in whole language?* Portsmouth, NH: Heinemann.

Graves, D. (1983). *Writing: Teachers and children at work.* Portsmouth, NH: Heinemann.

Graves, D. (1991). *Build a literate classroom.* Portsmouth, NH: Heinemann.

Handwriting: Basic skill and application (1987). Columbus, OH: Zaner-Bloser.

Hansen, J. (1987). *When writers read.* Portsmouth, NH: Heinemann.

Harste, J. & Short, K. (1988). *Creating classrooms for authors: The reading-writing connection.* Portsmouth, NH: Heinemann.

Harste, J., Woodward, V., & Burke, C. (1984). *Language stories and literacy lessons.* Portsmouth, NH: Heinemann.

Johnson, P. (1992). *A book of one's own: Developing literacy through book making.* Portsmouth, NH: Heinemann.

Newkirk, T., & Atwell, N. (1988). *Understanding writing: Ways of observing, learning, and teaching.* Portsmouth, NH: Heinemann.

Parry, J., & Hornsby, D. (1988). *Write on: A conference approach to writing.* Portsmouth, NH: Heinemann.

Read, C. (1971). Pre-school children's knowledge of English phonemes. *Harvard Educational Review, 41,* 1–34.

Reif, L. (1991). *Seeking diversity.* Portsmouth, NH: Heinemann.

Temple, C., Nathan, R., Burris, N., & Temple, F. (1988). *The beginnings of writing.* Boston: Allyn & Bacon.

Thurber, D. (1987). *D'Nealian handwriting.* Glenview, IL: Scott, Foresman.

Wilde, S. (1992). *You kan red this! Spelling and punctuation for whole language classrooms, K–6.* Portsmouth, NH: Heinemann.

7

The primary thing is now held to be the grasp of meaning—the ability to "make sense" of things and above all to make sense of what people do, which of course includes what people say.

(DONALDSON, 1978, p. 33)

Speaking and Listening

What is the proper role of speaking and listening in the elementary classroom?

What is the relationship between oral language and literacy and oral language and learning?

What are sound instructional practices that develop oral language?

How can teachers evaluate children's talking and listening?

*L*anguage, oral as well as written, is the basis for school and future life learning. It is the basis for all our business and social transactions and the primary means by which we represent our understanding of the world and come to know ourselves. It is one of the symbol systems we use to categorize, organize, and clarify our thinking. Language is the major tool for teaching.

Like written language, oral language learning is a constructive process. It occurs naturally as young children interact with others and with their environment. Oral language development does not stop with the beginnings of literacy development. It does not stop when children enter school. Even in classrooms where talking is discouraged, oral language continues to develop; however, it may not develop as fully as possible. The way talking and listening occur in schools tends to be very different from the way they occur at home. In school children are typically required to listen to someone talking to them for several hours each day; they are often discouraged from "chiming in" whenever they have a contribution, an observation, a suggestion, or a question. When they *are* allowed to talk, they are usually asked to respond in certain ways with very specific information. Further, talk in school may employ a different set of terms and standard phrases that is new and confusing to young children. But classroom practice does not have to be this way.

Teachers who want children to develop their oral language must themselves have something worthwhile to say, and they must be good listeners. Teachers who wish to promote oral language development must model what they value. They need to listen to children and hear what they have to say, treating children's offerings as important and worthy of attention. They must provide ample opportunities for children to engage in authentic discussions, group problem solving, and other events that naturally involve speaking and listening. These teachers examine with their children the characteristics of effective oral presentations and the characteristics of the good audience. Much of the talking and listening in their classrooms is a natural consequence of inquiry. Because the use of oral language is authentic and risk-free, students engage in it willingly. It is embedded in an atmosphere of mutual respect and cooperation.

This chapter addresses oral language development in the classroom. It describes the purposes of an instructional focus on talking and listening and suggests several theoretically sound teaching strategies. The chapter also addresses classroom management in a context in which a considerable amount of talking is encouraged as a necessary and natural part of inquiry. Issues of dialect, language variation, and shyness or reluctance are discussed. Finally, suggestions are provided for documenting and evaluating learner growth in oral language.

What Speaking and Listening Are

Listening and speaking are oral language processes. They are reciprocal; each reinforces the other. Indeed, one does not normally occur without the other. Listening is the receptive part of oral language and speaking, the productive. Listening is highly complex and transactive. It is invisible, taking place in the mind of the listener; yet it is actively constructive in that listeners construct the rules by which they comprehend speech just as readers figure out the rules for making sense of written language. To do this, listeners require ample instances of purposeful utterances to comprehend.

Likewise, speaking plays a critical role in children's lives both in and out of school. Talking is actively constructive in that learners construct the rules by which they organize verbal symbols to represent their meanings for others to understand. Through talking, children not only learn language, they also socialize and define themselves. They grow as individuals as they share not only their ideas, but their feelings, hopes, fears, and desires as well.

Since listening is making sense of talk, much of what young children learn before school is learned through listening. Once they are in school, however, listening may play an even more important role. Educators have suggested that perhaps half of children's instructional time is spent listening (Fisher & Terry, 1990). If that is true, then listening as a force in the curriculum should be closely examined.

Wolvin and Coakley (1985) point out that much of what happens in school requires the act of purposeful listening. Purposeful listening is the process of receiving, attending to, and making sense of spoken language. It is possible for a person to receive language sounds and not attend to them, not listen purposefully. If people's prior knowledge of the subject is limited or if the concepts are too complex or developmentally sophisticated, they may both receive and attend but be unable to make much sense of what is being said.

Authentic talking-listening experiences should relate to the learners' interests, backgrounds, age levels, and areas of study. They emerge naturally from an inquiry-based curriculum. As students discuss current events, good books, science projects, and the math calculations for something the class is building, opportunities for purposeful speaking and listening are naturally woven into all aspects of the instructional program.

Oral Language Development and Schools: Our Evolving Understanding

All of us learned at least one language, our native language, without formal instruction. This feat was perhaps our most successful learning endeavor, because language, with its layer upon layer of patterns and rules, is extremely complex. The focus in school on written language development often means that continued growth in oral language is frequently ignored. Yet elementary classrooms can and should be places where oral language continues to flourish. Group discussions, project planning, storytelling, choral readings, drama, debates, and interviews are some of the ways teachers may structure opportunities for natural, purposeful oral language with children.

According to the National Council of Teachers of English (1983, p. 246), several broad objectives for children's oral language should be considered in developing classroom events and evaluating students. These include helping children learn:

- to speak clearly and expressively about their ideas and concerns,

- to adapt words and strategies according to varying situations and audiences, from one-on-one conversations to formal, large-group settings,

- to participate productively and harmoniously in both small and large groups,

- to present arguments in orderly and convincing ways,

- to interpret and assess various kinds of communication, including intonation, pause, gesture, and body language that accompany speaking.

In this age of information explosion and rapid technological advancement, the ability to think logically, find and assess information, organize thoughts, and communicate effectively with others is essential. Intentionally engaging learners with demonstrations of purposeful talking and listening activities in authentic classroom events enhances oral language development in several ways—for example, expanded vocabulary, clarity and organization of thinking, ability to vary communication according to audience, and enhanced self-confidence. Purposeful talking and listening carry over into reading and writing development.

Oral Language, Literacy, and Learning: Current Perspectives

Indeed, children learn by doing. And what learners *do* must be purposeful and meaningful to them. This occurs naturally during the oral language development years. Children listen to what interests and affects them; they talk about what interests and affects them. They learn language and they learn through language simultaneously.

Literacy learning parallels and complements the processes of oral language development. The strategies children used during oral language development are the same ones they will use in acquiring written language and learning in general. But growth in oral language does not stop when reading and writing starts, and attention to oral language development should not cease when children begin formal schooling. Instead it should be incorporated into the successful elementary classroom. Hence, we have the language- and literature-based, learner-centered, inquiry-driven curriculum.

One way teachers incorporate oral language into the curriculum is through their knowledge of the functions of language. Knowledgeable teachers provide opportunities for all the uses of discourse children naturally employ. Children's oral language, instead of being taught as a separate subject, continues to develop when integrated with reading, writing, thinking, and subject matter areas. Each supports the others.

Young children use language as a tool for controlling their environments, and as a creative device as well. Using it as a creative device, they make new worlds through imagination; they entertain themselves and others with sounds and rhythms; they develop their own personalities; and they narrate their daily lives (Fisher & Terry, 1990). Used as a tool for controlling their environments, language indicates what children are personally interested in and attending to, offering keys to understanding their learning and language development (Donaldson, 1978). As Halliday (1978) has suggested, young children use language in at least seven different ways. These seven functions of language might produce the classroom talking and listening opportunities listed in table 7.1.

The Talking-Listening Curriculum: Major Approaches

The talking-listening curriculum is composed of the following three broad approaches or conditions:

1. Someone (teachers, other adults, other children) *talking to* children and children listening

2. Someone (teachers, other adults, other children) *talking with* children and listening to what the children have to say

3. *Children talking and listening to* each other, to teachers, and to other adults

Talking and listening are purposeful and natural in real discussions, literature response groups, planning and problem-solving ses-

TABLE 7.1
Classroom Applications from Halliday's Functions of Language

Functions of Language		Possible Learning Events
Instrumental	(I want)	Discussing choices and options/group planning time
Regulatory	(Do as I tell you)	Group leader/giving directions/directing plays and presentations
Interactional	(You and me)	Sharing time/small group problem solving/paired oral readings
Personal	(Here I come)	Dictated stories/oral presentations/author's chair
Heuristic	(Tell me why)	Questioning time for each new unit/questions that arise during units
Imaginative	(Let's pretend)	Oral storytelling/story retelling/acting out stories/role playing
Expressive	(I have something to tell you)	Journal sharing/oral reports/conferences/interviews

sions, presentations by classroom visitors, and classroom drama presentations. The two roles may be interactive, with speakers and listeners switching back and forth, or more separate, with part of the group listening and one or more persons speaking. However they occur, talking and listening are part of every subject, and every learning event may involve purposeful oral language. In this way, students' spoken language continues to grow. Knowledgeable teachers recognize the importance of oral language development in the total educational process. Through purposeful listening, learners encounter new language patterns, vocabulary, and concepts. Through speaking, they clarify and refine information and ideas and develop self-awareness and self-esteem.

The amount of oral language children possess is a strong determiner of the ease with which they acquire other knowledge and skills. Extent of oral language is also one of the best predictors of the ease with which children learn to read and write. Table 7.2 may help teachers as they think about expanding purposeful listening and speaking in their classrooms.

As learners participate in purposeful classroom talk, their contributions are respected and their language accepted. Teachers model "standard English," of course, but remember that each of us speaks a dialect variation of our language. Originally, we spoke the form of language that was modeled in our home and community. Some of these variations of English are labeled "good" or "standard" while others are labeled "poor" or "nonstandard." If language exists for the purpose of communication within a community of speakers, then all dialects communicate equally well. That is, meaning is conveyed whether a child says, "We didn't have no lunch" or "We didn't have any lunch." Judgments about the *acceptability* of one dialect over another reflect social values, not linguistic ones (Jaggar, 1980).

Acknowledging and celebrating differences is one of the hallmarks of a whole language philosophy. This does not mean that standard forms are not valued, they are; but children are ill served if they are labeled, insulted, and caused to feel inferior because of the way they talk. They are also ill served if they are left to cope with the realities of the larger society without the tools it takes to succeed. Educated adults in this society typically speak (and write) some form

TABLE 7.2   The Listener's Role in Listening and Speaking Contexts

Classroom Context Example	Listening	Listener Speaking
A discussion following a read aloud.	Conversational: Interacts with another, as roles switch back and forth from speaker to listener in a give-and-take communication.	Interacts with another, as roles switch back and forth from speaker to listener in a give-and-take communication.
A visiting expert presents information, photos, documents on the Holocaust.	Reactive: Attends to information, integrates concepts, reflects on the message.	Responds to the sender.
Several students present a case for becoming involved in a classroom campaign to raise money for the homeless in their community.	Reflective: Retains information while evaluating, drawing inferences, making connections, and predicting.	Perhaps responds to the sender or to others who were also listening respectively.
A local artist is visiting the classroom to explain how she does what she does.	Retentive: Comprehends and recalls messages presented by integrating ideas, grouping concepts, and organizing input for future use.	May also respond to the sender or to others who were also listening to retain information.
A speech given by a class member who is running for student council office.	Attentive: Pays attention to the cues provided by the speaker and constructs a meaning appropriate to the context.	May respond to the sender or to others who were also attending to construct an appropriate meaning.
An older child listens to a younger child read and discuss a story during cross-age tutoring.	Affectionate: Listens out of love or respect when the listener values the speaker and gives the speaker time and attention.	May respond briefly.
Children listen to a visiting grandparent tell a story.	Courteous: Hears another politely and patiently as a support when little response is expected or needed.	May respond briefly.
A classroom readers theater production.	Appreciative: Attends to persons presenting drama, music, storytelling, read alouds, becomes involved in the mood and meaning of the artistic presentation.	May respond to the sender or to others who were also listening to appreciate and enjoy the presentation.
A group project examines television advertising.	Critical: Listens for point of view, persuasion techniques, and to separate fact from opinion, truths from nontruths.	Responds to sender or to others in the group who were also listening to evaluate.

of standard English at will. Since children learn by immersion, demonstration, and engagement, teachers must model standard forms. Television provides some immersion in standard speech, and teachers engage learners in examining their own language. Children explore and practice standard forms through purposeful oral language events and through the writing process until language variations become just another part of their language repertoire (Smith, 1988).

Classrooms that establish nonthreatening, nondirective, cooperative environments have the best chance for encouraging continued oral language development in general and the development of standard language patterns in particular. For example, in a classroom where the environment was conducive and purposeful talk was encouraged and provided for, one teacher recorded twenty different types of problem-solving talk naturally employed by the children (Huff, 1991). She found that when the children were interested in the problem under discussion, both highly verbal and quiet children participated successfully. She concluded that children who believe their ideas have value to both their peers and teachers willingly share and participate in classroom events. When they engage in authentic speaking and listening, they take risks and acquire confidence in themselves. They find their own voices and take greater control over their self-expressions and over their own learning.

Disciplinary difficulties are kept to a minimum when children's natural drives to socialize are incorporated into the daily routine and life of the classroom. By more closely reflecting the elaborated oral language conditions of most homes, rather than the language-restricted conditions of many classrooms, whole language classrooms become places where children feel comfortable (Dillon & Searle, 1981). They feel less need to act out their frustrations when they can talk or write about them, and when those frustrations are not being exacerbated by authoritarian and dominating adults (Knapp, 1991).

In one inner-city third grade, for example, the teacher and the children decided to study the solar system and outer space because they had tickets to the local planetarium. Just as the unit was getting under way, plans for the outing fell through because transportation was not available. The children were upset. They voiced their displeasure during morning check-in time, but chose, somewhat less than enthusiastically, to continue the unit of study anyway.

The teacher suggested that they each select a planet to learn about and report on. This idea was met with much moaning and groaning. Several children said they thought that would be boring. So the teacher asked the group what they would like to do instead, how they would like to organize their unit. The students had already listed what they knew about the solar system, outer space, and space travel, and they had posed some of their own questions as well. After a moment of muffled conversation among themselves, one child suggested that since they could not go to the museum, that they turn their classroom into one. They could schedule tours for other classes and present all the information they could find about outer space and the solar system to their schoolmates and even parents.

Once more the children were excited and enthusiastic about learning. Once more the classroom was theirs. They began to describe how to arrange the room into concept areas, what materials they were going to need, what projects and displays they might create, how to organize tours and publicize their museum, and so on. What began as a disruptive event was channeled into a learning experience. In schools such as this one where discipline all too frequently detracts from learning, children in this type of classroom fare better than most.

Documenting and Evaluating Speaking and Listening

"Kidwatching" is a hallmark of whole language classrooms (Y. Goodman, 1991). Watching for kids' growth in purposeful listening and meaningful talking is essential for the whole language teacher. Teachers who are engaged in observing children's responses to instructional events in the classroom are necessarily observing all four language modes. They are collecting and analyzing information they need to plan curriculum and adapt their plans responsively. Reflective observation for purposes of planning and evaluation is continuous and documented.

As with reading and writing, checklists may initially prove helpful for recording and analyzing observations of children's speaking and listening performance. Figures 7.1 and 7.2 are examples of the types of checklists teachers might use in documenting learners' growth in oral language.

Selected Strategies: A Cooperative Learning-Based Classroom

In whole language classrooms, students work together exploring their own writing, high-quality literature, and informational content. The two most obvious classroom events that naturally improve listening and speaking are listening to someone read aloud and listening to student authors read their own writing. Listening to someone read aloud is the first and most important kind of listening students do (see figure 7.3). Hearing good stories and information pieces read aloud gives learners models of literate texts that they need for their own reading and writing. Purposeful listening also occurs when authors share their working drafts for peer evaluation. When listeners know the author wants and expects a response, automatically a purposeful and authentic reason for listening exists.

Tompkins, Friend, and Smith (1984) assert that children say they listen in schools for only two reasons: to learn and to avoid being punished. A broader view of the purposes of listening might help us enhance the language curriculum. Generally, these purposes can include appreciative, discriminative, comprehensive, therapeutic, and critical listening. Appreciative listening is listening for enjoyment. Discriminative listening develops the ability to distinguish among sounds (for example, dogs barking or traffic noises) and to distinguish general sounds from the patterned sounds that constitute oral language. Comprehensive listening is listening in order to interpret the speaker's message. Therapeutic listening involves listening to another person talk through a problem. Critical listening is listening to both understand and evaluate the meaning of the spoken communication (Wolvin & Coakley, 1985).

As with other learning, an awareness of the processes involved in

---

STUDENT PROFILE: SPEAKING

Name: _____   Date: _____

Grade: _____   Setting: _____

	Always	**Sometimes**	**Not Yet**
1. Speaks clearly and distinctly			
2. Expresses self logically			
3. Uses inflection			
4. Uses language in appropriate ways			
5. Relates experiences in school to personal life			
6. Speaks in complete sentences when appropriate			
7. Uses language in variety of ways			
8. Speaks with confidence			
9. Has well-developed vocabulary			
10. Other(s)			

Teacher Comments:

---

listening appears to have a positive effect on it. And, as with reading and writing, listening develops best when it serves the learner's needs from the learner's point of view. A reciprocal relationship also appears to exist between growth in listening and growth in reading comprehension (Pearson & Fielding, 1982).

Discussing and Storytelling   In addition to read aloud, authors' circle, and author's chair, a number of authentic purposes for listening emerge in group sessions of storytelling discussions of a topic or discussions about a good book.

FIGURE 7.1
Sample Evaluation
Form for Speaking

Group Discussions   Small group discussion is the most frequent means of incorporating authentic talking and listening in the classroom (see figure 7.4). Group discussion may be informal, as in spur-of-the-moment planning for acting out a story. It may also be formal, as in literature study groups, peer editing, authors' circle, or project planning and presentation. Listening opportunities that are natural—that is, embedded in the context of authentic language experiences—develop listening most effectively. Authentic listening occurs when a person is speaking about a subject of interest to the audience.

FIGURE 7.2
Sample Evaluation
Form for Listening

STUDENT PROFILE: LISTENING

Name: _____   Date: _____

Grade: _____   Setting: _____

	Always	**Sometimes**	**Not Yet**
1. Hears clearly and accurately			
2. Understands main ideas			
3. Remembers important details			
4. Draws reasonable conclusions			
5. Makes reasonable predictions			
6. Makes logical judgments			
7. Retells complete stories			
8. Listens for variety of purposes			
9. Listens attentively			
10. Other(s)			

Teacher Comments:

FIGURE 7.3
Attentive Listening

Effective discussion and planning groups do not just happen. Teachers teach children how to conduct collaborative and cooperative groups by modeling group processes at the beginning of the year. As they work with small groups or even entire classes, they may ask someone to keep a record of what the group decides. They may ask the students to select a timekeeper, a moderator, or a group leader. The children and the teacher discuss what needs to happen for the group to accomplish its purpose. These procedures may be written and posted somewhere in the room so that the group processes that facilitate the accomplishment of the task are examined and made overt. For example, after several group events directed by the teacher, one second-grade class decided on the following procedures for successful groups: pick a leader, pick a recorder, discuss your topic, brainstorm, divide the work, meet when

FIGURE 7.4
Group Planning and Sharing

needed, be respectful, present findings to rest of class (optional). These were written on chart paper and displayed.

Teachers also model appropriate group behavior in peer-editing groups, literature study groups, and other small discussion groups that have a definite structure. Listening and speaking occur naturally within these groups, each reinforcing the other. Children learn language by using the language to make meaning with a purpose. As children negotiate, question, compliment, suggest, argue, and share their thinking on classroom problems and projects their oral language grows.

Children in problem-solving and project-planning groups benefit from prior group experience. They need only the slightest suggestions from the teacher about how to organize and get started if they have participated in peer editing, authors' circle, and other group discussions. (Also see The Research Paper or Project in chapter 10 for further help in breaking the process down into logical and manageable components.)

Panel Discussions   Another type of group discussion is the panel or round table discussion. Although panel discussions are most often employed by teachers in middle or upper grades, younger children are also quite capable of conducting them. Panel and round table presentations are an alternative to the individual and group report. Students researching subtopics of the same general topic may coordinate their findings and present their information to the larger group in the form of a panel discussion. In order to share their findings, they must talk and listen to each other.

One group of fifth graders researching African American literature subdivided their topic into these parts: Revolutionary War, slavery and the Civil War, current stories, music and poetry. When they finished reading and talking among themselves and with their teacher, they decided to present a panel discussion of their work. They developed a "program" for the session, with an overall title for their project and a more specific title for each presenter. They showed examples of the materials they had read and played samples of African American music, such as blues, ragtime, and rap. They shared audiotapes of two writers reading their own poetry and displayed pictures of the authors they were discussing. When the group presentations were finished, the panel presenters asked for questions and comments from the audience. In order for the members of the audience to ask meaningful questions they had to be active participants—they had to really hear, attend to, and think about what they were listening to. The panel presentation was so successful that the students were asked to present it to other classrooms.

Oral Storytelling   Enhancing children's sense of story and their self-confidence as performers aids in developing the whole child. These two areas are supported simultaneously when children are encouraged to tell stories. Young children may make up their own stories or retell familiar ones like "Little Red Riding Hood" or "The Three Pigs."

Oral storytelling is a valuable experience that may be used as an alternative to book reports. Teachers interested in exploring the potential benefits of regular oral storytelling might begin by telling stories to children. Many teachers choose to use oral storytelling very informally with young children.

Teachers may establish a place in the classroom, a raised platform perhaps, with a "storytelling chair." Props may be made available but probably should be kept simple—shoes, hats, scarves, and the like. At least one person per day or several persons on a designated day may sign up to tell a story during storytelling time.

When older children are planning to tell a story, the following steps might be helpful for them:

1. Select a story you especially want to tell.

2. Read the story several times until you are very familiar with it.

3. Jot down the major events of the story and arrange them in sequence, noting who did what to whom and why. (optional)

4. Lay the story aside and with eyes closed, visualize the story from beginning to end.

5. Then, return to the book and reread the story with expression as if an audience were listening and watching.

6. Finally, close the book and tell the story in your own words, bringing the characters and the action to life with your voice and your own inner vision of the story. A story may be practiced at home, with a friend, or on the tape recorder before it is performed for the class.

Telling Stories with Wordless Picture Books   One of the key elements in learning to read and write well is learning to think like an author. Thinking like an author is beneficial for young children, for children who appear to be word callers (those who do not fully comprehend when they read orally), and for children who have difficulty writing stories. Becoming the author is what happens when learners tell stories for wordless picture books.

Examine any good wordless picture book, for example, *Deep in the Forest* by Turkle or *Window* by Baker. Encourage the children to look closely at the details in the illustrations. Talk about how these carry the story line. As the story is initially explored, predict what is likely to come next. Then have the children help you tell the story the way a writer would write it. In large groups the illustrations may have to be shown with an opaque projector or a big book.

After the story has been told several times, the students may wish to write it. Several wordless picture books may be made available for the children to explore, perhaps at the listening center, where children can tape-record themselves. Children may also create their own wordless picture book by cutting pictures from magazines and arranging them in story form. These creations may be given to another group of children to tell.

The following is a short list of wordless or nearly wordless picture books. As you explore this genre, you may find several others written by the same authors.

Ahlberg, J., & Ahlberg, A. (1978). *Each Peach Pear Plum: An "I Spy" Story*. New York: Scholastic.
Alexander, M. (1970). *Bobo's Dream*. New York: Dial Press.
Anno, M. (1978). *Anno's Journey*. New York: Philomel.
Baker, J. (1991). *Window*. Sydney, Australia: Julia MacRae Books.
Briggs, R. (1978). *The Snowman*. New York: Random House.

Collington, P. (1987). *The Angel and the Soldier Boy.* New York: Knopf.

Day, A. (1985). *Good Dog Carl.* LaJolla, CA: Green Tiger Press.

de Paola, T. (1981). *The Hunter and the Animals.* New York: Holiday House.

Drescher, H. (1987). *The Yellow Umbrella.* New York: Bradbury.

Keats, E. (1982). *Clementina's Cactus.* New York: Viking Press.

McCully, E. (1988). *New Baby.* New York: Harper & Row.

Mayer, M. (1967). *A Boy, a Dog, and a Frog.* New York: Dial Press.

Mayer, M., & Mayer, M. (1975). *One Frog Too Many.* New York: Dial Press.

Ormerod, J. (1981). *Sunshine.* New York: Penguin Books.

Spier, P. (1982). *Peter Spier's Rain.* New York: Doubleday.

Turkle, B. (1976). *Deep in the Forest.* New York: Dutton.

Wiesner, D. (1988). *Free Fall.* New York: Lothrop, Lee & Shephard.

Wiesner, D. (1991). *Tuesday.* New York: Lothrop, Lee & Shephard.

Young, E. (1984). *The Other Bone.* New York: Harper & Row.

Zolotow, C. (1967). *Summer Is . . .* New York: Crowell.

The Listening Center   Many classrooms today have an area specially designated as the listening center. Usually a table or cubicle becomes the listening center and houses audiotape players and headphones. Students may listen to tapes without disturbing the rest of the class. Teachers stockpile tapes and corresponding written texts from stories, poems, and information materials. Choosing to read and listen to tapes of poems from Prelutsky's *The New Kid on the Block* as part of a unit on Things That Are New, or choosing to read and listen to tapes of Ashley Bryan telling African folk tales during a unit on Folk Tales from Around the World enhances students' comprehensive and appreciative listening. Student-made tapes of their own oral or written stories expands the classroom collection.

Show and Tell   Show-and-tell time, a familiar part of many kindergarten and primary classrooms, establishes the relationship between things the child prizes and finds interesting outside of school and the learning and sharing that occur in school. Show and tell also establishes the relationship between talking and listening. After the presenter has shared, a question-and-answer time ensues. Show and tell is not just the presenter telling about an item and then sitting down. When children ask thoughtful questions and receive meaningful responses, real listening and talking have occurred.

Teachers may structure show and tell by asking for specific types of items, such as artifacts related to the current unit of study. They may have a sign-up sheet for "Tomorrow's Show and Tell." Show and tell may take place daily or only two or three times a week. To take advantage of time constraints, some teachers divide the class into groups so that more people have an opportunity to share. Yet even when show and tell is highly structured, finding time for an occasional unannounced show and tell may be valuable (one child who had been out of school for surgery brought his appendix in a jar of formaldehyde).

Since whole language teachers look for ways to connect good books with other school and home learning, many teachers find *Show and Tell* by Munsch an enjoyable and instructive way to introduce this activity at the beginning of the year. This book is useful for exploring what types of items are appropriate for show and tell and which are better left home. In the book a child brings his new baby brother to school in his book bag.

Telephone Conversations   More than just play in the primary grade classroom, playing telephone is authentic language experience. Not only do children learn about the importance of speaking clearly and taking turns during a conversation, they also develop many other vital skills. By role playing what to do if someone is injured and needs assistance, they learn how to use the telephone in an emergency situation. By exploring these situations, they discover the need for listening to instructions and providing accurate and complete directions.

They may also learn how to use the telephone as a research tool. As adults, we gather a great deal of information by phone. For example, we use the phone to find out about air fares and schedules, city bus routes, movie times, the comparative cost of a new appliance, or where to have the car repaired. Thoughtful teachers identify purposeful ways for children to gather information from several sources, using a variety of tools and techniques.

After reading *Michael Bird Boy* by de Paola, a first-grade class wanted to know if there were any women bosses in the local factories and businesses. Their teacher helped them prepare, practice, and conduct a telephone survey. He also helped the children make sense of the information they gathered and develop ways to share it with other people in the school. Speaking, listening, reading, and writing were all used in preparing the survey, implementing the project, gathering and analyzing the information and reporting the findings. These first graders were researchers, in a rather formal sense.

Oral Clozure   Most teachers instinctively know that oral clozure is helpful to young readers. That is, when reading aloud from a predictable book, most teachers will pause on highly predictable words and wait for the children to supply the meaningful text. For example, "There is a house, a napping house, where everyone is _____" (from *The Napping House* by Wood).

This strategy, common during guided reading in the early grades, causes learners to use all the cueing systems—graphophonic, syntactic, and semantic. Good books, even those that do not have repetitious lines or rhyming patterns, contain predictable words and ideas. For example: "The bridge was my most prized possession. . . . All I had to do was fly over it for it to be mine forever. I can wear it like a giant diamond _____" (from *Tar Beach* by Ringgold). Oral clozure helps learners understand the active part that listeners play in comprehending the message.

Creative Dramatics   Drama in all its forms encourages self-expression; it is also another way learners come to know their world. *Creative dramatics* is an umbrella term for the many types of creative and dramatic activities teachers may encourage. These include acting, improvisation, mime and movement, role playing, and puppetry. Creative dramatics helps children develop stage presence, control body movements, develop visual imagery, identify the salient features of a concept or an event, and think and plan sequentially. Different activities allow for the integration of each of the language arts as students plan, practice, produce, and perform their works. A variety of drama activities used along with good literature helps children develop a sense of story, of action and characters, and of the power of their own imaginations. But perhaps most fundamental of all, drama turns vicarious experiences into active and concrete experiences. This is especially important for elementary-age learners.

Pantomime   Actions that are designed to convey ideas without words are called pantomime (sometimes referred to as mime, from the word *mimic,* and movement). Because it is nonverbal, it is highly imaginative. Pantomime helps children solve problems together and attend to details. Teachers may use pantomime to represent a story that the children have read. Teachers encourage students to visualize what they want to present; they talk with students about how to do something without being able to tell the audience what they are doing. Teachers may create their own mimes for the students to watch and discuss, show a film on mime, or participate in group mimes with their students. Another popular example of pantomime is the game of charades. Book titles readily lend themselves to acting out in charades.

Role Playing and Acting Out Stories   Other forms of creative dramatics include role playing and acting out stories. They may be spontaneous and unrehearsed, like improvisation or make-believe, or they may result in complete theatrical productions with scripts, props, costumes, and scenery.

Teachers of young children may develop a Let's Pretend or make-believe area in the room, as shown in figure 7.5. Sometimes props are stored in the area for the children to use in their role playing. Much rich oral language naturally flows from these creative activities. The function and contents of the area change to meet children's needs, interests, or curricular goals. Familiar places of business provide the interest, and in many instances the props, for extended role play. For example, following a visit to the bank, the teacher and the children in one kindergarten created a teller's window from a cardboard box in their Let's Pretend area. They collected

FIGURE 7.5
Let's Pretend Center

forms from the bank: blank counter checks, savings account pass books, deposit slips, withdrawal slips, coin wrappers, and money pouches. With the addition of a little play money, the children were ready to be tellers, depositors, withdrawers, people in need of loans, and so on.

Role playing being a hairdresser, doctor, builder, veterinarian, dentist, grocer, teacher, bus driver, or pilot involves language and learning as children explore the world of possibilities and connect remote abstraction to present reality.

Role playing and other creative drama are frequently ways for learners to present their understanding of literature they have read; they can recreate the story, character and plot development, or emotional content.

After reading *Frank and Ernest* by Day, one group of third-grade students set up a "diner" in their classroom. They explored being short-order cooks and customers. They made menus and advertised their diner. They experimented with the slang terms in the book and created a few of their own. Their teacher encouraged them and took the opportunity to incorporate math as well.

Older students may also role play to examine good literature or act out their own or other students' stories. Improvisation, mime, and readers theater are ways for students to develop skits that explore the tone set by an author, expectations of the reader, or character motivations. Planned role playing, whether as general outline or as a complete written script, engages learners in the composing and creating process as well as in all modes of language. Acting out or role playing as a way to examine the relationship between Winnie Foster and Angus Tuck in Babbitt's *Tuck Everlasting* or that between the boy and his mother in Armstrong's *Sounder* make powerful and lasting impressions on participants and audience alike. Acting and role playing help foster the learner's personal experiences with books and build students' writing capabilities in character development, feelings, dialogue, and description.

Puppetry   Storytelling with such devices as puppets, flannel boards, and masks are variations of creative drama opportunities. Because these techniques remove the storyteller from direct contact with the audience, they may make storytelling a bit easier for the beginner. Puppets are popular with young children and are often highly motivating to reluctant readers. They help children work cooperatively, provide creative outlets for them, and allow for the integration of talking, listening, reading, writing, music, art, storytelling, and content.

Many elementary classrooms have a folding puppet theater, but even without a commercially prepared "theater," puppet productions are easy to arrange. A small draped table placed in front of a doorway quickly makes an excellent puppet stage. The children kneel behind the drape, and the action takes place on the table. Boxes that once held large appliances, such as refrigerators or automatic washers, make excellent puppet theaters. A large rectangle or square is cut into one side of the box, and two pieces of cloth are strung across the inside of the opening. The children presenting the drama hide inside the box; the audience views the action through the opening. The box may be covered with contact paper or heavy wallpaper to further strengthen and reinforce the cardboard, or it may be painted and decorated by the children.

A number of types of puppets may be constructed by students from inexpensive or discarded household materials, as shown in figure 7.6. Frequently these are more popular than puppets teachers buy. An important part of the learning resides in creating the puppets, masks, or flannel board characters. As children decide how their character will look, what materials they will use, and how to show certain character or story traits, decision making, cooperative planning, and problem solving become authentic experiences. For instance, figuring out how to show a magic pot forever boiling over requires some ingenuity.

According to Briggs and Wagner (1979), several criteria should be considered when helping children determine if a story is appropriate for a puppet presentation. Among them are briskly moving action, characters that allow the children to explore voice as well as movement, and familiarity of the story. The size of the stage or puppet theater may also need to be considered when selecting a story. Those with too many characters or too many different scenes may not work in homemade theaters.

After an appropriate story has been chosen, rehearsal is the second key to successful puppet theater. Each scene should be practiced so that each child can coordinate moving his or her puppet and speaking its lines. As with all informal classroom drama, improvisation is preferred over memorization. Improvisation allows children to participate in an activity in which risk taking and self-expression are encouraged and valued.

Choral Speaking and Choral Reading   Choral speaking and reading of literature involves learners with books and other literary forms in nonthreatening ways. It gives students practice memorizing text. It may help learners interpret literature as they make decisions about how to present selections they wish to read. It promotes a sense of the rhythm and flow of language. The simplest and most common format is for students to speak or read a text in unison. However, they may speak or read in groups as one responds to the

FIGURE 7.6   Easy-to-Make Puppets

FINGER PUPPETS

Finger Puppet
(with Velcro tabs)

Finger Puppet
(from old glove finger)

Toilet Paper Roller Puppet

STICK PUPPETS

Stick Puppet

Paper Cup Puppet

Paper Plate Puppet

HAND PUPPETS

Sock Puppet

Paper Bag Puppet

Cloth Puppet

other—for example, boys and girls or left side and right side of the room. Choral events may also involve individuals speaking or reading a part with the chorus joining in as in a refrain. Several groups may read as in a round, with two, three, or more groups joining in at certain intervals.

Poetry and nursery rhymes may be the most common material used for choral reading. *Animals Animals* by Carle, *Joyful Noise* by Fleishman, *Nathaniel Talking* by Greenfield, *Where the Sidewalk Ends* by Silverstein, and *Possum Come a Knockin'* by Van Laan are gold mines for choral presentations. Poems for older learners such as "The Creation" by James Weldon Johnson, "The Ballad of the Harpweaver" by Edna Millay, or *Spin a Soft Black Song* by Giovanni also make interesting group presentations. As with most projects, students are put in charge and are encouraged to experiment and explore. Helping students investigate combinations of group and solo voices, varied expressions, rhythm patterns, and arrangements to interpret their piece enhances not only oral language learning, but learning about written language as well.

Structured Talking and Listening Events

Most of the speech and listening events described above require some planning and may involve a degree of practice, but they are more spontaneous than the two strategies described next. Students can derive many benefits from opportunities to engage in planned interviews and formal and informal debates.

Interviews   A set of techniques with which most students are familiar is the interview. Through television, they have seen people interviewed for any number of reasons. Interviewers talk to persons who have survived a recent disaster, won a prestigious award, run for public office, or defended themselves against an impending indictment. Interviewers gain first-hand information as a way of coming to know and understand the world. They acquire experience organizing and presenting information, talking to unfamiliar persons, and asking appropriate questions. Both interviewers and interviewees must be active listeners in order to respond appropriately and meaningfully. Interviews may be conducted by groups or the entire class; they may take place between pairs of students as a way of presenting information to an audience.

Interviews logically consist of three parts: planning, conducting, and sharing or discussing. When an interviewee is scheduled to present for the group, the teacher and students may prepare by brainstorming what they already know or think they know about the speaker's subject. Then using their list, they may break into small groups to generate questions they want to ask the speaker. Questions are written on note cards to give to each student. If the speaker answers the question during the presentation, the student writes the answer on the card. If the speaker does not answer the question, the student asks it and records the answer during the follow-up question-and-answer or discussion time.

Interviewing helps build self-confidence and gives the learner practice in both oral language (asking questions) and written language (taking notes). Sharing the results of interviews requires organizing and synthesizing information. The actual words of the informant as well as impressions and perceptions of the interviewer will need to be shared. Learners may write out their reports or they may arrange their notes, add comments and perceptions, and present these orally. Oral presentation might take the form of television news interviews. They might be accompanied by posters, drawings, photographs, or other visual and textual displays.

The list of persons to interview is endless: family members, local historians, storytellers, businesspeople, community leaders, local artists, an award-winning scientist at the local university or the president of a local group. Interviews are most successful and appropriate when learners decide they have a need to know. Teachers may also see authentic opportunities and suggest conducting interviews as a means for learners to extend their knowledge and skills.

Debates   Another way learners develop language skills is through debates, which are controlled arguments by informed persons with opposing views. The purpose of a debate is to persuade the members of the audience. Debates may be informal or formal. Informal debates may be used when the entire class is excited about an issue and most or all of the students have taken a position either for or against the central problem or controversy (Hoskisson & Tompkins, 1987).

For example, as one group of fifth graders worked through a unit on ecology and rain forests, students encountered the issues related to clear-cutting of forests. Students disagreed with one another and occasionally the discussions became quite intense. Their teacher suggested an informal debate. Those who supported whatever was needed to preserve jobs for people took one side, and those who thought the federal government should intervene to save the forests and the endangered wildlife took the other side. Students were asked to state the reasons for their positions. Questions were then asked and answers given. Then students had an opportunity to change sides. Those who did were required to tell why.

Informal debates encourage self-expression in learners; in debates everyone's opinion is valuable. Debates allow teachers to gauge the extent of the information students have acquired and how well they have synthesized and organized it. They promote growth in speaking and listening as presenters work to make their positions clear and audiences follow arguments and draw conclusions.

Unlike informal debates, formal debates are highly structured and well-researched arguments between two teams taking opposing sides of a proposition. They are difficult to do well and are usually not attempted until high school. However, teachers who know the general guidelines for setting up and conducting formal debates may wish to offer older elementary students the opportunity.

Formal debates might be presented as a culminating activity at the end of a unit of study or as an event to present information in which students are intensely interested. A proposition suitable for formal debate is a statement calling for change in the status quo of some issue or condition. The affirmative team asks for the change. The negative team denies the need for the change. The affirmative team is responsible for devising a plan for implementing the "needed" change. They must demonstrate the advantages of the change and of their plan. The negative team attacks the plan and shows its disadvantages.

Formal debates take place in two parts. The first part is the construction in which each team member has eight to ten minutes to speak. Their job is to construct the team's case. This is followed by the rebuttal phase. At this time each team member speaks for four to five minutes. Teams consist of two members; the debate is usually conducted by a moderator who introduces each speaker and keeps track of time. Formal debates are arranged as follows:

Phase I: The Construction

1st affirmative speaker establishes the need for the change.

1st negative speaker denies the need for change and tells why.

2nd affirmative speaker presents the plan for change and its advantages.

2nd negative speaker attacks the plan and presents its disadvantages.

Phase II: The Rebuttal

1st negative speaker reiterates and attacks the case set up by the affirmative.

1st affirmative speaker reiterates and attacks the position of the negative team.

2nd negative speaker continues the attack and summarizes their position.

2nd affirmative speaker reiterates need for change and summarizes their position.

Teachers may modify these procedures. An excellent source for more in-depth information about helping students conduct formal debates is Ericson (1987).

Propositions for debate are expressed in terms of a resolution. For example, "Resolved, students should participate in setting school dress codes" or "Resolved, the federal government should develop a national health care system." Whether directly related to school events or not, for best results, the debates should address meaningful issues near and dear to the hearts of the students.

Many teachers who help students create and present formal debates also have them select judges. Sometimes the class as audience votes for the winning team. Discussing how the vote came out and why students voted as they did is frequently an interesting and valuable learning event. This provides teachers opportunities to explore criteria that a judge—that is, a critical listener—should use to determine which side actually presented the better case.

Miscellaneous Strategies: Having Fun with Language   A wealth of theoretically sound strategies are available for engaging learners in authentic talking and listening in the classroom. While oral storytelling and choral speaking are entertaining, debates and panel discussions are somewhat more intense. Here we describe briefly several strategies that are smaller in scope than a debate or a literature study and discussion. Nevertheless, they are instructive and enjoyable. Adapt them to fit your needs and purposes.

A Listening Walk   Taken early in the year, a listening walk helps young children become familiar with their surroundings and develops discriminative listening, especially if the group later discusses what they heard and how they knew. Using Paul Showers's *The Listening Walk,* teachers read the story aloud, then take their students on a neighborhood trek. The children are directed to listen carefully and to note all the different sounds they hear, where they hear them, and what they mean. Discussions of the children's discoveries take place when the group returns to the classroom. Children may wish to draw captioned pictures of their favorite sound. The group may decide to repeat the trip with an audiotape recorder and prepare a tape for their listening center with a narrator asking the listener to identify the sounds. Listening walks might evolve into color walks and smell walks to explore the senses and the environment.

Visual Imagery and Imagining   Constructing and retaining meaning require visual imagery and imagining. Visual imagery is one of the abilities proficient readers develop and one that may decline when children have too many images created for them in the form of television and movies. *Frederick* and *Fish Is Fish* by Leo Lionni are excellent illustrations of imagery teachers might use to engage learners in the concept initially.

To further explore visual imagery, children may close their eyes and visualize a concrete object such as a puppy. Ask them if they can "see" it, "touch" it, "smell" it. After each attempt at pretend sensory experiences, have the children talk about what happened. Ask them what words they might use to describe the object. Discuss how their descriptions differ.

Teachers may prepare a short talk about a place they are very familiar with—for example, the beaches of North Carolina's Outer Banks, the wheat fields of the Great Plains, or the giant redwood forests of northern California. Make sure the talk is full of details and description. Ask the children to draw mental pictures, to *imagine* the place, as you tell them about it. Then they might draw real pictures or make lists of the sights, sounds, and smells they heard. These may be compared with photos of the actual place. Students can follow suit by preparing to describe for their classmates a place with which they are very familiar.

Chain Stories   Learners may benefit from exploring the differences and inaccuracies that occur when groups or individuals listen. Teachers may select and rehearse the telling of a new story for the group. Before the first telling, four to six students are asked to participate. All but one leaves the room to wait outside in the hallway. The teacher then tells the story to the group, audiotaping the story. One of the students from out in the hall is asked to come back into the room. The student who remained in the classroom to hear the first telling of the story has to retell it. Then each student from the hallway hears the story from the preceding student, the last one telling the next one until all the students from the hallway have heard and retold the story. The final retelling is audiotaped.

The majority of students in the class have acted as audience and have been observing the chain of events. They lead the discussion, describing what went on and why they think the story changed the way it did. The teacher may play back both the original and the final versions. Learners are encouraged to decide when it is all right to alter a speaker's (or a writer's) message and when it isn't. They might relate this experience to their lives both in and out of school.

The strategies cited in this chapter are not isolated activities from workbooks or manuals of teaching ideas. Conducting practice activities in speaking and listening, no matter how well-formed the instruction, cannot be as effective as providing a great many opportunities for listening for *real* reasons to authentic speech events that are interesting to learners. However, teachers may occasionally introduce speaking and listening strategies to serve as a foundation for future application to reading and writing, as well as to broaden children's experiences with language.

SUMMARY

Speaking and listening are reciprocal aspects of oral language; each reinforces the other. Indeed, under normal circumstances one does not occur without the other. Like reading and writing abilities, oral language abilities are learned as they are used—in natural contexts, for real reasons.

Halliday (1978) identified seven functions for speaking in which children engage. Wolvin and Coakley (1985) found at least five purposes learners have for listening. This chapter has described the integration of natural speech and listening events into classrooms where students are using language in all its forms to explore the world around them.

Oral language learning is an active, constructive process. It does not stop when children enter school. However, the ways that schools treat speaking and listening are very different from the ways they naturally occur at home. Typically, oral language in school is more restrictive than natural development would indicate. Because oral language is crucial to the learning process, sound instructional practices teach listening and speaking as integrated with their purposes, each other, or the other forms of language.

THEORY-TO-PRACTICE CONNECTIONS

Speaking and Listening Theory

1. Oral language is learned as it is used.

2. Oral language is a symbolic system for representing meaning and our understanding of the world.

3. Listening and speaking reinforce each other, and they reinforce reading and writing.

Examples of Classroom Practice

1. Group discussion and storytelling events

2. Panel discussions and debates, group presentations

3. Play acting and choral speaking, readers theater

Speaking and Listening Theory	*Examples of Classroom Practice*
4. Listening, speaking, reading, writing, and thinking are integrated with content in authentic experiences for learners.	**4.** Interviews
5. Listening and speaking opportunities enhance self-expression and self-concept.	**5.** Pantomime, role play, and puppetry

SUGGESTED READINGS

Barrs, M., Ellis, S., Hester, H., & Thomas, A. (1989). *The primary language record: Handbook for teachers.* Portsmouth, NH: Heinemann.

Barton, R. (1986). *Tell me another: Storytelling and reading aloud at school and at home.* Portsmouth, NH: Heinemann.

Booth, D., & Thornley-Hall, C. (Eds.). (1991a). *Classroom talk.* Portsmouth, NH: Heinemann.

Booth, D., & Thornley-Hall, C. (Eds.). (1991b). *The talk curriculum.* Portsmouth, NH: Heinemann.

Daniel, A. (Ed.). (1992). *Activities integrating oral communication skills for students grades K–8.* Annandale, VA: Speech Communication Association.

SUGGESTED ACTIVITIES

1. Discuss how the instructional examples cited above put whole language theory into practice.

2. Identify several ways the teacher could engage students in functional math in the "diner in the classroom" described in this chapter.

3. List several props children would need for each of the role-playing jobs cited in the section Role Playing and Acting Out Stories. Name other types of role play children might enjoy. What props might facilitate these roles?

4. Obtain a copy of the Speech Communication Association's integrated activities book cited in Suggested Readings (Daniel, 1992). Read and select several that you find interesting and potentially useful in the elementary classroom. How do they fit your developing theory of learning and teaching? With what classroom content might you employ one of these integrated activities? Would it need to be adapted? If so, in what way?

5. Since we believe that teachers are learners and that they should engage in the same learning events they ask of their students, we suggest that you select a piece of high-quality children's literature that meets the criteria established on page 177. Working with a small group, create a flannel board story or puppet theater presentation from an appropriate piece of children's literature. Then present your creation; discuss what you learned.

REFERENCES

Barrs, M., Ellis, S., Hester, H., & Thomas, A. (1989). *The primary language record: Handbook for teachers.* Portsmouth, NH: Heinemann.

Barton, R. (1986). *Tell me another: Storytelling and reading aloud at home.* Portsmouth, NH: Heinemann.

Barton, R., & Booth, D. (1990). *Stories in the classroom.* Portsmouth, NH: Heinemann.

Booth, D., & Thornley-Hall, C. (Eds.). (1991a). *Classroom talk.* Portsmouth, NH: Heinemann.

Booth, D., & Thornley-Hall, C. (Eds.). (1991b). *The talk curriculum.* Portsmouth, NH: Heinemann.

Briggs, N., & Wagner, J. (1979). *Children's literature through storytelling and drama.* Dubuque, IA: William C. Brown.

Britton, J. (1976). *Language and learning.* London: Penguin.

D'Angelo, K. (1979). Wordless picturebooks: Also for the writer. *Language Arts, 56,* 813–814.

Daniel, A. (Ed.). (1992). *Activities integrating oral communication skills for students grades K–8.* Annandale, VA: Speech Communication Association.

Deglar, L. (1979). Putting words into wordless picturebooks. *The Reading Teacher, 30,* 399–402.

Devine, T. (1978). Listening: What we know after 50 years of theorizing. *Journal of Reading, 21,* 296–304.

Dillon, D., & Searle, D. (1981). The role of language in one first grade classroom. *Research in the Teaching of English, 15,* 311–328.

Donaldson. M. (1978). *Children's minds.* New York: W. W. Norton.

Ericson, J. (1987). *Debater's guide: Revised edition.* Carbondale, IL: Southern Illinois University Press.

Fisher, C., & Terry, A. (1990). *Children's language and the language arts: A literature-based approach.* Boston: Allyn & Bacon.

Fox, S., & Allen, V. (1983). *The language arts: An integrated approach.* New York: Holt.

Goodman, Y. (1991). Kidwatching: Observing children in the classroom. In D. Booth & C. Thornley-Hall (Eds.), *The talk curriculum.* Portsmouth, NH: Heinemann.

Guidelines for developing oral communication curricula in kindergarten through twelfth grade. (1991, September). Annandale, VA: Speech Communication Association.

Haley-James, S., & Hobson, C. (1980). Interviewing as a means of encouraging the drive to communicate. *Language Arts, 57,* 497–502.

Halliday, M. (1978). The functional basis of language. In B. Bernstein (Ed.), *Class, codes, and control. Vol. 2: Applied studies toward a sociology of language.* Boston: Routledge and Kegan Paul.

Hall, S. (1990). *Using picture storybooks to teach literary devices.* Phoenix: Oryx Press.

Hoskisson, K., & Tompkins, G. (1987). *Language arts: Content and teaching strategies.* Columbus, OH: Merrill.

Huff, S. (1991). Types of problem-solving talk in the classroom. In D. Booth & C. Thornley-Hall (Eds.), *Classroom talk.* Portsmouth, NH: Heinemann.

Jaggar, A. (1980). Allowing for language differences. In G. Pinnell (Ed.), *Discovering language with children* (pp. 25–28). Urbana, IL: NCTE.

Knapp, B. (1991). Talk and the quiet child. In D. Booth & C. Thornley-Hall (Eds.), *Classroom talk.* Portsmouth, NH: Heinemann.

Lundsteen, S. (1979). *Listening: Its impact on reading and the other language arts.* Urbana, IL: NCTE.

Martinez, M., & Rosen, N. (1985). The value of

repeated readings during storytime. *The Reading Teacher, 38,* 782–786.

McGee, L., & Tompkins, G. (1983). Wordless picturebooks are for older readers too. *Journal of Reading, 27,* 120–123.

National Council of Teachers of English (1983). Forum: Essentials of English, *Language Arts, 60,* 244–248.

Norton, D. (1993). *The effective teaching of language arts.* New York: Macmillan.

Pearson, P. D., & Fielding, L. (1982). Research update: Listening Comprehension. *Language Arts, 59,* 617–629.

Paley, V. (1985). *Wally's stories: Conversations in the kindergarten.* Cambridge, MA: Harvard University Press.

Peterson, R., & Eeds, M. (1988) *Grand conversations: Literature* groups in action. Toronto, Ontario: Scholastic.

Pinnell, G. S. (1975). Language in the primary classroom. *Theory into Practice, 14,* 318–327.

Roth, R. (1986). Practical use of language in the school. *Language Arts, 63,* 134–142.

Scher, A., & Verrall, C. (1992). *200+ ideas for drama.* Portsmouth, NH: Heinemann.

Siks, G. (1983). *Drama with children.* New York: Harper & Row.

Sloyer, S. (1982). *Readers' theater: Story dramatization in the classroom.* Urbana, IL: NCTE.

Smith, F. (1988). *Joining the literacy club.* Portsmouth, NH: Heinemann.

Spolin, V. (1986). *Theater games for the classroom.* Evanston, IL: Northwestern University Press.

Talking to learn: Classroom practices in teaching English. (1991). Urbana, IL: NCTE.

Tompkins, G., Friend, M., & Smith, P. (1984). Children's metacognitive knowledge about listening. Presentation at the American Educational Research Association Convention, New Orleans, LA.

Watts, I. (1990). *Just a minute: Ten short plays and activities for your classroom with rehearsal strategies to accompany multicultural stories from around the world.* Portsmouth, NH: Heinemann.

Wells, G. (1986). *The meaning makers: Children learning language and using language.* Toronto, Ontario: Unwin.

Wells, J. (1980). *Children's language and learning.* Englewood Cliffs, NJ: Prentice-Hall.

White, C. (1990). *Jevon doesn't sit at the back anymore.* Richmond Hill, Ontario: Scholastic.

Wilkinson, L. (1984). Research currents: Peer group talk in elementary school. *Language Arts, 61,* 164–169.

Willbrand, M. L., & Rieke, R. (1983). *Teaching oral communication in elementary schools.* New York: Macmillan.

Wolvin, A., & Coakley, C. (1985). *Listening.* Dubuque, IA: William C. Brown.

8

Bringing It All Together

What do whole language classrooms have in common?

How are they likely to be different from one another?

What can the beginning whole language teacher do to get started?

What questions arise as teachers move into whole language?

Children construct their own language and literacy, and they use language and literacy to learn about the world. From the beginning, classrooms should be designed to facilitate these constructive explorations. In traditional classrooms, textbooks, workbooks, tests, and other materials structure the content of what children learn. Most traditional teachers present directed lessons and organize activities by ability groups. In whole language classrooms, teachers structure the planning and organization to fit their philosophy. To a very great extent, the content emerges as children and teachers discuss, read, write, and study good literature, real issues, and important concepts and events.

However, teachers and students are rarely completely free to design a classroom curriculum. Bureaucratic requirements, budget and time limitations, and community concerns bring other considerations. Integrated, language- and literature-based classrooms are a constant interaction between theory, application, reflective observation (or kidwatching), and external constraints. Most whole language teachers find ways to adapt to these constraints while remaining true to their philosophy. Their classrooms accommodate children with different interests, needs, and backgrounds, celebrating these differences and employing them in a truly multicultural sense.

But teachers who are in transition and beginning teachers who wish to teach differently from the traditional models have many legitimate questions and concerns. Among these are: What attributes do most whole language classrooms share? What is the best way to get started? How can changes in practice be justified to parents and principals? Where will the additional materials come from? Will the children learn the "skills" they need? Can adequate structure and direction be provided? Will standardized test scores be adversely affected?

This chapter's three broad aims are: first, to summarize the commonalities on which most whole language classrooms are based; second, to identify what teachers can do to get started; and third, to answer some questions frequently asked by teachers considering a more holistic instructional alternative.

Like all learners, teachers also require immersion in and demonstrations of whatever they are trying to learn. They require hands-on (that is, engagement) experiences and experimentation in low-risk environments. Their approximations will, over time, more closely resemble the instruction of experienced whole language teachers, especially if adequate networking and support systems are available. And both beginning and proficient whole language teachers need to read professional literature to keep in touch with new ideas and information.

What Whole Language Classrooms Have in Common

Classrooms that support constructive exploration and inquiry are busy places. They are collaborative; children work in pairs, small groups, and large groups. These classrooms are rich in materials and may even appear cluttered at times. These classrooms are active, imaginative, exciting, and sometimes noisy places. How children work in these environments is determined by the nature of what is being accomplished. Students read and are read to; they write, learn about science, use computers, develop math skills, and use information from social studies in projects that integrate content. Learners are not seated in straight rows, nor do they work in silent isolation on filling in the blanks in workbooks or copying from the chalkboard or textbooks. Whole language classrooms do not sound or look like traditional classrooms.

The work, movement, and noise in these classrooms are not aimless. Whole language classrooms are not chaotic (Cambourne, 1989). A difference exists between chaos and the noise of purposeful learning, the bustle of children going in different directions to accomplish various tasks. These classrooms buzz with the noise of students engaged in collaborative problem solving, group discussions, and creative projects, and interactions with teachers. Of course, some children do work independently, and, at times these classrooms are absolutely quiet.

However, directives such as "Please open your books to page 33" or "Jenny, pay attention!" are rarely heard. Teachers talk with individuals and small groups of children about what they are doing. They do relatively little ordering of children; rather, they do a great deal of listening, guiding, suggesting, negotiating, and encouraging. They often make comments or ask questions like these: "Good thinking!" "Tell me what you were imagining when you wrote this." "What do you plan to do next?" "How can I help?"

The classrooms themselves have a distinctive look (see figure 8.1). They are filled with print. Children's written work, art, lists, labels, charts, webs, and messages are abundant and prominently displayed. Poems, songs, and group stories are among the many examples of teacher-produced print in the room. Trade books, reference books, newspapers, magazines, catalogs, student-published books, and many other resources line the walls, shelves, and tabletops. The furniture, which is arranged for flexible grouping, may reflect what is going on that day. Some have no desks at all, only tables and perhaps one larger surface for projects. Some have areas where children can read and write in comfort. Certain spaces may be for general use, for conducting all kinds of projects; others may be devoted to specific uses, such as a science center, computer area,

FIGURE 8.1
The Look of One
Whole Language
Classroom

class grocery store, math center, listening center, editing table, or
free reading corner. Work materials, paper, pencils, markers, scis-
sors, and paint are stored openly for easy access. Some teachers keep
many of these items in small containers at each table; this arrangement eases the occasional student disagreement over availability of
supplies and relieves some of the need for shelf and drawer storage
space in these typically crowded classrooms.

Storage is nearly always a problem in whole language classrooms. The majority of schools were built when classrooms needed to house only a few sets of texts, workbooks, and desks for thirty students. Nevertheless, materials and other resources must be plentiful, because in these classrooms textbooks are used only as a resource (see figure 8.2). Science and social studies equipment—such as magnifying glasses, magnets, microscopes, globes and maps—are ideally in every room. Functional and environmental print is also prominent; lists of class activities, sign-up forms, observation logs, product labels, street and highway signs, newspapers, advertisements, and a written record of the class field trips are just a few examples (see figure 8.3). For very young children, classroom articles are often labeled in phrases or sentences, such as "our front door," "the east windows," "This is Ms. Smith's desk." Other needed materials may include a wealth of math manipulatives, art supplies, musical instru-

FIGURE 8.2
Shelves at the End of the Day

On signs,
On labels,
And in a book,
Words are
everywhere
you look.

FIGURE 8.3
Environmental Print
Display

ments, creative shelving for a wide range of children's literature, animal cages, and items supporting the current unit of study.

Much of the literature needed in whole language classrooms is expensive and has to be accumulated over a period of years. To do so, teachers may obtain small grants, use bonus points from children's book clubs, have bake sales, spend money from their own pockets, and so on. However, some of the printed materials needed in classrooms are cheap if not free. As fluent adult readers, we read a variety of materials on a daily basis. Catalogs, junk mail, bus schedules, phone books, product packages, bills, and other household reading materials can be brought in for children to read. Paper (colored paper, construction paper, butcher paper, chart paper) and a variety of writing implements (pens, pencils, markers, paints) are also necessary. Discarded computer paper is good for rough drafts and children's artwork.

The backdrop for all whole language classrooms is an environment rich in print and content. In *Creating the Child-Centered Classroom*, Susan Schwartz and Mindy Pollishuke (1991) list the print resources that a whole language classroom could include (the list is reprinted by permission):

fiction books	predictable books	picture books
wordless books	pattern books	big books
poetry	anthologies	novel sets
books with tapes or records	non-fiction books	lists
student writing	challenge cards	recipe books
message boards	felt boards	magnetic boards
encyclopedias	dictionaries	thesauri
telephone directories	writing center	mailboxes
newspapers	magazines	catalogues
television guides	student author displays	signs
library corner	drama area	puppets
labels	posters	audio-visual stuff

Children read to find out information and for pleasure. They write to convey information, record their reflections, express themselves, and for many other reasons. Nearly all these activities can and do go on simultaneously. When the teacher engages in direct teaching, it is usually in small group settings and in the context of these activities, although occasions for large group teaching do occur.

Children's needs and interests form the basis for choices among authentic events. For example, many classrooms developed and extended a natural curiosity about Christopher Columbus in the fall of 1992 when several new books and films marked the five hundredth anniversary of his famous voyage. Much questioning and rethinking of who Columbus was took place. Students asked about Native Americans' rights and consequences for them of the European invasion that followed Columbus. Many learners wondered about the possibility of earlier discoveries of the "new world" before Columbus. Student-generated questions were followed by reading, investigating, writing, sharing, and talking.

Since the children inform the curriculum, each classroom necessarily differs with their needs and interests, as well as with the teacher's style and personality. Most teachers spend time each day negotiating, planning, and arranging with the children what they will do that day. Choices may be very broad and numerous or narrowed to only three or four. Daily group planning may take place on the rug during large group sharing time. Each classroom forms its own routine. Some classes like poetry, so each day begins with one or two poems. Others prefer to start the day singing. In some classrooms, the day begins with a discussion of yesterday's events or of family and neighborhood news. Some teachers begin by sharing a new book or inviting a student to.

Whole language classrooms are frequently described as "inviting." This means they are bright and well lighted, clean, well organized and neat, and appealing to the eye. They are comfortable places to be. Above all, there is ample evidence that the children are co-creators of the space (see figure 8.4).

The sights, sounds, and materials of the classroom reflect the theoretical base of the teacher. Teachers believe in the collaborative nature of learning, in immersing children in good literature and rich content, in learner choices, and in the learner's taking responsibility. So they demonstrate strategies and processes; they engage children in active learning and they respect children's language, culture, and interests.

Teachers model what they want children to be able to do. They also demonstrate positive attitudes about the children and the children's abilities to learn. They value knowledge, thinking, and co-operative problem solving. They treat children with respect and kindness and require those same behaviors of the children. They expect children to do their best, and they maintain high but reachable standards for learning. Teachers who are curious and eager learners themselves find it easier to engage children in intellectual activity. Teachers who keep clean, organized, neat, and tastefully decorated classrooms provide inviting and predictable environments. When the children's work is mounted on colorful paper and carefully displayed, teachers demonstrate to their children that they value their children's work and their workplace.

Children spend most of their time finding information, interacting with others, reflecting on what they are learning, and presenting or sharing their learning in some way. Teachers spend most of their time explaining, facilitating, encouraging, counseling, demonstrating, attending, observing, documenting, evaluating, gathering materials, and collaborating. Activities revolve around thinking, content, and the use of language.

FIGURE 8.4
Whole Language
Classroom Display of
Children's Work

The classroom reflects the teacher's belief that learning is fun, continuous, useful, and important. Teachers do not spend hours preparing the classroom alone; they believe the room is the responsibility of the children. The walls, typically bare at the beginning of

FIGURE 8.5
Rug Time

the year, are bare again at the start of each new unit of study. They quickly fill up with children's plans, written work, lists, notes, artwork, new words, and materials for the unit. These are learner-centered environments where children may create an airport in one corner, or a rain forest or space museum throughout the entire room. These classrooms are highly literate, ever renewing and changing—places where children and their teachers celebrate learning and the world around them.

These classrooms are also places where teachers really talk with children. They talk about ideas and share information; they talk about books and about each other's lives (see figure 8.5). They discuss individual pieces of writing, topics of individual interest, and current events; they plan many events and activities together. Teachers encourage children to explore and take risks with language and learning; they negotiate not only what the children will study but how they will be evaluated.

The teachers have a thorough knowledge of language and language learning; they also know their learners, the materials and resources available, and the major approaches and strategies that fit their philosophy. In these classrooms authentic oral language and literacy events occur as children engage with rich content (K. Goodman, 1986). Central to everything, teachers read to and read with children; they write to and write with children; and the children read and write with one another every day.

Figure 8.6 summarizes the whole language teachers' knowledge base. It shows how they use their knowledge of learners, resources, and approaches to create classrooms rich in language, literature, and content.

Getting Started

There is no single way to start a whole language curriculum, but some commonalities do exist among teachers who have changed their practice to more closely reflect their philosophy. Many teachers started by realizing that there must be a seemingly better way. Many began with an assessment of their own educational beliefs and philosophy. What teachers believe is the key. Once you have decided to attempt a more holistic, language- and literature-based instructional program, the task of getting started may appear enormous. The following are suggestions gleaned from what many teachers have done.

- ▫ Pick an area to explore or expand that you feel comfortable with:
  read aloud
  writing
  literature studies
  using the basal reader in a more natural way

- ▫ Then decide what you want to omit from your existing program:
  ditto sheets
  the suggested reading lesson format and sequence
  workbooks

- ▫ See how it goes. Make adjustments as needed. Keep focusing on

FIGURE 8.6   Whole Language Teachers' Knowledge Base

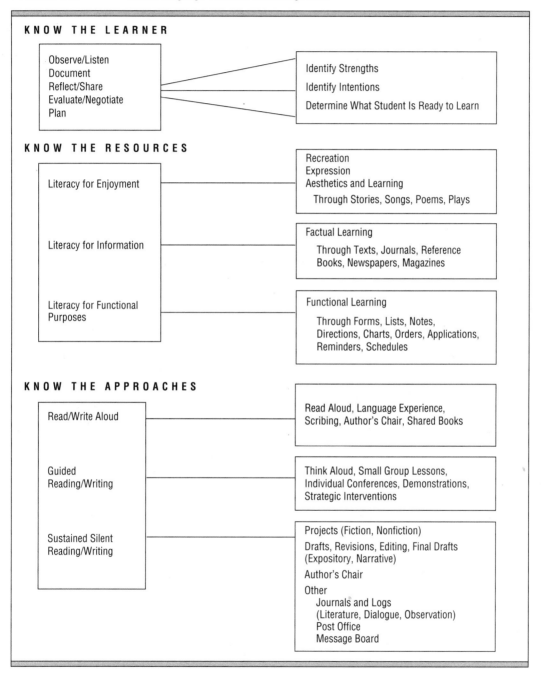

how your changes fit your theory, on what your goals are for the learners.

□ Decide what to try next:
a holistic checklist
more literature
more writing
a strategy idea or two
a mini-unit

□ In order to add more, you must omit something else. Decide what you will omit now. Continue this omit-and-add process to gradually transform your curriculum.

□ Visit a whole language classroom or two. Talk to whole language teachers about how they got started. Join a support group if one is nearby. If not, link up with a whole language teacher from another school. Phone or write to share your celebrations and frustrations.

□ Read professional books (for a comprehensive list, see appendix B). Attend whole language workshops and conferences.

□ Take a university course if one is available.

□ Enlist the support of your principal. Tell the principal what you are doing and why. Invite the principal to your classroom to observe, to take part in authors' celebrations, to listen to children read aloud.

□ Educate parents. Explain what you are doing, and ask for their help.

□ Take a running record or do a miscue analysis on the reading of some of your less proficient students. Determine what their strengths are and what they may be needing help with.

□ Keep a teaching log or journal. As you reflect on each day, and each week, record your observations, insights, and frustrations. What worked? Why? What didn't? Why? Teaching, like learning, is inquiry based, and what you are trying to do is answer the questions that naturally arise. A teaching journal will be invaluable to you over time.

▫ Find time during each school day for the basic whole language components:
  read aloud to your children
  write with your children
  read silently with your children

▫ The more you are able to integrate these with content into units of study, the better. Determine what your goals are, what you want your classroom to be like. Make an effort to know the approaches, know the resources, and know the learners you have.

▫ And *give yourself time.* Like all other learning, becoming a language- and literature-based teacher is an active, constructive process.

The Questions of Emerging Whole Language Teachers

Teaching is an act of inquiry, a research process itself; the dynamics of real teachers and real children coming together generate a variety of questions about particular transactions. Obviously, these cannot be answered here. That's why joining a support group, keeping a reflective teaching journal, reading professional books, and attending conferences and workshops are so important. However, we can address some of the typical issues encountered by teachers as they move toward whole language. These include concerns about scheduling, evaluating, planning, communicating with parents and administrators, discipline, standardized test scores, and assigning grades.

Scheduling   Scheduling is an important part of every teacher's planning. In whole language classrooms, blocks of time are large in order to give children ample time to attend to activities such as shared books, independent reading and writing, and author's chair. Scheduling in this manner allows children opportunities to become involved in the content and concepts of a book, to practice being an author, and to explore using language and other forms of self-expression for their own purposes. The integration of the curriculum through themes makes the large blocks of time necessary.

Conference time or instructional time (as in guided reading or guided writing) must be worked into the day. Figure 8.7 is a general schedule that emerging teachers might consider. It will very likely need to be altered to accommodate the needs of the group or the school schedule.

Room Arrangement Just as time frames are altered, so must the physical arrangement of the classroom reflect the teacher's philosophy. The arrangement must be flexible enough to support a variety

FIGURE 8.7
Sample Daily
Schedule

8:00–8:30	Journal writing or read aloud to children
8:30–8:45	Community meeting or rug time (what's going on, assignments, create projects, follow-up, family matters)
8:45–10:00	Language workshop: sustained reading and writing; guided reading and writing; authoring (revising, editing, publishing)
10:00–10:15	Break
10:15–10:50	Physical education/music/art/library/special explorations/computers
10:50–11:50	Math workshop: concepts, games, and practice
11:50–12:30	Lunch break, mailbox, talk with adults, etc.
12:30–2:00	Projects (theme study in science, social studies, etc.): silent reading and writing, group work, shared reading
2:00–2:30	Read aloud to children/author's chair/peer conferences/storytelling, etc.
2:30–2:50	Community meeting (review day, solve problems, plan next day, assign homework, etc.)
2:50–3:00	Clean up
3:00	Dismissal

of working conditions. The classroom setup should allow children opportunities to communicate with each other. Desks, if they are present, are pushed together to form groups. Accessibility to materials and to the many different forms of print on display is crucial. Children must be able to pursue various types of projects, so centers must be easy to get to. Figure 8.8 is a diagram of a typical classroom arrangement.

Experiment to gauge what is appropriate for the day's events. For instance, in one second/third-grade classroom the children became engrossed in Graeme Base's *The Eleventh Hour: A Curious Mystery* (1988). After lengthy discussions and two days of thorough investigation during shared book and silent reading time, the children solved the mystery. Then they wanted to create projects based on the book. Some chose to plan a party. Invitations were written, recipes for party foods collected and written, and party games devised. Others chose to write the author. Another group of children decided to create a mystery game complete with gameboard and rules for play. One group of children wanted to write a play based on the book. The class voted to present the play to the first graders. They also created a wall display of all their interpretations and creations emanating from this story.

Scheduling became important in this rich activity. Blocks of time were large, with ample opportunity for children to study the book, talk about their discoveries, test their hypotheses, catch the thief, and plan and execute projects. Space was also crucial. Work space for the party planners was needed. The children writing the play wanted a private place where they could write, talk, and try out various scenes. The children developing the game needed a tabletop work area and materials. All of these activities and arrangements reflected both the teacher's concern for flexibility and children's interests and choices. Their mini-unit lasted more than a week and culminated in a play and class party.

Discipline   The issue new teachers bring up most often is discipline. What will happen, they ask, when children have all these choices and opportunities? Talking and collaboration are legitimate ways of coming to know. When children have a voice in what hap-

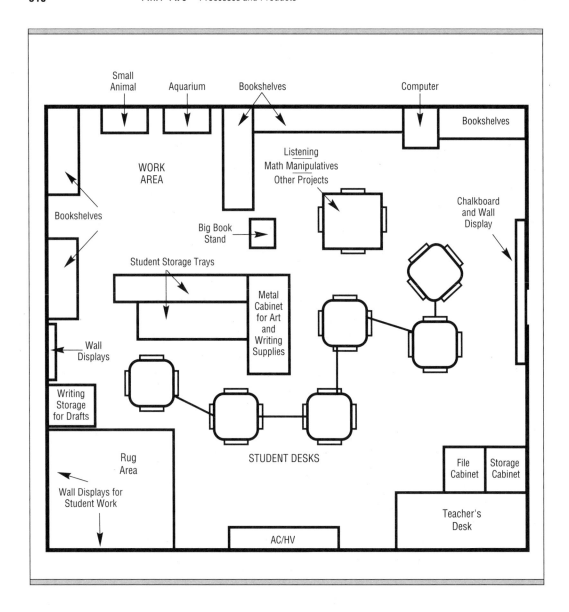

Small
Animal

Aquarium

Bookshelves

Computer

Bookshelves

WORK
AREA

Listening
Math Manipulatives
Other Projects

Chalkboard
and Wall
Display

Bookshelves

Big Book
Stand

Student Storage Trays

Metal
Cabinet
for Art
and
Writing
Supplies

Wall
Displays

Writing
Storage
for Drafts

Rug
Area

STUDENT DESKS

File
Cabinet

Storage
Cabinet

Wall Displays for
Student Work

Teacher's
Desk

AC/HV

FIGURE 8.8
Floor Plan of
Classroom

pens to them in school, they become empowered. Children do better
in cooperative and low-risk environments than in competitive classrooms (Goodman, Goodman, & Hood, 1989). They do better when
they are learning about things in which they are interested. A growing sense of ownership and responsibility reduces behavior prob-

lems, as children learn that power is not only what they *can* do, but also what they *should* do for their own and others' welfare.

Skills   Because of the integration of language, content, and learning, a frequent question asked of whole language teachers is "How can you be sure all the skills are covered?" Many teachers assume that since skills are assessed in isolation they must be taught in isolation. Indeed, many of the materials commonly found in traditional classrooms—basal readers, language arts textbooks, spelling textbooks—do present certain skills at certain times. However, no hierarchy or sequence of skills exists. Rather, children use all the cueing systems all the time.

In whole language classrooms, skills are naturally integrated into the language, thinking, and content in which the students engage. In other words, they learn the skills as they read and write, negotiate and discuss, and plan and present their learning. So the issue is not whether to teach skills, it is *when* and *how*.

Basal Readers   Because most whole language teachers do not use basal readers, questions about using them in whole language classrooms often arise. In 1990, the Commission on Reading of the National Council of Teachers of English (NCTE) prepared a position statement on basal readers and the state of American reading instruction (see appendix H for the NCTE position statement). The commission cited the significant gap between what is known about how people learn to read and how reading is typically taught. Most whole language teachers don't use basal readers because basals are not simply anthologies of good literature. They are collections of stories and other literature forms written or rewritten to teach children about reading.

However, some school districts mandate the use of the basal reader. When the basal reader series *must* be used, the materials may be used as multiple copies of the best stories in the book. The stories selected should be as complete as possible. Unfortunately, most stories are both abbreviated and rewritten by grade-level formula for specific skills instruction. Original versions of some of the stories may be made available to the children for comparison. In selecting stories, notice the relationship between the text and the illustrations. Too often the illustrations in the original text are altered or missing. In at least one instance, a recent Caldecott winner was included in a new literature-based series, but more than half of the illustrations were omitted.

Since teachers do not have to assign every story in the reader, they may give learners choices. Teachers who want to rely less on the basal reader can explore the enrichment activities with the children. The suggested activities in the teacher's manual do not have to be followed. The workbooks do not have to be used at all. Skills will be developed through guided reading and guided writing.

Communicating with Parents   Communicating with parents about their child's learning is an essential element of whole language classrooms. Typically, parents hear from schools only when there is a problem (Epstein, 1988). However, most parents really want to know what is going on in the classroom and how their children are doing. When teachers communicate with parents on a regular basis about the good things as well as the problems, parents typically are very pleased. There are countless ways to accomplish this. Consider one or more of these suggested ways to communicate with parents:

1. Invitations to school to review portfolios so that a child's progress and strengths may be emphasized

2. Newsletters, class newspapers, flyers that explain coming events, etc.

3. Notes home that emphasize good things children do, so that the occasional note about something negative will not stand out so strongly

4. A report card scheme that includes anecdotes as well as grades (the report card should reflect how the teacher sees the child and should invite parents to come in if their views differ)

5. A parent volunteer program

6. Invitations to parents to observe the classroom at work several times a year

7. Home visits

8. A home reading program (parents reading to children) that is administered from school with cheerful letters home and awards for families

9. A phone call schedule on which teachers call and report on how a child is doing so that each home gets a call on a regular basis

10. Involving both children and parents in projects such as community service outside the school

11. Three-way conferences among the child, parent, and teacher to set goals and share accomplishments

Communicating with Principals   The administrator may set the tone for the entire school. Keep the principal and other administrators posted on your philosophy and your developing program. Provide information about how the children are progressing, and regularly invite the principal into the classroom to see children's work. Keeping the principal informed about what is happening in your classroom increases the potential for his or her support and reduces the possibility of misunderstanding. Even when problems do arise, principals who know what their teachers are doing and why they are doing it tend to be more supportive.

Standardized Testing   Both parents and principals are concerned about standardized tests; everyone recognizes their influence. Children in whole language classrooms nearly always score at least as well, if not better, than children in traditional classrooms (Gunderson & Shapiro, 1987; Hagerty, Hiebert, & Owens, 1989; Ribowsky, 1986; Stice & Bertrand, 1990). Frequently, the reading comprehension scores of children in whole language classrooms are higher than the word identification scores. This is because of the nature of the tests and the nature of instruction. The standardized tests used in most public schools tend to assess subskill types of knowledge and to focus on assessing factual information. For these reasons, teachers do not risk lowered test scores in adopting a whole language curriculum. In fact, the likelihood is that scores will increase.

Evaluating: Becoming a "Kidwatcher"

The area that reportedly causes emerging whole language teachers the greatest difficulty is evaluation. The root of the word *evaluation* is the word *value.* Evaluation ought to be a systematic means of showing what we value in children's school experiences (Goodman, Goodman, & Hood, 1989). A theoretically sound view of evaluation involves activities in which the teacher and students collect, analyze, and interpret several types of data to judge how well learners are reaching educational goals. This is called *process evaluation.* The gathering of quantitative data only, from measures such as testing, is a *product assessment.*

Teachers need both types of information about students. However, product assessments are of little practical value in the actual planning of student's learning experiences. For one thing, they typically address lower order thinking and lower order analysis in ways that are meaningless outside schools (Smith, 1990). Product assessments separate students into categories based on scores. Process evaluations, on the other hand, allow teachers to make informed judgments about their students' growth and capabilities.

Many forms of performance do not lend themselves to product assessment (Heald-Taylor, 1989). Real knowledge and skills are difficult to evaluate. Teachers realize that often the test scores that go home and grades they give reflect children's ability to take tests as much as their underlying knowledge and real competence.

Individual assessment by objective measures—that is, teaching the test—limits the curriculum severely. It reduces opportunities for children to learn and places artificial constraints on the amount and rate at which teachers introduce information into the classroom. Traditional testing has been justifiably criticized for providing too small and artificial a sample of what children know. These constraints also act as stages through which children have to pass. In other words, tests can control the curriculum; and when that happens, education ceases to exist. Schools where the curriculum is driven by standardized tests pay little or no attention to such processes as synthesis, summary, observation, analysis, classifying, self-expression, application, creativity, diverse thinking, and critical thinking. They rob learners of their potential and of the real abilities they will need outside of school (Smith, 1990).

In process-oriented, learner-centered classrooms, evaluation is based on a different philosophy, that of empowering learners and teachers. Since the purposes of evaluation are different from traditional assessment, the practices are also different. Whole language evaluation procedures reflect what is known about learning, language learning, and literacy. They employ informed teacher judgment, document strategies learners are developing, focus on learner growth over time, serve to encourage learners, and become an integral part of the classroom.

Teachers' informed judgment stems from two sources, what teachers know and what children "tell" them. First, teachers look at children with their knowledge of child development, language, learning, and the outside world. Second, teacher judgment is informed by children's responses to classroom events. Informed teachers come to know each child intimately. They do this by "kidwatching" to discover what the children are doing, what their interests and intentions are, and what they are learning. This type of evaluation involves both literacy and content learning (Baskwill & Whitman, 1988; Eggleton, 1990; Goodman, Goodman, & Hood, 1989; Graves & Sunstein, 1992).

The major question the concerned teacher addresses in evaluation is, How can I find out what the students have learned? The following principles give guidance in this area:

1. Evaluation of performance should be over time using regular observation and informed perspectives.

2. Evaluation should be nonpunitive.

3. Evaluation does not control teachers; teachers control evaluation.

4. Evaluation should be reliable and valid.

5. Evaluation is a dual agenda that encompasses both evaluation of learners and evaluation of instruction.

6. Evaluation should be carried out using forms and instruments that resemble those learners may encounter outside of school.

7. Evaluation should include children's collaborative efforts.

8. Good evaluation brings the child into the process.

9. Evaluation that reflects what the teacher knows and has observed should serve as the basis for assigning grades.

10. Evaluation is holistic and does not fragment language or learning.

Teachers use what they learn about their students as they reflect on their instructional programs and make decisions about future classroom events and activities. Reflective teachers carry on an internal dialogue that constantly questions what students are accomplishing (Goodman, 1985). In general, evaluation revolves around six activities: goal setting, observing, reflective observation, record keeping, planning, and assigning grades.

Goal Setting   Teachers are actually the final arbiters of the goals and values for their classrooms. Teachers' goals derive from their philosophy and from what they value for learners. This is not a responsibility held solely by teachers. Parents and children are partners in goal setting and evaluation. However, teachers are the trained professionals and the only ones in the classroom milieu who have the opportunity to truly know the children and their needs, to serve as the advocate for parents' desires, and to protect children from inappropriate demands. Setting attainable, meaningful, and realistic goals is one of the main purposes of kidwatching.

Observing   Teachers become sensitive, reflective "kidwatchers" (Goodman, 1985). Learning what to look for and what to look at takes time and experience, as does learning what to listen for and what to focus on. Looking for children's learning strategies and identifying their strengths is the main goal. The following guidelines were developed by Yetta Goodman (1991, p. 274) to help teachers become better kidwatchers:

1. Know what, how, and when to observe.

2. Know how language and learning operate in order to observe.

3. Observe in a variety of social/cultural settings. What's the student reading in stories, streets, homes, libraries? Relate to interests.

4. Observe reading by watching and listening to kids read things usually read. Base evaluation on what is known about reading.

5. Observe writing by watching kids write. Base evaluation on what is known about writing.

6. Explore the nature of miscues (errors)—miscues are indicators of all language developmental processes.

   a. Everyone makes miscues, has misconceptions.

   b. Miscues reveal interpretative differences.

   c. Miscues reveal editing process, change process, version process, folk process.

   d. Focus on high level miscues which indicate reading effectiveness and efficiency.

7. Listen and observe what many different adults do.

8. Understand responses in relation to social/cultural view of learner.

9. View "right" answers with care.

10. Ask "Why is this happening? What does this tell me about the intellectual functioning of the learner?"*

Reflecting   Reflective observation is at the heart of what holistic teachers do. Only through intimate knowledge of the children can a teacher structure classroom programs to truly meet children's needs, interests, and intentions. Teachers "kidwatch" in a variety of ways and settings. Conferences, shared work, journals, letters, and conversations are some of the ways children reveal what is in their heads and hearts. Whole language teachers engage in continuous evaluation; they set up situations that allow them to observe children's responses to learning events.

---

*Reprinted with permission of Yetta Goodman.

For instance, when teachers hear two children reading together, they focus on the strategies the children use. They watch as the children select books. They listen to see if the children predict based on meaning. They determine if retellings show evidence that readers are constructing meaning. They record their observations anecdotally or on a form or checklist. What will the teacher do with this information?

As teachers study the notes they have made about children's learning or the materials they have collected to represent children's work, a coherent, overall picture of each student emerges. No single right way exists to explain how teachers reflect. Some peruse their collection of anecdotes, papers, samples of work, and/or student-published books, looking for evidence of learning. Others log events in a journal and refer to it frequently for evidence of student growth. Still others use a small tape recorder to record rough notes they later organize and transcribe, reflecting as they transcribe. Whatever techniques teachers use, the act of making sense out of the events and materials from the classroom is the evaluation process.

Record Keeping   Keeping records is essential for all teachers, but whole language teachers are set apart by the kinds of records they keep. Most whole language teachers keep at least three kinds of records. (Additional sample record-keeping devices are found in appendix G.)

First, representative samples of each child's work are dated and retained to serve as examples of growth over time. This allows teachers to gauge both children's overall ability to get and make meaning and their developing control over the conventions of language. For instance, whole language teachers would probably not address rules of capitalization with a lesson in front of the class followed by several worksheets filled with unconnected sentences. Rather, they might use examples from children's writing as springboards for both exploration and discussion.

Jorld's story in figure 8.9 can be celebrated because it represents a reluctant writer's first complete story. It might also be used to teach capitalization and end marks to the young writer as he revises and edits.

FIGURE 8.9   Jorld's Story

The dead man

rinun dy
Jorld

September
3

he got shat
in th horet 3
tims and shat
in the legg
and brock hes
orm the poles
came ond
the amlins
came

evre bide
rad after
the poles
to see what
wus going
on Thay
See shuting
and bud

he is going
to get bered
thay is going

to hav a frunr
thay is going t
crie then
they is going
to go home

they is going
to set bie
the frie
and tok a
bout it it is
going to be
sad thin thay
is going to
rest

the mon
that celd he
is bad I hot
he if I see
he I am
going to
col he a
Name

Second, teachers keep informal observation records, including quick notes to oneself, checklists, observation summary forms, and charts or graphs of the learner's progress. Checklists and other systematic recording devices can be developed or adapted for children's creative projects, their oral reading, and their writings. Narrative summaries of children's experiences are prepared by many teachers every week or two. Sometimes teachers write anecdotal notes to remind themselves of seminal events in the classroom life of children.

Third, teachers make formal observations. These include miscue analyses, running records, finished products such as published books, records of conferences, and other activities that lend themselves to evaluation of end products. A benefit of good record keeping is that it not only fulfills a purpose in evaluation, but it models the behaviors that teachers want children to learn. Record keeping is a real and contextual use for literacy.

All records, anecdotal or more quantitative, should be summarized periodically. The bits and pieces of paper used to record informal, anecdotal notes may be discarded. Many teachers prefer to collect these bits and pieces during the week, dropping them into each student's folder once or twice a day. Then they are compiled on a simple summary once a week. Summary forms, checklists, and graphs are dated and kept in the learner's folder. Good record keeping acts as a secondary memory for teachers, giving them an accurate picture of what has transpired over time. Documentation of children's growth is the teacher's best tool. Reflection is the teacher's most important endeavor, and it depends on keeping good records.

Planning   The purposes for evaluation are documenting children's growth, planning for instruction, and assigning grades—in that order. In addition to informal evaluation techniques such as "kidwatching" and keeping anecdotal records, teachers use a variety of other instruments and procedures. Several devices can gather in-depth data—both qualitative and quantitative—about children's reading, writing, and learning. Teachers use this kind of information to help plan guided reading, guided writing, and teacher-pupil conferences. Evaluation data inform teachers. Teachers use these data to work with individuals and to bring together ad hoc groups of children with common needs. The knowledge and understandings that students possess can inform teachers and determine the direction the classroom curriculum will take.

Daily lesson plans by experienced classroom teachers look rather like short notations. When substitute teachers come into most whole language classrooms, they typically need only follow the daily schedule, because the students know what they are working on. But beginning teachers need to keep more detailed plans that focus on the choices learners have within the framework of the daily schedule. (For a sample lesson plan format, see appendix G.) These choices include short-term events (conduct the experiment with the popcorn during language workshop time; meet with Billy, Marcus, and Fran to help them with their letter to the editor) and also activities based on long-term goals (set up the art project for painting scenery for the play, read the new book on dinosaurs, encourage writing about favorite dinosaur).

Daily lessons are typically written in large blocks by time frames from the daily schedule, as in figure 8.10. They may cover a page in the plan book for each day because they track a great amount of information and materials.

Table 8.1 summarizes the major options available to teachers for gathering information for observational evaluation. The types of activities to observe as the children are engaged with print are identified, as are the numerous settings in which reading and writing occur. Teachers inform themselves about children's reading and writing development through on-the-spot observations and also through formal, planned observations, and continual, informal kid-watching opportunities.

Teachers may make their own observation and evaluation forms, many of which are composites from a variety of sources. In figure 8.11, the teacher selected categories she felt were most appropriate for her second graders. She assessed Tabitha's writing with a checklist (figure 8.11a). She counted Tabitha's invented and conventional spellings both at the beginning of school and again in early October (figure 8.11b); she also kept a list of Tabitha's spelling errors for individualized instruction in spelling (figure 8.11c). She created her own form for evaluating oral reading and retelling (figure 8.11d).

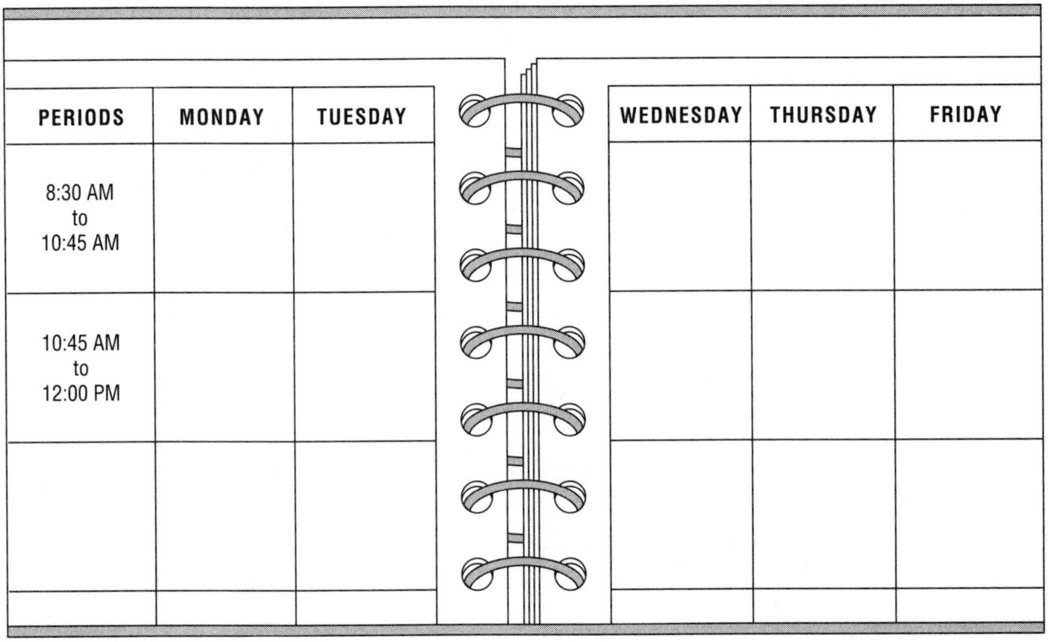

PERIODS	MONDAY	TUESDAY		WEDNESDAY	THURSDAY	FRIDAY
8:30 AM to 10:45 AM						
10:45 AM to 12:00 PM						

FIGURE 8.10
Block Format for
Daily Lesson Plans

She made anecodotal notes on Tabitha's attitude and special needs (figure 8.11e).

Whole language evaluation is individual. It aims to identify what each learner can do, what each learner knows, and what each learner may be ready to work on next. Classroom instruction is planned to help learners, not to penalize them. It starts with what they know and what they appear to need. Children are evaluated based on their ability to grow, rather than on impersonal norms that create labels serving no good purpose. Rather than a separate, artificial system in the classroom, evaluation is a continuous, integral part of the daily activities (see figure 8.12). It is used to inform and guide teachers as they plan instruction, select materials, and develop programs (Baskwill & Whitman, 1988; Eggleton, 1990; Goodman, Goodman, & Hood, 1989; Heald-Taylor, 1989).

Good evaluation does not control teachers, it informs them. Teachers control evaluation. Testing, informed judgments, samples and records, checklists, observations, reflections, and collaborative evaluation with students and their parents combine to form good evaluation. Sometimes in traditional classrooms the teachers an-

To Be Observed and Evaluated	On the Spot	Regular, Formal	Continual, Informal
Use of reading cues and strategies	Paired reading SSR	Taped readings Miscue analysis Running record Reading conferences	Shared book Author's chair
Reading comprehension	Paired reading Group discussion	Taped retellings Reading conferences	Literature study groups
Writing process	Paired writing SSW	Writing conferences	Author's chair Journal entries Drafts
Mechanics of written language	SSW Message board Notes Pen pal letters	Initial writing conferences Peer conferences Final editing conferences	Journal entries Drafts Revisions
Attitudes, values, self-concepts	Self-selections Difficulty levels of books Projects attempted	Interest inventories Interviews Portfolio presentations	Child's comments and contributions
Other	Work in progress	Tests	Projects

nounce a test and then "prepare" the children by going over the answers. And still a number of children will do poorly. Children may correctly perceive that the material is meaningless and devoid of application to their lives. Even many who "pass" merely memorize material long enough to restate "answers" and cannot apply what was "learned." The type of data collected for process evaluation is kept and analyzed by reflective kidwatchers. These data are more authentic; they represent what learners have done and where they are in their development.

TABLE 8.1
Settings and Literacy Events Teachers May Use for Kidwatching and Evaluation

Assigning Grades

Most teachers have the responsibility of assigning grades. Grading with test scores is easy. Turning anecdotal, narrative data, checklists, and other more qualitative process evaluations into letter or number

FIGURE 8.11a   Writing Assessment

WRITING ASSESSMENT				
Student Name: _Tabitha_			D: Developing	
Age: __8__			C: Consistently used	
Quality of Writing	Aug.	Oct/Nov.		
Is willing to write	C			
Self-selects topics	C			
Takes risks		C		
Uses original ideas				
Uses expansive vocabulary				
Writes complete simple sentences	C			
Writes complete compound sentences				
Writes complete complex sentences				
Ties thoughts together				
Stories have beginning, middle, end				
Revises own writing				
Revision techniques:				
A. erases				
B. crosses out				
C. uses arrows				
D. cuts apart				
E. writes over				
Uses environment for reference	Sept. C			
Uses peers for reference				
Uses another text as model	Sept. C			
Seeks conferences		C		
Demonstrates sense of audience				

grades is more difficult. Grades reflect children's work and progress, and the reporting form of choice for many whole language teachers is the narrative with samples of the child's work attached.

However, most school systems still require teachers to report children's progress in the form of a grade on a report card. In some cases, progress in the primary grades is reported as E for Excellent, S for Satisfactory, N for Needs Improvement, and U for Unsatisfactory, but in the middle and upper grades progress is usually reported by the traditional A, B, C, D, F scheme or by percentage scores that mean the same thing. Regardless of the scheme used to report grades, teachers have developed techniques for determining grades. Figures 8.13 and 8.14 are examples of how teachers may accomplish this task for reading and writing. A similar format can be applied to grading in other subject areas.

FIGURE 8.11b
Record of Invented-to-Conventional Spellings

TEXT	INVENTED SPELLING	CONVENTIONAL SPELLING
9/14/92 Little Red Riding Hood 53 words "everyone loved her. Her grandmother loved her most of all." 10/19 Much Bigger Than Martin (105 words!) Tabitha	55% 30% % of invented spelling (circled at end of each item).	45% 70%! % of conventional spelling (circled at end of each item).

SPELLING EVALUATION

NAME: Tabitha

mask   Mask

dollar   Dolre

morning   Mnring

yard   yrd

carry   Kare

brought   brot

homemade   Home made

I've   I'v

wheel   Wil

those   Tose

FIGURE 8.11c
Record of Spelling
Errors

Note that the grading in figures 8.13 and 8.14 has been set up on base ten so that conversion to percentages is simple. Since letter grades usually reflect percentages (an A might be 90–100), assigning letter grades is simplified as well.

Assisting Students' Self-Evaluation and Portfolios

Good evaluation brings the learner into the process and encourages independence. Teachers serve children well when they find ways to help them take responsibility for their own learning and their own evaluation. A large part of all classroom evaluation should be self-evaluation. A realistic appraisal of one's own work, aided by the teacher, is often the most perceptive. Teacher-pupil conferencing, peer conferencing, portfolios, and three-way conferencing (with parent, teacher, and child) are among the techniques that promote realistic self-evaluation.

FIGURE 8.11d
Oral Reading and Retelling Assessment

Student _____ Tabitha _____ Date _____ Sept. _____

Book _____ Small Deer _____ Pages Aloud _____

_____ Overuse of graphophonic cues

_____ Nonwords

_____ Predictions _____ syn. acc. _____ sem. acc.

_____ Syntactically acceptable substitutions

_____ Omissions _____ acc. _____ unacc.

_____ Corrections _____ yes _____ no _____ over

__X__ Unacceptable punctuation omits .

_____ Fluent

_____ Appropriate intonation

Predictions have 1st consonent same - not for meaning

Many miscued sentences had same words - never corrected, even in diff. contexts - weather - water long - log smiled - small

Didn't trust her

Character recall/development	1	2	3	4	(5)	Book sharing: understanding
Setting remembered	1	2	3	4	5	
Events sequence parts not	1	2	(3)	4	5	
Plot statement in order	1	2	(3)	4	5	
Theme/purpose	1	2	3	(4)	5	
Inferences	1	2	3	4	5	

"I think I said the wrong word, but it didn't sound right - it sounded like he was a nice deer, but he was foolish because he tried to make the crocodile eat his stick ("log" for long) so he wouldn't bite his foot - put the stick in his mouth"

FIGURE 8.11e   Observation/Anecdotal Record

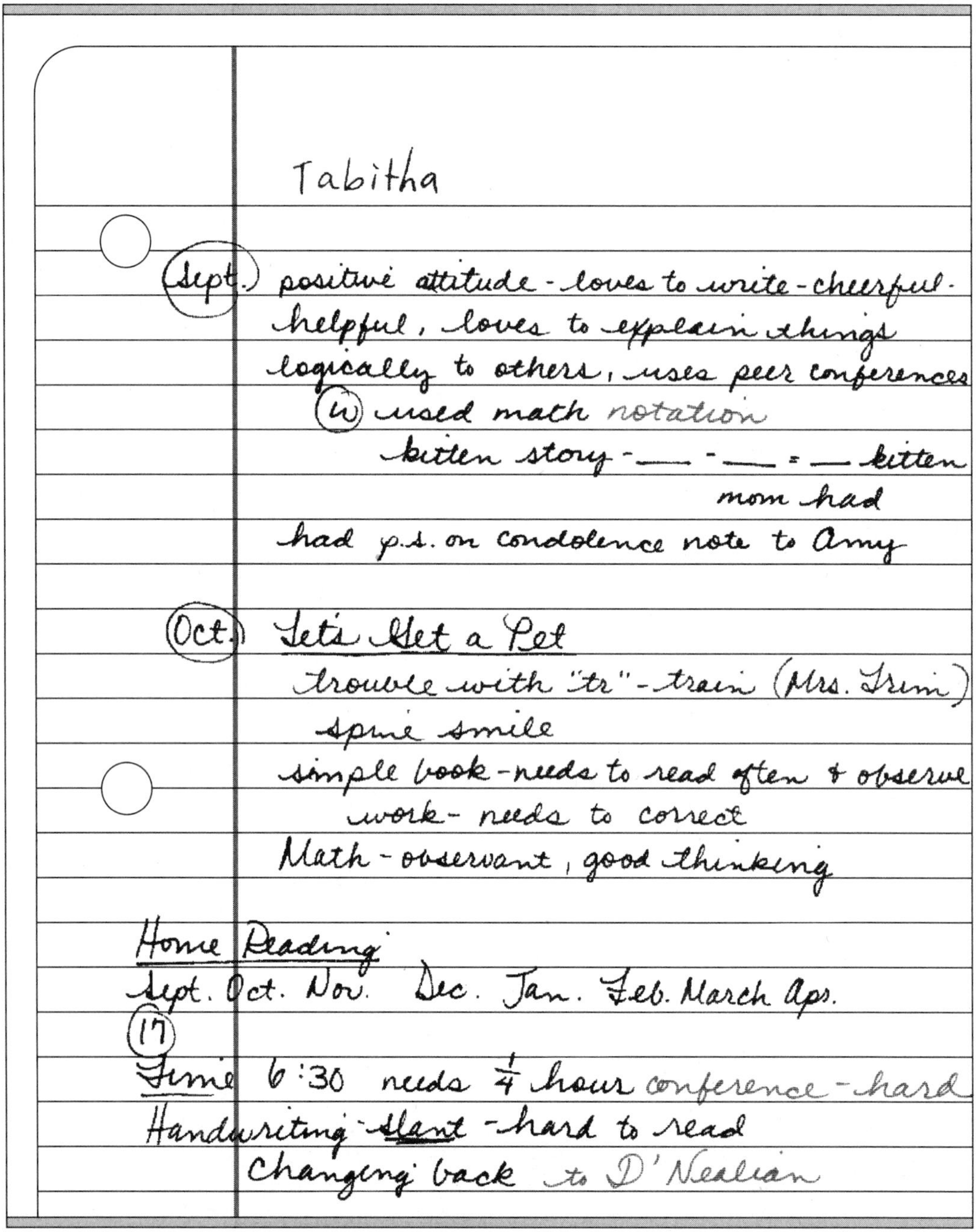

Tabitha

(Sept.) positive attitude - loves to write - cheerful.
helpful, loves to explain things
logically to others, uses peer conferences
(w) used math notation
     kitten story - ___ - ___ = ___ kitten
                              mom had
had p.s. on condolence note to Amy

(Oct.) Let's Get a Pet
     trouble with "tr" - train (Mrs. Trim)
     spure smile
     simple book - needs to read often + observe
     work - needs to correct
Math - observant, good thinking

Home Reading
Sept. Oct. Nov. Dec. Jan. Feb. March Aps.
(17)
Time 6:30 needs ¼ hour conference - hard
Handwriting Slant - hard to read
     Changing back to D'Nealian

FIGURE 8.12
Kidwatching

Good evaluation is structured to address literacy and subject matter learning as they interact with each other. Evaluation is most informative when it occurs as students work on authentic events of their own choosing. Whole language teachers believe children need to reflect on and evaluate their own learning so they can become more consciously aware of the processes they go through in their own learning. Learning is thereby enhanced. As we examine our own

FIGURE 8.13   Assigning Grades for Reading

GUIDE FOR GRADING READING

Name: _____ Date: _____

Observing the Learner	Always 10/9	Often 9/8	Occasionally 8/7	Not Yet 6–
1. Views reading as language, i.e., expects reading to make sense; reads for pleasure, information, etc.; makes reading sound like language instead of word-by-word decoding.				
2. Uses prior knowledge, i.e., demonstrates that personal experience and information help readers understand what is being read.				
3. Makes predictions based on prior knowledge, i.e., previews material, reads title, looks at pictures, uses picture clues during reading.				
4. Makes predictions while reading, i.e., makes reasonable predictions based on grammar and meaning, confirms or disconfirms predictions.				
5. Self-corrects, i.e., when reading does not make sense, when it does not sound like language, reader rereads and attempts corrections.				
6. Reads with fluency, i.e., oral reading is natural in intonation, speed, and rhythm; reader adjusts to various materials.				
7. Grammatical acceptability, i.e., reader produces sentences that are grammatically acceptable in English within the reader's dialect.				
8. Semantic acceptability, i.e., reader produces sentences that are meaningful within the context of the story.				
9. Use of graphophonic information, i.e., reader uses letter-sound relationships to help identify unknown words.				
10. Retellings, i.e., reader's retellings include information directly stated and inferred that is important to a full understanding of the text.				

SOURCE: Adapted from M. Kemp (1987), *Watching Children Read and Write: Observational Record for Children with Special Needs* (Portsmouth, NH: Heinemann).

GUIDE FOR GRADING WRITING

Name: _____   Date: _____

Observing the Learner	Always 10/9	Often 9/8	Occasionally 8/7	Not Yet 6–
1. Writes a complete story, i.e., story has beginning, middle, and end.				
2. Selects and revises drafts, i.e., works on content.				
3. Edits drafts, i.e., works on mechanics.				
4. Attempts to use "best" word.				
5. Uses appropriate suggestions from others.				
6. Uses multiple resources for drafts and editing.				
7. Exhibits growing control over conventions of spelling.				
8. Writes willingly on a daily basis.				
9. Writes for a variety of purposes.				
10. Writings show sense of different audiences.				
11. Writings show originality and imagination.				
12. Writer is developing own "voice."				

---

reading behavior and that of others, our reading tends to improve. When we examine our own writing processes and strategies, as well as how other authors write, we find new avenues for improving our writing. It is important for children to know how they are really doing. Identifying evidence of their own learning and changes in their skills and knowledge improves self-concept and offers children a purpose for continued learning.

When education consists of a series of arbitrary assignments, such as memorizing the states and their capitals, children see little purpose

FIGURE 8.14
Assigning Grades for Writing
SOURCE: Adapted from M. Kemp (1987), *Watching Children Read and Write: Observational Records for Children with Special Needs* (Portsmouth, NH: Heinemann).

or relevance. However, when learners are involved in helping choose what they will do and when they have a voice in examining their own achievements, purpose and relevance are clear. Simply asking children what they like about their work encourages self-reflection. Giving children choices of what they will work on or asking them to listen while the teacher reads a piece of their writing are examples of ways to encourage children's thinking about their learning.

A popular form for self-evaluation in many classrooms is the portfolio (Graves & Sunstein, 1992; Tierney, Carter, & Desai, 1991). Portfolios are collections. Artists use portfolios to represent their best work; models, architects, and some pre-service teachers keep them to impress prospective employers. Even professors are developing portfolios. They are not scrapbooks; they represent highly selective artifacts that have meaning for the individual. Because of the emphasis on self-evaluation, authenticity, and the personal-social nature of learning, portfolios are promising additions to process-oriented classrooms.

Portfolios are *not* used in grading. Rather, they are self-evaluative in that they allow children to present themselves through their learning. Teachers use portfolios in a variety of ways. For instance, children may choose to develop portfolio presentations for the end of each unit of study, for every six-week grading period, across each semester, or throughout the year. After examining different types of portfolios, children may list some of the categories they want for their own portfolio collections. They decide how to make their portfolios best present their work and their learning. These could include any of the following items:

1. A letter at the beginning describing what the learners thought this year would be like and what they hoped to learn

2. Their best artwork, dated and arranged by topics

3. First drafts and finished products of their favorite writing, both stories and information

4. Any poems, raps, or free verse they wrote

5. Lists of books they read during SSR

6. Lists and samples of all their published work

7. Copies of any formal letters they might write, or favorite pen pal letters

8. Copies of tests, both formal and informal

9. Lists of all the words they learned to spell, or lists of favorite vocabulary words

10. Science projects or photos or written descriptions of them

11. Copies of any math games or other products they created

12. A letter at the end describing what the learner thought she or he had learned

13. Photographs that represent important class events, field trips, displays

Portfolios are organized by the presenter to reflect a purpose. Some of the more obvious organizational structures include time, events, and concepts. The teacher may require that the children develop a table of contents and number the pages. Portfolios can be fun when treated as both a culminating event and a time to show off. While they are the property of the learner and are the learner's personal expression, they may also provide teachers with information and insight.

SUMMARY

Whole language classrooms are busy places full of children's books, their writings, and their imaginations. They do not sound or look like traditional classrooms. In these classrooms, children do not merely learn about their favorite dinosaur, they may "become" their favorite dinosaur, and the classroom their cave away from home. Children learn to read and write; they learn to use reading and writing to further their learning and to open a multitude of worlds. Learners explore the physical world, the world of computers, literature, math, history, geography. These classrooms are learner centered and risk-free. They are places children want to be.

Teachers interested in moving toward the whole language paradigm must first set goals for themselves and their students by acquiring current information about learning, child development, and language. They decide what they believe and make decisions based on what they know and value. They decide where to begin and they give themselves time. Becoming a whole language teacher is a process of inquiry.

Evaluation is an integral part of the process. Evaluation focuses on documenting and describing children's growth. Teachers use evaluation to inform their theory, to make informed judgments about their children, and to tailor their program to the needs, interests, and intentions of the children. They also use evaluation to learn about themselves as teachers.

THEORY-TO-PRACTICE CONNECTIONS

Organizing Teaching Theory	*Examples of Classroom Practice*
1. Teaching is also a learning process.	1. Keeping a teaching journal for reflecting on and assessing own theory and practice; observing other whole language teachers
2. Start where the child is.	2. Looking for the learner's strengths, the learner's interests, and what the child appears ready to learn next
3. Teachers know their learners.	3. Observing (watching and listening), recording and reflecting on what each child is doing or trying to do
4. Teachers know the approaches.	4. Reading and writing to, with, and by children every day
5. Teachers know the available resources.	5. Filling the classroom with appropriate books, newspapers, magazines, lists, catalogs, art supplies, reference materials, science equipment, etc.
6. Learners benefit from becoming aware of their own learning.	6. Facilitating children's portfolios, conducting self-assessment conferences

SUGGESTED READINGS

Barrs, M., Ellis, S., Hester, H., & Thomas, A. (1989). *The primary language record: Handbook for teachers.* Portsmouth, NH: Heinemann.

Base, G. (1988). *The eleventh hour: A curious mystery.* New York: Harry N. Abrams.

Baskwill, J., & Whitman, P. (1988). *Evaluation: Whole language, whole child.* New York: Scholastic.

Bird, L. (1989). *The Fair Oaks story: Becoming a whole language school.* Katonah, NY: Richard C. Owen.

Cambourne, B. (1988). *The whole story: Natural learning and the acquisition of literacy in the classroom.* New York: Ashton Scholastic.

Crafton, L. (1990). *Whole language: Getting started and moving forward.* Katonah, NY: Richard C. Owen.

Cutting, B. (1990). *Getting started in whole language: The complete guide for every teacher.* San Diego, CA: Wright Group.

Goodman, K., Bird, L., & Goodman, Y. (1992). *The whole language catalog: Supplement on authentic assessment.* Santa Rosa, CA: American School Publishers.

Goodman, Y., Hood, W., & Goodman, K. (Eds.). (1991). *Organizing for whole language.* Portsmouth, NH: Heinemann.

Graves, D., & Sunstein, B. (Eds.). (1992). *Portfolio portraits.* Portsmouth, NH: Heinemann.

McVitty, W. (Ed.). (1989). *Getting it together: Organizing the reading-writing classroom.* Rozelle, Australia: PETA.

Massam, J., & Kulik, A. (1986). *And what else?* Auckland, New Zealand: Shortland Publications.

Mills, H., & Clyde, J. (Eds.). (1990). *Portraits of whole language classrooms: Learning for all ages.* Portsmouth, NH: Heinemann.

Tierney, R., Carter, M., & Desai, L. (1991). *Portfolio assessment in the reading-writing classroom.* Norwood, MA: Christopher-Gordon.

SUGGESTED ACTIVITIES

1. Design your ideal classroom. How would you arrange student desks or tables? What materials would you want? Where would you put the various elements necessary in a child-centered, literature-based program? Present your design to the class and discuss.

2. Explore a basal reader series that incorporates children's literature. Compare the basal version of the text to the original. What, if anything, has been changed? How do the changes affect the meaning and quality of the reading experience?

3. Write a letter to parents telling them about the new curriculum you are going to be implementing in the upcoming school year. Share your letters.

4. Prepare a persuasive statement for your principal explaining to him or her what changes you want to make in your classroom program and *why*. Share your statements with classmates and add any ideas from others that you think you should include in your request.

5. Many teaching applications ask for a brief statement of your philosophy of teaching. What could you say about your philosophy of teaching and learning?

6. How have you been evaluated in schools up to now? Have you ever had the opportunity to contribute to your own evaluations? If so, to what extent or under what circumstances? What was the purpose of students' input? How did it work? What do you believe to be the purpose of evaluation? In school settings, who has the right and the obligation to evaluate?

7. Plan and present a portfolio of your learning in this course. You may wish to work together to plan this activity. Your instructor may provide you with information on portfolio assessment and may ask persons with business portfolios to come to class to share them with you.

8. Compile your own portfolio. It can be of your school experiences from college, high school, or elementary school. It could be a portfolio of your experiences in becoming a teacher. It should represent several aspects of your life, perhaps including a description of who you were at the beginning of your undergraduate education, what your most memorable experiences are, what you are most proud of, and who you are now as a result of these experiences. It could include samples of your work, written explanations, photographs or other pictures, grade cards, and interviews with former teachers. What do you want to accomplish with your portfolio? Will it help you decide what you want to do next? Do you feel good about yourself as a result of this experience? Why or why not? If you do create portfo-

lios with children, how can you ensure they will have a positive and productive learning experience?

9. Talk to a good student about his or her school experiences. Then talk to a poor student. What kinds of things do they tell you? If you were their teacher and had to work with them to evaluate their learning and plan for their next learning, what would you do and why? Share these findings and conclusions with classmates. Discuss. Be able to explain your perceptions.

10. Using one of the guides for assigning grades (figures 8.11 and 8.12), ask a local whole language classroom teacher to determine one or two of their students' grades. Discuss the process with him or her. How might you use this or a similar procedure for determining letter or number grades?

REFERENCES

Baskwill, J., & Whitman, P. (1988). *Evaluation: Whole language, whole child.* New York: Scholastic.

Cambourne, B. (1989). *Coping with chaos.* Portsmouth, NH: Heinemann.

Eggleton, J. (1990). *Whole language evaluation.* San Diego, CA: Wright Group.

Epstein, J. (1988). How do we improve programs for parent involvement? *Education Horizons, 66,* 58–59.

Freppon, P., and Dahl, K. (1991). Learning about phonics in a whole language classroom. *Language Arts, 68,* 190–197.

Goodman, K. (1986). *What's whole in whole language?* Portsmouth, NH: Heinemann.

Goodman, K., Bird, L., & Goodman, Y. (1992). *The whole language catalog: Supplement on*

authentic assessment. Santa Rosa, CA: American School Publishers.

Goodman, K., Goodman, Y., & Hood, W. (1989). *The whole language evaluation book.* Portsmouth, NH: Heinemann.

Goodman, Y. (1978). Kidwatching: An alternative to testing. *National Elementary Principal, 57* (4), p. 45.

Goodman, Y. (1991a). Evaluation—kidwatching. In J. Poeton (Ed.), *A child's window to the world: Creating child-centered classrooms* (p. 276). Peterborough, NH: Society for Developmental Education.

Goodman, Y. (1991b). Observation and evaluation: Kidwatching. In J. Poeton (Ed.), *A Child's window to the world: Creating child-centered classrooms* (p. 274). Peterborough, NH: Society for Developmental Education.

Goodman, Y. (1985). Kidwatching: Observing children in the classroom. In A. Jaggar & M. Smith-Burke (Eds.), *Observing the language learner*. Newark, DE: International Reading Association.

Graves, D., & Sunstein, B. (Eds.). (1992). *Portfolio portraits*. Portsmouth, NH: Heinemann.

Gunderson, L., & Shapiro, J. (1987). Some findings on whole language instruction. *Reading Canada Lecture, 5*, 22–26.

Hagerty, P., Hiebert, E., & Owens, M. (1989). Students' comprehension, writing, and perceptions in two approaches to literacy instruction. In S. McCormick & J. Zutell (Eds.), *National Reading Conference Yearbook*.

Heald-Taylor, G. (1989). *The administrator's guide to whole language*. Katonah, NY: Richard C. Owen.

Kemp, M. (1987). *Watching children read and write: Observational records for children with special needs*. Portsmouth, NH: Heinemann.

Mills, H., O'Keefe, T., & Stephens, D. (1992). *Looking closely: Exploring the role of phonics in the whole language classroom*. Urbana, IL: NCTE.

Ribowsky, H. (1986). *The comparative effects of a code emphasis approach and a whole language approach upon emergent literacy of kindergarten children*. Unpublished doctoral dissertation, New York University, New York.

Schwartz, S., & Pollishuke, M. (1991). *Creating the child-centered classroom*. Katonah, NY: Richard C. Owen.

Smith, F. (1986). *Insult to intelligence*. New York: Arbor House.

Smith, F. (1990). *To think*. New York: Teachers College Press.

Stice, C., & Bertrand, N. (1990). *Whole language and the emergent literacy of at-risk children*. Nashville, TN: Tennessee State University, Center of Excellence for Research in Basic Skills (ERIC Document Reproduction Service No. ED 324-636).

Tierney, R., Carter, M., Desai, L. (1991). *Portfolio assessment in the reading-writing classroom*. Norwood, MA: Christopher-Gordon.

PART THREE

Content and Curriculum

EXPANDING THEORY INTO
PRACTICE ACROSS THE GRADES

9

Primary and Elementary Grades

Although whole language classrooms vary and have their own personalities, . . . certain strategies are included. . . . These strategies . . . reflect teachers' respect and regard for story, learner, community of learners, and for the learner's life outside the classroom.

(WATSON, 1989, p. 134)

STRATEGY IDEAS

What are some theoretically sound instructional strategies in addition to the ones already described?

What is the difference between an instructional strategy and strategic teaching?

Strategy Lesson Ideas
Oral Storytelling
Wordless Picture Books
Alphabet and Counting Books
Sing-Along
Class Grocery Store
Reading, Writing, and Imagining
Sequencing Story Events
Sketch to Stretch
Macro-Structure
Webbing
Reciprocal Questioning

Text Sets
A Holiday Text Set
Book Baskets, Bags, and Backpacks (BBB)
Readers Theater

Strategic Teaching

SUMMARY
THEORY-TO-PRACTICE CONNECTIONS
SUGGESTED READINGS
SUGGESTED ACTIVITIES
REFERENCES

The basic approaches common to most whole language classrooms involve reading and writing to students, reading and writing with students, and students' reading and writing on their own. But beginning teachers may wish to have a few theoretically sound, interesting instructional ideas at their disposal. Literacy events involving reading, writing, talking, listening, and thinking with good books are at the heart of the activities described in this chapter. Each idea is centered on the learner and designed for a literature-based, integrated curriculum. As teachers begin implementing this type of classroom instruction, they may wish to explore these and other strategy ideas. As teachers gain experience with this curricular philosophy, they employ fewer and fewer strategy ideas in favor of supporting learners who are pursuing units of study they have chosen themselves. Teachers also develop strategic interventions for individuals or small groups of students.

Strategy Lesson Ideas

Encouraging children's varied reading and writing experiences helps build their confidence and also demonstrates some of the possibilities for self-expression, making connections, and extending learning. Strategy ideas generally have three parts: (1) what you do with the children *before* they read and write, (2) what happens *while* they read and write, and (3) what they do *after* they have read and written. We can also conceptualize the strategy idea as showing them how to do it, helping them do it, and then letting them apply it for themselves.

The first part of an activity may consist of shared book, a demonstration, brainstorming, previewing, a simulated experience of some sort, or a combination of any of these. The second part of the learning event consists of reading and perhaps writing in a guided small group or individual setting. The experience is usually shared, examined, reflected on, repeated, or otherwise experimented with. Finally, children are given an opportunity to expand their self-expression and concept development.

These strategy ideas are all "kid-tested" learning events. They all integrate reading and writing, and many integrate subject matter content as well. Each is explained in terms of a specific material. These ideas are meant as prototypes, designed to be employed in the lower grades but not necessarily limited to those levels. They may be adapted to the interests and needs of any class.

Oral Storytelling   Recall from the description of storytelling in chapter 7 that whole language strategy encourages students to compose in one medium and share, rehearse, or revise in other media. During storytelling time, readers may retell stories, create puppet shows, put poems to music, draw pictures of favorite scenes and characters, or express strong emotions in pantomime or dance. Writers may retell their own written stories, act them out, illustrate them, and connect them to subject matter in various ways. For example, they may create a map of where their story takes place.

Sometimes poor readers find they are very good storytellers. When working with less proficient readers, teachers may have someone read a chosen story to them, then read it with them. Poorer readers are then able to work on the rest of the steps for storytelling alone. They can also choose from several other ways to present a well-liked story.

To enable students to tell longer stories, teachers may suggest a group with a narrator, characters, dialogue planned in outline form, and background scenes painted on long butcher paper. Chapter books from a literature study group can be told this way over the course of several days.

Wordless Picture Books

Wordless picture books, which are described in detail in chapter 7, are helpful for poor and reluctant readers. One of the key elements in learning to read and write well is learning to think like an author. Storytelling with wordless picture books is beneficial for beginning readers, older and less able readers, and children who are word calling, that is, children who read aloud with few miscues and with good inflection but who do not construct meaning.

Inexpensive coloring books that tell a story, old discarded basal readers with good illustrations, or trade books can be used to write a story from the pictures. Tape plain paper over the text. Following the procedure outlined above, let the children create their own story and print the edited version in the actual book. Old basal readers can be taken apart and each story "bound" into an individual booklet with heavy wallpaper or construction paper. With the text cut away, or covered, some of these stories make excellent wordless picture books from which children may tell and write stories.

Alphabet and Counting Books

Most primary level curricula require the teaching of the names of the letters. Children need experiences with the letters, their names, and the sounds most commonly associated with them. Most children do not really understand the "letter-a-week" technique; however, they do like and appreciate many of the beautiful alphabet books on the market. Good alphabet books are a staple of the primary classroom and may be used in meaningful and interesting ways.

One of the most interesting and fun alphabet books is *Q Is for Duck* by Elting and Folsom. As you read it, invite the children to join in and to guess.

A is for zoo. Why?
Because . . . *animals* live in the zoo.

B is for dog. Why?
Because . . . dogs *bark.*

Discuss with the children that the authors made choices, but that those weren't the only words the authors could have used. The authors could have said "Because dogs eat *bones,*" for instance. Sometimes the children's words may be different, but they may be just as good or even better than the one the authors chose.

Brainstorm animal names. Write the children's list on the board. Tell the children that they are going to write a new alphabet book for their classroom. Sometime during the day select four to six animals from the list and write the pattern from *Q Is for Duck* on ditto paper or on separate sheets of blank paper.

_____ is for alligator. Why?
Because . . . alligators _____.

Working as a group, have the children call out possibilities and together fill in the blanks on the first two or three. Then, if possible, let the children work in pairs or small groups to fill in the blanks on the rest of their new "book." If the children are interested, this book can be expanded over time to include all the letters.

After the children have completed their own *Q Is for Duck,* the pattern can be repeated with foods, for example, instead of animals. This pattern can also be used to produce a counting book. For example:

One (1) is for puppy. Why?
Because . . . we got *one* puppy for Christmas.

Older, poorer readers can make such alphabet and counting books for the kindergartners and first graders. Another variation can be written using all the members of the class. For example:

M is for Billy. Why?
Because . . . Billy has a new *minibike.*

When the children have exhausted their interest in *Q Is for Duck,* explore other alphabet and counting books and use them for dictating and for writing. Each of the alphabet and counting books listed here is a learning experience that lends itself to expanding children's language and thinking. Some of these alphabet and counting books may also be appropriate for older children.

Alphabet Books

Alpha-Bakery: Children's Cookbook. (1991). Minneapolis, MN: General Mills.

Asimov, I. (1971). *ABCs of the Earth.* New York: Walker.

Base, G. (1986). *Animalia.* New York: Harry N. Abrams.

Bayer, J. (1984). *A My Name is Alice.* New York: Dial.

Brennan, J. (1984). *A Is for Australia.* Baronia, Australia: J. M. Dent.

Bridwell, N. (1983). *Clifford's ABC.* New York: Scholastic.

Elting, M., & Folsom, M. (1980). *Q Is for Duck.* New York: Clarion Books.

Hepworth, C. (1992). *Antics! An Alphabetical Anthology.* New York: Putnam.

Isadora, R. (1983). *City Seen from A to Z.* New York: Greenwillow Books.

Jonas, A. (1990). *Aardvarks, Disembark!* New York: Greenwillow Books.

Lear, E. (1983). *An Edward Lear Alphabet.* New York: Lothrop, Lee & Shephard Books.

Lobel, A. (1981). *On Market Street.* New York: Greenwillow Books.

Mayer, M. (1989). *The Unicorn Alphabet.* New York: Dial.

Musgrove, M. (1977). *Ashanti to Zulu: African Traditions.* New York: Dell.

Owens, M. (1988). *The Caribou Alphabet Book.* Brunswick, ME: Dog Ear Press.

Pallotta, J. (1989). *The Yucky Reptile Alphabet Book.* Watertown, MA: Charlesbridge.

Seuss, Dr. (1963). *ABC.* New York: Random House.

Wildsmith, B. (1962). *Brian Wildsmith's ABC.* New York: F. Watts.

Counting Books

Anno, M. (1975). *Anno's Counting Book.* New York: Thomas Y. Crowell.

Anno, M. (1983). *Anno's Mysterious Multiplying Jar.* New York: Philomel Books.

Bang, M. (1983). *Ten, Nine, Eight.* New York: Greenwillow Books.

Carle, E. (1968). *1, 2, 3 to the Zoo.* New York: Philomel Books.

Gerstein, M. (1984). *Roll Over!* New York: Crown.

Haskins, J. (1987). *Count Your Way through Russia.* Minneapolis, MN: Carolrhoda Books.

Howe, C. (1983). *Counting Penguins, 0–9.* New York: Harper & Row.

Leedy, L. (1985). *A Number of Dragons.* New York: Holiday House.

Noll, S. (1984). *Off and Counting.* New York: Greenwillow Books.

Pomerantz, C. (1984). *One Duck, Another Duck.* New York: Greenwillow Books.

Tudor, T. (1956). *1 Is One.* Chicago: Rand McNally.

Wild, R., & Wild, J. (1978). *The Bears Counting Book.* New York: Harper & Row.

Sing-Along   Music is another symbol system that humans have invented to represent meaning. Integrating music and reading helps some students find music a more comfortable form of self-expression than talking, drawing, or writing. This activity provides functional and repetitious language in enjoyable situations. Young children need to be immersed in meaningful written language, and that language must be whole and related to what the children are doing in the classroom.

As part of the regular morning routine, the teacher may plan a sing-along time. To prepare for this segment of the day's activities, teachers collect and copy several songs onto chart paper. A sign-up form may be displayed in the room for children who want to be morning leader. The person who leads selects the songs to be sung. Using a pointer, the leader (with assistance from the teacher when necessary) walks the children through the song a time or two by pointing to the words. The class reads the text in unison, and after this practice, they sing the song once or twice.

This helps children see and experience such aspects of the reading process as left-to-right tracking, voice-print matching, sound-letter associations, and capital letters at the beginning and end marks at the ends of sentences. Children can also explore how words and word forms have to change sometimes across a text. The rehearsal of the song also helps build vocabulary. In addition, experienced teachers know that when a child is having difficulty memorizing something, for instance the multiplication tables, music can help.

Several lengthy pieces of written language that every child can "read" and enjoy should become part of the literate environment of the classroom through songs, poems, and rhymes. Teachers add to the collection throughout the year. Patriotic songs, nursery rhyme songs, holiday and seasonal songs, songs from other cultures and other languages, and songs connected to units of study become part of the children's repertoire.

Older students may explore writing down the lyrics to popular music. They can listen to tapes and records of favorite songs, then copy some of these lyrics and make their own song books, which can be illustrated and used in the classroom or for a class presentation. Students may want to collect lyrics and make other books of songs—perhaps songs about animals, foods, or holidays. The students can tape-record their songs and put the books and the music in the listening center for everyone to enjoy. Teachers and children can collect music they like for the listening center. "Composer of the month" may become part of the life of a classroom as learners explore various types of music and learn about the people who wrote the pieces. The children may try writing their own lyrics to a favorite tune. And songwriting might lead to investigating poetry.

Class Grocery Store   One way to immerse children in print that they can make sense of is to include examples of the wealth of written language that is part of everyday life. One example of the print in the natural environment of all children is the product labels and packages they use in their homes. A classroom grocery, which is inexpensive and easy to set up, utilizes this form of print. Teachers and children collect empty boxes, cans, cartons and other packages for the "store." The children bring in cleaned and empty household food and product containers for their store.

Read such stories as *Neat-O, the Supermarket Mouse* by Tichenor, *Something Good* by Munsch, or *The Little Old Man Who Couldn't Read* by Black. Talk with the class about the times that reading and writing are useful to people. The children may mention paying bills, riding the bus, driving a car, going to the store. A reading walk through their "new grocery store" will provide opportunities for the children to "read" items such as Coke, Tide detergent, Crest toothpaste, Cheerios cereal, Skippy peanut butter, and so on. Create a checkout stand so the children can take turns buying items from the class store. Shopping lists can be written and math can then be incorporated.

Investigate prices of the products and add up the cost of the groceries children want to buy. Act out doing the family shopping. Students can make items for their store that they have not been able to bring in but that they want. These can then be priced and sold along with the regular items. Examining product ingredients, nutrition information, advertisements, and coupons might prove interesting and instructive. A field trip to a real supermarket could provide an opportunity for the teacher to model shopping, list writing, counting, adding, estimating, and reading at the grocery store.

Here are a few ways the class store can be used to teach children about reading, writing, math, and so on.

1. Students might make a window display of magazine and newspaper ads for grocery store items.

2. In a game of being a shopper, each child buys items and tries not to spend more than some specified amount. Or each child has to find items in the store that say _____ or items that contain _____.

3. After reading product advertisements over the course of several weeks, children can make up their own ads for favorite items. They may also want to make up new products, creating labels and ads for these items.

4. Older children may want to explore nutrition and ingredient labeling. This may begin a unit on food additives or natural and artificial foods—an excellent opportunity to read *Michael Bird Boy* by de Paola to the children.

Reading, Writing, and Imagining   Comprehension is not an end in itself. People read for many purposes. Good literature has the potential to create a love of reading and of good books if children can experience stories that stay with them and have an effect on their lives long after the book is closed. Of course, teachers must be familiar with high-quality children's literature; they also need a large number of good books in the room at all times. Some of these books might be related to a theme or central subject.

For instance, teachers may collect several bedtime books. *Bedtime for Frances* by Hoban, *Mortimer* by Munsch, *There's a Nightmare in My Closet* by Mayer, *There's an Alligator under My Bed* by Mayer, *Nightmares* by Prelutsky, *Where the Wild Things Are* by Sendak, *Clyde Monster* by Crowe, *Just Go to Bed* by Mayer, and *Ira Sleeps Over* by Waber are a few excellent selections.

The teacher reads one during read-aloud time, *There's a Nightmare in My Closet,* for instance. The story and the illustrations are discussed with the children. Then the teacher might present the children with "what if" situations:

What would you do if you found a nightmare in your closet?

What would you do if you found a nightmare under your bed?

What would you do if you found a nightmare in the bathtub?

What would you do if you found a nightmare in the refrigerator?

And so on . . .

The children select the situation they would like to respond to, imagine what they would do, and then tell, write, or act out a "what if." Read another bedtime book, *There's an Alligator under My Bed,* for example. Discuss and play with this story. Bring in nonfiction books about alligators. Show a film about alligators if you can. A secondary unit on amphibians or reptiles might be organized if some of the children are interested.

Read another bedtime book, perhaps *Ira Sleeps Over* or *Clyde Monster.* Both books also deal with fear of going to sleep. Discuss nighttime fears and nightmares. Read some of Prelutsky's *Nightmares.* Invite the children to write poems or stories about their nightmares and draw pictures of them.

Read *Where the Wild Things Are.* Let the children discuss what they would do if they could turn their nightmares into their favorite adventure and fantasy. Reread the Sendak book and invite the children to choose between writing their own "wild things" book or dictating a "wild things" group story. Encourage the children to develop their own ideas from these books. Suggest that they read, write, draw, investigate, and create projects of their own design. This mini-unit on bedtime stories might end with the children preparing a readers theater production and acting out *Mortimer* or *Bedtime for Frances* for the class. Figure 9.1 shows a wall display that grew out of a favorite book in one classroom.

Bedtime Books

Crowe, R. (1976). *Clyde Monster.* New York: Dutton.

Prelutsky, J. (1976). *Nightmares: Poems to Trouble Your Sleep.* New York: Greenwillow Books.

Hoban, R. (1960). *Bedtime for Frances.* New York: Harper & Row.

Mayer, M. (1983). *Just Go to Bed.* Racine, WI: Western.

Mayer, M. (1987). *There's an Alligator under My Bed.* New York: Dial.

FIGURE 9.1
Literature Study Group Display

Mayer, M. (1965). *There's a Nightmare in My Closet.* New York: Dutton.

Munsch, R. (1985). *Mortimer.* Toronto, Ontario: Annick Press.

Sendak, M. (1970). *In the Night Kitchen.* New York: Harper & Row.

Sendak, M. (1963). *Where the Wild Things Are.* New York: Harper & Row.

Waber, B. (1972). *Ira Sleeps Over.* Boston: Houghton Mifflin.

Sequencing Story Events   Summarizing the events of the story into a plot statement and sequencing story events are abstract and difficult tasks for some children. Teachers select a story that has a clear, marked sequence of events. Stories such as "Mother Meadowlark and Brother Snake" in *Sounds of a Storyteller* by Bill Martin, Jr. (1972), or *Murmel, Murmel, Murmel* by Munsch (1982) fit this category. The children may act out each episode. Cue cards might be written to prompt each new episode or scene. The students can create the cue cards and direct the action. This basic strategy can be expanded in these ways:

1. Students may create webs and other graphic displays of the story structure. Story webs can be posted in the classroom. The title of each book, perhaps the book jacket or an illustration and caption about the book can accompany the web. (Webs are described in detail later in this chapter.)

2. Students could write a press release advertising their favorite story. They could design a poster and caption to sell the story. It must be intriguing without really disclosing the plot.

3. Students might write a book of ads, like a catalog, for their favorite stories from a set of related stories or for the works of their favorite author.

Sketch to Stretch   Proficient readers integrate new material into their own background of experiences, and proficient learners view the world from more than one perspective. Engaging learners in generating new insights and meanings gained from their readings expands their learning, as does giving them experiences in looking at the world in new and perhaps unusual ways. Inviting learners to express their understandings in a variety of sign and symbol systems—for example, pantomime, art, music, and movement—also enhances learning.

In sketch to stretch, a strategy originated by Harste, Burke, and Siegel (1988, p. 64), the teacher selects a piece of high-quality literature, one with a lesson or moral. Three books that could be used are Merriam's *The Wise Woman and her Secret,* Silverstein's *The Giving Tree,* and de Paola's *Nana Upstairs, Nana Downstairs.* Students read the story for themselves or it is read aloud to them.

The students are given a sheet of paper and asked to sketch or draw what the story meant to them. The teacher tries not to give them any more information, but encourages them to do whatever they think is best. The students share, explain, and discuss their sketches. Teachers accept any graphic display. This allows students to set the parameters on their attempts and makes the activity essentially a risk-free event. Some students may include writing on their sketches; some students will be more concrete than others. A few students may not have an idea what to do at first. Some students will draw highly abstract representations of meaning they derived from the text. Each time sketch to stretch is an option, more students will express their understandings in abstract ways. Sketch to stretch drawings may also be used in author's chair or during oral storytelling.

Sketches may be collected and bound into a booklet. These might be placed at the recreational reading table along with a copy of the story. Teachers may add their own sketches of favorite stories. Chances are these will not be appreciably better than many of the children's sketches. Teachers can ask students to examine the sketches for levels of interpretation from literal to more abstract.

Macro-Structure Readers use cohesive ties and other structural cues across the entire text to help them weave the thread of the story or of informative material into a meaningful whole. Children need to know that they do this, and they may benefit from experiences that allow them to examine how they do it.

The strategy described here is adapted from one originated by

Dorothy Watson (1988, p. 65). Teachers select materials that have clearly identifiable organizing structures—a beginning, a middle, and an end or a setting, plot development, climax, and resolution. Most well-written stories and pieces from books and children's magazines, such as *Weekly Reader, Cricket, Highlights for Children, Scope,* and *World,* would fit this description.

Selections from fiction and nonfiction in children's magazines and from social studies and science textbooks, as well as newspaper articles can provide rich experiences for children. Stories from old basal readers may not be a viable source because they frequently are written to formula and do not retain the natural organizing structures found in good literature. However, they could be used to compare with well-written stories.

The selected passage is copied and cut into several sections, typically three to six sections for young children's material and six to ten sections for more lengthy material with older students. The selections are cut apart at highly predictable and natural breaking points. Each section is mounted on a piece of heavy construction paper. Each child or pair of children in the group is given one piece of the story. They then read their section silently, thinking about what might have come before or after their passage.

The discussion might begin by determining who has the beginning of the story. That child then reads the first section aloud. The second section is identified and read aloud. The rest of the passages are read in order. The children figure out how the pieces go together. They have the original text available to check after they have reassembled the story. Children will begin to see how texts naturally fit together and what cues authors provide.

A variety of types of texts may be explored in this way. One interesting possibility is recipes. Pick a recipe and copy the ingredients randomly on a sheet of paper. Copy the directions onto strips, one statement at a time. Give the children the name of the dish, and the list of ingredients; then give one piece of the directions to each child in the group. Ask the children to figure out how the dish is made. The process may be repeated with a no-cook food such as fresh fruit roll ups (if you live where it's hot and dry) or "ants on a log" (made from celery, homemade peanut butter, and raisins) or with simple cooked recipes prepared on a hot plate—for example, a cheese and vegetable spread for crackers. The children are given the actual ingredients and asked to reconstruct the directions and then make the dish for everyone in the class to taste.

Another alternative is to prepare several copies of a particularly good story or chapter from a textbook. Each copy is cut into the same sections and mounted on heavy paper. Every student or pair of students in the group is then given the entire stack shuffled, and asked to reconstruct the text. Students compare the results and discuss any differences in their versions.

Webbing   This strategy allows the teacher and the children to relate a story to themselves and to other subject areas. Webbing accommodates a wide variety of activities that extend children's language, thinking, and learning. It uses good books in a multitude of ways.

Teachers read a story that has a variety of aspects. After the story has been read at least twice, the teacher can begin to brainstorm with the children to draw a web of its elements and categories. Figure 9.2 shows a web for *Michael Bird Boy* by Tomie de Paola. A teacher and his students constructed this web together after they read the story. It gave them direction as they began to explore various components of the book and to develop projects.

Each identified area may lend itself to activities in reading, writing, art, drama, math, science, music, health, and social studies. Project ideas are developed jointly by the teacher and the children; the children choose what they want to do. Examples of interdisciplinary projects that could be undertaken are listed here.

Communication

1. Children plan a "taste of honey" party, at which they will serve things made of honey. They write invitations.

2. Children conduct a telephone poll to see how many factories in their community have women bosses. (They need to find out how many factories there are, how many "bosses" there are in each factory, and how many of these are women. They need to practice ask-

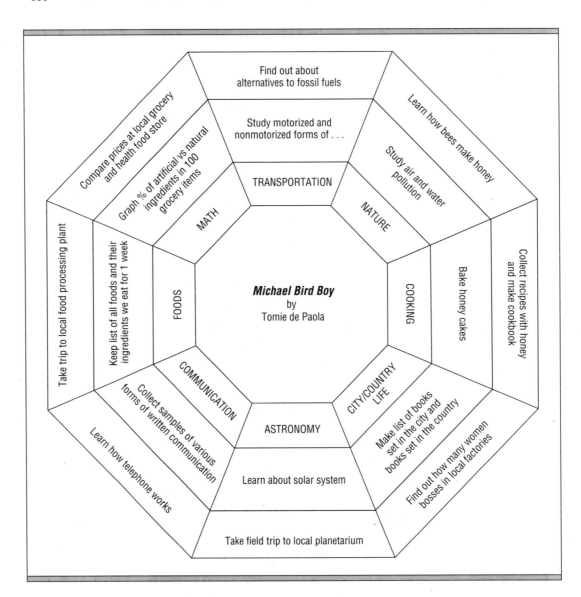

FIGURE 9.2
Web of *Michael Bird Boy*

ing questions and to decide how to record and present their findings.)

Food

1. Children collect food labels and find out what the ingredients in foods actually are. Their goal is to define *artificial* and *natural* and to determine what food additives are supposed to do and which ones may be harmful. (They will have to decide how to collect this information—whether from libraries, guest speakers, or manufacturers—and how to present their findings.)

Science

1. Children learn about how bees make honey. They contact local wildlife agents, find films and other materials in the library, and arrange through the wildlife agent for the class to visit a bee farm.

2. Children collect information on air and water pollution. They want to determine how much better or worse things are now than they were 100 years ago. They want to find out what causes pollution and what is being done about it. They begin by reading and they end by having someone from an ecology department at a nearby university visit their classroom.

Music

1. Children listen to a recording of "Flight of the Bumblebee" by Ippolitov-Ivanov. They are invited to "become bees" and do the things they have learned about bees as they listen to the music.

One of the children created a second web for this story during the week the group worked with this story (see figure 9.3). The study that developed from *Michael Bird Boy* was clearly successful for this student.

Reciprocal Questioning   Proficient readers ask themselves internal questions as they read. Encouraging less able readers to ask questions of themselves and demonstrating how to do that will help them better understand the reading process. Students who are having difficulty comprehending will benefit from this strategy, adapted from one developed by Anthony Manzo (Manzo & Manzo, 1993, pp. 313–314).

Teachers select a piece of material that has fairly long sentences with little or no dialogue. Tell the children they are going to read this story differently. Explain that readers ask themselves questions when they read. Usually these questions are only in our heads, but this time they will be asked out loud.

For example, in Rafe Martin's *Foolish Rabbit's Big Mistake* (1985), the first sentence is, "Early one morning a foolish little rabbit lay sleeping under a tree in the forest." The teacher might begin by saying, "When I read that, I asked myself, 'Who was sleeping in the forest?' I answered, 'A foolish little rabbit.' Then I asked myself, 'What was he doing?' and I thought to myself, 'He was sleeping.'

"What did you ask yourself?"

The teacher has an opportunity to model internal questioning and other thought processes that go into understanding text. This thinking aloud, question-answer pattern may be continued until the group can provide reasonable hypotheses about what happens in the remainder of the story. Try this strategy as a written conversation between teacher and students or between pairs of students. Repeat the strategy often with less proficient readers.

FIGURE 9.3
Another Way to
Construct a Web

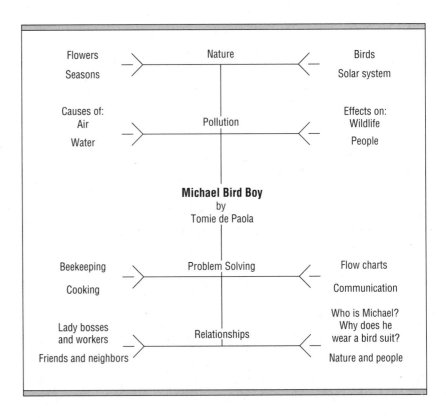

Text Sets   Text sets are conceptually related books assembled for children to read and discuss. The children are encouraged to explore the commonalities and related features among the books. This activity is appropriate for all children and is especially helpful to learners who do not relate what they read to themselves or to other information. The strategy described here is adapted from one originated by Lynn Rhodes (1987, pp. 22–23).

Everyone in the group reads pairs of books or sets of several selections that are connected in some way. They may be read aloud by the teacher or by the students taking turns. They may be read silently over time until everyone has read all the books. The teacher may make the books available at the recreational reading center so that they can be read silently during the course of a day or two. When the books have been read, the class meets to talk about the set.

Teachers may ask one or two questions to initiate discussion, or they may find they achieve better results if they simply encourage the children to talk about how these books are alike and how they are different. The sets they read may be made up of information or of expository materials. Both narrative and expository books on the same subject can be used.

After discussing similarities between or among texts, students can be guided to rank order their findings from most to least important. The children may then proceed to locate other texts that could be added to the original set. They can read the book they suggest and explain why they think it fits. Students can produce a group or individual story that fits into the set they have been working with. These stories could be shared, revised, edited, and bound to add to the classroom library. The types of text sets that are appropriate are as many as the teacher has time to come up with, including books on the same theme, with the same problem, or similar characters, or by the same author or illustrator. The examples listed here are but a few of the possibilities.

Books with the same theme form the largest set. The variations, from books about Native Americans to books about death and dying, are nearly limitless. Retold tales and similar stories from different cultures are among children's favorites. This strategy may be used regularly to acquaint children with a wealth of good literature.

Encourage the children to discuss the books and to question the reader further, extracting all major similarities and differences.

Multiple Versions

Blegvad, E. (1980). *The Three Little Pigs.* Hartford, CT: Wadsworth Atheneum.
Brenner, B. (1972). *The Three Little Pigs.* New York: Random House.
Galdone, P. (1970). *The Three Little Pigs.* New York: Scholastic.

Retold Tales

Briggs, R. (1970). *Jim and the Beanstalk.* New York: Coward, McCann & Geoghegan.
Howe, J. (1989). *Jack and the Beanstalk.* Boston: Little, Brown.

Contrasting Theme

McDonald, J. (1991). *Homebody.* New York: Putnam.
Moore, I. (1991). *Six Dinner Sid.* New York: Simon and Schuster.

Similar Theme

Pinkwater, D. (1977). *The Big Orange Splot.* New York: Scholastic.
Yashime, T. (1955). *Crow Boy.* New York: Viking.

Carrier, L. (1985). *There Was a Hill.* Natick, MA: Alphabet Press.
Clement, C. (1986). *The Painter and the Wild Swans.* New York: Dial.
Yoshi, (1987). *Who's Hiding Here.* Natick, MA: Picture Book Studio.

Bailey, C. (1988). *The Little Rabbit Who Wanted Red Wings.* New York: Putnam.
Howe, J. (1985). *I Wish I Were a Butterfly.* San Diego, CA: Harcourt Brace Jovanovich.
McDermott, G. (1975). *The Stone Cutter.* New York: Viking.

MacGill-Callahan, S. (1991). *And Still the Turtle Watched.* New York: Dial.

Wood, D. (1992). *Old Turtle.* Duluth, MN: Pfeifer-Hamilton.

Patterned Language

Boone, R., & Mills, A. (1961). *I Know an Old Lady.* New York: Rand McNally.

Kellogg, S. (1974). *There Was an Old Woman.* New York: Parents' Magazine Press.

▫

de Paola, T. (1986). *Teeny Tiny.* New York: Putnam.

Seuling, B. (1976). *The Teeny Tiny Woman.* New York: Viking.

Accumulated Pattern

Emberly, B. (1967). *Drummer Hoff.* Englewood Cliffs, NJ: Prentice-Hall.

Wood, D., & Wood, A. (1984). *The Napping House.* San Diego, CA: Harcourt Brace Jovanovich.

Same Story, Different Culture

Edens, C. (1989). *Little Red Riding Hood.* San Diego, CA: Green Tiger Press.

Young, E. (1989). *Lon Po Po.* New York: Philomel Books.

▫

Ehrlich, A. (1985). *Cinderella.* New York: Dial.

Climo, S. (1989). *The Egyptian Cinderella.* New York: Harper Trophy.

Similar Information

Jordan, H. (1960). *How a Seed Grows.* New York: Thomas Y. Crowell.

Krauss, R. (1945). *The Carrot Seed.* New York: Harper & Row.

▫

Cowcher, H. (1988). *Rain Forest.* New York: Farrar, Straus & Giroux.

Cherry, L. (1990). *The Great Kapok Tree.* San Diego, CA: Harcourt Brace Jovanovich.

Craig, J. (1990). *Wonders of the Rain Forest.* Mahwah, NJ: Troll Associates.

George, J. (1990). *One Day in the Tropical Rain Forest.* New York: Thomas Y. Crowell.

Point of View

Brett, J. (1989). *Beauty and the Beast.* New York: Clarion Books.

Hastings, S. (1985). *Sir Gawain and the Loathly Lady.* New York: Mulberry Books.

▫

Marshall, J. (1989). *The Three Little Pigs.* New York: Dial.

Scieszka, J. (1989). *The True Story of the Three Little Pigs.* New York: Viking.

▫

Howe, J. (1989). *Jack and the Beanstalk.* Boston: Little, Brown.

Paulson, T. (1990). *The Beanstalk Incident: The Giant's Story.* New York: Citadel Press.

Same Author

Herriot, J. (1986). *The Christmas Day Kitten.* New York: St. Martin's Press.

Herriot, J. (1984). *Moses the Kitten.* New York: St Martin's Press.

Herriot, J. (1990). *Oscar, Cat-about-Town.* New York: St. Martin's Press.

A Holiday Text Set   Teachers are often looking for new, enjoyable, and instructive ideas around holidays. This particular strategy combines poetry, story versions, and retold tales with a secular Christmas theme. While most school districts must avoid the religious aspects of religious holidays, most teachers search for holiday ideas that are new, are interesting, and engage learners in authentic activities and good literature. Other holiday themes that might employ a text set format are Hanukkah, Chinese New Year, Earth Day, Halloween, and Mother's Day. This text set is offered to provide examples of the types of activities and events that might emerge. This strategy was developed by Cathy Clarkson, an early childhood classroom teacher in Franklin, Tennessee.

The teacher began by talking to the children about their Christmas memories. She asked them to close their eyes as she read *The Night before Christmas.* The children talked about the pictures they saw in their heads as she was reading the poem. She gave everyone a copy of the poem and they read it together. She used a recording of the poem so the children could hear various voice effects.

She shared books illustrated by different artists (the versions illustrated by de Paola and Lobel were the children's favorites). She invited the children to bring in and share any versions of the poem they found in magazines, newspapers, greeting cards, and other books.

The teacher and the children developed several activities for further interaction with the poem, including the following:

Make a big book version of *The Night before Christmas.*
Make a readers theater script and present the poem.
Make a flannel board or puppet show version.
Write a play and act it out.

Then the teacher read a different retelling of the poem. She selected James Rice's *Cajun Night before Christmas.* In this book the reindeer are alligators with French names. The children loved the language play in this book. Then she read the "Hillbilly" version. Before reading the "Texas" version, the children predicted what the reindeer might be and what they might be named. Ultimately the children wrote their own language play versions such as: "The Rock 'n Roll Night before Christmas," "The Simpsons' Night before Christmas," "The Gremlins' Night before Christmas," "The Space Invaders' Night before Christmas," and "The Ninja Turtles' Night before Christmas." These were revised and edited, illustrated, bound, and given as Christmas gifts.

Some children experimented with rewriting the poem as it would sound if it were set in another country—for example, "The Japanese Night before Christmas" or "The Night before Christmas in Mexico." In order to do this they had to find information about these countries, their customs, language, indigenous animals, and common names.

Some of the different versions of this story we have found are listed here.

Rice, J. (1986). *Texas Night before Christmas.* Gretna, LA: Pelican.

Rice, J. (1982). *Cajun Night before Christmas.* Gretna, LA: Pelican.

Rice, J. (1983). *Hillbilly Night before Christmas.* Gretna, LA: Pelican.

Budar, V. (1987). *Hawaiian Night before Christmas.* Honolulu, Hawaii: Hawaiian Isles.

Van Bebber, C. (1987). *Desert Night before Christmas.* Tucson, AZ: Treasure Chest.

James, E. (1988). *The Night after Christmas.* New York: Greenwillow Books.

Some students also chose to research the life of Clement Moore to find out why he wrote the poem. They presented their findings to the class.

Book Baskets, Bags, and Backpacks (BBB)   The literate behaviors that different families practice in the home can be extended with books. The book baskets, bags, and backpacks (BBB) strategy is designed to put books and other literature into children's hands at home and to provide parents with a few guidelines or ideas for using these materials with their children. BBB promotes children's familiarity with books as well as positive experiences with books in the home. This enjoyment may in turn foster an interest in reading and a love of books.

Organized around a concept or theme, an author, or a genre, an assortment of books and related materials are collected and put into baskets, canvas bags, backpacks, or even decorated boxes. A list of the materials, along with one or two (or more) ideas for parents and children to do together, is included on a card and inserted along with the paperbound and hardcover books. Teachers may even add audiotapes, videotapes, maps, pictures, a toy, and other materials appropriate to the collection. Each basket or pack is given a title— for example, Bedtime Books and Stories, The Rain Forest, Humorous Poems, Bear Book, Dr. Seuss Books, or American Folk Tales.

A teacher may prepare five or ten baskets to be checked out by the children from Thursday to Monday. When every child has taken a basket home, they can be changed and another set of five or ten theme baskets developed. The baskets are checked out and returned along with a note from the parents stating how they liked the set and what they did with it. Each basket, bag, or backpack should also be labeled with the name and address of the school and classroom to which it belongs, in case it is lost. Some teachers arrange for older students to check the contents of the baskets and straighten them up on Tuesday or Wednesday, getting ready for the children to check them out again the next day.

This is not an inexpensive project for classroom teachers to undertake; however, it can be extremely effective. Many teachers secure small grants to fund the creation of book bags. In addition to the bags or baskets, teachers sometimes order audiocassette players with rechargeable batteries for the children who need to check them out with the books. Many teachers report that not only do the children love to take the bags home, but the teachers enjoy the creative effort of putting the collections together.

Readers Theater Readers theater is designed to expand students' language and creativity. As this strategy develops characters and moves the plot along, it helps students understand dialogue. Any student in grades 2–8 who is having trouble comprehending or who doesn't relate personally to the characters and situations in stories may benefit from this event.

Select stories that are good-quality literature or that deal with important concepts. Read the story together or individually and discuss who the characters are, what is said in the story, and how the plot develops and is then resolved. Some of this information is probably provided in the dialogue. Invite students to write and present the story like a play without movement, with students reading the script as if they were the characters talking.

Students then begin to make decisions about how the story might be arranged if it were a play. Copies of several plays may be brought into the classroom and examined by the group. They may decide that while most of the information can be given in dialogue, some of it might best be read by a narrator. They have to decide how to begin, possibly with a narrator setting the scene. The teacher may guide the exploration by asking questions: "What would happen next?" "What would that character say?" "What does the audience have to know to understand?" The students write their script like a play—complete with dialogue, stage directions, props, and scene descriptions.

The script is shared, revised, and edited until everyone is satisfied with the final product. Then the script is cast, and the readers practice their parts. The small amount of scenery that is called for is created, and the few props that are needed are gathered. When everything is ready, stools or chairs are arranged on the "stage" and the readers present their production to the rest of the class or to another group.

The story can be redone with another cast so that more than one group has a chance to perform, and the story can be presented to more than one audience. This production can be one of several for a week-long drama festival in the classroom or school. Several favorite stories could be turned into readers theater productions, one by each of the groups in the classroom or one by each participating classroom (Sloyer, 1982).

If students decide they like this form of expression, have them select an interesting event in history. They can read about the event in several texts and reference books, then write a script for a readers theater presentation. Some classes might wish to make readers theater a regular event for presentation to a younger class.

Strategic Teaching

Whole language teachers strive to help children develop the strategies they need to comprehend and produce written language. As we have already discussed, these are essentially the same strategies all learners use to organize information and solve problems. Strategic teaching expands learners' strengths. It takes place in the context of real literacy events and employs meaningful written language.

The strategy ideas and activities described in this and previous chapters all require meaningful written language in authentic literacy events with students. Some of the ideas are helpful for developing efficient use of language cues, some for developing attitudes toward good literature or writing that students need for school and future life success. However, teachers can also develop strategic interventions that are specific to individual learner needs. (For one sample lesson plan format, see appendix G.)

To be a strategic teacher, teachers must be kidwatchers. They must watch closely, listen carefully, and ask thoughtful questions about what their students are doing. A strategic intervention may be a well-placed explanation, demonstration, or instructional activity intentionally planned by an informed teacher. Strategic teaching may be developed for use in a guided reading or writing session or during conferencing. It is aimed at one child or a small group of children with a similar problem.

For example, a teacher discovers that one or two students confuse the words *was* and *saw* or *on* and *no*. Since these words look so similar and may operate in sentences in the same grammatical way, further work with the words together will *not* end the learners' habit of confusing them. Rather, a knowledgeable teacher might write a brief story or passage in which only one of the two words fits and makes sense. The students read the passage and are supported to self-correct. That is, when they miscue, they discover that the story doesn't make sense and are led by the text to correct.

What We Saw

[Child's name] and her [or his] parents went to the mountains on a vacation. She saw lots of different animals. She saw a bear, a skunk, and two deer. She also saw beautiful mountains, wild flowers, and a waterfall. The family took many pictures so we can all see what they saw on their trip.

This lesson helps the children build their predicting, confirming, and correcting strategies. It is important not to call the reader's attention to the individual words, since the goal is to support the development of their own system for separating, sorting out, and dealing with the words based on meaning and function. The passage helps the learner differentiate. A teacher might have to write more than one such passage (Goodman, 1986).

SUMMARY

Strategy ideas are designed to support and expand students' reading, writing, and thinking processes. They may also improve a learner's attitude toward learning and good literature. Teachers who are kidwatchers know their children, the children's strengths and problems, what they are trying to learn to do. The strategy lesson ideas offered throughout this book may be adapted to fit learners and available resources. Teachers should use them as prototypes for developing other ideas. It is important to work toward becoming a strategic teacher. Strategic teaching is part of the whole language teacher's repertoire.

THEORY-TO-PRACTICE CONNECTIONS

Literacy and Learning Theory

1. Learners learn to read and write by really reading and really writing.

2. Learning takes place best in a low-risk environment of cooperation rather than competition.

3. Learning best occurs as learners explore making meaning with a purpose.

4. Strategy ideas involve immersion, demonstration, approximation, and the other conditions for natural learning.

5. Classrooms invite learners' language and culture to become part of the curriculum.

6. Learners need to explore self-expression in a variety of media, with a variety of symbol systems.

7. Good teachers help learners have personal experiences with books and make connections across texts and across content.

8. Strategic teaching involves kidwatching and requires that teachers be informed and intentional.

Examples of Classroom Practice

1. Readers theater

2. Sing-along

3. Text sets

4. Class grocery store; book bags and baskets

5. Holiday text set

6. Sketch to stretch

7. Webs and projects

8. "What We Saw" passage

SUGGESTED READINGS

Chow, M., Dobson, L., Hurst, M., Nucich, J. (1992). *Whole language: Practical ideas.* Portsmouth, NH: Heinemann.

Cullinan, B. (Ed.). (1987). *Children's literature in the reading program.* Newark, DE: IRA.

Goodman, Y., & Burke, C. (1980). *Reading strategies: Focus on comprehension.* Katonah, NY: Richard C. Owen.

Korbin, B. (1988). *Eyeopeners! How to choose and use children's books about real people, places, and things.* New York: Penguin.

Monson, D. (1985). *Adventuring with books: A booklist for pre-K–grade 6.* Urbana, IL: NCTE.

Routman, R. (1991). *Invitations.* Portsmouth, NH: Heinemann.

Watson, D. (Ed.). (1989). *Ideas and insights.* Urbana, IL: NCTE.

SUGGESTED ACTIVITIES

1. Discuss how each of the classroom practices cited in this chapter reflects the whole language theory of language and learning.

2. If you are observing and working with students in a local elementary classroom, try some of the suggested strategies with your children. Share your experiences and observations.

3. Working in collaboration with classmates, develop one strategy idea that engages learners in an authentic experience with meaningful print. Share your ideas.

4. If you are observing and working with students in a local elementary school, identify one student who is a less proficient reader than his or her classmates. Identify one area of confusion or misunderstanding for that learner and develop a strategic intervention. What did you have to do to find this kind of problem? How did you go about creating an intervention lesson? What happened when you tried it out? Would you do it differently next time? Why? Share your experiences with your fellow students.

5. Using the strategy ideas in this chapter as samples, develop your own strategy idea either from a piece of children's literature, a type of literature, or a concept. Share among your classmates. Critique each other's ideas for theoretical fit and redesign as indicated.

REFERENCES

Burton, R. (1986). *Tell me another.* Portsmouth, NH: Heinemann.

Goodman, K. (1986). *What's whole in whole language?* Portsmouth, NH: Heinemann.

Harste, J., Burke, C., & Siegel, M. (1988). Sketch to stretch. In C. Gilles, M. Bixby, P. Crowley, S. Crenshaw, M. Hendricks, F. Reynolds, & D. Pyle (Eds.), *Whole language strategies for secondary students.* Katonah, NY: Richard C. Owen.

Manzo, A., & Manzo, U. (1993). *Literacy disorders: Diagnosis and remediation.* Fort Worth, TX: Harcourt Brace Jovanovich.

Paley, V. (1972). *Wally's stories.* Cambridge, MA: Harvard University Press.

Rhodes, L. (1987). Text sets. In D. Watson

(Ed.), *Ideas and insights.* Urbana, IL: NCTE.

Sloyer, S. (1982). *Readers theater: Dramatization in the classroom.* Urbana, IL: NCTE.

Watson, D. (1989, November). Defining and describing whole language. *Elementary School Journal, (90),* 2, 129–141.

Watson, D. (1988). Schema stories. In C. Gilles, M. Bixby, P. Crowley, S. Crenshaw, M. Hendricks, F. Reynolds, & D. Pyle (Eds.), *Whole language strategies for secondary students.* Katonah, NY: Richard C. Owen.

10

Middle and Upper Grades

CURRICULUM ISSUES AND STRATEGY IDEAS

Can a whole language philosophy be applied to middle and upper grades?

What are the particular problems teachers encounter at upper grade levels?

Is an integrated, language- and literature-based program as effective with older learners as with younger children?

What types of instructional strategies are more suited for older learners?

*M*ost primary grades are self-contained classrooms, but schools for the middle and upper grades in the United States tend to be organized by departments. Basically all schools are managed horizontally as well as vertically. In such a management scheme, a teacher has responsibility to both the department or grade level (horizontal) and to the principal and supervisor (vertical), as shown in figure 10.1.

School Organization

With a few exceptions, teachers in middle and upper grades teach sections of classes, often seeing as many as 160 children for as little as fifty minutes a day each. Some teachers in middle and junior high schools do not even teach the homeroom they meet each morning for roll taking. Their teaching experience is quite different from that of the teacher who keeps the same children all day and who is able to integrate lessons across subject areas.

At in-service training sessions, the first questions asked by many teachers in the middle and upper grades who are interested in whole language are: "How can I develop a whole language curriculum when I teach five sections a day in two subjects?" "Since early adoles-

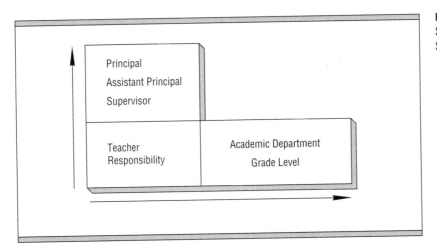

FIGURE 10.1
School Management Scheme

cents are different from younger children, do they learn language and literacy differently?"

This chapter answers these questions. It addresses the particular needs of teachers in departmentalized settings and of adolescent learners. We examine the effectiveness of an integrated, language- and literature-based curriculum for middle- and upper-grade classrooms, and we provide strategies appropriate for older students and for lengthy, more complex texts.

Departmentalization   Teachers in departmentalized settings can implement integrated programs even when they are required to address specific content within certain subjects. Most subjects are broad and general enough to allow teachers and students flexibility and creativity. Teachers may be able to choose from several alternatives to create an integrated curriculum. These include working alone, working with another teacher or group of teachers, working across grades or departments, and creating larger blocks of time that combine some subjects.

Some schools are currently experimenting with a variation on departmentalization in which math and science are combined for at least two periods a day and language arts and social studies are similarly blocked. This arrangement supports teachers who want to work with themes that integrate subjects. Teachers also have fewer total students to get to know, so they can establish better rapport with and learn in greater detail about the ones they do have. However, in most departmentalized schools teachers must try to develop themes alone or with one or two colleagues in one subject area. Teachers who are limited to one grade level or subject may begin by webbing their textbooks and grade level curriculum guide to determine what concepts and information might be explored and integrated.

In presenting ancient history, for example, many textbooks follow a predictable course from the Babylonian to the Greek to the Roman empires. One sixth-grade teacher found that his students became interested in architecture because of a local drive to save and restore historic structures. The students wanted to know why a particular building was referred to as a Greco-Roman structure with Byzantine flourishes. They learned about architecture as they studied their local buildings. They studied ancient civilizations to discover the origins of and reasons for building design. They read mythology as well as factual information. The thematic unit that developed lasted several weeks and involved reading, writing, and problem solving in several different subjects. The classroom became an environment rich in literature and information on ancient civilizations.

Teachers usually have some latitude in what they do. Imagination, the students' as well as the teacher's, intentionally applied to subject matter can lead to some wonderful learning experiences. The possibilities are endless. For example, the students in one eighth-grade English class were introduced to *To Kill a Mockingbird.* Their teacher went to the social studies teacher for help. Collaboration between these two teachers and the students led to an in-depth study of the 1920s. Students read a great deal of both fiction and nonfiction about this era; they interviewed people who could remember the 1920s and they wrote a local history of that time. They developed a "feel" for what life was like in the era of their grandparents.

When students in one fifth-grade science class created a rain forest in their classroom, the study of ecology spread throughout their school. Students from the science class became experts on various aspects of the rain forest and related ecosystems, and they shared their knowledge with English and social studies classes in both the fifth and sixth grades. The English teachers working with the science teachers began incorporating what the students were learning in science into their daily writing. The social studies teachers worked with the English and science teachers to facilitate study of the ecological impact of the destruction of rain forests. Frequent trips to the library, much map reading, writing, group work, and many lively discussion groups ensued.

While a great deal is gained by developing a more integrated curriculum, most teachers, regardless of subject, experience similar difficulties when they attempt to do so. The two most pressing problems are scheduling and subject matter requirements.

Scheduling   Unless an entire grade level in a school decides to change to a more integrated curriculum, it is difficult to alter the schedule very much. When colleagues choose a more traditional means of meeting classes (which is certainly their right), whole language teachers do not have the luxury of large blocks of time in which students can investigate, study, compose, reflect, and present. These teachers must find alternatives.

Teachers in departmentalized schools may have to think of scheduling in class periods across weeks, perhaps for fairly long sequences of time. A mini-theme might take a week or two in a self-contained classroom, but it could take several weeks in fifty-minute increments, even though roughly the same number of hours might ultimately be devoted to the study. The potential difficulty here is loss of focus by both teachers and students. Many teachers who must bridge across five class periods a week find they need to keep a flow-chart of students' activities to ensure that day-to-day tasks get attended to and that students do not lose the thread of what they are trying to accomplish. Figure 10.2 is an example of such a chart.

When more than one teacher in a department or grade level is interested in an integrated approach, classes can be combined and team taught. Team teaching may allow teachers to better support students working in flexible groups. However, team teaching is not easily accomplished for a variety of reasons, including space constraints. If several teachers wish to work together, there are more options. Collaborative planning and flexible scheduling can accommodate large time frames. Groups of variable sizes are among the alternatives to consider.

Larger blocks of time allow some students to write and some to work collaboratively in the library. Others may be involved in cross-age tutoring, developing project presentations, or working directly with one or more teachers. Groups work in different areas in (or even outside) the building. Working student choice into the program is the key to success. Unusual time, space, and grouping arrangements require administrative support and sometimes additional planning and meeting time; however, they may also produce exciting results for both teachers and students.

Subject Matter Requirements   Teachers in the upper grades often have little latitude in selecting areas of study, yet they usually do have a fair amount of freedom in deciding how that subject will be presented. The scope and sequence of the textbooks contain no absolutes and areas of study can be addressed in a multitude of ways. When learning is approached as inquiry and when students and teachers become investigators, tremendous changes occur in classrooms. One of the changes is the modeling of democratic processes, in which all members of the group have a voice. Students see teachers as co-learners and themselves as co-creators of both the environment and the curriculum. For instance, students in a science class may choose to study the three types of rocks in a unit on geology, dividing the subject and their responsibilities among the members of the group. Although this unit may or may not be covered in the sci-

FIGURE 10.2
Sample Flowchart

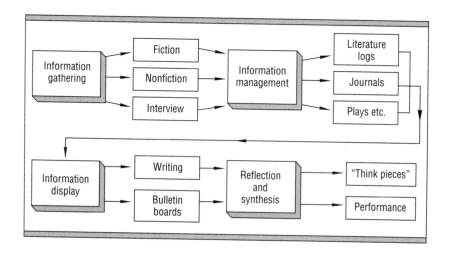

ence book, ample information, literature, books, and other materials can be gathered to allow students to learn what they want to know about the geology of the earth.

Employing the Basic Approaches

Teachers in the middle and upper grades may employ some form of the basic approaches for teaching reading and writing discussed in chapters 5 and 6. Every day they read aloud from a variety of genres, and they engage students in silent, self-selected reading and writing. However, since the texts are longer and more complex than those in primary grades, guided reading changes. The skills and abilities needed for reading short stories, novels, and expository texts are demonstrated and examined through literature study explorations and techniques that build metacognition, or an awareness of the processes employed in thinking and learning. The writing process remains intact across the curriculum.

For example, a seventh-grade reading class studying *Borrowed Children* by George Ella Lyon listened and read along as the teacher read the text aloud. When the group selected this book, the teacher began by asking them to keep a literature log; the reflections written in these logs were used every day as the basis of discussion and prediction. First, the teacher asked them to write what they thought the book was about based on the title. She wrote, too. Then the students shared their ideas. Most students thought it would be about adoption, the loss of one or both parents, or child stealing. After reading each chapter, students and teachers wrote in their logs again. They shared these comments at the end of each class and talked about what would be likely to happen in the next chapter.

Several aspects of reading narrative fiction were explored through this book—for example, characterization, settings, and conflict resolution. However, the students focused most on the unfolding of a family's history repeating itself. This led students to investigate with their relatives how history had repeated itself in their own families. While some students chose to construct their family trees, others wrote biographies, and still others presented pictorial histories. *Bor-*

rowed Children was the basis of a successful experience with a high-quality piece of literature for this group. It eventually led the students in two directions: some chose to explore other books by Lyon and the remainder chose to read more books about family history.

Students in one fifth-grade science class were taught several study techniques for learning from their textbooks. They were invited to experiment with the techniques over several days and then asked to choose the one they each preferred. Every day for two weeks their teacher provided time during class for the students to study using their favorite study method. When the chapter test was given, grades were calculated and scores compared to previous chapter tests taken without benefit of a systematic approach to studying. Almost everyone's score improved. The students created a rather large class bar graph of their scores with and without a study method. Then they posted the graph on a wall in their classroom to remind themselves that purposefully working through a text improves learning.

Students in the middle and upper grades are still developing their oral and written language abilities. They need to be read to, and they enjoy it. They need experiences that enhance their awareness of process, and ample opportunities to read and write for authentic purposes are essential. Time to discuss, plan, and share is vital. Students in the upper grades still require help in revising and editing manuscripts and possibly in planning and carrying out projects. While middle- and upper-grade students are becoming more sophisticated learners, they are still engaged in developing and refining their language and their thinking. They are still in the process of coming to know and understanding the world around them.

Selected Strategy Ideas: A Content-Rich Classroom

Many of the strategy ideas presented in earlier chapters may be adapted for use in the middle and upper grades—for example, text sets, role playing, literature logs, art projects, author's chair, and shared book. However, some activities are really more appropriate for younger learners. Most of the suggestions in this section are not aimed at teaching reading and writing per se. Rather, their goal is to provide students with the tools to inquire into subject matter. These suggestions are offered as examples and prototypes. The books and articles listed in Suggested Readings and References are recommended as sources of other practical and theoretically sound strategies for older students.

Middle- and upper-grade teachers can develop learner-centered rather than subject-centered classrooms. A learner-centered curriculum is by definition inquiry based because it evolves from the interests and intentions of the learners. An inquiry-based curriculum is one in which learners pose and answer questions for themselves. Students of all ages need support and guidance with inquiry. Encouraging children to ask and answer their own questions assumes that learners are interested in and curious about the world, that they want to learn. Inquiry-based classrooms engage students in their own research. "Research is not an activity reserved only for university scholars" (Short & Burke, 1991, p. 55). Systematically finding, organizing, hypothesizing, synthesizing, and sharing information with others *is* the research process, and that is what learners do. In other words, learning may be thought of as finding out. It is important to remember that teachers are learners and researchers too. They do not have to know everything about a subject to be able or willing to help students launch into a particular exploration.

The Research Paper or Project   Students determine their own study focus. Teachers facilitate this process with group discussion, recording students' questions, brainstorming, and narrowing topics. Helping students learn how to conduct classroom, field, and library research is a time-consuming process. Teachers who view learning as inquiry based are committed to helping learners think of themselves as researchers in both the physical and the social sciences.

When done well, a research project may take several weeks. Teachers should by no means feel they must hold to a ten-week format. The guidelines that follow suggest a schedule of activities; however, some activities may take more time to complete and others may take less time. Adapt this plan to fit your students' needs and capabilities.

Week 1. Topic selection, brainstorming, and initial discussions. Share background information, look for sources, take notes, and keep bibliography.

Week 2. Continue reading. Continue taking notes. Teacher structures time for sharing notes within groups. Teacher helps students narrow topics.

Week 3. Continue reading and taking notes. Choose tentative main theme or focus. Each student shares main ideas.

Week 4. Continue reading and aim note taking at main idea. Meet with group to discuss direction research is going. Arrange note cards in logical order and outline (outline is optional).

Week 5. Write first draft.

Week 6. Share draft with peers for suggestions. Make revisions.

Week 7. Write second draft. Cut and paste if that helps.

Week 8. Meet in groups and read each other's pieces. Offer advice. Revise if needed.

Week 9. Have conference with teacher and address mechanics.

Week 10. Write final copy.

Student research can then be presented orally to the class, published in book format, or displayed in the room, hallway, or library. Research projects often become part of students' portfolios because they reflect their best efforts.

Study Guides and Methods   Students (and adults) rarely become so proficient that they need no organizers for their work. Study guides are valuable when we investigate areas that stretch the mind. Probably the most widely known study method is SQ3R (survey, question, read, recite, review) or SQ4R (survey, question, read, recite, review, reread). The following strategy describes an alternative study method that many students like.

The E-Z Study Technique   After the teacher has introduced the material (which might include examining the title and the pictures and scanning the text), students are asked to work in pairs or small groups. As they read, they list the key words, terms, or phrases they encountered, writing them on the inside left column on a folded piece of paper. When the students are ready, each term or phrase is turned into a question and written on the right column. Working together, the students answer each of the questions; answers may be written on the back of the folded paper or on another sheet. Questions and answers are then used by the students as they help each other study. Other study methods for nonfiction, informative material include outlining, note taking, and summarizing. Studying fiction requires a somewhat different approach.

ERRQ   Students who like to read and who read willingly probably have had many personal experiences with books. Those who are able to connect new information and experiences with information and experiences they have already had are more likely to comprehend. Students who have not had intense personal relationships with text and who do not read willingly will benefit from experiences that engage them in making connections between a piece of reading material and their own thinking and feelings.

Developed by Watson and Gilles (1988), ERRQ stands for estimate, read, react, question. Although ERRQ is meant to show students how to relate to narrative, it can be applied to nonfiction as well. ERRQ is not an activity designed to be applied continuously. Students are asked to preview a piece of material they have selected and to estimate how far they can go in reading it with complete understanding. A Post-it note or light pencil mark can identify the stopping place. Students then read and are asked to be mindful of how they are feeling, what images and memories come to mind, and what thoughts flash through their heads as they read the passage. Students may read silently or as a paired reading activity. After reading, students react to the material and share the feelings, thoughts, and other experiences sparked by the text. Finally, students ask at least two questions about the text. These questions may be used to begin the next session, or they may be discussed at the time. Students who have experimented with ERRQ may then be better prepared for more in-depth literature studies (Watson & Gilles, 1988, p. 65).

Literature Studies with Chapter Books   Talking about good books leads to literature studies. As we have said earlier, when books become personally meaningful, children learn to love reading. Good literature transcends time and educates. It presents information, ideas, and attitudes about the world that help children grow. Good literature stretches the imagination and helps students bring meaning to their worlds. To benefit fully from a reading experience, students need good books, time to read and reflect, and time to share.

Literature studies are appropriate at all grade levels. In the middle and upper grades, literature study groups engage in in-depth studies of high-quality literature. First, teachers may read one book aloud to the class and create discussion groups after each reading. Then they may select several books and introduce them to the students by reading the title, looking at the cover, and briefly describing the subject of each book. Students may sign up for the literature group they want to join, indicating on the sign-up sheet their first and second choices. Middle- and upper-grade students read lengthy chapter books that may be selected on the basis of similar theme, author, or any other criteria.

Groups are organized at least three ways. Students may read the entire book first, then come together to discuss it. They may read a predetermined section or chapter, then come together to discuss that. Or they may meet to both read aloud and discuss as a group. Groups may last several weeks, depending on the interest generated in the discussions and the length of the book.

Some teachers prefer to initiate discussion by sitting with each group and asking the students to talk about their book. Others give students one or more open-ended questions as a point of departure. "What were your favorite parts?" "What would you change about the story and why?" "What was something you did not understand?" "What surprised you as you read the story?" "How did you feel about _____?"

Teachers turn over leadership of the group to the students as soon as possible. Students may decide to dispense with discussion questions and "get into the book." At the end of each group meeting, they decide what to read and/or discuss the next time.

Some teachers incorporate response logs as part of literature study. A group reading a chapter book may not meet every day, but the students will probably read some of their book every day. They can record their reactions daily as they read and use them as reminders of what they want to talk about when their group meets.

Some books provide better material for extending learning than others. If the group chooses, they plan how they will present their book to the rest of the class. The group may choose readers theater, puppetry, artwork, panel discussion, or any number of ways the students think of.

Selected Chapter Books—Middle and Upper Grades

Armstrong, W. (1969). *Sounder.* New York: Harper & Row.

Babbitt, N. (1975). *Tuck Everlasting.* Toronto, Ontario: Collins Pub.

Blume, J. (1970). *Are You There God? It's Me Margaret.* New York: Dell.

Blume, J. (1972). *Tales of a Fourth Grade Nothing.* New York: Dell.

Blume, J. (1974). *Blubber.* New York: Dell.

Bosse, M. (1993). *Ordinary Magic.* New York: Sunburst Books.

Childress, A. (1973). *A Hero Ain't Nothin' But a Sandwich.* New York: Putnam.

Cleary, B. (1983). *Dear Mr. Henshaw.* New York: Dell.

Collier, J., & Collier, C. (1981). *Jump Ship to Freedom.* New York: Dell.

Collier, J., & Collier, C. (1987). *Who Is Carrie?* New York: Dell.

Dahl, R. (1975). *Danny, the Champion of the World.* New York: Bantam.

Dahl, R. (1982). *The BFG.* New York: Viking Penguin.

Fleischman, S. (1986). *The Whipping Boy.* Mahwah, NJ: Troll Books.

Fox, P. (1973). *The Slave Dancer.* New York: Dell.

Fox, P. (1984). *One-Eyed Cat.* New York: Dell.

Gardiner, J. (1980). *Stone Fox.* New York: Harper & Row.

Hamilton, V. (1990). *Cousins.* New York: Scholastic.

Hansen, J. (1986). *Which Way Freedom?* New York: Avon Books.

Highwater, J. (1985). *Eyes of Darkness.* New York: Lothrop, Lee & Shepard.

Howe, J., & Howe, D. (1979). *Bunnicula.* New York: Avon Books.

Hunt, I. (1976). *The Lottery Rose.* New York: Scribner's.

King-Smith, D. (1986). *Pigs Might Fly.* New York: Puffin Books.

Lowry, L. (1989). *Number the Stars.* New York: Dell.

MacLachlan, P. (1985). *Sarah, Plain and Tall.* New York: Harper & Row.

MacLachlan, P. (1992). *Journey.* New York: Delacorte Press.

Mathis, S. (1975). *The Hundred Penny Box.* New York: Scholastic.

Merrill, J. (1986). *The Pushcart War.* New York: Dell.

Naidoo, B. (1985). *Journey to Jo'burg.* New York: Knopf.

Paterson, K. (1977). *Bridge to Terabithia.* New York: Harper & Row.

Paterson, K. (1978). *The Great Gilly Hopkins.* New York: Harper & Row.

Paterson, K. (1985). *Come Sing, Jimmy Jo.* New York: Dutton.

Paulson, G. (1984). *Tracker.* New York: Scholastic.

Paulson, G. (1987a). *The Crossing.* New York: Orchard Books.

Paulson, G. (1987b). *Hatchet.* New York: Penguin.

Reynolds, P. (1991). *Shiloh.* New York: Atheneum.

Rockwell, T. (1973). *How to Eat Fried Worms.* New York: Dell.

Rylant, C. (1986). *A Fine White Dust.* New York: Dell.

Sachar, L. (1987). *There's a Boy in the Girls' Bathroom.* New York: Knopf.

Smith, M. (1973). *A Taste of Blackberries.* New York: Thomas Y. Crowell.

Spinelli, J. (1990). *Maniac Magee.* New York: Scholastic.

White, E. (1952). *Charlotte's Web.* New York: Scholastic.

Yep, L. (1975). *Dragonwings.* New York: Harper & Row.

Yolen, J. (1988). *The Devil's Arithmetic.* New York: Puffin Books.

Zindel, P. (1968). *The Pigman.* New York: Bantam.

Poetry in the Classroom Exploring poetry is a regular if not a daily element of many whole language classrooms. Rather than pursuing academic exercises in which students learn about metaphor or rhyme and rhythm patterns, teachers invite students to be poetic, to take risks with poetry as a mode of self-expression. Like creating a drawing that represents a particular meaning for a student, writing a poem is one way to release images and impressions that may otherwise go unrealized.

In the lower grades children tend to love poetry naturally. They clap and move to the beat, they laugh, they memorize favorite poems, and they join in when one is read aloud (Hickman & Cullinan, 1989). Poetry in the middle and upper grades can elicit just as much enthusiasm as younger children display in hearing and writing their own poetry.

When Tasha, a nine-year-old African American student, entered a local fourth-grade classroom near the middle of the year, she was withdrawn and appeared to be unhappy. The teacher was quite concerned about her and offered repeated invitations for Tasha to join in various group activities in the classroom. Tasha's mother told the teacher that Tasha was homesick and had not wanted to move, leaving her home and friends behind. The other students also tried to include Tasha in their collaborations. She remained very quiet and on the fringes of classroom events for several days.

The teacher and the students were working in a unit on the geography of the United States. There were many books, photos, and maps related to the theme available throughout the classroom. Written projects, student art, posted copies of American folk songs, lists of related vocabulary, and poems covered the walls and lined the shelves. Several students had written poems about their favorite place or favorite scene. One morning Tasha hesitantly handed the teacher a poem she had written at home the night before (it is reproduced to the best of the authors' recollection in figure 10.3). She wanted to know if the teacher would put her poem on the wall with the other student writing. The teacher was thrilled, and Tasha's classmates realized they had a poet in their midst. Tasha, of course, continued to miss her old home, but she made a new school home and new friends with the help of a teacher who understood that all students have to find their own voice, their own way of expressing who they are and what is happening to them.

FIGURE 10.3
Tasha's Poem

The following is a brief list of illustrated and bound poems and collections of poems appropriate for intermediate, middle, and junior high school students.

Poetry

Adoff, A. (1986). *Sports Pages.* New York: Lippincott.

Baylor, B. (1982). *The Best Town in the World.* New York: Aladdin.

Brewton, J., & Blackburn, L. (Eds.). (1978). *They've Discovered a Head in the Box for the Bread and Other Laughable Limericks.* New York: Thomas Y. Crowell.

Buchanan, E., Cochrane, D., Cochrane, O., Potter, J., & Scalena, S. (1982). *Where Buttlerflies Go.* Katonah, NY: Richard C. Owen.

Cameron, P. (1961). *"I Can't" Said the Ant.* New York: Coward, McCann & Geoghagen.

Cassedy, S. (1985). *Behind the Attic Wall.* New York: Avon.

Cochrane, O. (1985). *Blue Frog and Other Poems.* Katonah, NY: Richard C. Owen.

Cochrane, O. (1987). *The Golden Unicorn.* Katonah, NY: Richard C. Owen.

Dahl, R. (1982). *Roald Dahl's Revolting Rhymes.* New York: Bantam.

Dennis, L. (1975). *Alligator Pie.* Boston: Houghton Mifflin.

Feelings, T. (1993). *Soul Looks Back in Wonder.* New York: Dial.

Fleischman, P. (1983). *Path of the Pale Horse.* New York: Harper & Row.

Fleischman, P. (1988). *Joyful Noise: Poems for Two Voices.* New York: Harper & Row.

Forrester, V. (1985). *A Latch against the Wind.* New York: Atheneum.

Frost, R. (1978). *Stopping by Woods on a Snowy Evening.* New York: E.P. Dutton.

Frost, R. (1988). *Birches.* New York: Henry Holt.

Greenfield, E. (1988). *Nathaniel Talking.* New York: Black Butterfly Children's Books.

Kennedy, X. (1985). *The Forgetful Wishing Well.* New York: Atheneum.

Kennedy, X. (1986). *Brats.* New York: Atheneum.

Koch, K. (1985). *Talking to the Sun.* New York: Henry Holt.

Lewis, R. (1988). *In the Night, Still Dark.* New York: Atheneum.

Little, L. (1988). *Children of Long Ago.* New York: Philomel.

Morrison, L. (1988). *Rhythm Road: Poems to Move To.* New York: Lothrop, Lee & Shepard.

Prelutsky, J. (1984). *The New Kid on the Block.* New York: Scholastic.

Prelutsky, J. (1990). *Something Big Has Been Here.* New York: Greenwillow.

Ryder, J. (1985). *Inside Turtle's Shell and Other Poems of the Field.* New York: Macmillan.

Service, R. (1987). *The Cremation of Sam McGee.* New York: Greenwillow.

Sleator, W. (1986). *Interstellar Pig.* New York: Bantam.

Silverstein, S. (1981). *Where the Sidewalk Ends.* New York: Harper & Row.

Silverstein, S. (1983). *Who Wants a Cheap Rhinoceros?* New York: Macmillan.

Spinelli, J. (1986). *Who Put That Hair in My Toothbrush?* New York: Dell.

Thayer, E. (1988). *Casey at the Bat.* New York: Putnam.

Thomas, D. (1985). *A Child's Christmas in Wales.* New York: Holiday House.

Tripp, W. (1985). *Marguerite, Go Wash Your Feet.* Boston: Houghton Mifflin.

Turner, A. (1986). *Street Talk.* Boston: Houghton Mifflin.

Van Laan, N. (1990). *Possum Come a-Knockin'.* New York: Alfred A. Knopf.

Viorst, J. (1981). *If I Were in Charge of the World and Other Worries.* New York: Atheneum.

Anticipation: An Advance Organizer   This activity is designed to activate students' thinking *before* they read a selection, so that learners are ready to react to the text at a personal level and make the connections necessary for comprehension. All middle- and upper-grade students could benefit occasionally from advance organizer strategies. While teachers always model previewing a text prior to reading, this strategy stimulates more than general knowledge and interest in the material. The best type of text for this strategy is a well-written chapter book, one with important concepts and one to which the children can relate emotionally. These examples start with books appropriate at grades 4 or 5 and progress to books more appropriate for grades 7 and 8: *Bridge to Terabithia* by Paterson, *Number the Stars* by Lowry, *The Lottery Rose* by Hunt, *Tuck Everlasting* by Babbitt, and *A Fine White Dust* by Rylant.

If there are enough copies for everyone in class to read the same book, prepare the anticipation guide only once. If, however, each group is going to read a different story, either because of the number of copies, or because the children want to have a choice, then begin by introducing separately and briefly each book from which they might choose.

After selections have been made and the children are grouped by their choices, give each group a list of statements that has been prepared ahead of time. These statements should be stated in direct and absolute terms, either in the negative (for example, Students should never . . .) or in the positive (Families should always . . .). These statements are not meant to reflect the beliefs and values of the teacher; rather, they are designed to make the students take a stand and reasonably defend what they say they believe.

Examples of a few statements a teacher might use with Hunt's *The Lottery Rose* are:

1. Parents by law should not be allowed to spank children.

2. Children should stay with their natural parents no matter what.

3. Every teacher should have to go visit every child's home and meet the parents.

The children read the statements and discuss them one at a time. The list should probably contain no more than ten and no fewer than four such statements. After the controversies are over, students are asked to predict what they think the book is likely to be about. They are then asked to read the story and to consider if, when, and why they changed their minds about any of the statements they discussed before they read the story. The story can be read aloud by the teacher, silently by each child, or as a literature study in a small group.

Each group can present their book in some form to the rest of the class. Students might research and develop a "kangaroo court" in which they indict and bring to trial one of the characters in a story. Students might stage a panel discussion or a debate of one of the issues raised.

Simulations and Role Plays   Role playing helps students personalize their learning. Mock trials, debates on issues arising from narrative stories and history or current events, and other simulation experiences provide instructional opportunites for the creative and flexible teacher. For instance, one seventh-grade teacher suggested to her American history class that had studied the causes of the

American Civil War for several weeks that they form a "government committee of interested and representative parties" to solve the nation's problems and avoid the war. The students were enthusiastic and began by creating a list of characters and persons who should be appointed to the committee. They identified ten specific persons (including Thaddeus Stevens and Jefferson Davis) and ten types of characters representing various interests (slave, slave owner, abolitionist, northern manufacturer). The students selected the person or character they wanted to be, and determined what those persons would be interested in and concerned about and what they might say. Each person was represented by one student; each character type was represented by one or more students. Every student had a role. While the students found this experience difficult because they had to really grapple with the issues, they were successful in their charge to find a legitimate way to solve the problems and avoid civil war.

Another variation on role play is a "Meeting of the Minds" or "You Are There" experience. In this type of event, students create a scenario involving two historical figures from different times who come together to discuss a current event—for example, Gandhi and Dr. Martin Luther King, Jr., meeting to discuss the Los Angeles riots of 1992. The meeting of two or more fictional characters to create a plausible dialogue also provides interesting possibilities. For example, what would happen if Judy Blume's Blubber and Katherine Paterson's Gilly got together? What might they write if they were pen pals? What makes you think so? Helping students make connections within and across texts is important, and role plays are one avenue for encouraging such explorations.

Graphic Organizers

Concept Mapping   Learning has been variously described as building cognitive schemata, creating knowledge structures, and making connections as in scaffolding. Concept maps attempt to make internal knowledge structures, or scaffolds, overt so learners can explore them in metacognitive ways. Concept maps are word diagrams that differ from webs in two ways: first, concept maps are more structured, forming a hierarchy from most general to most specific; second, the links between words are labeled to show what the connections are. Concept maps help students organize, categorize, and visualize the relationships of concepts. They can be used for increasing understanding of complex stories and for studying textbooks. However, they are most powerful for examining whole concept areas, the ways knowledge is structured, and the ways knowledge structures interrelate.

Key terms (nouns) and relational words (conjunctions, prepositions, and verbs) are used in forming concept maps. More information on concept mapping may be found in Novak and Gowin (1984) and Alvarez (1989). The following list describes one procedure for developing concept maps:

1. *Read:* Students read the text or material related to topic to be mapped.

2. *Select:* Students select the most important or broadest idea to which all other concepts are related.

3. *Write:* Students write the main idea and a list of words related to the main idea found in the material they are reading or studying.

4. *Rank:* Students rank the words hierarchically from most inclusive to least inclusive.

5. *Arrange:* Students arrange the words from the hierarchical list to form relationships.

6. *Link:* Students link concepts by drawing lines between them. Lines are labeled with words or phrases that explain the relationship.

7. *Review:* Students review or read their maps. They may add information as it is acquired. They may revise or completely restructure a map to better represent the topic.

8. *Summarize:* Students may write summarizing paragraphs to accompany their maps. Maps are displayed as part of the information and resources in the classroom.

Figure 10.4 is a concept map created by fifth graders as part of a unit on transportation.

Classifying and Categorizing   As students encounter complex information in their reading and explorations, they may need practice organizing, classifying, and otherwise relating facts. For example, students might become interested in material comparing toads and frogs or moths and butterflies. To make an advance organizer, they can fold a piece of paper in half lengthwise and list the characteristics of one animal down the left inside column and the characteristics of the other down the right.

A simple Venn diagram might also be used to show commonalities and differences (see figure 10.5). Concepts consisting of more

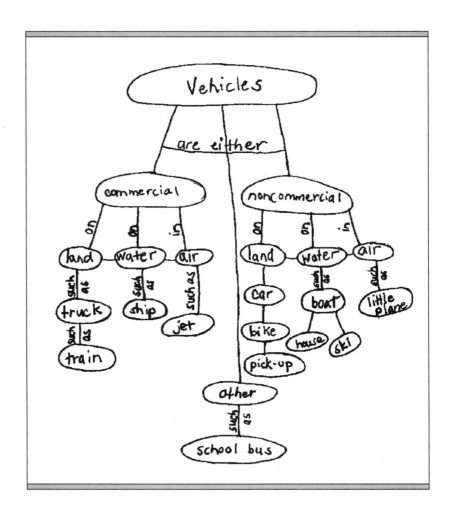

FIGURE 10.5
Venn Diagram

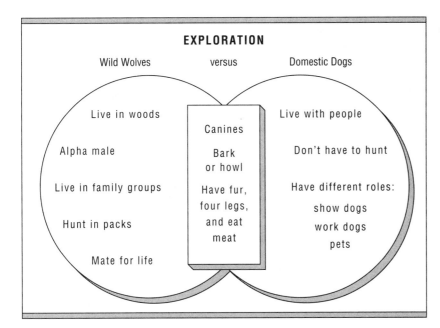

than two categories (for example, causes of disease or the basic food groups) might provide occasion to use other organizing techniques, such as webs or cluster diagrams (Hoskisson & Tompkins, 1987). An example of a cluster diagram is shown in figure 10.6.

When students encounter material involving cause and effect relationships (effects of poverty on young children or causes of the Civil War and its effect on the civilian population) an advance or graphic organizer like that shown in figure 10.7 might be employed.

Propaganda Devices   Caveat emptor or "Let the buyer beware!" could be the name for a series of strategies that engage learners with propaganda devices. In addition to identifying and analyzing types of these devices—for example, bandwagon, just plain folks, glittering generalities, snob appeal, name calling, and card stacking—learners may be directed to find examples of each in radio and television commercials and in magazine and newspaper advertisements. Subtle persuaders can be found in the news as well as in advertising. Students can look for: (1) logical fallacies such as shifting the subject, oversimplification, or beginning with false assumptions,

(2) loaded words, such as "new and improved" or "maximum strength," (3) euphemisms or doublespeak, such as "forced liquidation" or "on sale," (4) general persuasive devices, such as "If you are a good person, you will agree" or "If you are a smart person, you will agree," and (5) fallacies of relevance, such as appeal to threat— "If you don't agree, some harm will come to you." Students may experiment with using these devices in their own advertisements for made-up products, favorite books, or classroom elections.

Students may begin keeping a list of devices and examples meant to persuade, fool, and conceal. They may create a display of the examples they have found. They may become aware of the ways in which publications and advertisements use pictures to persuade and

FIGURE 10.6
Cluster Diagram

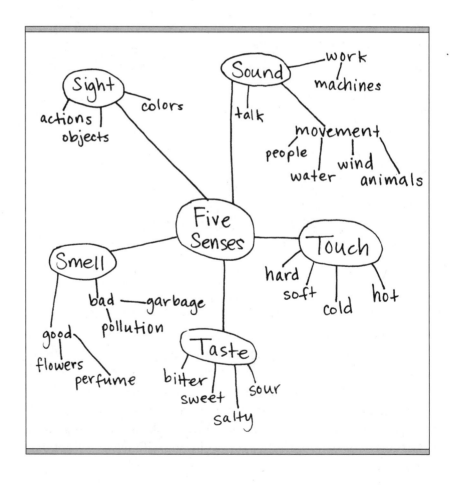

FIGURE 10.7   Cause and Effect Relationships

A. ONE CAUSE, ONE EFFECT

Cause

Effect

Example:
Baking soda and water

↓

Carbon dioxide gas

B. ONE CAUSE, MULTIPLE EFFECTS

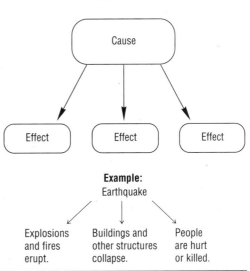

Example:
Earthquake

Explosions and fires erupt.

Buildings and other structures collapse.

People are hurt or killed.

C. MULTIPLE CAUSES, ONE MAIN EFFECT

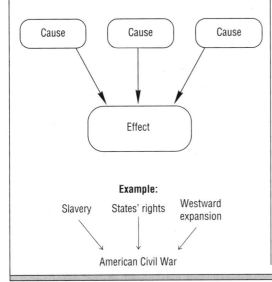

Example:

Slavery   States' rights   Westward expansion

American Civil War

D. CHAIN OF EVENTS:

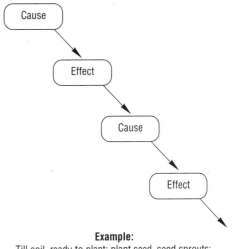

Example:
Till soil, ready to plant; plant seed, seed sprouts; water and add fertilizer, plant grows; weed garden and water, plant produces vegetables

create the desired effect. While any one project on persuasion and propaganda may be short-lived, the focus on propaganda frequently recurs throughout the school year. Again and again students will encounter other ways that propaganda devices relate to new areas of their learning. Teachers may encourage students to explore propaganda and persuasive devices in politics. Gaining insights into how dictators like Hitler come to power, cult leaders develop control over their followers, or politicians manipulate public opinion is a worthwhile learning experience.

Retrospective Reading Miscue Analysis   Retrospective miscue analysis is a technique in which readers listen to their own oral reading miscues to expand their understanding of and control over their reading. Readers audiotape their oral reading; then they evaluate their reading by listening to themselves and identifying difficulties. They are directed to ask, "Does that sentence sound right?" "Does it make sense?" "What does it mean?" This enables them to build on their own strengths as readers.

By the middle grades, students are in many ways their own best teachers. As they listen to themselves read, they make their own decisions about the quality and acceptability of their miscues. Teachers first demonstrate this procedure with their own reading. Together teachers and students discuss strategies they might use with each miscue to construct meaning. Students need to understand that reading need not be error-free, that not all miscues need to be corrected. Examples of overcorrections as well as syntactically and semantically acceptable miscues may be discussed (Goodman, Watson, & Burke, 1987).

SUMMARY

The philosophy and instructional approaches of whole language are appropriate for middle- and upper-grade students. The school organization, complexity of the materials studied, and developing abilities of the students, however, mean that applications will differ from those in the lower grades. Nevertheless, the major teaching tools pertain to upper grades just as to lower grade levels: read aloud to students daily, and students read and write daily. Many concerns that teachers in the upper grades express can be dealt with using whole language techniques, but a different approach to planning is needed.

Teachers and students in middle and upper grades find integrating the curriculum rewarding. Giving students choices empowers them;

they take control of their own learning. They make connections that might go unrecognized in more traditional settings. They experience increasing control over their reading and writing. Teachers also become more empowered; they control their own teaching and they begin to see new ways of helping children make sense of the world.

THEORY-TO-PRACTICE CONNECTIONS

Learning Theory for Older Students	*Examples of Classroom Practice*
1. Learning as inquiry.	1. Thinking like a scientist or historian, doing field, library, and classroom research
2. Learning as exploration.	2. Anticipation, literature study
3. Learning as scaffolding and making connections.	3. Concept mapping

SUGGESTED READINGS

Atwell, N. (1987). *In the middle: Writing, reading, and learning with adolescents.* Portsmouth, NH: Heinemann.

Atwell, N. (1990). *Coming to know: Writing to learn in the intermediate grades.* Portsmouth, NH: Heinemann.

Cordeiro, P. (1992). *Whole learning: Whole language and content in the upper elementary grades.* Katonah, NY: Richard C. Owen.

Gilles, C., Bixby, M., Crowley, P., Crenshaw, S., Henrichs, M., Reynolds, F., & Pyle, D. (Eds.). (1988). *Whole language strategies for secondary students.* Katonah, NY: Richard C. Owen.

Peterson, R., & Eeds, M. *Grand Conversations: Literature groups in action.* Toronto: Scholastic.

Reif, L. (1992). *Seeking diversity.* Portsmouth, NH: Heinemann.

Short, K., & Burke, C. (1991). *Creating curriculum: Teachers and students as a community of learners.* Portsmouth, NH: Heinemann.

Short, K., & Pierce, K. (Eds.). (1990). *Talking about books: Creating literate classrooms.* Portsmouth, NH: Heinemann.

SUGGESTED ACTIVITIES

1. Discuss the theoretical basis of the strategies and classroom activities in this chapter. What are some other instructional strategies described earlier in this book that reflect these same theoretical considerations?

2. If you are able to observe in classrooms in your area and work with students, spend time kidwatching. Identify a student who is having some difficulty reading and learning from the text materials provided. Create a strategic intervention, a strategy idea designed specifically to help one student develop an understanding, a process, or a strategy that will be useful to that student now and later. Share what you did, how you determined what to try, how it worked, and what you learned from the experience.

3. If you are able to observe in classrooms and work with students, try one or two of the strategies cited in chapters 9 or 10. Note how they are received. What needs to happen for students to have successful experiences? What should happen next to follow up or extend learning in the classroom in which you have been working?

REFERENCES

Alvarez, M. (1989). Using hierarchical concept maps. In W. Pauk (Ed.), *How to study in college.* Boston: Houghton Mifflin.

Goodman, Y., Watson, D., & Burke, C. (1987). *Reading miscue inventory: Alternative procedures.* Katonah, NY: Richard C. Owen.

Hickman, J., & Cullinan, B. (1989). *Children's literature in the classroom: Weaving Charlotte's Web.* Norwood, MA: Christopher Gordon.

Hoskisson, K., & Tompkins, G. (1987). *Language arts: Content and teaching strategies.* Columbus, OH: Merrill.

Lyon, G. (1988). *Borrowed children.* New York: Bantam.

Novak, J., & Gowin, D. (1984). *Learning how to learn.* New York: Cambridge University Press.

Short, K., & Burke, C. (1991). *Creating curriculum: Teachers and students as a community of learners.* Portsmouth, NH: Heinemann.

Vygotsky, L. (1978). *Mind in society: The development of higher psychological processes.* Cambridge, MA: Harvard University Press.

Watson, D., & Gilles, C. (1988). ERRQ. In C. Gilles, M. Bixby, P. Crowley, S. Crenshaw, M. Henrichs, F. Reynolds, & D. Pyle (Eds.), *Whole language strategies for secondary students.* Katonah, NY: Richard C. Owen.

11

Thematic Teaching

INTEGRATING THE CURRICULUM

What is an integrated curriculum?

How can teachers integrate some subject areas and still remain organized?

How can teachers be certain that children are learning all the necessary skills?

What might a completely integrated unit look like?

Whole language teaching is based on a philosophy of education that integrates language and thinking with rich content in authentic experiences for children (Goodman, 1992). Rich content requires a multitude of books and other resources, as well as ideas and information. Authentic experiences are what people do with reading and writing in the real world. When children really read, they must read about something. Teachers provide opportunities for them to experience a wide variety of high-quality materials and resources. When teachers ensure that the curriculum supports children's interests and intentions, it begins to naturally integrate itself.

For example, when a teacher read two versions of "The Three Little Pigs" to a group of second graders, the children talked about the differences and similarities between the stories. This eventually led some of the children to find other versions of the story. Some children found other stories about pigs, and some took the opportunity to bring information about real pigs to class. Reading, sharing those materials, and discussing them led to a field trip to a pig farm. One of the class members found *The True Story of the Three Little Pigs* by A. Wolf (as told to Jon Scieszka) and shared it.

This in turn led to a discussion of wolves, writing informative books about wolves and pigs, developing a survey of students who favored the pigs' version versus those who believed the wolf, and presenting the findings in graph form. Together the teacher and the children expanded the focus to an investigation of story versions for several standard fairy tales. This produced several story versions of traditional fairy tales in which the students experimented with point of view. Ultimately, the unit involved reading and writing, as well as cooking, art, music, geography, health, and some math.

The children created a newspaper they called "The Grimm Facts," a fairy tale cookbook including recipes for "wolf stew," "no lumps porridge," and "Grandma's goodies." The unit culminated with a project that combined characters, plots, settings, and story problems from several fairy tales into one play that the children wrote, revised, edited, cast, practiced, and performed for the entire school.

While some study may be given to individual "subjects," as teachers make informed judgments about learner needs, authentic learning events necessarily cut across subject matter boundaries. Lessons for individuals, small groups, and even large groups in specific skills or subjects may certainly take place from time to time. When teachers introduce children to the concept of fractions, for instance, they may choose to do so with the entire class. However, this does not necessarily mean a lesson at the board followed by ditto sheets. Rather, the class may spend a couple of days making pizzas, with the children counting and figuring out how to cut them so that everyone gets the same amount. This activity might be followed by a discussion and looking for other ways to "see" fractions in the classroom and in the environment.

Theme Teaching: One Perspective

Unlike traditional scheduling, which fragments and isolates the curriculum, theme teaching integrates it. Integrating the language, thinking, and content experiences of children helps produce learners who are better educated, who have a connected understanding of their world.

Consider this situation faced by a parent trying to decide between two schools for her daughter. She encountered these descriptions of classroom focus and content. In one school, the principal encouraged the mother to consider his school by saying that her daughter would enjoy the third grade classroom she would go into. They were studying primates and the children were involved in doing and learning all sorts of things about primates around the world. In the other school, the principal encouraged the mother to consider his school by saying that her child would certainly learn a great deal. The third grade into which she would be placed was currently studying pronouns. The classroom practice sheets worked on pronouns, and homework assignments focused on pronouns in stories and workbooks.

There are perhaps more schools like the second one. But the mother in this scenario preferred the school in which the principal thought good teaching and learning resulted when children were engaged in authentic experiences that interested them. Surely, most of us would rather have our children studying primates and in the process learning concepts from social studies, science, and mathematics, studying primates and in the process acquiring greater skill as readers, writers, and thinkers. Surely inquiry into primates produces more usable knowledge and learner capabilities than identifying pronouns on worksheets and in books.

The "real world" is not fragmented into disciplines, and disciplines are not fragmented into facts and subskills. That is, one does not memorize what pronouns are in order to be a better reader and writer. One does not live history apart from mathematics or science. Rather, language in use is whole, and events in politics and science affect daily existence. When you bake a cake, reading, math, and science are all part of the process that leads to the final product. We don't have to take a test on cake baking—we can taste the cake to know whether learning has occurred.

In this book we have outlined the conditions for natural learning and described how these can be realized in the classroom regardless of the grade level or abilities of the learners. We have established the underlying framework for whole language classrooms and described the three major elements: (1) the basic approaches to instruction, (2) the major resources needed, and (3) the ways teachers come to know their students.

We have encouraged teachers to begin slowly, incorporating this philosophy a little at a time and reflecting on their process and progress. As children's interests and intentions lead teachers to explore various questions, the curriculum will gradually become more integrated. Many whole language classrooms accomplish this goal through unit teaching. The purpose of this chapter is to help teachers explore the creation of integrated, thematic teaching. With theme teaching, teachers are viewed as both a resource and a collaborator in the learning process, and students are encouraged to be the principal investigators.

Through theme teaching, all the elements of a whole language philosophy come together as depicted in figure 11.1. Students choose to read and write about things in which they are interested. Teachers provide an environment in which learners use their natural inclinations to make and represent meaning in the ways most productive for them. Theme teaching enables students to make connections within and among knowledge structures as they build their ever-widening view of the world. Finally, theme teaching allows classrooms to live the multicultural values they promote and to reflect and celebrate the pluralistic reality of our nation.

Multicultural Implications

Classrooms that reflect our diverse cultures help students develop a better sense of themselves and the world they live in. Whole language philosophy is multicultural by nature, in that it respects and celebrates learners' language and backgrounds of experience, it invites students to share who they are, and it attempts to create risk-free environments for this sharing.

Integrating multicultural education into all facets of learning is one of the purposes of American public schools, according to Lewis and Doorlag (1987), who suggest that

1. Commonalities among peoples cannot be recognized unless differences are acknowledged.

2. A society that interweaves the best of all its cultures reflects a truly mosaic image.

3. Multicultural education can restore cultural rights by emphasizing cultural respect and equality.

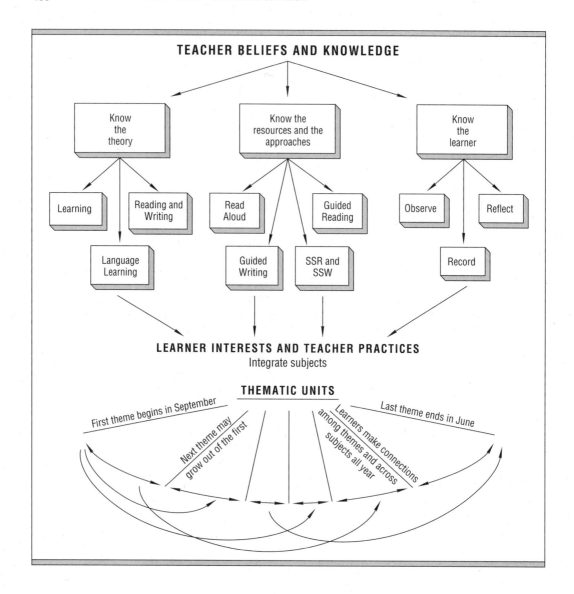

TEACHER BELIEFS AND KNOWLEDGE

Know the theory

Know the resources and the approaches

Know the learner

Learning

Reading and Writing

Read Aloud

Guided Reading

Observe

Reflect

Language Learning

Guided Writing

SSR and SSW

Record

LEARNER INTERESTS AND TEACHER PRACTICES
Integrate subjects

THEMATIC UNITS

First theme begins in September

Next theme may grow out of the first

Learners make connections among themes and across subjects all year

Last theme ends in June

FIGURE 11.1
Weaving the Fabric of the Curriculum through Thematic Teaching

4. Multicultural education enhances the self-concepts of all students because it provides a more balanced and realistic view of American society.

However, multicultural education is not found in workbook exercises through which students "learn about others," followed by a set of test items to see if the appropriate facts have been acquired.

Multicultural education is a part of everything that happens in the elementary classroom. It is one of the essential underpinnings of the integrated curriculum. Certainly theme teaching is well suited to developing a deeper and broader understanding of the multicultural nature of society.

Literature studies organized by author—such as all the folk tales by Tomie de Paola or the rhyming stories by Bill Peet—lead to connections with other books, information, and concepts. Themes like The Holocaust or Hispanic Americans of the Southwest become broad lesson formats that connect information, experiences, and resources across time and across several subject areas. Such themes weave threads of varied interests into the fabric of learning throughout the curriculum. Themes blend into one another so that what begins as a theme about Native Americans may become a study of celebrations and rituals that leads to a theme on clothing and native dress around the world.

Where Theme Ideas Come From

Unit teaching is nothing new; many good teachers have used it for years (Davis, 1990). At various times in our history, education in general has emphasized teaching by some sort of integrated unit. However, the actual implementation of teaching by thematic unit, which was never widespread, tended to reflect the school's organization rather than any underlying instructional philosophy.

In some schools, for instance, one teacher teaches both math and science in a large block of time, while another teacher handles social studies and language arts together. Theoretically, the blocked subjects can be combined into units; but in reality, the block is typically divided by the teachers into separate subjects with lessons that follow a textbook.

We believe that education at the elementary level should be as broad as possible, producing students who know a great deal and who enjoy learning. We support classrooms that treat learners as active participants in constructing their own knowledge. Children are constantly trying to make sense of their world. We do not want them to conclude that school learning is boring, meaningless, and something you do only to please others. Implementing theme teaching is one way to avoid the development of this attitude.

Themes spring from one of four basic sources. First, theme ideas may come from the teacher and/or the prescribed curriculum. Some teachers attempt a thematic unit because they think the children at that age need it and tend to be interested in it—for instance, a solar system unit for sixth graders. Some unit ideas are part of the curriculum because the school system requires them at given grade levels. For example, a unit on the state the children live and go to school in is required before eighth grade.

A second source for theme ideas is the wealth of high-quality children's literature. Children may wish to pursue reading from one genre as a unit. Reading folk tales and fables is a common unit of study in many classrooms and may lead to exploring how folk tales and fables vary across cultures. One teacher encouraged the study of books by the same author, beginning the year with her favorite children's author and then letting the children vote for each consecutive author thereafter.

Another teacher read *A House Is a House for Me* by M. Hoberman, as requested by one of the children. She then added D. Burn's *Henry Andrew's Meadow* and D. Pinkwater's *The Big Orange Splot*, making a text set. The ideas in those books sparked children's interest in learning about different types of houses people live in, and a theme study was born.

A teacher may choose to use a particular chapter book for one reason and then find the students expressing interest in an entirely different concept from the story. For example, one teacher shared with her first graders several books about giants, beginning with *Fin M'Coul* by de Paola. This led to a unit on giants that evolved into a study of Things Both Big and Little in the World.

Another teacher read *Dragonwings* by Yep to her junior high class to encourage their exploration of China and the history of Chinese Americans. During their study, the students also expressed an interest in aerodynamics, planes and kites, and the history of powered flight. The unit evolved and expanded in a variety of significant ways.

Objects and events occurring in the school or classroom are a third area from which theme ideas may be generated. When the local science and nature museum hosted an exhibit on dinosaurs, one classroom scheduled a field trip to see it. This proved to be a perfect time to embark on a unit that tapped children's natural fascination with creatures from earth's distant past. On another occasion, a child brought an "abandoned" hornet's nest to class one winter day, only to discover as it heated up in the warm classroom that it was not empty at all. After the exterminators left and calm was restored to the room, a unit on Insects, Their Habits and Habitats seemed to be unavoidable.

Finally, current events may lead to the creation of theme studies. Since many whole language teachers subscribe to a daily newspaper for their classrooms, the children spend some part of each day gathering and sharing news items. Local community, state, nation, and world events provide fertile ground for thematic ideas. Newsworthy events and articles that have led some classes into units of study include a whale trapped in a North Atlantic ice floe (a unit entitled Whaling Around the World); the financial plight of an African American ballet company in New York (Dance and Other Nonverbal Forms of Self-Expression); discoveries of the warming of the earth's surface (Global Warming and the Greenhouse Effect); the changing map of Eastern Europe (History in the Making); the destruction of tropical rain forests (They Can't See the Forest for the Trees—see figure 11.2); an adoption plan to save wild horses and burros (Beasts of Burden); the relationship between divorce, teen drug abuse, and teen suicide (The Big D's: Drugs, Divorce, and Death); local concerns over a new city dumpsite (Down in the Dumps); and community concerns about newly discovered levels of radon gas (Check This: Unseen Dangers in the Environment!).

What Thematic Teaching Is

Thematic teaching leads to a curricular organizational plan that provides a central focus and framework so children can successfully tackle complex issues in the classroom. Thematic units are developed by the children with the teacher acting as supporter, facilitator, resource, and guide. They are designed to accomplish several educational goals: (1) to reflect how children naturally learn, (2) to depict the way information about the world is structured, (3) to help children explore and discover how knowledge is structured and interrelated, (4) to help children become independent learners, (5) to stretch children's minds as they grapple with important issues, ideas, and questions, and (6) to simultaneously expand and refine children's language development as they extend their world view.

Thematic teaching allows children to construct their own understandings, to ask questions, to solve problems by generating and testing their hypotheses, and to present and evaluate their own learning. The best learning comes from "the having of wonderful

FIGURE 11.2
Rain Forest Display

ideas" (Duckworth, 1987). This means that classroom content must come from what the children already know and are interested in. The more they know about an area and the more interested they are in it, the more ideas they will generate and the more complex and detailed their personal, internal schemata are likely to become (Pappas, Kiefer, & Levstik, 1990).

Thematic units are usually lengthy in nature. Although a class may sometimes spend only a few days on a mini-unit that develops from an interest of the children, thematic units generally last several weeks. They incorporate most subject areas, and they evolve as the children become involved so that the activities in the unit cannot be planned in great detail beyond the first few days.

Basic Elements of Thematic Teaching

Subjects that are potential themes generally meet several criteria. They must be interesting to the children and be broad enough to be divided into smaller subtopics. The relationship of the subtopics to the broader theme must be clear. The subjects must lend themselves to comparing and contrasting of ideas, allow for extensive investigation of concrete situations, materials, and resources, and permit learners to use the surrounding world as a laboratory for part of their study (Gamberg, Kwak, Hutchings, & Altheim, 1988).

For example, children living near one of the country's national parks might be curious about national parks and forests. Some subtopics of this theme might be the history of our national parks system, other countries' ways of preserving their natural lands, problems and disputes over government-controlled lands, locales and purpose for each of the major national parks in the system, or conservation and the issue of clear-cutting by lumber companies.

When selecting a theme, evaluate its possibilities in these areas:

1. Personal interest of students and teacher

2. Suitability for age group

3. Resource availability, in print and other forms

4. Relevance and importance of the central subject

5. Potential for concept development

6. Subdividability

7. Potential for developing independence

8. Time available

Since student interest is key to the success of any thematic unit, the subject must be broad and flexible enough to allow for a great deal of student choice and creativity. Whatever the unit, it must be rich enough to allow each of the children to manipulate the central concepts in various ways so they can make sense of what they are learning. The resource materials must be plentiful and should cover a wide range of age and ability levels. Even the inclusion of adult level reference or nonfiction materials is acceptable if they contain pictures and if the teacher helps the children use the materials to further their study.

Planning and Organizing the Theme   Theme teaching in whole language classrooms differs from other types of integrated unit teaching in two very basic ways. Themes reflect the conditions for natural learning, and they are developed by the children (and the teacher) as they go. The units of inquiry that are requested or selected by the students are probably the most successful.

Here are eight steps to follow in preparation of a theme:

1. Brainstorm

2. Subdivide by categories

3. Locate initial resources

4. Plan initial activities

5. Set goals

6. Allow children to make choices

7. Plan initiating event

8. Plan evaluation

Webbing   Planning a unit begins with *selecting the theme*. After a topic for study has been decided upon, children and their teacher then *brainstorm and web* (Corwin, Hein, & Levin, 1976) the theme for possible subtopics, questions the children have, interesting learning activity ideas, compare-and-contrast ideas, and the availability of known and needed resources (see figure 11.3). As the theme grows, a *framework* will begin to take shape. Teachers will continue to employ large blocks of time for reading and writing and for conferencing—that is, the units occur within the classroom schedule that we have already presented. Teachers may find a generic web for conceptualizing unit development, as shown in figure 11.4, to be helpful.

Reviewing webbing as described in chapter 9 might also be helpful. There we see students webbing the elements in one piece of children's literature and developing ways in which they can respond to

FIGURE 11.3
Pre-Unit Questions

FIGURE 11.4
Generic Web for
Organizing Unit
Teaching

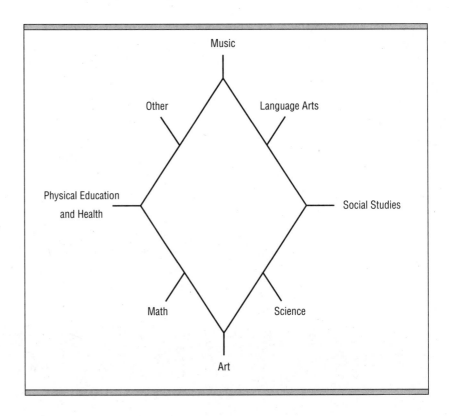

the story, categorizing them by subject areas. The same general principle may be applied here, except that we are now dealing with an entire concept rather than a single piece of text.

Listing Resources   Lists of resources may be compiled by category. The categories may include books and other printed materials, artifacts, community resources, media, the children themselves, and their parents. The children check the school library, and the teacher may use the school system's resource and media center for additional materials, equipment, "props," and other aids. Everyone combs the local public libraries and consults pertinent information clearinghouses or perhaps local or state historical societies, tourist bureaus, government offices, and chambers of commerce.

Children may solicit from parents any relevant experiences, expertise, or artifacts that a parent might share with the class. Involvement of parents and other family members encourages and facilitates children's learning and their enthusiasm for the unit. Children and teachers also investigate other community resources such as people, groups, and places that might contribute to their understanding of the theme in the larger world.

Another category of possible resources is the arts. Paintings, music, drama, and dance offer another form of self-expression to the integrated unit. Local art galleries and museums, as well as local colleges and universities, may provide resources in the graphic and performing arts.

Many teachers may be concerned about the availability of ample materials and resources in their schools and communities to support theme teaching. In one way the more resources, especially in terms of printed matter, the better. This allows learners to view their subject from many perspectives and to acquaint themselves with a multitude of facts and details. From another point of view, however, too many materials may lead to a somewhat shallow approach to learning. Teachers and students can be overwhelmed, unable to organize the materials and use them to their best advantage.

One good resource, for example, *Journey into China,* by the National Geographic Society (Danforth & Dickinson, 1982), may become the central source that supports and propels children's inquiries for weeks. As students and their teacher explore this type of document they look for additional related materials in school and public libraries. They may find advertisements, local experts on their subject, magazine articles and photos, interesting objects and artifacts, and other resources and materials to further their writings, projects, readings, and discussions. The teacher brings books and other resources to add to the class collection. But they all return again and again to the main book that has so much wonderful information in it. Theme teaching and theme learning really require in-depth information, a variety of materials, and opportunities for learners to express what they are learning. The total amount or number of resources does not have to be great. The material produced by the students—their journals, stories, artwork, and other displays—will fill the classroom.

Major resources are usually identified early and are supplemented while the unit is going on. As materials are collected and activity and project ideas developed, these lead to other materials and project or activity ideas. The unit soon appears to have a life of its own. That is the sign that the theme has "taken off." If this doesn't happen within the first few days, then the unit is not really of interest to the children, or has been developed in such a way that the children felt no sense of ownership. At that point, the teacher and children need to decide whether or not they wish to restructure or choose another subject.

Implementing the Unit   There are many ways to begin a thematic unit. When one unit is winding down, the next is already identified by the children. For instance, as a unit on the Laura Ingalls Wilder books was ending in one third-grade classroom, the children asked the teacher if they could study the Wild West. They wanted to do a unit on cowboys, outlaws, and American Indians of the West. The children and the teacher removed from walls and display areas all the children's work and other materials relating to *Little House on the Prairie*. Permanent materials were stored and the rest were sent home with the children. The classroom was bare, ready for the next set of children's work.

The next day, following the regular morning routine, the teacher read aloud two legends, one Navaho and one Sioux. The children talked about the stories and the similarities and differences of the two legends. The children divided into groups and began to talk about and list stories they already knew about the American West. They shared what each group had listed, created an initial web for their unit, and made some choices about where to begin. The new unit was under way.

When initiating a unit of study, teachers may consider making the following preparations:

1. Select one or more books for read aloud.

2. Find an object or artifact for the children to examine.

3. Plan a simulation activity.

4. Begin to collect several books (and other materials if possible) related to the theme.

5. Prepare a display area in the classroom using the books, objects, and photographs collected.

If a *simulation activity* is planned, it may be the first thing the teacher does with the children. The activity would then be discussed. If the teacher has brought an object or *artifact*, it might be passed around for the children to examine, describe, and discuss.

Following the experience with an object of interest or a group event, the next step might be to *brainstorm and create a web* on butcher or chart paper to be displayed. The brainstorm list is an excellent way to develop vocabulary for the new unit. It reveals the children's prior knowledge about the topic and allows them to decide how the central concept should be subdivided. Ultimately the web can be redesigned or expanded as the children learn more about the subject.

The next step is for the *children to divide themselves* by interest in the subtopics. One teacher calls these groups clubs, and the children name their club before they begin to outline what they want to do. One teacher calls these special interest groups (SIGs), and again the children name their SIGs. One teacher refers to these groups as "research and development committees" (R&Ds). Whatever the particular designation, the children choose the part of the unit they wish to be involved with. Some teachers encourage the children to select two groups to belong to. This is an excellent idea but does carry with it additional organization and record-keeping requirements for both students and teacher.

Each day, sometimes several times a day, the teacher and children enjoy *shared book* time. The first read aloud for the new unit should be selected carefully. The book should be interesting and include either a wide range of relevant information or some in-depth aspect of the unit. In the lower grades, the book or books may be read more than one time. In the upper grades, the first read aloud may be a chapter book that will be read along as the theme develops. Guided reading and writing are built into the day, just as with read aloud, sustained silent reading (SSR), and sustained silent writing (SSW). Instruction in reading and writing is still important and must occur throughout the unit.

Some teachers prefer to initiate a unit with read aloud, but others prefer an activity or group event followed by brainstorming and discussion. Teachers may begin each new school year simply by asking the children what they want to learn about. The children would be invited to brainstorm and list the topics in which they are interested. Then groups might be formed and the children encouraged to discuss in their small groups. The children could be asked to decide on a hierarchy of topics from most to least important. They might be told they could add to the base list as ideas occur to them. Each group could then present their prioritized list to the entire class and a final list could be drawn up.

The first item on the list should represent the topic of most interest to the greatest number of students. During the unit, time is still set aside each day for the children to *read* related materials, *talk* about books, and *write* about what they are learning. Also, during the first day or two of a unit, the children typically go to the library to begin their search for information about their subtopic. The teacher helps with planning the projects and activities. Each is logically ordered so that the children see the connections, and each is supported with the necessary materials and equipment. Most of the activities develop naturally as the children become engaged (see figure 11.5).

Teachers find ways to incorporate *subject areas* into the unit. They may prepare math-related activities, and the children may create their own math activities or games. A map or globe might be part of the teacher-suggested learning events. Teachers could provide the materials for hands-on projects, perhaps in art, music, science, or cooking.

The overall "goal is to open for children the many possibilities that exist in even the simplest of ideas such as 'houses' and to help move them toward new and exciting insights and understandings" (Pappas, Kiefer, & Levstik, p. 67). Thoughtful, reflective teachers working with children who are encouraged to have and share their wonderful ideas accomplish this goal and more.

One Classroom's Exploration   Even though these guidelines will differ from teacher to teacher, it can be helpful to see how one teacher developed and implemented a thematic unit with her third-

FIGURE 11.5
Planning a Project

and fourth-grade combined class. The children decided they wanted to learn about Australia when they became interested in koalas and kangaroos after a field trip to the city's new zoo. The children and the teacher together collected a variety of pictures, music, storybooks, maps, and other printed materials. The school library, local public libraries, and the Australian Booksource in Davis, California, provided most of the resources. The teacher received money from a mini-grant she had proposed to purchase support materials for thematic units. The study of Australia ultimately led to studying about the American Wild West, explorers and colonization around the world, and strange and amazing animals.

The Web   When the unit began, the teacher helped the students create a web of what they already knew and wanted to learn. Figure 11.6 is one such effort. The unit was eventually titled Exploring Down Under.

The Resources   The resources gathered for the thematic unit on Australia are listed here by category. The categories are nonfiction, fiction, and audiocassettes.

Nonfiction

Tourist Map: Australia. Australian Surveying and Land Information Group. (1988). Cairns, Australia: Tropical Publications.

Clarke, H., Burgess, C., & Braddon, R. (1988). *Prisoners of War.* N. Sydney, Australia: Time-Life Books.

Clark, M. (1983). *A Short History of Australia.* Ringwood, Victoria, Australia: Penguin Books, Australia.

Condreu, K. (1987). *The Ridge Didge Guidebook to Australia.* Queensland, Australia: New Brighton Press.

Dixon, M. (1976). *The Real Matilda.* Victoria, Australia: Penguin Books, Australia.

Gelman, R. (1986). *A Koala Grows Up.* New York: Scholastic.

Grant, T. *The Platypus: A Unique Animal.* Kensington, New South Wales, Australia: Union Press.

Grunwald, H. (1986). *Australia.* Alexandria, VA: Time-Life Books.

FIGURE 11.6
Web at Beginning of
Australia Unit

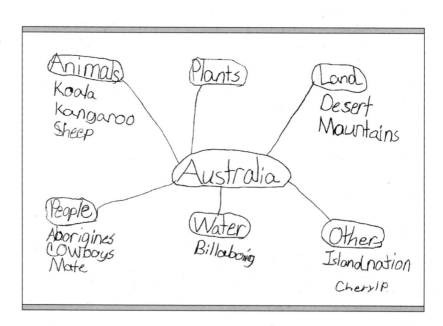

Haddon, F., & Oliver, T. (1986). *Living Australia, Animals and Their Homes.* Lane Cove, New South Wales, Australia: Hodder & Stoughton.

Hughes, R. (1966). *The Art of Australia.* Victoria, Australia: Penguin Books, Australia.

Lee, A., & Martin, R. (1988). *The Koala, A Natural History.* Kensington, New South Wales, Australia: New South Wales University Press.

Martin, D. (1987). *Australians Say G'Day.* Melbourne, Australia: Ozmarket. (Includes cassettes.)

Miller, J. (1985). *Koori: A Will to Win.* North Ryde, New South Wales, Australia: Angus & Robertson.

Moffat, A. (1985). *Handbook of Australian Animals.* Sydney, Australia: Bay Books.

Neidjie, B. (1986). *Australia's Kakadu Man.* Darwin, Northern Territory: Resource Managers.

Newman, G. (1987). *The Down Under Cookbook.* New York: Harrow and Heston.

Pride, M. (1989). *Australian Dinosaurs.* San Diego, CA: Mad Hatter Books.

Reader's Digest Services (1988). *Reader's Digest Visitor's Guide to the Great Barrier Reef.* Surry Hills, New South Wales, Australia.

Reader's Digest Services (1989). *Reader's Digest Motoring Guide to Australia.* Surry Hills, New South Wales, Australia.

Roberts, M. (1988). *Echoes of the Dreamtime: Australian Aboriginal Myths in the Paintings of Ainslie Roberts.* Melbourne: J. M. Dent.

Schouten, P. (1987). *The Antipodean Ark.* North Ryde, New South Wales: Angus & Robertson.

Terrill, R. (1978). *Australians.* New York: Simon & Schuster.

Treborlang, R. (1985). *How to Survive Australia.* Potts Point, Australia: Major Mitchell Press.

Vandenbeld, J. (1988). *Nature of Australia: A Portrait of the Island Continent.* New York: Australian Broadcasting Company.

Wilkes, G. (1978). *A Dictionary of Australian Colloquialisms.* Sydney: Collins Pub.

You Can Draw a Kangaroo (1988). Canberra, Australia: Australian Government Publishing Service.

Fiction

Baker, J. (1991). *Window.* Sydney: Julia MacRae Books.

Base, G. (1983). *My Grandma Lives in Gooligulch.* Davis, CA: Australian Book Source.

Brennan, J. (1984). *A Is for Australia.* Baronia, Victoria, Australia: J. M. Dent.

Burt, D. (1984). *I'm Not a Bear.* Ashburton, Victoria, Australia: Buttercup Books.

Cox, D. (1985). *Bossyboots.* New York: Crown.

Factor, J. (Ed.). (1983). *Far Out, Brussel Sprout!* South Melbourne: Oxford University Press.

Factor, J. (Ed.). (1985). *All Right, Vegemite!* Kew, Victoria, Australia: Oxford University Press.

Factor, J. (Ed.). (1986). *Unreal, Banana Peel!* South Melbourne: Oxford University Press.

Fox, M. (1983). *Possum Magic.* Nashville, TN: Abingdon Press.

Fox, M. (1989). *Koala Lou.* San Diego, CA: Gulliver Books.

Generowicz, W. (1982). *The Train.* Ringwood, Victoria, Australia: Penguin Books.

Green, M. (1984). *The Echidna and the Shade Tree.* San Diego, CA: Mad Hatter Books.

Heseltine, H. (Ed.). (1972). *The Penguin Book of Australian Verse.* Victoria, Australia: Penguin Books, Australia.

Heseltine, H. (Ed.). (1976). *The Penguin Book of Australian Short Stories.* Victoria, Australia: Penguin Books, Australia.

Lavery, H. (Ed.). (1985). *The Kangaroo Keepers.* Queensland, Australia: University of Queensland Press.

Mowalijarlal, D. (1984). *When the Snake Bites the Sun.* Gosford, New South Wales, Australia: Mad Hatter Books.

Pugh, J. (1985). *Wombalong.* San Diego, CA: Mad Hatter Books.

Small, M. (1986). *The Lizard of Oz.* Ashburton, Victoria, Australia: Buttercup Books.

Steele, M. (1985). *Arkwright.* Melbourne: Hyland House Publishing Ltd.

Trinca, R., & Argent, K. (1982). *One Woolly Wombat.* Brooklyn, NY: Kane/Miller Books.

Utemorrah, D. (1983). *Dunbi the Owl.* Sydney: Mad Hatter Books.

Wheatley, N., & Rawlins, D. (1987). *My Place.* Long Beach, CA: Australia in Print.

Wilson, B. (Ed.). (1987). *Australian Stories and Verse for Children.* Melbourne: Thomas Nelson of Australia.

Winch, G. (1986). *Enoch the Emu.* Adelaide, Australia: Childerset.

Audiocassettes

Larrikin Records (1982). *Seven Creeks Run: Songs of the Australian Bush.*

Mackness, B. *Fossil Rock and Other Prehistoric Hits.* Larrikin/Rascal Records.

Maza, B. *Music of My People: Australian Aboriginal Music.* Twintrack Productions.

Day One   On the first day, following the morning routines, the teacher read *Possum Magic* by Mem Fox. She read the book to her children twice, and they talked about the animals, place names, and foods in the story. The teacher asked the children what they thought vegemite tasted like, and they talked about that. Then she brought out a jar of Marmite, which she purchased at a local East Indian market (Marmite is essentially identical to vegemite). She gave each child a half slice of bread spread with "vegemite." Everyone tasted vegemite, then they wrote or drew their reactions to it—what the taste reminded them of. That afternoon, the teacher read *My Grandma Lives in Gooligulch* by Graeme Base. The children talked about the books and listed all the animals mentioned in both. They expanded their initial webs (as in figure 11.7). The children selected an animal from the list and began small group projects to study them.

The unit grew and eventually involved all the subject areas. It was extremely successful from the teacher's perspective, and everyone seemed to enjoy it and learn from it (see figures 11.8 and 11.9). Actually, everyone wanted to go to Australia (fair dinkum), even if everyone didn't like vegemite.

FIGURE 11.7
Expanded Web on
Australia

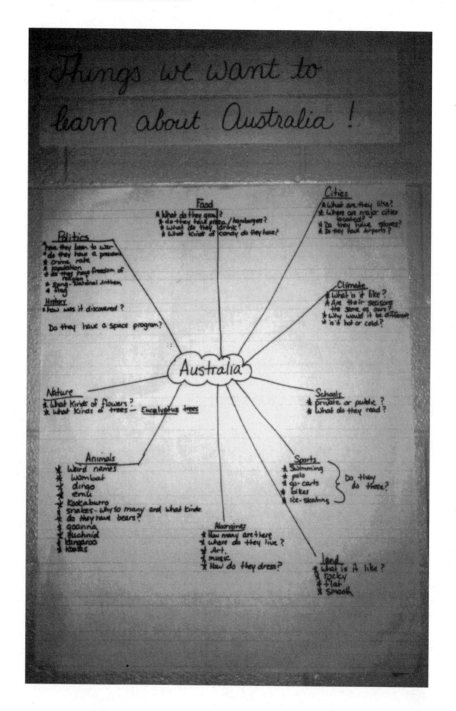

Products of the Theme Study   Activity and project ideas that the children developed and participated in are listed here:

The Arts

A display of crafts indigenous to Australia was created.

A presentation entitled "What We Learned about Aboriginal Art" was made.

A presentation entitled "What We Learned about Australian Art and Famous Australian Artists" was made.

Children did their own dreamtime paintings with oral explanations.

A calendar for next year with Australian animals and another with Australian birds were prepared.

FIGURE 11.8
Artifacts and Art in Australia Unit Wall Display

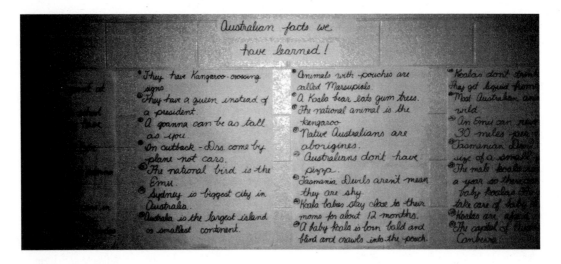

Australian facts we
have learned !

* They have Kangaroo-crossing signs
* They have a queen instead of a president
* A goanna can be as tall as you
* In outback - Drs. come by plane not cars.
* The national bird is the Emu.
* Sydney is biggest city in Australia.
* Australia is the largest island or smallest continent.

* Animals with pouches are called Marsupials.
* A Koala bear eats gum trees.
* The national animal is the kangaroo
* Native Australians are aborigines.
* Australians don't have pizza.
* Tasmania Devils aren't mean they are shy.
* Koala babies stay close to their moms for about 12 months.
* A baby koala is born bald and blind and crawls into the pouch.

* Koalas don't drink they get liquid from
* Most Australian are wild
* An Emu can run 30 miles per
* Tasmanian Dev
* The male koala
  a year so there
  baby koalas th
  take care of baby
* Koalas are afra
* The capital of
  Canberra

FIGURE 11.9
Compilation of Facts about Australia

"Our Favorite Australian Animals," an information book with illustrations, was created for the classroom.

A set of drawings of what aboriginal music made one group think of was done with captions.

A large map of Australia with topographical features and printed labels was painted for the wall.

A rather primitive, homemade musical instrument was made out of wood, metal, and rubber bands.

Literature

A discussion of Australian stories and poems for children covered how they are the same as and different from stories and poems we might read in America.

Dreamtime stories were written and illustrated.

An Australian alphabet book for the kindergartners was made.

One group did an Australian counting book for younger children.

A comparison of Australian humor to American humor for kids was presented.

A story using Aussie slang language became a readers theater presentation.

A favorite Australian children's story was turned into a puppet show.

An interview with an Australian about Australia and the way Australians talk was done and shared with the class.

Fictionary, a word game, was played with Australian terms and plausible definitions.

Two children created a "new" Australian animal, described and illustrated it, and shared it with the class.

Health (Foods and Recreation)

A trip into the outback to hunt opals was planned, with thought given to what would be needed to survive and why.

Each group made (or bought) and shared in a taste test of one of the foods mentioned in *Possum Magic.*

Math

A poll was taken of the number of students in the school who liked vegemite (Marmite) on crackers, compared to peanut butter. A bar graph was constructed and added to as each pollster's data came in.

A report was prepared on how Australia compares to the United States in size, population, miles of roads, miles of coast, annual rainfall, highest point, lowest point, numbers of cities over 100,000, and so on. Charts, graphs, and diagrams were used to present the comparisons.

Each student made up a word problem from the information above. These were illustrated and placed on the wall outside the classroom for passersby to solve.

Social Studies (Peoples, History, Prehistory, Geography)

The European settling of Australia was compared to the settling of North America. Some of the children wrote a poem to share their feelings and discoveries.

Prehistoric Australia was the subject of a relief map made of clay with plastic dinosaurs.

A motoring trip around Australia was planned. It included an estimate of the time the trip would take, cost of fuel, food and lodging, and what the group wanted to see.

Science (Ocean, Land, Plants, and Animals)

One group of children painted a giant underwater mural of the Great Barrier Reef, and they labeled all the plants and animals for their classmates.

One group created a display of poisonous animals and insects from Australia.

SUMMARY

Over the years, many educators have pointed out that young children enter school successful learners of language, eager to learn more, and curious about the world around them. Yet, by the middle grades or earlier, too many of these same children appear to have learning difficulties; they are bored and they dislike school. An integrated, inquiry-based language and literature perspective on teaching and learning— that is, whole language—is one way to change schools and keep more students engaged.

Such a change may feel risky. It requires support and transition time. However, teachers who are interested in developing learner-centered classrooms in an inquiry-based curriculum will find that thematic teaching can begin to pull it all together.

THEORY-TO-PRACTICE CONNECTIONS

Learning Theory	*Examples of Classroom Practice*
1. Learning as inquiry	1. Themes are selected by students and they pursue their own interests in the unit as much as possible.
2. Learners as active constructors of their own knowledge	2. The theme evolves as learners become interested and as they find and share information and resources, make connections, and as their study becomes more involved.
3. Learning as generative, as in making connections and figuring out how the world works	3. Learners pursue their own questions and the theme expands to encompass the entire curriculum.

SUGGESTED READINGS

Atwood, V. (Ed.). (1986). *Elementary social studies: Research as a guide to practice.* Washington, DC: National Council for the Social Studies.

Baratta-Lorton, M. (1976). *Mathematics their way.* Menlo Park, CA: Addison-Wesley.

Baskwill, J., & Whitman, P. (1986). *Whole language source book.* Toronto, Ontario: Scholastic.

Butler, A., & Turbill, J. (1988). *Towards a reading-writing classroom.* Rozelle, Australia: PETA.

Crouse, P. & Davey, M. (1989, November). Collaborative learning: Insights from our children. *Language Arts, 66*(7), 756–766.

Gamberg, R., Kwak, W., Hutchings, M., & Altheim, J. (1988). *Learning and loving it:* *Theme studies in the classroom.* Portsmouth, NH: Heinemann.

Hughes, M. (1986). *Children and numbers: Difficulties in learning mathematics.* New York: Basil Blackwell.

Hyde, A., & Bizar, M. (1989). *Thinking in context: Teaching cognitive processes across the elementary curriculum.* White Plains, NY: Longman.

Manning, M., Manning, G., & Long, R. (1994). *Theme immersion: Inquiry-based curriculum in elementary and middle schools.* Portsmouth, NH: Heinemann.

Pappas, C., Kiefer, B., & Levstik, L. (1990). *An integrated language arts perspective in the elementary classroom.* White Plains, NY: Longman.

SUGGESTED ACTIVITIES

1. If you were teaching the unit on Australia, what would you do with the children on the first day? Why? Share and discuss.

2. Select a high-quality piece of adolescent literature like MacLachlan's *Journey* and read it thoroughly. Discuss the story in small groups.

Then web the story by categories and begin to create project ideas that you might set up and/or suggest to students if you were using this book in the classroom as a literature study. Think about how such a book might lead into several projects or into a mini-unit.

3. Select a favorite author. Collect and read several of his or her books. Repeat the process outlined above.

4. Examine subject area textbooks at your favorite grade level. Select a theme topic covered in science, social studies, or math, for instance, and begin to create a thematic unit. Web the concept, identify resources, develop project ideas, and describe what you might do on the first day of class with the children. Exchange theme ideas with classmates. Evaluate yourselves by asking whether your project ideas and starting activity are consistent with the theory presented in this book.

5. Interview at least ten children at a given age or grade level. Ask them what they would most like to learn about or most like to study in school if they could. Arrange it so you and your classmates' choices cover all the elementary grades. Compile a list of children's favorite theme interests by age. Share with your classmates.

REFERENCES

Corwin, R., Hein, G., & Levin, D. (1976). Weaving curriculum webs: The structure of non-linear curriculum. *Childhood Education, 52* (5), 248–251.

Danforth, K., & Dickinson, M. (Eds.). (1982). *Journey into China.* Washington, DC: National Geographic Society.

Davis, D. (1990). The world of Miss Daisy Boyd: Memories of a teacher's voyage through the mind. *Teacher Magazine, 1*(5), 8–10.

Duckworth, E. (1987). *The having of wonderful ideas and other essays on teaching and learning.* New York: Teachers College Press.

Gamberg, R., Kwak, W., Hutchings, M., & Altheim, J. (1988). *Learning and loving it: Theme studies in the classroom.* Portsmouth, NH: Heinemann.

Goodman, K. (1992). A question about the future of whole language. In O. Cochrane (Ed.), *Questions and answers about whole language.* Katonah, NY: Richard C. Owen.

Harste, J. (1992). Inquiry-based instruction. *Primary Voices, 1*(1), 3.

Lewis, R., & Doorlag, D. (1987). *Teaching special students in the mainstream* (2nd ed.). Columbus, OH: Merrill.

Pappas, C., Kiefer, B., & Levstik, L. (1990). *An integrated language arts perspective in the elementary classroom.* White Plains, NY: Longman.

12

Special Needs Learners

Learning to read and to write ought to be one of the most joyful and successful of human undertakings. Notoriously, it is not so. . . . [However], there is a tradition of sanity and deep concern for the children who need not fail.

(HOLDAWAY, 1979, p. 11)

Who are the special needs learners?

How are they different from learners in regular education classrooms?

How are they like the learners in regular classrooms?

What do special learners need to know to be successful readers and writers?

Scene 1: "My student teacher is really going to have quite an experience in this classroom," the teacher of the class next door to mine said, lifting her eyes to the ceiling.

"Why is that?" I asked.

"Well, you see those seven children over there? They're learning disabled. And those two are on Ritalin. And poor little Jimmy," she said as she nodded toward a small boy scrunched down in his desk, "he's mentally retarded, but he's in here anyway. And see him?" she glared directly at a boy too large for his desk, "Both of his parents are deaf and he's so slow." He looked down, ashamed that she would single him out. His parents might be deaf, but he wasn't. "Anyway," she continued, "nine of my children go to Chapter 1 Reading and three to a math support class."

By second grade, almost one-third of these children had been labeled with some type of handicapping condition.

Scene 2: "Wow! How many students do you have this year?" I asked my teacher friend as we watched a room full of active children playing together.

"Twenty-five kindergartners, all ready to go," she enthusiastically replied, "and nineteen of them do not speak English. I have several Japanese, Laotian, Cambodian, and Vietnamese children, one Polish child, and one who speaks Spanish."

I was amazed. I would have been panic-stricken if most of my children could not speak English, but my friend was not. She welcomed the challenge and looked forward to watching the children learn and grow.

These are accounts of actual exchanges that occurred at different times with two regular education teachers in the same school. The two teachers teach down the hall from each other but they are worlds apart in their attitudes toward children with special learning needs. A great deal has been written about children who are at-risk of school and later life failure. Certainly special needs children are at-risk, but the children in the first teacher's classroom are more at-risk than the children who are lucky enough to have been placed in the second teacher's room.

Who Are Special Needs Learners?

Typically an elementary classroom has twenty-five to thirty children from a variety of backgrounds and experiences. Most classrooms contain children who have been certified as special learners. That is, they have been tested and have scored two standard deviations beyond (above or below) the mean (Cartwright, Cartwright, & Ward, 1989). Children who are physically impaired or sensory-impaired or who speak English as their second language are also considered to be special needs learners.

In many cases, a child may have more than one label, including but not limited to attention deficit/hyperactive disorder (ADHD), learning disabled (LD), emotionally disturbed (ED), gifted and talented (GT), educable mentally retarded (EMR), remedial, reluctant, at-risk, underachiever, developmentally delayed, slow learner, and gifted LD. These special needs labels and categories are used in federal legislation and funding formulas.

In the late 1950s, grants of federal money, called *categorical aid*, were created for the purpose of improving American education. The National Defense Education Act (NDEA), passed during the Eisenhower years, was established to improve achievement in mathematics, the sciences, and foreign language learning. This governmental action was taken in response to a national assessment of education that determined American students were performing less well than students in competing countries, specifically the Soviet Union. The United States was in the "race for space" at the time, and we believed we were losing.

In 1965, the Elementary and Secondary Education Act (ESEA) was passed as part of President Johnson's "war on poverty." It was designed specifically to improve the school achievement of educationally deprived children. Presented as the way to ensure full contribution to society by all its members, and in so doing to end poverty in the United States, ESEA earmarked 75 percent of the millions set aside yearly for the education of the nation's disadvantaged young people. Specific categories, Title I, Title II, and Title VI of ESEA, spelled out how the money was to be spent (Spring, 1991). These entitlement programs created support classrooms such as remedial reading, which are now referred to as Chapter programs.

ESEA was restructured during the 1970s with legislation such as Public Laws 89–10, 89–313, and 89–750. These laws amended ESEA to provide money to state and local education agencies specifically for the education of "handicapped" children (Haring, 1982). Then, in 1975, Public Law 94–142 was passed, guaranteeing a *free* and *appropriate* public education for all "handicapped" children. This act was viewed as a continuation of the attempt to ensure full opportunities for all citizens and to prevent loss of the gifts and talents of "disabled" citizens.

As helpful as this legislation has been in many ways, it and subsequent laws have increased the number of special needs categories that are recognized as deserving of funding. However, simply providing money for a recognized problem does not necessarily solve it. Teachers solve educational problems, in collaboration with other teachers, and with support in terms of information, time, and funding. But money is frequently the only element of the equation that is available. Too often teachers are not even asked what they think or what they need to solve an educational problem.

Because of the categorical nature of federal funding, some states now recognize as many as thirty separate labels of special needs.

Labeling children is a full-time job for one or more persons in many school districts. Unfortunately, labels do not tell the teacher anything about the child's learning outside the school or testing situation. They do not tell a teacher how to work with that child. They only tell the teacher that the child is entitled to receive special services under the law. They also enable the school system to receive the federal funds (Gilles, 1992).

The variety of different assistance or compensatory programs established by the federal government is a source of both support and frustration for classroom teachers. The programs provide support for children who really need specialized help or for children who cannot function in the regular classroom for the entire day. But they are frustrating as teachers struggle to keep track of which children are missing during what part of the day's learning events.

The diversity among learners is certainly one of the most demanding issues classroom teachers encounter. How can teachers be expected to meet the needs of so many different types of learners? Perhaps the most confounding problem embedded in this situation is the difficulty many children have in learning to read and write. Children who have serious problems learning to read and write have concerned educators for decades, dating back to the time when the systematic teaching of reading and writing began in our schools (Lipa, 1983).

In this chapter, we will explore learners who are different. Some of these children are served by special education classes, some by Chapter 1, and some by other types of remedial programs. Should regular education classroom teachers be held accountable for the achievement of so many children with so many different labels? Our purpose is *not* to focus on the deficits of groups of children, but rather to share what is known about how these children learn and what classroom practices are most successful.

As in previous chapters, we will focus on helping teachers know their learners, know the approaches and strategies, and know the materials appropriate for special needs children.

As we discussed in chapter 1 of this book, human learning is social. Human beings do not learn best in contrived settings where they are isolated from their peers, but rather they learn in rich and varied environments that include other people (Rhodes & Dudley-Marling, 1988). What and how human beings learn is affected by what they already know. Likewise, what human beings know is affected by what they learn. This is because "all knowledge is 'embedded' in other knowledge" (Caine & Caine, 1991, p. 36). Therefore, learning cannot be understood by focusing on the learning task in isolation. Nor can it be understood by focusing on specific bits and pieces of information fragmented from their natural contexts.

Traditional American classrooms are designed to focus on individual learning tasks and fragmented bits of information. Standardized tests measure what has been "learned" in these kinds of classrooms; this means that learning is defined as a measurable outcome. This view of how learning occurs has been called behaviorism or "reductionism" because, in this view, learning is broken down or reduced to small parts that are presumably easier to learn. Teachers teach the parts one at a time, and then the learner is left to put the parts back together to form the whole again. Learning is seen as additive.

But higher forms of human learning, such as learning to talk, learning to read, and learning to write are not additive. In fact, when we separate language into "skill" activities, we strip away meaning and destroy language. We obscure the process, the whole. Learning becomes more difficult, instead of less difficult, because children's ability to construct meaning, to apply what they already know to making sense of the new, is taken away. Learners then have nothing to use to make sense of the learning activity (Rhodes & Dudley-Marling, 1988).

Most human learning occurs in context. Learning to talk, for example, is natural and happens because children are in situations that facilitate learning to talk, where they are surrounded by talk and where they use talk to get what they want and need. Under the right conditions, learning to read and write occur as naturally as learning to talk. We now know that learning is constructive, occurring within a context. It is possible that schools that employ a reductionist view of learning actually cause some of the need for remedial education.

Most children in the United States enter formal schooling at age five. While kindergarten is still not mandatory in some states, most children attend public school kindergarten when it is available to them. The vast majority of kindergarten-age children cannot read or write yet. They do, however, know a great deal about written language in their environments, and they have learned many more things without benefit of formal, planned instruction. Before they start school, most five year olds have learned to

Walk, run, hop, skip, jump

Talk in sentences, many with extensive vocabulary

Tie their shoes

Ride a bicycle

Draw or write, perhaps scribble, make some letters, spell some words

Recognize their name in print

Recognize words in the environment, such as McDonald's signs, name of their favorite cereal or toy

Find their way home from a friend's house

React appropriately to signs, such as walk/don't walk

Select the appropriate restroom in restaurants

Use the telephone

Typical five year olds learned these skills and much, much more in the context of meaningful experiences. They learned with little effort and little or no instruction. Why, then, do so many children enter school knowing so much, yet fail to do well once there?

One of the major purposes of kindergarten is to prepare children for reading and writing instruction in the first grade. In first grade, children will likely encounter programs that employ a reductionist view of learning, where reading and writing are presented as a hierarchy of "skills" to be mastered. They may complete hundreds of ditto sheets or workbook pages for practice in making letters and sounds, matching rhyming words, identifying pictures, filling in blanks—all in the name of teaching children to read. "Skills" are also presented in stories in basal readers that may be written by formula so they don't sound like literature any more. Unfortunately, this mode of instruction frequently continues well into the primary grades. Some teachers, for example, will not allow the children to even try reading the next story in their basal reader until they have memorized all the "new" words. In some cases, children are not even given their initial readers in first grade until they can recite all the vocabulary words used in the books. Word lists are sent home, and only when the children can recognize the words in isolation may they proceed.

Practices like these confuse some children and lead them to approach reading as though it were a matter of saying all the words correctly one a time—that is, that reading is an additive process. They also cause some children to read as though getting the words right were a matter of sounding them out or memorizing them and nothing else. Children are taught to read without being taught to use what they already know about their spoken language and about the world around them. In other words, reductionist forms of instruction may actually teach some children to read badly.

But we know this is not how the reading process works. We know that isolated skill and drill is not how children learn best. And the problem is compounded for children who fall behind. Very early on, children who do not perform well on these types of activities are put into "the low group" with other children who also do not perform well. In this group they devote even more time to working on isolated skills because they have not yet "mastered" them. They do more ditto sheets, more workbook pages, more word lists; they spend more time on drill and practice, and less time reading stories. They spend less of their school day reading and writing because they do not know how yet. They have not accumulated the necessary skills.

Many of these children are subsequently scheduled for testing to determine what special programs and help they need. When they are tested, a label is affixed to their permanent school records. What's worse, the labels tend to stick to children, regardless of later performance. It is difficult for children to live down labels such as "slow learner" or "learning disabled" when those labels are on the permanent record. Often children categorize and label themselves. "I can't write, I'm LD" or "I can't learn, I'm in the dumb kid's class" (Gilles, 1992). Labels tend to become self-fulfilling prophecies, and children are regularly placed in low groups in later grades based on early assessments. Labels can take on a reality of their own (Taylor, 1991). As Wuthrick (1990) pointed out, children who were labeled "crows"— children in low ability reading groups—continued to do poorly in reading while their counterparts, the "bluejays," excelled. Indeed, the rich get richer and the poor get poorer.

Children who come to school who are exposed at home to a variety of literacy experiences at an early age normally do well in school in spite of the isolated instruction they receive. But what becomes of children who enter school without these experiences? What are they learning about reading and writing? What about children who come from linguistically different homes? What about children who do not score well on initial screening tests for kindergarten or first-grade placement? For them, reading may forever be sounding out words, memorizing lists, and working in workbooks (Goodman, 1986).

How Are Special Learners Different?

Some children do come to school with problems that are deep-seated and difficult to deal with. However, the majority of children who are labeled as being in need of special or remedial education are not distinguishable from their peers when they enter school (Cartwright, Cartwright, & Ward, 1989; Goodman, 1991; Smith, 1986). Often, these are children who came from homes where no one read to them, where there were few books or magazines to look through, where little experimentation with writing occurred. So, the children who most need to be read aloud to, who most need the time to explore print, and who most need context to make sense of learning in school are given the least time and opportunity to have enjoyable, meaningful experiences with print. It is ironic and tragic that many children have no recognizable problems at all until they enter school (Smith, 1986, 1988).

Regular education classrooms are heterogeneous places made up of children with varied experiences. Teachers cannot really teach one child at a time with methods customized for that particular learner (Caine & Caine, 1991). Therefore, children who are identified as having learning problems are often pulled out of the regular classroom for special help only to find themselves in instructional programs like those in which they first experienced difficulties. While the materials and their degree of difficulty may be different, the basic philosophy and methods may not be. Regardless of the differences among these learners, the instruction will almost certainly be the same as what they've already had (Weaver, 1991).

Some children are pulled out of their regular classrooms and taken to special classrooms where they receive more drill and practice on isolated skills. While pull-out programs do enable teachers to work with small groups of children with similar labels, pull-out programs have not proven very effective. Children's progress is assessed with scores on tests that are designed to measure knowledge of isolated skills, rather than their application. And the cycle continues.

Children are also tested with a variety of diagnostic instruments to identify their deficits. Instruction focuses on what these measures show that children cannot do. Rarely do children find themselves in programs that allow them to use their previous learning, to use what they already know. Most schools do not focus on what students are good at and build from there; they do not encourage children to pursue their own interests and thereby learn the information and skills they need. Schools that do provide these kinds of programs tend to reserve them for the academically gifted and talented students.

The commonly used reductionist approach provides few opportunities for children to engage in real literacy events. Many special students become passive learners because drill and practice do not require them to be active constructors of their own knowledge (Rhodes & Dudley-Marling, 1988). A continual barrage of practice with abstract skills that have not been mastered focuses on children's deficits and treats them as deficient and defective learners. Children are constantly reminded of their inadequacies and shortcomings. These instructional methods and what they imply may have a devastating effect on the children's lives (Rhodes & Dudley-Marling, 1988; Taylor, 1991).

Special education and remedial classrooms tend to be like regular classrooms in their curriculum and philosophy, but their culture is different. Special classes are likely to contain children with a wide range of age and cognitive abilities. They are less stable because children are phased in and out throughout the day and across the school year. Attempts to individualize instruction in special education classrooms also decrease the social aspects of literacy development. The children are isolated from each other as they work on their workbooks and ditto sheets; they are also separated from their peers in the regular classroom.

Whether in regular education classrooms, special education classrooms, or remedial classrooms, the instructional emphasis is frequently on what the children can't do. "They can't make all the letters. They make some letters backwards. They are so messy. They can't spell. So, of course, they can't write." The belief persists that successful literacy experiences for these children are achieved by limiting the amount of reading and writing they do. The notion is that children will experience more success by doing less.

The expectation for these learners tends to be lower than for their regular education counterparts. Many teachers have been taught that they must wait until children are able to read and write before giving them opportunities to actually read and write. Many have been taught that unless children can read and write error-free, they are not learning to read and write well. This practice places children in general, and special needs children in particular, at a decided disadvantage. What would happen if we thought children should be able to walk and talk well before we gave them opportunities to actually walk and talk? What sense does that make?

Many children experience problems in the regular classroom because of the restricted curriculum in reductionist programs. When they experience problems, many children are tested, certified, and labeled. From 1978–1979 to 1986–1987, the number of special education children increased from 3.9 million to 4.4 million. This was largely due to the number of children classified as "learning disabled." Growth in population, an increased awareness by parents of the rights of special children under the law, and increased federal funding for the learning disabled category have all contributed to this expansion. Growth in LD certified cases "exceeds all other handicapping conditions combined" (Hardman, Drew, Egan, & Wolf, 1990, p. 173). A whole language curriculum from the beginning of formal schooling could reduce the number of children labeled with "learning difficulties."

However, whole language classrooms cannot prevent every problem. Some children have severe sensory, physical, and neurological conditions and may be best served in special education classrooms, while many children challenged with such handicapping conditions are more appropriately served in the regular classroom for all or part of the school day. Most special education and remedial classrooms are still reductionist, although many are moving toward more meaning-making, holistic practice. But even whole language special and remedial classrooms cannot solve all the problems of labeled children.

Students with learning difficulties may still have problems reading and learning in certain subject areas. If they are separated from their peers for much of the day, they may experience difficulties with social relationships. Their learning may be slowed and their progress intermittent. Nevertheless, what whole language classrooms can do—whether they are regular, special, or remedial education—is help special learners experience success. When children's confidence and self-concepts are enhanced, they are likely to try harder and improve more rapidly (Gilles, 1992; Weaver, 1994).

Knowing the Learner

Special education children, especially those encountered in most classrooms, are more similar to than different from regular education children. Like all children, special children also actively construct their own knowledge. They are subject to the same conditions of natural learning. The reading and writing processes are the same for labeled children as for regular students.

In order to know the special needs learners in our classes, we have changed the way we look at children. First, we have done away with the practice of focusing on what children cannot do, on their weaknesses. Now we look for what children *can do* as they construct meaning for themselves. We identify their strengths, build instruction based on what they can do rather than what they cannot do, and encourage their interests and decision making. To that end, the observation and evaluation procedures for reading and writing described in chapters 5 through 7 are as appropriate for special need students as for any other group.

Second, we acknowledge that special and remedial education children *are learners,* too. Our expectations may be different—they may allow more time or provide more supports—but it is important not to expect less than what the child *can do.* Children tend to perform to the level they believe their teachers and their parents set for them.

Third, we celebrate risk taking as it leads to learning. As George Bernard Shaw reportedly quipped, "The person who has never made a mistake has never made anything." Special children may be less likely to try, they may be less likely to take risks, because many of them have been severely treated and criticized when they did (Rhodes & Dudley-Marling, 1988). They may have been ridiculed in front of their peers or made fun of by other children; they have already been singled out as needing to go to a "special" class for extra help. Taking risks is part of learning anything and everything. All children and all adults make approximations—they make mistakes—when they attempt to do anything new.

Teachers make very carefully documented, informed decisions about children in their classrooms. Reflective observation of children is critical. What teachers know and believe about how children learn and what language is will guide them in the instructional decisions they make. Teachers are the ones who decide *what* is needed and *how* to facilitate children's learning. Teachers must *know their learners.*

Knowing the Approaches

Teachers must also know the major approaches and strategies that are theoretically sound and appropriate for a whole language setting. Teachers are responsible for applying the approaches and choosing the strategies that best suit their students. In chapter 5, we discussed the major approaches and other strategies used to teach reading: read aloud, guided reading, sustained silent reading (SSR), and language experience.

Read aloud is used when the material presents more challenges to than supports for the reader. In other words, the text is too difficult for readers to tackle by themselves. Teachers select a text to share with an individual or with a small group of children who have similar reading strengths and needs. Big books originated as part of this book-sharing approach. Some children enter school not having experienced being read to or "lap-reading." Don Holdaway (1979) wanted to devise a way for these children to experience lap-reading in the classroom setting. He developed big books, books big enough for as many as three children to "get into" as they shared the book on the floor. Because the writing and pictures are larger than a regular-sized book, the big book can be shared with small groups. In general, big books are not intended to be used in large group settings because in these groups learners' abilities will vary widely. Choosing a text that has more challenges than supports offers a way to introduce children to new words and new strategies for figuring out words. As teachers and children explore new information together, teachers can demonstrate ways to construct comprehension so that learners develop useful strategies for reading on their own.

Guided reading is used with texts in which the amount of support and challenge is approximately equal. While the text contains many supports and the learner could achieve some degree of success from attempting it, the text also contains some stumbling blocks or challenges that could frustrate the reader. So teachers "guide" readers through the text. They demonstrate strategies (or skills) useful to readers as they work their way through more difficult text. They may stop to discuss how to figure out an unknown word, ask a question about what is being read, or predict what comes next. The teacher may choose to work with an individual or with a small group of readers who have similar strengths and needs.

Independent reading is used with material where the supports are more numerous than the challenges. If you believe that children learn to walk by walking, to ride a bicycle by riding a bicycle, to water ski by water skiing, and to read by reading, then you must offer time for the children to read. Since this is time set aside for learners to work independently, it is important that the text chosen not be too difficult for readers to handle alone.

Unfortunately, for learners with a difference, independent reading is either seldom used as an approach or is used little because many teachers believe that children who have learning difficulty cannot read independently. Independent writing is encouraged even less. SSR and SSW (sustained silent writing) are just as important for less proficient readers and writers as they are for the more able. Independent reading and writing events give children opportunities to explore printed materials. Selecting materials that present many supports gives special learners positive experiences with text. It engages them in the reading and writing strategies they are learning. Materials with many supports also help special learners build their sense of themselves as readers and writers.

Learners who do not speak English as their native language are also at a decided disadvantage in school. According to Rigg and Allen (1989), bilingual and non-English-speaking, monolingual students benefit from being read to. They also benefit from the rich environment of whole language classrooms, with their natural talking and problem solving. The question of whether English as a second language (ESL) students should receive instruction in their native language or in English alone is one that is still hotly debated in many circles. Most whole language teachers would agree with Au (1993) that "ESL students will be more successful in school if they receive instruction in their native language. Proficiency in the native language serves as the basis for developing students' proficiency in English. The goal . . . is to have students develop oral fluency and literacy in both the native language and in English" (p. 145).

In addition, recent research suggests that bilingual students, while at a disadvantage initially, especially in traditional classrooms, are ultimately advantaged in several cognitive areas over their mono-lingual counterparts (Lanauze & Snow, 1989). Certainly, ESL students have a better chance of having their instructional and social needs met in language- and literature-based classrooms. Classrooms where language learning is supported—where immersion and demonstration are natural, and where engagement is encouraged—are more likely to benefit special needs learners including ESL students.

Knowing the Materials and Resources

Many companies publish sets of high-quality literature that have been "kid-tested" and are appropriate for whole language classrooms. They typically consist of four to six small paperback copies and one enlarged text. The stories are not written by a formula that controls certain elements of text, such as spelling patterns or sentence types and lengths. The stories do become progressively more complex. That is, stories designed to be read early in the year have a large number of supports and few challenges, and those designed to be presented later in the year contain more challenges. Teachers find these materials very helpful for building their collections of children's literature. Multiple copies of stories are needed for small group instruction.

Teachers must know the materials well enough to be able to determine what supports and what challenges each offers. An example of a text with a great many supports is *Not Now, Bernard* by McKee. This story is both patterned and repetitive. The bold illustrations also give readers sufficient information to predict what the next line will be.

A second text that offers some of the same supports but involves a bit more challenge for the developing reader is Verna Aardema's *Who's in Rabbit's House?* While this text is both predictable and repetitive, more challenges are present because of the length and complexity of the language. This particular story provides added supports if the refrain is acted out. Texts that are not patterned or repetitive or that have fewer illustrations to aid prediction tend to offer the reader many challenges. Readers may be better able to use the supports that are provided if the teacher previews the story with the students before they read it. An example of a story with a good many challenges for a developing reader is Robert McCloskey's *Make Way for Ducklings.*

Selected Strategies: The Inclusive Classroom

The major approaches and selected strategies founded on whole language theory and research are as viable with special needs learners as with their regular education peers (see figure 12.1). Teachers select the materials and approaches to match the learners and they apply selected strategies as needed. Next we present a few strategies described in earlier chapters that have been altered slightly for special learners.

FIGURE 12.1
The Inclusive Classroom

Language Experience   Language experience begins with an event shared by the children and the teacher. The teacher leads the children into talking about the event, writing about it, reading about it, and sharing a written product. Language experience enables learners to see that the language they use in talking may be used in writing. It is also an excellent way to write a class big book that can be published and kept in the classroom library.

Language experience allows the teacher to demonstrate and children to explore written language. Teachers demonstrate elements such as reading from left to right and from top to bottom, voice-print match, and sound-letter cues. Children explore spelling strategies, punctuation and capitalization, vocabulary, and grammatical acceptability.

An especially useful type of language experience is the dictated story (see figure 12.2). Because some special needs children may have trouble physically producing print (they might be vision impaired, for instance), teachers, teaching assistants, parent volunteers, or other students may scribe for the children as they dictate. Dictated stories may be simple or complex. Journal entries may also be dictated. In figure 12.3, David wrote his own journal entry. David is a very bright fourth grader who has cerebral palsy. Figure 12.4 is a sample of an entry that the teacher assistant wrote for David when he asked for help writing about his feelings on the war in the former Yugoslavia.

Shared Reading   Shared reading with special children may take many forms. The teacher will read to the children every day from a variety of genres and as many times a day as possible. But shared reading is not limited to the teacher's reading to the children. Shared reading may occur child to child, child to small group, or even children to children. Particularly effective for building self-esteem in special needs children is having an older child with special needs prepare and read a story to a younger child. We suggest that older children be matched with younger children with whom they may work all year. Perhaps each Friday the pairs could meet together to talk, to share stories, and to learn from one another.

FIGURE 12.2   Justin's Caterpillar Book

Written by Justin

Illustrated by Justin

I like Caterpillars
because they are nice.

They have 16 legs.

They shed their skin.

They eat too much.

FIGURE 12.3
David's Journal Entry
in His Own Writing

Assisted Reading One of the most effective techniques specifically designed for children who are having difficulty reading is assisted reading. This technique is categorized as guided reading because the teacher guides the child in a one-on-one session through a selected text. Assisted reading is a variation of a technique called the neurological impress method, which was developed for severely disabled adolescent readers (Rhodes & Dudley-Marling, 1988), but is effective for younger readers as well. The method is designed to simulate lap-reading. If employed as little as five minutes, three times a week, assisted reading yields measurable results over time.

Assisted reading works best with an entire text or story that the less able reader has heard before and likes. Although it is not imperative that a familiar text be chosen, a predictable text is recommended. If the less able reader has not heard the story before, the instructional session might begin with the teacher reading the book to the child. In this way, the child can hear the text read fluently and can begin to build a knowledge of the text by hearing it in its entirety. The teacher may repeat the reading, this time inviting the child to read along. If the child needs less assistance or is familiar with the text, the session may begin with the child reading along with the teacher.

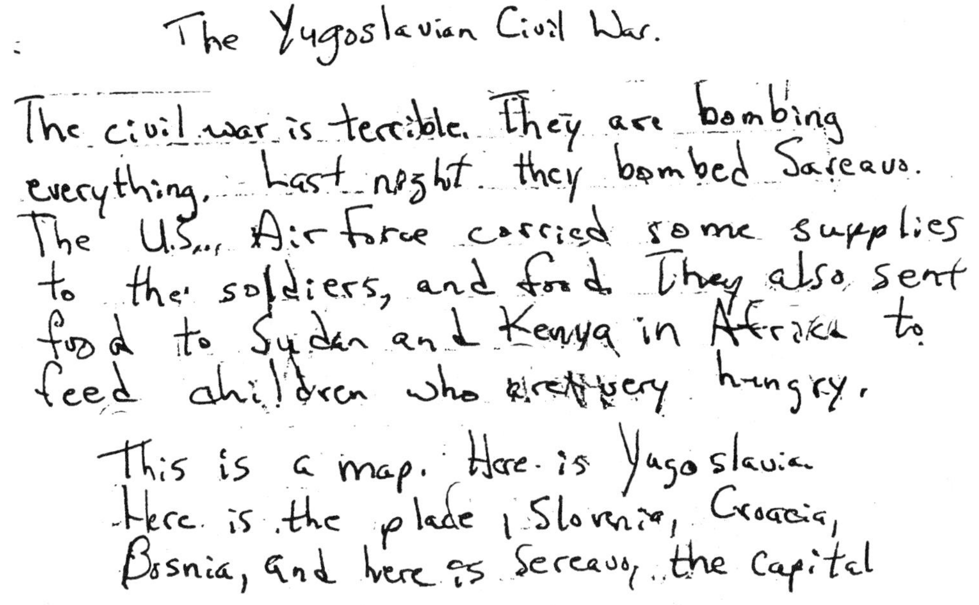

The Yugoslavian Civil War.

The civil war is terrible. They are bombing everything. Last night they bombed Sareavo. The U.S., Air Force carried some supplies to the soldiers, and food. They also sent food to Sudan and Kenya in Afrika to feed children who are very hungry.

This is a map. Here is Yugoslavia. Here is the plade Slovenia, Croacia, Bosnia, and here is Sereavo, the capital

As the text is being read, the teacher reads smoothly and with expression. As the child shows evidence of controlling the text, the teacher's voice lowers so that the child's voice is louder. If the child falters, the teacher reads louder to provide the reader more help. As the child again gains control, the teacher's voice again diminishes, and so on. The reading of the text is never interrupted. If discussion of individual words is needed, it is done only after the entire text has been read.

To employ this technique, the teacher must know the needs of the learner. For example, if the child needs help with voice-print matching, the teacher points to the words in the text as they are read. Initially word-by-word pointing by the reader may be encouraged to ensure voice-print match. As the reader becomes more proficient in voice-print matching, pointing should no longer be done on a word-by-word basis. Instead, the reader and the teacher move across the

FIGURE 12.4
David's Dictated Journal Entry

line of print in a smooth and even manner. Eventually, all pointing becomes unnecessary.

Text Sets   Another useful assisted-reading strategy is using text sets in a guided-reading format. By guiding the readers through the ways stories in the set are alike and different, the teacher demonstrates useful strategies in relating across texts and relating new information to existing knowledge. Large pieces of butcher paper on which the comparisons are written can be displayed in the classroom and can become part of the literate environment.

Text sets may be used with groups as guided or assisted reading or in conference settings with individuals. They may also be used in a literature study. Teachers might also have the children examine several different books, reading and talking about their similarities and differences. Examining several related books in this way might continue for a week or more. Groups may meet for a few minutes every day to read, examine, and discuss their discoveries. For example, children exploring all the books written by Robert Munsch discovered that he likes the words *seventeen, enormous, no,* and *wap*. Children studying the books of Ezra Jack Keats found a dachshund in every story.

Listening Experience   On days when the teacher does not work individually with children using assisted reading, they may listen to a prerecorded tape of the text. Headphones are recommended to cut down on distraction; multichannel wireless systems give readers the opportunity to hear both the tape and themselves reading (Rhodes & Dudley-Marling, 1988).

Teachers may also read a story to a group of children once, tape-recording it as they read. Children can then listen to the tape and follow along in their books at least two more times during the morning. That afternoon, the children can retell the story in writing. These writings may be shared among the children. They may also be used by teachers as part of their continuous evaluation of children's writing and story comprehension.

The Authoring Classroom   While the discussion so far has centered primarily on reading, writing is an important part of literacy development as well. Many programs specifically designed to help children struggling with reading have ignored the importance of writing.

Special learners may need additional supports as they write. Certainly, it is important that they engage in all facets of the writing process from topic selection to publication. In addition, special learners need many and varied opportunities to write for authentic, functional purposes. The approaches that are an integral part of whole language classrooms—write aloud, guided writing, and SSW —should also be employed with special learners whether they are in regular, special, or remedial classrooms.

In whole language classrooms, children are encouraged to write every day. Children with special needs are not excluded. Their writing is encouraged and celebrated just as is everyone else's. Granted, their spelling may not look conventional and their letters may not all face the right way. Their writing may be "messy," but the content may be remarkable. Special children are capable of constructing meaningful and often highly creative texts. Frequently, all they need is opportunity, demonstrations, and supports. Expect that labeled learners can write and they will. Many times children with special needs have risked writing only to feel humiliated because their writing was unreadable. The following strategy is designed to offer the writer more supports than challenges.

Assisted Writing   Using a variety of ways to demonstrate how writing works may be helpful. For example, ask the children to draw a picture of themselves, then ask them to write one sentence about their picture. If children are unsure of their writing, scribe for them, but encourage them to write what you have written underneath. The following day, children may be asked to draw another picture, perhaps of their family or their home, and another sentence is written about the picture. If this process is continued for a week, each day's writing can be bound together and "published" for the classroom library or for the children to take home (see the example in figure 12.5).

FIGURE 12.5   All about Me, by Justin

For children who do not need quite that much support, a variation of this strategy is useful. Begin the first week by having the children write one sentence each day about their chosen topic. The second week, they write two sentences each day to expand the topic, and so on. As the writers begin to develop confidence, less support is needed. Reading leads to writing so what children read and hear read aloud is very important (McCarter, 1989).

Message boards, a classroom post office, logs and journals, written conversations, and other authentic writing opportunities are important for special needs children. Most special learners develop literacy the same way as other children; therefore, they need the same kinds of experiences with print.

Multisensory Activities   While special needs children learn the same way that regular education children do, on the surface the approach may be a little different. The children may require more time and more support, but little need exists to design special learning programs that are markedly different from whole language classrooms. Many special and remedial programs focus on "multisensory" learning activities to compensate for regular programs that tend to favor learners whose primary mode was visual. The tactile and kinesthetic modes were commonly ignored in these programs. Special multisensory programs were developed to involve these two modalities because it was believed they would be successful with labeled learners.

Whole language classrooms are multisensory by definition. While reading is certainly visual, nothing is more tactile or kinesthetic than writing. Children in whole language classrooms are constantly engaged in using all their senses and their different modes of learning as they construct meaning for themselves. They are not confined to a single mode of learning or to a single mode of presenting their learning. Therefore, whole language classrooms are viable for special learners. Special needs students may require more assistance and they may take a little longer, but they are all learners, too. What applies to regular whole language classrooms is appropriate for special and remedial whole language classrooms as well: teachers must *know their learners, know the approaches,* and *know the materials and resources.*

The strategies presented in this chapter are theoretically sound for all students. And while they are being recommended for learners with special needs, they are not intended only for special learners, any more than the strategies suggested in the preceding chapters were intended solely for regular learners.

□

The same summer that Jenny learned to water ski, she attended summer camp. While there, she wrote the letter in figure 12.6 to her parents. Can you read it? Not very many of the words are spelled correctly, and some of the letters are made backwards. She doesn't

FIGURE 12.6
Jenny's Letter and
Word Search

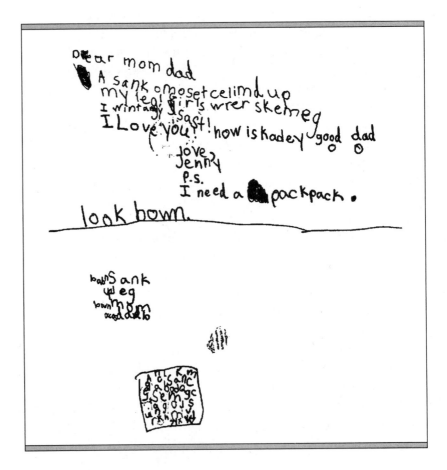

have a strong sense of the space between words. Can she write or not? What can she do as a writer?

Jenny's letter says:

Dear mom dad
A snake almost climbed up
my leg! Girls were screaming
I went away fast! How is Katy? good ☐   bad ☐
I love you!
    Love,
    Jenny
    P.S.
    I need a backpack.
look down

Below the letter, Jenny created a word search for her parents. She included words from the letter in the puzzle. She listed the ones she had included so they would be easier to find. One supposes she didn't want her parents to be bored in her absence, so she provided them with an activity they might enjoy.

Jenny is an extremely competent child and an excellent problem solver. She has above-average intelligence and an extensive speaking vocabulary. Her self-image was bolstered by learning to water ski. However, because her ability to use conventions of written language has not developed as quickly as for some other children her age, she has found her traditional-style school a punitive place. How do you think she would respond to a holistic language- and literature-based classroom?

The world is full of children like Jenny.

SUMMARY

Special learners are more similar to than different from regular learners. All children learn in the same basic way. They use what they already know to develop strategies for finding out what they want to know. They construct hypotheses, test them, and confirm or refute them. They connect new learning to existing knowledge. They do all these things best when the conditions that support learning are present. Learning is easy when it is personal and social, when learners are immersed in what they want to know, and when the environment is rich and low-risk—whether it be water skiing or reading, writing, and arithmetic. They learn as more proficient learners demonstrate the knowledge and processes being acquired. They learn because they are provided with many opportunities to engage in what they are trying to learn, to use what they are trying to learn in meaningful ways. They learn because they are praised as their approximations become more proficient. They learn when they take the responsibility for learning and make their own choices. They learn because they expect they will and because the people around them expect they will.

Many educators view reading and writing as performance on tests, exercises, and workbooks. Putting aside these reductionist views of reading and writing, we come instead to see literacy as making sense of written language. What a learner brings to the literacy event—experiences, attitudes, concepts, cognitive schemata—is as important as what the writer brought. Reading and writing are creative acts because meaning is created in response to a text. After all, making meaning is what human beings do best. Approaching the teaching of reading and writing from a language- and literature-based, holistic view is as appropriate for special learners as it is for everyone.

THEORY-TO-PRACTICE CONNECTIONS

Language and Learning Theory

1. Special needs learners are more like regular education students than they are different.

2. Special needs learners have many of the same instructional needs as regular education students.

Examples of Classroom Practice

1. Group projects, class discussions in the inclusive classroom

2. Read aloud/write aloud, guided reading and writing, SSR and SSW

SUGGESTED READINGS

Carrier, J. (1986). *Learning disability: Social class and the construction of inequality in American education.* Westport, CT: Greenwood Press.

Coles, G. (1989). *The learning mystique.* New York: Fawcett.

Rhodes, L., & Dudley-Marling, C. (1988). *Readers and writers with a difference: A holistic approach to teaching learning dis-* abled and remedial students. Portsmouth, NH: Heinemann.

Shannon, P. (1988). *Broken Promises: Reading instruction in twentieth-century America.* Westport, CT: Bergin & Garvey.

Weaver, C. (Ed.). (1994). *Success at last: Helping students with attention deficit (hyperactivity) disorders achieve their potential.* Portsmouth, NH: Heinemann.

SUGGESTED ACTIVITIES

1. Read about and report on the characteristics and instructional needs of ESL, LD, or ADHD children.

2. Read about and report on such techniques as the neurological impress method, the Fernald approach, the Montessori method, or the Slingerland materials for teaching phonics and word-identification skills.

3. Read about and discuss learning styles research.

REFERENCES

Aardema, V. (1977). *Who's in rabbit's house?* New York: Dial.

Au, K. (1993). *Literacy instruction in multicultural settings.* Fort Worth, TX: Harcourt Brace Jovanovich College.

Caine, R., & Caine, G. (1991). *Making connections: Teaching and the human brain.* Alexandria, VA: Association for Supervision and Curriculum Development.

Cartwright, G., Cartwright, C., & Ward, M. (1989). *Educating special learners* (3rd ed.). Belmont, CA: Wadsworth.

Gilles, C. (1992). How can whole language help the "labeled" learner? In O. Cochrane (Ed.), *Questions and answers about whole language.* Katonah, NY: Richard C. Owen.

Goodman, K. (1986). *What's whole in whole language?* Portsmouth, NH: Heinemann.

Goodman, K. (1991). Revaluing readers and reading. In S. Stires (Ed.), *With promise: Redefining reading and writing for "special" students.* Portsmouth, NH: Heinemann.

Hardman, M., Drew, C., Egan, M., & Wolf, B. (1990). *Human exceptionality* (3rd ed.). Boston, MA: Allyn & Bacon.

Haring, N. (1982). *Educating exceptional children and youth.* Columbus, OH: Merrill.

Holdaway, D. (1979). *The foundation of literacy.* Portsmouth, NH: Heinemann.

Lanauze, M., & Snow, C. (1989). The relation between first- and second-language writing skills: Evidence from Puerto Rican elementary school children in the mainland. *Linguistics and Education, 1*(4), 323–328.

Lipa, S. (1983). Reading disability: A new look at an old issue. *Journal of Learning Disabilities, 16,* 453–457.

McCarter, C. (1989). Encouraging the reluctant writer: A one-sentence approach. *Tennessee Reading Teacher, 17*(2), 34–37.

McCloskey, R. (1941). *Make way for ducklings.* New York: Viking.

McKee, D. (1980). *Not now, Bernard.* New York: Puffin Books.

Rhodes, L., & Dudley-Marling, C. (1988). *Readers and writers with a difference: A holistic approach to teaching learning disabled and remedial students.* Portsmouth, NH: Heinemann.

Rigg, P., & Allen, V. (Eds.). (1989). *When they don't all speak English: Integrating the ESL student into the regular classroom.* Urbana, IL: NCTE.

Smith, F. (1986). *Insult to intelligence.* New York: Arbor House.

Smith, F. (1988). *Understanding reading.* Hillsdale, NJ: Lawrence Erlbaum.

Spring, J. (1991). *American education: An introduction to social and political aspects.* White Plains, NY: Longman.

Taylor, D. (1991). *Learning denied.* Portsmouth, NH: Heinemann.

Weaver, C. (1991). Potential for developing readers. *Topics in language disorders. Whole language theory and practice: Implication for the language impaired, 11*(3), 28–44.

Weaver, C. (Ed.). (1994). *Success at last: Helping students with attention deficit (hyperactivity) disorders achieve their potential.* Portsmouth, NH: Heinemann.

Wuthrick, M. (1990). Bluejays win! Crows go down in defeat. *Phi Delta Kappan, 71*(7), 553–556.

Love yourself before you Love Anyone else

Chelsea Henson

May 5, 1980–September 5, 1992

APPENDIX A

Phonic Patterns

As an alphabetic system, the patterns of letter-sound relationships are one of the three sets of cues readers must become aware of and use when reading and writing. This store of information is most usable to learners who have developed their phonemic awareness *as* they engaged in real reading and writing. Merely memorizing the multitude of letter-sound associations in drills and on worksheets causes many children to misunderstand the reading process and fail to fully develop their ability to read.

The alphabetic code for English is complex. For instance, there are at least ten ways to spell the long /ā/ sound as in the word *baby*. These include the *ay* as in *day*, the *a* + silent *e* as in the word *game*, the *ai* as in the word *mail*, the *ey* as in *they*, the *ea* as in *break*, the *ei* as in the word *rein*, the *eigh* as in *neighbor*, the *aigh* as in *straight*, and the *et* as in *bouquet*. This complicates things for the young writer.

The young reader has a slightly different concern. That is, every time the letter [a] appears in a word (such as *machine*), how does the reader know what sound is being represented if he or she doesn't recognize the word? For instance, the letter [a] represents at least seven different sounds in standard pronuncia-tion alone. The letter [a] as in *idea*, in *mountain* or *around*, in *said* or *any*, in *swallow* or *father*, in *spinach* or *village*, in *talk* or *draw*, or in *apple* or *plaid* represents a different sound in each example.

Vowel Sounds

The following is a list of most of the common spelling patterns in fairly common words for vowel sounds in "standard" English.

/ā/ as in date	/ē/ as in be
a shady	e me
ay lay	ea mean
a + (e) date	y happy
ey they	ee + (e) freeze
ai mail	ie field
eigh eight	ee seen
aigh straight	ie + (e) achieve
ai + (e) raise	ea + (e) peace
au + (e) gauge	i ski
ee matinee	ae algae
ea steak	e + (e) these
ei rein	ey key
et bouquet	eo people
	ei + (e) seize

/ī/ as in die
i mild
i + (e) time
igh night
y sky
ie pie
y + (e) type
ey geyser
ay bayou
ei stein
eigh height
ai + (e) aisle
oy coyote

/ō/ as in go
o gold
o + (e) those
ow know
oa coal
ou soul
oe toe
ough though
eau plateau
ew sew

/ü/ as in to
o who
oo noon
ou you
ew threw
u + (e) rule
ue blue
oo + (e) choose
o + (e) whose
oe shoe
ou + (e) rouge
ough through
ui + (e) bruise

/ă/ as in at
a cat
ai plaid

/oi/ as in boil
oi coil
oy toy
oi + (e) noise

/a/ as in hot
o odd
a father
o + (e) dodge

/au/ as in hour
ou out
ow owl
ough drought
ou + (e) house
ow + (e) browse

/ĕ/ as in yes
e get
ea head
a many
u bury
ai said
e + (e) edge
ea + (e) cleanse
ei heifer
eo leopard
ie friend

/ə/ as in about
a around
i happily
e listen
o lemon
ou famous
u study
ai certain
ie ancient
e + (e) sentence
o + (e) purpose
eo pigeon

/u/ as in look
oo book
u put
o wolf

/o/ as in off
aw draw
o off
a walk
au author
oa broad
augh daughter
ough thought
a + (e) false
au + (e) cause

/ĭ/ as in if
i in
y system
a spinach
i + (e) give
e + (e) privilege
a + (e) village
ui build
ie + (e) sieve

Consonant Sounds

The following is a list of the most common spelling patterns for consonant sounds in "standard" English.

/b/ as in bib
b bib
bb ebb

/ch/ as in church
ch churn
tch pitch
t nature

/d/ as in did
d do
dd add
ld could

/f/ as in for
f for
ff effort
ph graph
gh laugh

/g/ as in gag
g go
gg egg
gh ghost
x example

/h/ as in high
h home
wh whole

/j/ as in judge
j project
g digest
dg edge
d educate

/k/ as in king
c cap
k keep
ck crack
cc occur
ch chorus
lk chalk
que antique

/l/ as in lull
l low
ll allow

/m/ as in mom
m some
mm summer
mb climb
lm calm
mn condemn

/n/ as in <u>n</u>o<u>n</u>e

n   no
kn   knee
nn   announce
gn   gnat

/ng/ as in ri<u>ng</u>

ng   singer
n   sink

/p/ as in <u>p</u>o<u>p</u>

p   pup
pp   puppy

/r/ as in <u>r</u>ea<u>r</u>

r   roar
rr   correct
rh   rhyme
wr   wrap

/s/ as in <u>s</u>a<u>ss</u>

s   so
ss   pass
c   cent
sc   scent
st   whistle
ps   psychology
sw   sword

/sh/ as in <u>sh</u>u<u>sh</u>

sh   rush
t   action
ch   chef
c   ocean
s   sure
sc   conscious
ss   tissue

/t/ as in <u>t</u>o<u>t</u>

t   to
tt   better
ed   cracked
cht   yacht
bt   debt
ct   indict
pt   recipt

th/ as in <u>th</u>is and <u>th</u>in

th   bathe
th   bath

/v/ as in <u>v</u>ote

v   valve
f   of
lv   calves

/w/ as in <u>w</u>o<u>w</u>

w   water
u   aqua

/y/ as in <u>y</u>et

y   yet
i   senior

/z/ as in <u>z</u>ero

z   zeal
ss   dessert
zz   buzz
cz   czar
s   poison

/zh/ as in vi<u>s</u>ion

s   usual
g   beige

Other Sound-Letter Patterns

There are several other ways of viewing phonic patterns in addition to how sounds are spelled. These include the numbers of sounds that any one spelling pattern reflects. For example, an [e] by itself in a syllable may represent long /ē/ as in *penal* and *fetal,* or it may represent short /ĕ/ as in *metal* and *petal.* Phonemic awareness also includes knowledge that some single vowel sounds are spelled with two letters. These are called vowel digraphs (for example, *ea* as in *<u>ea</u>ch, oa* as in *<u>oa</u>k, ie* as in *fr<u>ie</u>nd).* Some single consonant sounds are spelled with two letters. These are called consonant digraphs (for example, *ch* as in *per<u>ch</u>, ph* as in *<u>ph</u>one, ng* as in *si<u>ng</u>).* Some vowel sounds are actually two sounds blended together. These are called diphthongs (for example, *oi* as in *b<u>oi</u>l, ai* as in *t<u>ai</u>l).*

Some consonants are blended in words as well. These are called consonant blends. English has three basic varieties of consonant blends: consonant + *r* as in *<u>br</u>ick* or *<u>dr</u>op,* consonant + *l* as in *<u>bl</u>ow* or *<u>fl</u>ip,* and *s* + consonant as in *<u>st</u>ick* or *<u>sp</u>ot.* Three-letter blends are combinations of the above (*s* + consonant + *l* as in *<u>spl</u>ash* or *s* + consonant + *r* as in *<u>str</u>ipe).* A few consonant blends occur in final position within words and syllables. These are exceptions to the three patterns described above, for example, the *ld* as in *fo<u>ld</u>,* and the *nk* as in *dri<u>nk</u>.*

Other sound-letter patterns include: (1) double consonants (for example, *dd* as in *mi<u>dd</u>le, gg* as in *wi<u>gg</u>le, bb* as in *bu<u>bb</u>le, tt* as in *bu<u>tt</u>er*); (2) silent letters (*kn* as in *<u>kn</u>ow, mb* as in *thum<u>b</u>, pt* as in *recei<u>pt</u>*); and (3) the letter [c] sounded like /s/ before *e, i,* and *y* (*<u>c</u>ent, <u>c</u>ity,* and *<u>c</u>ycle*) or sounded like /k/ everywhere else (*<u>c</u>at, <u>c</u>ot,* and *<u>c</u>ut*).

Finally, phonic "rules" have been created in an effort to identify highly consistent letter-sound patterns. These include little rhymes such as, "When two vowels go walking, the first one does the talking," as in *g<u>oa</u>l* and *b<u>ea</u>n,* or simply stated observations such as, "When the letter [r] follows a vowel, the vowel is neither long nor short," as in *b<u>ur</u>n* or *f<u>ir</u>.* Research has concluded that there are only a few rules that have sufficiently high utility to be useful, and that children's reading ability is not enhanced by their memorizing such generalizations (Rosso & Emans, 1981).

Highly Predictive Phonic Generalizations

The following sound-letter patterns or phonic generalizations are applicable at least three out of four occurrences, or 75 percent of the time.

1. A single vowel in the middle of a one-syllable word is usually short, as in c*a*t.

2. The [r] causes the preceding vowel to be neither short nor long, as in j*e*rk.

3. In words having an [oa], the long sound of the /o/ is heard and the [a] is unvoiced, as in s*oa*p.

4. In words with [ee] the long sound of /e/ is usually heard, as in fl*ee*.

5. In words with an [ay], the [y] is unvoiced and the long sound of /a/ is usually heard, as in m*ay*be.

6. When the letter [i] is followed by the letters [gh], the long sound of /i/ usually heard and the [gh] is unvoiced, as in fl*igh*t.

7. When the letter [y] is the final letter in a word, it usually represents a vowel sound, as in sk*y* and mone*y*.

8. When the letters [ch] are next to each other in a word, they represent only one sound, as in chur*ch*.

9. When a word begins with the letters [wr], the [w] is unvoiced, as in *wr*ong.

10. When two of the same consonants are next to each other in a word, only one sound is voiced, as in ma*rr*y.

11. When a word ends with [ck] only the /k/ is voiced, as in sti*ck*.

12. In most two-syllable words, the first syllable is stressed, as in *on*ly.

13. The syllables [ture] and [tion] appearing as second syllables in two-syllable words are unaccented, as in na*ture* and na*tion*.

14. In words that end in [le], the consonant preceding the [le] usually begins the syllable, as in sta*ble*.

15. When the last syllable in a word is the sound /r/, the syllable is unaccented, as in wond*er*.

REFERENCE

Rosso, B., & Emans, R. (1981). Do children use phonic generalizations and how? *Reading Teacher, 34,* 653–658.

APPENDIX B

Recommended Whole Language Reading List: Books, Journals, and Newsletters

Books

Philosophy and Theory

Cambourne, B. (1988). *The whole story.* Toronto, Ontario: Ashton-Scholastic.

Collis, M., & Dalton, J. (1990). *Becoming responsible learners: Strategies for positive classroom management.* Portsmouth, NH: Heinemann.

Edelsky, C., Altwerger, B., & Flores, B. (1991). *Whole language: What's the difference?* Portsmouth, NH: Heinemann.

Goodman, K. (1986). *What's whole in whole language?* Portsmouth, NH: Heinemann.

Goodman, K. (1988). *Report card on basal readers.* Katonah, NY: Richard C. Owen.

Goodman, K., Smith, E., Meredith, R., & Goodman, Y. (1987). *Language and thinking in schools.* Katonah, NY: Richard C. Owen.

Goodman, Y. (1990). *How children construct literacy: Piagetian perspectives.* Newark, DE: IRA.

Graves, D. (1990). *Discover your own literacy.* Portsmouth, NH: Heinemann.

Holdaway, D. (1979). *The foundations of literacy.* Portsmouth, NH: Heinemann.

Newman, J. (1985). *Whole language: Theory in use.* Portsmouth, NH: Heinemann.

Shannon, P. (1989). *Broken promises: Reading instruction in twentieth-century America.* Granby, MA: Burgin & Garvey.

Shannon, P. (1990). *The struggle to continue: Progressive reading instruction in the U.S.* Portsmouth, NH: Heinemann.

Short, K., & Burke, C. (1991). *Creating curriculum: Teachers and students as a community of learners.* Portsmouth, NH: Heinemann.

Smith, F. (1983). *Essays into literacy.* Portsmouth, NH: Heinemann.

Smith, F. (1985). *Reading without nonsense.* New York: Teachers College Press.

Smith, F. (1988). *Joining the literacy club.* Portsmouth, NH: Heinemann.

Smith, F. (1990). *To think.* New York: Teachers College Press.

Stephens, D. (1991). *Research on whole language: Support for a new curriculum.* Katonah, NY: Richard D. Owen.

Stephens, D. (1990). *What matters? A primer for teaching reading.* Portsmouth, NH: Heinemann.

Watson, D., & Harste, J. (1989). *Whole language: Inquiring voices.* Toronto, Ontario: Scholastic.

Weaver, C. (1990). *Understanding whole language: From principles to practice.* Portsmouth, NH: Heinemann.

Wilson, J., & Jan, L. (1994). *Thinking for themselves: Developing strategies for reflective learning.* Portsmouth, NH: Heinemann.

Reading Process

Harste, J. (1989). *New policy guidelines for reading.* Urbana, IL: NCTE.

Hornsby, D. (1988). *Read on: A conference approach to reading.* Portsmouth, NH: Heinemann.

Mooney, M. (1990). *Reading to, with, and by.* Katonah, NY: Richard C. Owen.

Smith, F. (1985). *Reading without nonsense.* New York: Teachers College Press.

Smith, F. (1988). *Understanding reading: A psycholinguistic analysis of reading and learning to read.* Hillsdale, NJ: Lawrence Erlbaum.

Weaver, C. (1988). *Reading process and practice.* Portsmouth, NH: Heinemann.

Writing Process

Atwell, N. (1990). *Coming to know: Writing to learn in the intermediate grades.* Portsmouth, NH: Heinemann.

Calkins, L. (1986). *The art of teaching writing.* Portsmouth, NH: Heinemann.

Calkins, L., with Harwayne, S. (1991). *Living between the lines.* Portsmouth, NH: Heinemann.

Clay, M. (1975). *What did I write?* Portsmouth, NH: Heinemann.

Fletcher, R. (1991). *Walking trees: Teaching teachers in the New York City schools.* Portsmouth, NH: Heinemann.

Graves, D. (1983). *Writing: Teachers and children at work.* Portsmouth, NH: Heinemann.

Graves, D. (1989a). *Experiment with fiction.* Portsmouth, NH: Heinemann.

Graves, D. (1989b). *Investigate nonfiction.* Portsmouth, NH: Heinemann.

Ledoux, D. (1994). *Turning memories into memoires: A handbook for writing lifestories.* Portsmouth, NH: Heinemann.

Murray, D. (1984). *Write to learn.* New York: Holt, Rinehart and Winston.

Newkirk, T., & Atwell, N. (1988). *Understanding writing: Ways of observing, learning, and teaching.* Portsmouth, NH: Heinemann.

Newman, J. (1984). *The craft of children's writing.* Portsmouth, NH: Heinemann.

Parry, J., & Hornsby, D. (1988). *Write on: A conference approach to writing.* Portsmouth, NH: Heinemann.

Rule, R., & Wheeler, S. (1992). *Creating the story: Guides for new writers.* Portsmouth, NH: Heinemann.

Turbil, J. (1982). *No better way to teach writing.* Portsmouth, NH: Heinemann.

Reading-Writing Connection

Butler, A., & Turbil, J. (1984). *Toward a reading/writing classroom.* Portsmouth, NH: Heinemann.

Chow, M., Dobson, L., Hurst, M., & Nucich, J. (1992). *Whole language: Practical ideas.* Portsmouth, NH: Heinemann.

Cochrane, O., Cochrane, D., Scalena, S., & Buchanan, E. (1984). *Reading, writing, and caring.* Katonah, NY: Richard C. Owen.

Hansen, J. (1987). *When writers read.* Portsmouth, NH: Heinemann.

Harste, J., Short, K., & Burke, C. (1988). *Creating classrooms for authors.* Portsmouth, NH: Heinemann.

Harwayne, S. (1992). *Lasting impressions: Weaving literature into writing workshop.* Portsmouth, NH: Heinemann.

Hudson-Ross, S., Cleary, L., & Casey, M. (1993). *Children's voices: Children talk about literacy.* Portsmouth, NH: Heinemann.

Loughlin, C., & Martin, M. (1987). *Supporting literacy.* New York: Teachers College Press.

McKenzie, M. (1986). *Journeys in literacy.* Huddersfield, England: Schofield & Sims.

Classroom Environment

Glasser, W. (1986). *Control theory in the classroom.* New York: Harper & Row.

Graves, D. (1991). *Build a literate classroom.* Portsmouth, NH: Heinemann.

Hill, S., & Hill, T. (1990). *The collaborative classroom.* Portsmouth, NH: Heinemann.

Jackson, M. (1994). *Creative display and environment.* Portsmouth, NH: Heinemann.

Mills, H., & Clyde, J. (1990). *Portraits of whole language classrooms: Learning for all ages.* Portsmouth, NH: Heinemann.

Nelson, J. (1987). *Positive discipline.* New York: Ballantine Books.

Peterson, R. (1992). *Life in a crowded place: Making a learning community.* Portsmouth, NH: Heinemann.

Becoming a Whole Language Teacher and School

Bird, L. (1989). *Becoming a whole language school: The Fair Oaks story.* Katonah, NY: Richard C. Owen.

Edelsky, C., Altwerger, B., & Flores, B. (1991). *Whole language: What's the difference?* Portsmouth, NH: Heinemann.

Newman, J. (1990). *Finding our own way.* Portsmouth, NH: Heinemann.

Routman, R. (1991). *Invitations.* Portsmouth, NH: Heinemann.

Stephens, D. (1991). *What matters? A primer for teaching reading.* Portsmouth, NH: Heinemann.

Weaver, C., & Henke, L. (Eds). (1992). *Supporting whole language: Stories of teachers and institutional change.* Portsmouth, NH: Heinemann.

Wells, G. (Ed.). (1993). *Changing schools from within: Creating communities of inquiry.* Portsmouth, NH: Heinemann.

Early Literacy

Avery, C. (1994). *And with a light touch: Learning about reading, writing, and teaching with first graders.* Portsmouth, NH: Heinemann.

Barron, M. (1990). *I learned to read and write the way I learned to talk.* Katonah, NY: Richard C. Owen.

Bissex, G. (1980). *Gyns at wrk: A child learns to read and write.* Cambridge, MA: Harvard University Press.

Bruner, J., & Cole, M. (1990). *Early literacy: Developing child.* Cambridge, MA: Harvard University Press.

Calkins, L. (1983). *Lessons from a child.* Portsmouth, NH: Heinemann.

Cambourne, B., & Turbil, J. (1987). *Coping with chaos.* Portsmouth, NH: Heinemann.

Clay, M. (1991). *Becoming literate.* Portsmouth, NH: Heinemann.

Ferriero, E., & Teberosky, A. (1982). *Literacy before schooling.* Portsmouth, NH: Heinemann.

Harste, J., Woodward, V., & Burke, C. (1984). *Language stories and literacy lessons.* Portsmouth, NH: Heinemann.

Meek, M. (1986). *Learning to read.* Portsmouth, NH: Heinemann.

Teale, W., & Sulzby, E. (1989). *Emergent literacy.* Norwood, NJ: Ablex.

Temple, C., Nathan, R., & Burris, N. (1982). *The beginnings of writing.* Boston: Allyn & Bacon.

Integrating Art

Ernst, K. (1994). *Picturing learning: Artists and writers in the classroom.* Portsmouth, NH: Heinemann.

Johnson, P. (1992). *A book of one's own: Developing literacy through making books.* Portsmouth, NH: Heinemann.

Olson, J. (1992). *Envisioning writing: Toward an integration of drawing and writing.* Portsmouth, NH: Heinemann.

Integrating Poetry

Denman, G. (1988). *When you've made it your own.* Portsmouth, NH: Heinemann.

Graves, D. (1992). *Explore poetry.* Portsmouth, NH: Heinemann.

Heard, G. (1989). *For the good of the earth and the sun.* Portsmouth, NH: Heinemann.

McClure, A. (1990). *Sunrises and songs.* Portsmouth, NH: Heinemann.

Integrating Drama

Heinig, R. (1992). *Improvisation with favorite tales: Integrating drama into the reading/writing classroom.* Portsmouth, NH: Heinemann.

Mallan, K. (1992). *Children as storytellers.* Portsmouth, NH: Heinemann.

Proter, S. (1989). *Play it again: Suggestions for drama.* Portsmouth, NH: Heinemann.

Scher, A., & Verrall, C. (1992). *200+ ideas for drama.* Portsmouth, NH: Heinemann.

Sloyer, S. (1982). *Readers' theater: Story dramatization in the classroom.* Urbana, IL: NCTE.

Watts, I. (1990). *Just a minute: Ten short plays and activities for your classroom with rehearsal strategies to accompany multicultural stories from around the world.* Portsmouth, NH: Heinemann.

Integrating Math

Baker, A., & Baker, J. (1990). *Mathematics in process.* Portsmouth, NH: Heinemann.

Baker, D., & Semple, C. (1990). *How big is the moon? Whole maths in action.* Portsmouth, NH: Heinemann.

Charles, L., & Brumett, M. (1989). *Connections: Linking manipulatives to mathematics (grades 1–6).* Sunnydale, CA: Creative Publishers.

Rowan, T., & Bourne, B. (1994). *Thinking like mathematicians.* Portsmouth, NH: Heinemann.

Stoessiger, R., & Edmunds, J. (1992). *Natural learning and mathematics.* Portsmouth, NH: Heinemann.

Whitin, D., Mills, H. & O'Keefe, T. (1990). *Living and loving mathematics.* Portsmouth, NH: Heinemann.

Whitin, D., & Wilde, S. (1992). *Read any good math lately? Children's books for mathematical learning.* Portsmouth, NH: Heinemann.

Integrating Science

Balding, G., & Richards, N. (1990). *Springboards: Ideas for science.* Albany, NY: Delmar Publishers.

Butzow, C., & Butzow, J. (1989). *Science through children's literature.* Englewood, CO: Teacher Ideas Press.

Harlin, W., & Jelly, S. (1990). *Developing science in the primary classroom.* Portsmouth, NH: Heinemann.

Marcuccio, T. *Science and children.* Washington, DC: National Science Teachers Association.

Saul, W., & Jagusch, S. (1992). *Vital connections: Children, science, and books.* Portsmouth, NH: Heinemann.

Scott, J. (1993). *Science & language links: Classroom implications.* Portsmouth, NH: Heinemann.

Integrating Spelling

Bean, W., & Bouffier, C. (1988). *Spell by writing.* Portsmouth, NH: Heinemann.

Bolton, F., & Snowball, D. (1994). *Teaching spelling: A practical resource.* Portsmouth, NH: Heinemann.

Buchanan, E. (1989). *Spelling for whole language classrooms.* Katonah, NY: Richard C. Owen.

Gentry, R. (1987). *Spel . . . is a four letter word.* Portsmouth, NH: Heinemann.

Wilde, S. (1991). *You kan red this! Spelling and punctuation for whole language classrooms, K–6.* Portsmouth, NH: Heinemann.

Integrating Social Studies

Ammon, R., & Tunnell, M. (1992). *The story of ourselves: Teaching history through children's literature.* Portsmouth, NH: Heinemann.

Richards, N. (1989). *Springboards: Ideas for social studies.* Albany, NY: Delmar Publishers.

Walsh, H. *Social studies and the young learner.* Washington, DC: National Council for the Social Studies.

Integrating across the Curriculum

Gamberg, R., Kwak, W., Hutchings, M., & Altheim, J. (1988). *Learning and loving it: Theme studies in the classroom.* Portsmouth, NH: Heinemann.

Manning, M., Manning, G., & Long, R. (1994). *Theme immersion: Inquiry-based curriculum in elementary and middle schools.* Portsmouth, NH: Heinemann.

Pappas, C., Kieffer, B., & Levstik, L. (1990). *An integrated language arts perspective in the elementary school.* White Plains, NY: Longman.

Weaver, C., Chaston, J., & Peterson, S. (1994). *Theme explorations: A voyage of discovery.* Portsmouth, NH: Heinemann.

Special Needs Children

Au, K. (1993). *Literacy instruction in multicultural settings.* Fort Worth, TX: Harcourt Brace Jovanovich.

Freeman, Y., & Freeman, D. (1992). *Whole language for second language learners.* Portsmouth, NH: Heinemann.

Hayes, C., Bahruth, R., & Kessler, C. (1991). *Literacy con carino.* Portsmouth, NH: Heinemann.

Lee, C., & Jackson, R. (1992). *Faking it: A look into the mind of a creative learner.* Portsmouth, NH: Heinemann.

Piper, T. (1994). *And then there were two: Children and second language learning.* Portsmouth, NH: Heinemann.

Rhodes, L., & Dudley-Marling, C. (1988). *Readers and writers with a difference: A holistic approach to teaching learning disabled and remedial students.* Portsmouth, NH: Heinemann.

Rigg, P., & Allen, V. (1992). *When they don't all speak English: Integrating the ESL student into the regular classroom.* Urbana, IL: NCTE.

Stires, S. (Ed.) (1991). *With promise: Redefining reading and writing for special students.* Portsmouth, NH: Heinemann.

Taylor, D., & Dorsey-Gaines, C. (1988). *Growing up literate: Lessons from the inner-city.* Portsmouth, NH: Heinemann.

Weaver, C. (Ed.). (1994). *Success at last: Helping students with attention deficit (hyperactivity) disorders achieve their potential.* Portsmouth, NH: Heinemann.

White, C. (1990). *Jevon doesn't sit at the back anymore.* Jefferson City, MO: Scholastic.

Evaluation

Barrs, M. (1990). *The primary language record.* Portsmouth, NH: Heinemann.

Baskwill, J., & Whitman, P. (1989). *Evaluation: Whole language, whole child.* Toronto, Ontario: Scholastic-TAB.

Goodman, K., Goodman, Y., & Hood, W. (1989). *The whole language evaluation book.* Portsmouth, NH: Heinemann.

Graves, D., & Sunstein, S. (1992). *Portfolio portraits.* Portsmouth, NH: Heinemann.

Harp, W. (Ed.) (1991). *Assessment and evaluation in whole language programs.* Norwood, MA: Christopher-Gordon.

Heald-Taylor, G. (1989). *The administrator's guide to whole language.* Katonah, NY: Richard C. Owen.

Rhodes, L., & Shanklin, N. (1992). *Windows into literacy: Assessing learners K–8.* Portsmouth, NH: Heinemann.

Tierney, R., Carter, M., & Desai, L. (1991). *Portfolio assessment and the reading-writing classroom.* Norwood, MA: Christopher-Gordon.

Using Children's Literature

Brown, H., & Cambourne, B. (1990). *Read and retell.* Portsmouth, NH: Heinemann.

Cullinan, B. (1987). *Children's literature and the reading program.* Newark, DE: IRA.

Hickman, J., & Cullinan, B. (1989). *Children's literature in the classroom: Weaving Charlotte's web.* Norwood, MA: Christopher-Gordon.

Moss, J. (1990). *Focus on literature.* Katonah, NY: Richard C. Owen.

Peterson, R., & Eeds, M. (1990). *Grand conversations: Literature groups in action.* Jefferson City, MO: Scholastic.

Rudman, M. (1989). *Children's literature: A resource for the classroom.* Norwood, MA: Christopher-Gordon.

Short, K., & Pierce, K. (1990). *Talking about books: Creating literate communities.* Portsmouth, NH: Heinemann.

Middle and Upper Grades

Atwell, N. (1987). *In the middle: Writing, reading, and learning with adolescents.* Portsmouth, MH: Heinemann.

Benedict, S., & Carlisle, L. (1992). *Beyond words: Picture books for older readers and writers.* Portsmouth, NH: Heinemann.

Reif, L. (1991). *Seeking diversity: Language arts with adolescents.* Portsmouth, NH: Heinemann.

Journals

Elementary School Journal
University of Chicago Press
P.O. Box 37005
Chicago, IL 60637
5 issues per year

This journal covers all subject areas, reports research, and presents think pieces for and by teachers, researchers, administrators, and teacher educators.

Holistic Education Review
Holistic Education Press
39 Pearl Street
Brandon, VT 05733–1007
2 issues per year

This is a forum for innovative, experimental, leading-edge ideas in education. It explores and challenges traditional assumptions and methods of mainstream education. The journal seeks to explain humanistic alternative approaches to education.

The Horn Book
14 Beacon Street
Boston, MA 02108
6 issues per year

This journal presents announcements of forthcoming works and reviews of children's literature. Covering both fiction and nonfiction, the magazine also offers articles on using literature in the classroom.

Language Arts
NCTE Press
1111 Kenyon Road
Urbana, IL 61801
8 issues per year

This journal is the elementary language arts journal for the National Council of Teachers of English. Each monthly issue has a theme. The journal contains articles dealing with issues in language arts and literacy development.

The New Advocate
Christopher-Gordon Publishers
480 Washington Street
Norwood, MA 02062
4 issues per year

This journal promotes children's literature in the classroom and issues related to more humanistic instruction. Reviews of children's literature are also included.

The Reading Teacher
International Reading Association Publishers
800 Barksdale Road
P.O. Box 8139
Newark, DE 19714–8139
9 issues per year

This journal focuses on practical application articles. It is the elementary journal of the International Reading Association. Included in this publication is "Children's Choices," a list of books chosen by children as their favorites.

Young Children
National Association for the Education of
    Young Children
1509 16th Street N.W.
Washington, DC 20036–1426
6 issues per year

Covering the ages from preschool through the
primary grades, this journal offers articles
dealing with critical issues of early childhood
education.

Newsletters

Administrators Applying Whole Language
WLU interest group newsletter
Contact: Gordon Gulseth
Franklin Elementary School
410 West Second Street
Junction City, KS 66411

*Book Links: Connecting Books, Libraries and
Classrooms*
American Library Association Publication
Contact: Barbara Elleman
Subscription Services B11203
American Library Association
50 East Huron Street
Chicago, IL 60611
(800) 545–2433

The Colorado Communicator
The Colorado Council of the International
    Reading Association
Contact: Joan B. Ripple
7672 Olive Circle
Englewood, CO 80112

Connections
C.E.L. Inc., Winnipeg
(Child-Centered Experience-Based Learning)
Contact: Hazel Stoyko
C.E.L. Inc.
246 Barker Boulevard
Winnipeg, Manitoba R3R 2E4
Canada

*Genessee Valley Developmental Learning Group
Newsletter*
Genessee Valley Developmental Learning
    Group
Contact: Barbara Carder, Newsletter Editor
233 Walker Road
Hilton, NY 14468
(716) 392–5782

Illini TAWL Newsletter
Illini TAWL
Contact: Barbara Varadian
4 Keeneland Court
Edwardsville, IL 62025
(618) 288-7080

The Literacy Connection
Contact: Kathleen Taps
1018 Bricker Boulevard
Columbus, OH 43221–1644

Mid-Missouri TAWL Newsletter
Mid-Missouri TAWL
Contact: Mary Jo Stockbauer
2301 Sears Court
Columbia, MO 65202

Network News
Granite State Integrated Language Network
Granite State Council
Kimball School
North Spring Street
Concord, NH 03301

New Mexico TAWL Newsletter
New Mexico TAWL
Contact: Carolyn Doughdrill
Montezuma Elementary School
or P.O. Box 27651
Albuquerque, NM 87125–7651

R-C-S Whole Language Newsletter
Ravena-Coeymans-Selkirk
Central School
Contact: Nancy Andress
Director of Special Programs and
Instructional Services
Selkirk, NY 12158
(518) 767–2516

TAWL News
Greater Kansas City TAWL
Contact: Glenn Owen
5825 Oak
Kansas City, MO 64113

*Teachers Networking: The Whole Language
Newsletter*
Richard C. Owen Publishers, Inc.
P.O. Box 585
Katonah, NY 10536
(800) 336–5588

The WEB (Wonderfully Exciting Books)
The WEB
Ohio State University
200 Ramseyer Hall
29 West Woodruff Avenue
Columbus, OH 43210–1177
(614) 292–0711
4 issues per year

The Whole Idea
The Wright Group Newsletter
Contact: John M. Hostvedt
18916 North Creek Parkway, Suite 107
Bothell, WA 98011
(800) 331–4524

The Whole Language Advocate
Minnesota TAWL
Contact: Dave Heine
1101 22nd Avenue North
Saint Cloud, MN 56303

Whole Language Newsletter
Scholastic, Inc.
P.O. Box 7502
Jefferson City, MO 65102
(800) 325–6149

The Whole Language Newsletter
Contact: Rita Tenorio
The Whole Language Council of
Milwaukee Public Schools
Milwaukee, WI 53208

*Whole Language Special Interest Group
Newsletter*
WLSIG Newsletter
International Reading Association
800 Barksdale Road
Newark, DE 19714–8139
(302)731–1600
or
WLSIG
Grace Vento-Zogby
125 Proctor Boulevard
Utica, NY 13501
2 issues per year

The Whole Language Umbrella Newsletter
WLU Newsletter
Contact: Jerry Harste
Ed. 3024 Indiana University
Bloomington, IN 47405
3 issues per year

Newbery and Caldecott Award Winning Books

Newbery Award

Year	Title	Author	Year	Title	Author
1994	*The Giver*	Lowry	1976	*The Grey King*	Cooper
1993	*Missing May*	Rylant	1975	*M.C. Higgins, The Great*	Hamilton
1992	*Shiloh*	Naylor			
1991	*Maniac Magee*	Spinelli	1974	*The Slave Dancer*	Fox
1990	*Number the Stars*	Lowry	1973	*Julie of the Wolves*	George
1989	*Joyful Noise*	P. Fleischman	1972	*Mrs. Frisby and the Rats of NIMH*	O'Brien
1988	*Lincoln: A Pictography*	Freedman			
1987	*The Whipping Boy*	S. Fleischman	1971	*Summer of the Swans*	Byars
1986	*Sarah, Plain and Tall*	MacLachlan	1970	*Sounder*	Armstrong
1985	*Hero and the Crown*	McKinley	1969	*The High King*	Alexander
1984	*Dicey's Song*	Voight	1968	*From the Mixed-up Files of Mrs. Basil E. Frankweiler*	Konigsburg
1983	*Dear Mr. Henshaw*	Cleary			
1982	*William Blake's Inn*	Willard			
1981	*Jacob Have I Loved*	Paterson	1967	*Up a Road Slowly*	Hunt
1980	*A Gathering of Days*	Blos	1966	*I, Juan de Pareja*	de Trevino
1979	*The Westing Game*	Raskin	1965	*Shadow of a Bull*	Wojciechowska
1978	*Bridge to Terabithia*	Paterson	1964	*It's Like This, Cat*	Neville
1977	*Roll of Thunder, Hear My Cry*	Taylor	1963	*A Wrinkle in Time*	L'Engle
			1962	*Bronze Bow*	Speare

Year	Title	Author
1961	*Island of the Blue Dolphins*	O'Dell
1960	*Onion John*	Krumgold
1959	*Witch of Blackbird Pond*	Speare
1958	*Rifles for Waitie*	Keith
1957	*Miracle on Maple Street*	Sorenson
1956	*Carry On, Mr. Bowditch*	Latham
1955	*The Wheel on the School*	de Jong
1954	*And Now Miguel*	Krumgold
1953	*The Secret of the Andes*	Clark
1952	*Ginger Pye*	Estes
1951	*Amos Fortune, Free Man*	Yates
1950	*The Door in the Wall*	de Angeli
1949	*King of the Wind*	Henry
1948	*The Twenty-One Balloons*	du Bois
1947	*Miss Hickory*	Bailey
1946	*Strawberry Hill*	Lenski
1945	*Rabbit Hill*	Lawson
1944	*Johnny Tremain*	Forbes
1943	*Adam of the Road*	Gray

Year	Title	Author
1942	*Matchlock Gun*	Edmonds
1941	*Call It Courage*	Sperry
1940	*Daniel Boone*	Dougherty
1939	*Thimble Summer*	Enright
1938	*The White Stag*	Seredy
1937	*Roller Skates*	Sawyer
1936	*Caddie Woodlawn*	Brink
1935	*Dobry*	Shannon
1934	*Invincible Louisa*	Meigs
1933	*Young Fu of the Upper Yangtze*	Lewis
1932	*Waterless Mountain*	Armer
1931	*The Cat Who Went to Heaven*	Coatsworth
1930	*The Trumpeter of Krakow*	Kelly
1929	*Hitty, Her First Hundred Years*	Field
1928	*Gay Neck*	Mujkerji
1927	*Smokey, the Cowhorse*	James
1926	*Shen of the Sea*	Christmas
1925	*Tales for Silver Lands*	Finger
1924	*The Dark Frigate*	Hawes
1923	*The Voyages of Dr. Dolittle*	Lofting
1922	*The Story of Mankind*	van Loon

Caldecott Award

Year	Title	Author/ Illustrator
1994	*Grandfather's Journey*	Say
1993	*Mirette on the High Wire*	McCully
1992	*Tuesday*	Weisner
1991	*Black and White*	Macaulay
1990	*Lon Po Po*	Young

Year	Title	Author/ Illustrator
1989	*Song and Dance Man*	Ackerman/ Gammell
1988	*Owl Moon*	Yolen/ Schoenherr
1987	*Hey Al*	Yorinks/ Egielski

Year	Title	Author/Illustrator	Year	Title	Author/Illustrator
1986	Polar Express	Van Allsburg	1962	Once a Mouse	Brown
1985	St. George and the Dragon	Hodges/Hyman	1961	Baboushka and the Three Kings	Robbins
1984	The Glorious Flight	Provenson	1960	Nine Days to Christmas	Ets/Labastida
1983	Shadow	Brown	1959	Chanticleer and the Fox	Cooney
1982	Jumanju	Van Allsburg			
1981	Fables	Lobel	1958	Time of Wonder	McCloskey
1980	The Ox-Cart Man	Hall/Cooney	1957	A Tree Is Nice	Udry/Simont
1979	The Girl Who Loved Wild Horses	Goble	1956	Frog Went A-Courtin'	Langstaff/Rojanlovsky
1978	Noah's Ark	Spier	1955	Cinderella	Brown
1977	Ashanti to Zulu: African Traditions	Musgrove	1954	Madeline's Rescue	Bemelmans
			1953	The Biggest Bear	Ward
1976	Why Mosquitoes Buzz in People's Ears	Aardema	1952	Finders Keepers	Nicholas
			1951	The Egg Tree	Milhous
1975	Arrow to the Sun	McDermott	1950	Song of the Swallows	Politi
1974	Duffy and the Devil	Zemach	1949	Big Snow	Hader
1973	The Funny Little Woman	Mosel	1948	White Snow, Bright Snow	Tresselt/Duvoisin
1972	One Fine Day	Hogrogian	1947	Little Island	MacDonald/Weisgard
1971	A Story, a Story	Haley			
1970	Sylvester and the Magic Pebble	Steig	1946	Rooster Crown	Petersham
			1945	Prayer for a Child	Field/Jones
1969	Fool of the World and the Flying Ship	Ransome	1944	Many Moons	Thurber/Slobodkin
1968	Drummer Hoff	Emberley	1943	The Little House	Burton
1967	Sam Bangs and Moonshine	News	1942	Make Way for Ducklings	McCloskey
1966	Always Room for One More	Leadhas/Hogrogian	1941	They Were Strong and Good	Lawson
1965	May I Bring a Friend?	de Regniers	1940	Abraham Lincoln	d'Aulaire
1964	Where the Wild Things Are	Sendak	1939	Mei Li	Handforth
			1938	Animals of the Bible	Lathrop
1963	The Snowy Day	Keats			

APPENDIX D

Favorite Big Books

Bartel, P. (1989). *The Fair.* Chicago: Riverside.

Bartel, P. (1989). *The Quarrel.* Chicago: Riverside.

Cochrane, O. (1986). *The Great Grey Owl.* Katonah, NY: Richard C. Owen.

Cochrane, O. (1988). *The Legend of the Goose and Owl.* Katonah, NY: Richard C. Owen.

Cowley, J. (1980). *Mrs. Wishy Washy.* San Diego: Wright Group.

Cowley, J. (1986). *Turnips for Dinner.* New York: Modern Publishing—Unisystems.

Cowley, J. (1989). *Quack, Quack, Quack.* San Diego: Wright Group.

Drew, D. (1989). *Animal, Plant, or Mineral?* Crystal Lake, IL: Rigby.

Hoberman, M. (1987). *A House Is a House for Me.* New York: Scholastic.

Martin, B. (1980). *Brown Bear.* New York: Holt, Rinehart, and Winston.

Mayer, M. (1980). *What Do You Do with a Kangaroo?* New York: Ashton-Scholastic.

Nelson, J. (1989). *Peanut Butter and Jelly.* Cleveland: Modern Curriculum Press.

Nelson, J. (1989). *There's a Dragon in My Wagon.* Cleveland: Modern Curriculum Press.

Numeroff, L. (1985). *If You Give a Mouse a Cookie.* Toronto, Ontario: Scholastic.

Parkes, B., & Smith, J. (1985). *The Three Little Pigs.* Crystal Lake, IL: Rigby.

Parkes, B., & Smith, J. (1984). *The Ugly Duckling.* Crystal Lake, IL: Rigby.

Parkes, B., & Smith, J. (1987). *The Three Billy Goats Gruff.* Crystal Lake, IL: Rigby.

Schwartz, D. (1985). *How Much Is a Million?* New York: Scholastic.

Wells, R. (1980). *Noisy Nora.* New York: Scholastic.

APPENDIX E

Predictable Books for Young Children

Predictable books are books that support young children's reading. They are books with one or a combination of the following: a repetitious line or repetitive pattern, a rhyming scheme, or an accumulated pattern that continues throughout the story.

Repetitive Line

Balina, L. (1982). *Mother's Mother's Day.* Nashville, TN: Abingdon Press.

Barrett, J. (1980). *Animals Should Definitely Not Act Like People.* New York: Atheneum.

Barrett, J. (1981). *Animals Should Definitely Not Wear Clothes.* New York: Atheneum.

Barrett, J. (1983). *A Snake Is Totally Tail.* New York: Atheneum.

Berenstain, S., & Berenstain, J. (1970). *Old Hat New Hat.* New York: Random House.

Brown, M. (1947). *Goodnight Moon.* New York: Harper & Row.

Brown, R. (1981). *A Dark Dark Tale.* New York: Dial.

Caldwell, M. (1984). *Henry's Busy Day.* New York: Viking.

Carle, E. (1977). *The Grouchy Ladybug.* New York: Thomas Y. Crowell.

Carle, E. (1981). *The Very Hungry Caterpillar.* New York: Philomel.

Carle, E. (1988). *The Very Busy Spider.* New York: Philomel.

Domanska, J. (1971). *If All the Seas Were One Sea.* New York: Macmillan.

Eastman, P. (1960). *Are You My Mother?* New York: Random House.

Eastman, P. (1972). *Go, Dog, Go!* New York: Random House.

Ginsburg, M. (1972). *The Chick and the Duckling.* New York: Macmillan.

Harper, A. (1977). *How We Work.* New York: Harper & Row.

Hutchins, P. (1972). *Goodnight Owl.* New York: Macmillan.

Kalan, R. (1981). *Jump, Frog, Jump!* New York: Scholastic.

Krauss, R. (1945). *The Carrot Seed.* New York: Harper & Row.

Krauss, R. (1952). *A Hole Is to Dig.* New York: Harper & Row.

Langstaff, J. (1977). *Oh, A-Hunting We Will Go.* New York: Atheneum.

Martin, B. (1970). *Brown Bear, Brown Bear.* New York: Holt, Rinehart, & Winston.

Martin, B. (1970). *The Haunted House.* New York: Holt, Rinehart, & Winston.

Martin, B. (1970). *Up the Down Escalator.* New York: Holt, Rinehart, & Winston.

Mayer, M. (1973). *What Do You Do with a Kangaroo?* New York: Scholastic.

Mosel, A. (1968). *Tikki Tikki Tembo.* New York: Holt, Rinehart, & Winston.

Paterson, D. (1977). *If I Were a Toad.* New York: Dial.

Polushkin, M. (1978). *Mother, Mother, I Want Another.* New York: Crown.

Preston, M. (1978). *Where Did My Mother Go?* New York: Four Winds Press.

Quackenbush, R. (1975). *Skip to My Lou.* New York: Lippincott.

Rosen, M., & Oxenbury, H. *We're Going on a Bear Hunt.* New York: McElderry Books.

Watanabe, S. (1981). *I Can Ride It.* New York: Philomel.

Williams, B. (1977). *Never Hit a Porcupine.* New York: Dutton.

Wood, A. (1982). *Quick as a Cricket.* Trenton, NJ: Crane.

Rhyming Pattern

Aliki. (1968). *Hush Little Baby.* Englewood Cliffs, NJ: Prentice Hall.

Cameron, P. (1961). *I Can't Said the Ant.* New York: Scholastic.

Hawkins, C. (1983). *Pat the Cat.* New York: Putnam.

Hoberman, M. (1978). *A House Is a House for Me.* New York: Puffin Books.

Schermer, J. (1979). *Mouse in a House.* Boston: Houghton Mifflin.

Seuss, Dr. (1937). *And to Think I Saw It on Mulberrry Street.* New York: Vangard Press.

Seuss, Dr. (1957). *The Cat in the Hat.* New York: Random House.

Shaw, N. (1986). *Sheep in a Jeep.* Boston: Houghton Mifflin.

Spier, P. (1967). *London Bridge Is Falling Down.* New York: Doubleday.

Withers, C. (1967). *Favorite Rhymes from a Rocket in My Pocket.* New York: Scholastic.

Zolotow, C. (1969). *Some Things Go Together.* New York: Thomas Y. Crowell.

Repetitive or Cumulative Pattern

Aardema, V. (1975). *Why Mosquitoes Buzz in People's Ears.* New York: Scholastic.

Aardema, V. (1981). *Bringing the Rain to Kapiti Plain.* New York: Dell.

Berenstain, S. (1968). *Inside Outside Upside Down.* New York: Random House.

Charlip, L. (1964). *Fortunately.* New York: Four Winds Press.

Dodd, L. (1983). *Hairy Maclary from Donaldson's Dairy.* Chicago: Gareth Stevens.

Emberley, B. (1967). *Drummer Hoff.* Englewood Cliffs, NJ: Prentice-Hall.

Ets, M. (1972). *Elephant in a Well.* New York: Viking.

Galdone, P. (1960). *The Old Woman and Her Pig.* St. Louis: McGraw-Hill.

Gordon, J. (1992). *Two Badd Babies.* Honesdale, PA: Boyds Mills Press.

Granowsky, A. (1974). *Pat's Date and a Plate.* Lexington, MA: D.C. Heath.

Hogrogian, N. (1971). *One Fine Day.* New York: Collier.

Kent, J. (1973). *Jack Kent's Twelve Days of Christmas.* New York: Scholastic.

Kent, J. (1971). *The Fat Cat.* New York: Scholastic.

Lobel, A. (1984). *The Rose in My Garden.* New York: Greenwillow.

Peppe, R. (1970). *The House That Jack Built.* New Orleans: Delacorte.

Sadler, M. (1983). *It's Not Easy Being a Bunny.* New York: Random House.

Seuss, Dr. (1960). *Green Eggs and Ham.* New York: Random House.

Shulevitz, U. (1967). *One Monday Morning.* New York: Scribner.

Silverstein, S. (1964). *A Giraffe and a Half.* New York: Harper & Row.

Tolstoy, A. (1968). *The Great Big Enormous Turnip.* New York: Franklin Watts.

Wildsmith, B. (1978). *What the Moon Saw.* London: Oxford University Press.

Wildsmith, B. (1982). *Cat on a Mat.* London: Oxford University Press.

Wildsmith, B. (1983). *All Fall Down.* London: Oxford University Press.

Wood, A. (1984). *The Napping House.* San Diego: Harcourt Brace Jovanovich.

Wood, A. (1985). *King Bidgood's in the Bathtub.* San Diego: Harcourt Brace Jovanovich.

Wordplay Books

Gwynne, F. (1970). *The King Who Rained.* New York: Windmill Books.

Gwynne, F. (1976). *A Chocolate Moose for Dinner.* New York: Simon & Schuster.

Gwynne, F. (1988). *A Little Pigeon Toad.* New York: Simon & Schuster.

Gwynne, F. (1980). *A Sixteen Hand Horse.* New York: Simon & Schuster.

Hanson, J. (1972). *Antonyms.* New York: Lerner.

Hanson, J. (1973). *Homographic Homophones.* New York: Lerner.

Parish, P. (1972). *Amelia Bedelia.* New York: Scholastic.

Parish, P. (1977). *Teach Us, Amelia Bedelia.* New York: Scholastic.

Steig, W. (1984). *CDB.* Toronto, Ontario: Collins.

Pop-Up Books

Berger, M. (1976). *Prehistoric Mammals.* New York: Putnam.

Meggendorfer, L. (1980). *The Doll's House.* New York: Viking.

Pienkowski, J. (1981). *Dinner Time.* Los Angeles: Price Stern Sloan.

Pienkowski, J. (1986). *Little Monsters.* Los Angeles: Price Stern Sloan.

Willey, S., & Roffey, M. (1985). *There Was an Old Woman.* New York: Harper & Row.

Colors

deRico, U. (1978). *The Rainbow Goblins.* New York: Warner Communications.

Johnson, C. (1955). *Harold and the Purple Crayon.* New York: Harper & Row.

Klamath County YMCA Family Preschool. (1993). *The Land of Many Colors.* New York: Scholastic.

Miller, J., & Howard, K. (1978). *Do You Know Colors?* New York: Random House.

O'Neill, M. (1961). *Hailstones and Hallibut Bones.* New York: Doubleday.

Rossetti, C. (1971). *What Is Pink?* New York: Macmillan.

Stinson, K. (1983). *Red Is Best.* Toronto, Ontario: Annick.

Stinson, K. (1985). *Those Green Things.* Toronto, Ontario: Annick.

Days of the Week

Clifton, L. (1974). *Some of the Days of Everett Anderson.* New York: Holt, Rinehart & Winston.

Domanska, J. (1985). *Busy Monday Morning.* New York: Greenwillow Books.

Elliott, A. (1980). *On Sunday the Wind Came.* New York: William Morrow.

Hooper, M. (1985). *Seven Eggs.* New York: Harper & Row.

Shulevitz, U. (1967). *One Monday Morning.* New York: Scribner.

Weisner, D. (1991). *Tuesday.* New York: Lothrop, Lee & Shepard.

Yolen, J. (1978). *No Bath Tonight.* New York: Thomas Y. Crowell.

Months and Seasons

Clifton, L. (1974). *Everett Anderson's Year.* New York: Holt, Rinehart & Winston.

Considine, K., & Schuler, R. (1963). *One, Two, Three, Four.* New York: Holt, Rinehart & Winston.

de Paola, T. (1977). *Four Stories for Four Seasons.* Englewood Cliffs, NJ: Prentice-Hall.

Lionni, L. (1981). *Mouse Days.* New York: Pantheon Books.

Sendak, M. (1962). *Chicken Soup with Rice.* New York: Scholastic.

Tafuri, N. (1983). *All Year Long.* New York: Puffin Books.

APPENDIX F

Bookbinding

DIRECTIONS FOR MAKING A BOOK

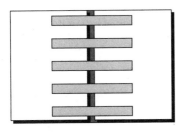

1. Using pattern on next page, place backboards 5/8" apart. Leave center space open.

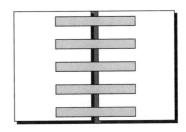

2. Place five pieces of masking tape (4" strips) horizontally, starting at top and bottom, then in between. Note: Boards must be at least 5/8" apart for taping.

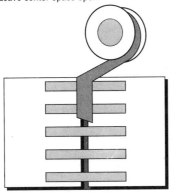

3. Turn boards over and repeat taping on reverse side.

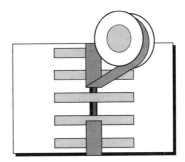

4. Using 36" length of masking tape, cover spine vertically from front to back. Continue wrapping until tape is used up.

Developed by Dr. Elizabeth Brashears, Professor Emeritus, Middle Tennessee State University. Reprinted with permission.

Pattern

(5/8")

Place boards against the lines, not over this space.

(mark the dots for punching holes)

5. Spread glue smoothly on wrong side of cloth. Cover surface completely with glue. Dip fingers in water to spread smoothly if using white glue. Rubber cement may be used instead of white glue, but should be used over surface of boards.

On back of cloth, spread glue evenly with fingers that have been dipped in water. Keeping fingers damp, spread glue into corners.

7. Fold sides of cloth and press to backboard to complete cover.

6. Center taped backboards on glued side of cloth. Fold corners of cloth down first, pressing carefully to glue corners to backboards.

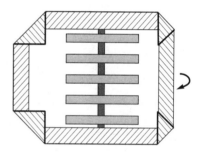

8. Lay this aside to dry. A heavy book placed on it may be used to help flatten out bookback, but be sure to place wax paper between to keep book from sticking.

9. Fold six sheets of 8 1/2"-x-11" paper to make writing pages.

10. Fold two sheets of construction paper in half to make endpapers and flyleaf. Place writing pages inside endpapers as in illustration.

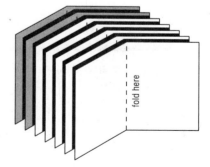

fold here

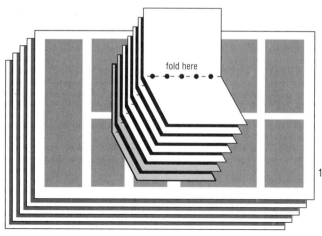

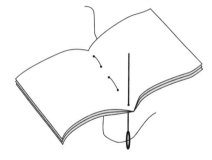

11. Using large needle, punch five holes on fold using pattern on previous page. Punch through writing pages and construction paper.

Place pages on pad of old newspapers to protect table. *Note:* Holes are shown greatly enlarged in picture.

12. Thread large needle with 30" of waxed dental floss. Push needle through first hole from back side. Tape end of thread to back side of construction paper or knot end to secure it.

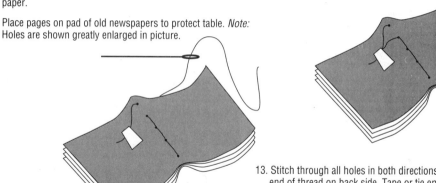

13. Stitch through all holes in both directions, leaving end of thread on back side. Tape or tie ends to secure stitches.

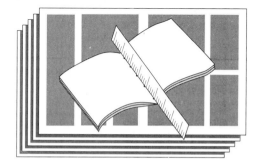

14. Cover inside of bookbacks completely with white glue or rubber cement. Smooth glue with just a few drops of water.

15. Glue fold into spine of cover, pressing hard with ruler to bond. Smooth endpapers onto backboards. Open and close book gently while drying to prevent creases.

These are some special effects that may be included when designing books.
The use of these enhances the feeling of ownership.

1. Write an original personal narrative or a story in draft.

2. Design a title page on the first writing page.

3. Design a dedication page.

4. Design and make a bookplate to glue on the inside front cover.

5. Design and make a bookmark.

6. Design the signature including the endpapers and flyleaf.

7. Design and make an "About the Author" (photo if possible).

8. Copy the story from your draft into the book.

9. Design a library pocket and library checkout card to place in the back of the book.

10. Place your copyright in your book.

11. Design the front cover (title and author).

12. Design chapters or the beginning of the story.

13. Plan a logical ending for the story.

14. Design illustrations, if any (photos, if appropriate).

15. Design a table of contents if appropriate.

16. Design an "Other Books by This Author" page.

When writing with young authors,
the following kinds of activities should be going on in the classroom:

17. Examining various trade books for ideas to use in designing books.

18. Sharing ideas for topics, word choices, writing styles, sentence patterns, characters, spelling, grammar, and other considerations.

19. Participating in an author's chair.

20. Editing and proofreading each other's drafts.

21. Bringing materials and making the book in class.

Designing the Title Page

The title page contains the title of the book and the name of the author. This information is usually found on the right side of the first writing page in the book.

Designing the Copyright

A piece of writing is copyrighted the moment it is put to paper and you indicate your authorship with the word "Copyright," the year, and your name. Children enjoy using this privilege and may also write in the name of their own personal publishing company. This information is usually found on the reverse side of the title page.

Designing a Dedication Page

The dedication statement is written by the author to dedicate the book to some very special person or persons. This information is usually placed on the right page facing the copyright page. Bookstores and libraries are excellent sources for books to examine for ideas concerning the expressions of dedication.

Designing the "About the Author" Page

A short autobiography of a few sentences is usually written by the author in third person. Sometimes a photograph is included. Also a list of other publications by the author is often included. This information is usually found on the last page of the book excluding the flyleaf.

Designing an "Other Books by This Author" Page

A list of other books and publications by the author is given either in the back or the front of the book.

MAKING LIBRARY CARDS AND POCKET FOR BOOK

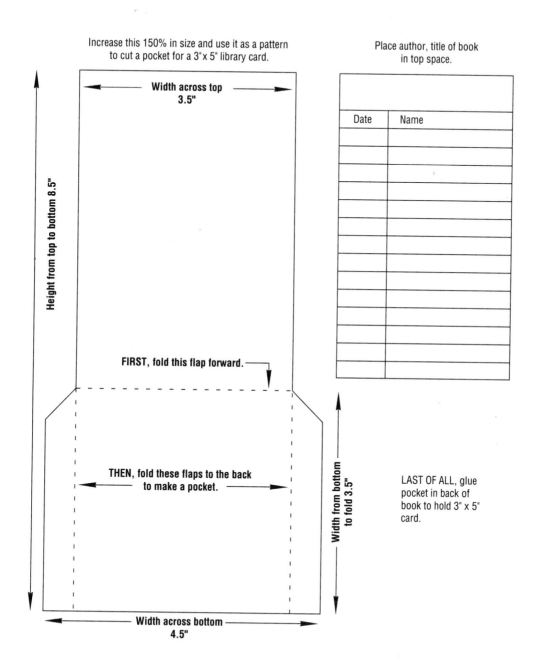

Increase this 150% in size and use it as a pattern
to cut a pocket for a 3" x 5" library card.

Place author, title of book
in top space.

Width across top
3.5"

Height from top to bottom 8.5"

FIRST, fold this flap forward.

THEN, fold these flaps to the back
to make a pocket.

Width from bottom
to fold 3.5"

Width across bottom
4.5"

Date	Name

LAST OF ALL, glue
pocket in back of
book to hold 3" x 5"
card.

This Book

Belongs To

_____

_____

A good book is the best
of friends, the same
to-day and for ever.

—Martin Tupper

This Book

Belongs To

_____

_____

_____

No entertainment is so cheap as reading:
nor any pleasure so lasting.

—Lady Mary Wartley Montagu

This Book

Belongs To

_____

_____

_____

The desire to read grows with reading.

—Erasmus

This Book

Belongs To

_____

_____

_____

What we read with pleasure we never forget.

—Alfred Mercier

Examples of Bookplates

ONE WAY TO MAKE A "BIG BOOK"

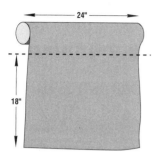

Step 1. Cut two pieces the same size from a roll of brown wrapping paper. A good size is 24" wide and 18" deep.

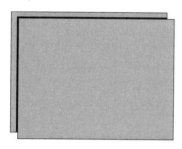

Step 2. Place the two pieces together so that the edges are exactly matching all the way around.

Step 3. Put masking tape around all four edges so that the two sheets are taped together. This makes one sheet double thick. Decorative tape may be used if desired.

Tape is folded in half and finished on the reverse side.

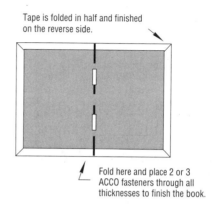

Fold here and place 2 or 3 ACCO fasteners through all thicknesses to finish the book.

Step 4. Make several more double-thickness pages until you have enough for your book. Stack them up neatly and fold all of them in half to make the spine for the book. Secure all thicknesses along the fold with ACCO paper fasteners.

GUIDELINES FOR MAKING "BIG BOOKS"

1. The story of a big book needs to be predictable—that is, children must be able to predict the language patterns as well as the story itself so they will know how to "join in" with the reading.

2. The print needs to be large so children may see words from a distance.

3. The pictures need to be large so children may see them from a distance.

4. The book needs to be easily manipulated. It needs to be heavy enough to hold pages in place when turning but not so heavy that it is difficult to pick it up. A big book does not need to be awkward to store and use naturally. It does not need to be so big that it loses its effectiveness.

5. Predictable themes may be divided into these (and other) broad categories:

   a. repetitive
   b. cumulative
   c. cause and effect
   d. rhyme and rhythm
   e. opposites
   f. numbers
   g. alphabet
   h. time sequence
      time of day
      days of week
      months
   i. Familiar story formats
      fairy tales
      fables
      sequels for popular stories
      wordless stories

HOW TO MAKE AN ALBUM-STYLE BOOK

Step 1. Obtain two sheets of **very** heavy 9" x 12" cardboard. Triple-weight illustration board is best, but use whatever is available. *Note:* Corrugated cardboard is **not** recommended as it "breaks" too easily. Cut a 1" strip off the left edge of each board. These dimensions, 9" x 12", are suggested because they fit standard-size paper. Other sizes and shapes may be used, but all other materials must be scaled to size.

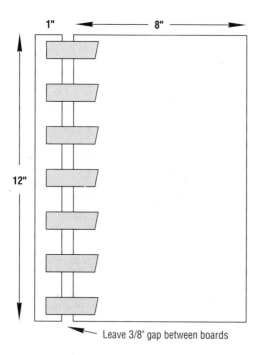

Leave 3/8" gap between boards

Step 2. Place the 1" strip about 3/8" away from the 8" piece. Place masking tape in short widths across the gap in seven or eight places as shown in the picture. Turn the piece over and tape the back the same way, matching the tape from the front side.

Step 3. Now take the other two pieces, the 8" x 12" and the 1" x 12", and tape them together the same way. This makes a front and a back cover with a hinged section for securing the pages.

Step 4. Cover the front first with a piece of cloth or wallcovering that is about 12" x 15". Use glue or rubber cement. After covering the front, complete the back by covering the same way.

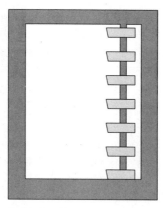

Inside front cover

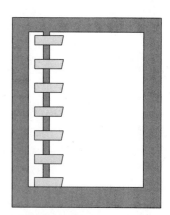

Inside back cover

Turn the corners of the material down and glue as in the sequence of the pictures below.

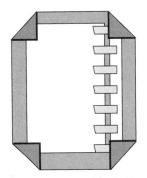

Step 5. Glue corners down inside both covers.

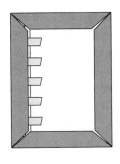

Step 6. Glue edges of cover material inside both covers.

Step 7. Glue endpaper inside covers of both front and back.

Step 8. Collate both front and back covers, the flyleaves, and all of the writing pages to form the book. Punch three holes in the 1" strip, the flyleaves, and all pages. Tie together by putting one end of the tie through each outside hole on the **front**. Pull tight to the back. Now push both ends back through the middle hole and secure them by tying a bow.

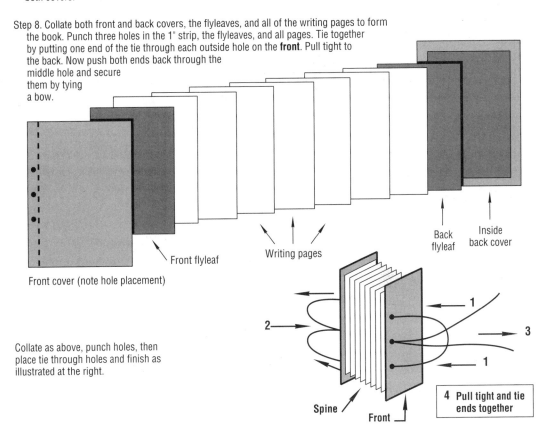

Front cover (note hole placement)

Front flyleaf

Writing pages

Back flyleaf

Inside back cover

Collate as above, punch holes, then place tie through holes and finish as illustrated at the right.

2

1

3

1

Spine

Front

4 Pull tight and tie ends together

APPENDIX G

Sample Record-Keeping Devices

Child Record-Keeping Forms

THINGS I DID THIS WEEK

Name: _____ Week: _____

| | Monday | Tuesday | Wednesday | Thursday | Friday |

Writing: _____

Books read: _____

Projects: _____

Art: _____

Science observation: _____

Other: _____

Teacher comments: _____

_____

_____

STUDENT READING RECORD

Name: _____ Date: _____

A. **Before reading**

What is the subject? _____

_____

_____

What do I know about this topic? _____

_____

_____

What does this remind me of? _____

_____

_____

What do I want to find out about this topic? _____

_____

_____

B. **During reading**

Things I want to remember and discuss later _____

_____

_____

_____

_____

C. **After reading**

What new information do I know now? _____

_____

_____

What else would I like to know? _____

_____

_____

What was the most interesting part? _____

_____

_____

How can I best represent what I like best about this book? (For instance, artwork, play, science project)

_____

_____

_____

Teacher Record-Keeping Forms

CLASS WRITING RECORD	Date:								
Children's Names	Nonwriting	Early	Emergent	Fluent	Spelling	Mechanics	Style	Variation	Audience

THE LESSON PLAN: STRATEGIC TEACHING

1. Who the lesson is designed for:
   (Specify the individual student, small group, or large group. Describe the characteristics of the learner or group.)

2. Rationale:
   (Explain why you want to do this activity with your students. Describe how the lesson is theoretically sound.)

3. Materials needed:
   (List the materials and resources you will need.)

4. The lesson:
   Before:
   (Specify what you will do to get the students ready for the lesson or activity.)

   During:
   (Describe the activity or learning event step by step.)

   After:
   (Explain how you will help learners make connections, evaluate the event, determine what to do next, etc.)

5. Expand:
   (List one or more appropriate ideas for follow-up or extension activities.)

6. Evaluate:
   (Describe how you will evaluate the success of your lesson.)

APPENDIX H

NCTE Position Statement

*A Statement of the Commission on Reading,
National Council of Teachers of English*

Basal Readers and the State of American Reading Instruction: A Call for Action

The Problem

As various national studies suggest, the problem of illiteracy, semi-literacy, and aliteracy in the United States appears to be growing, due at least in part to escalating standards of literacy in the workplace and in the civic area. And at a time when our information-age society demands increased literacy from all citizens, reading instruction is locked into a technology that is more than half a century out-of-date.

Basals: Part of the Problem

There is a significant gap between how reading is learned and how it is taught and assessed in the vast majority of our classrooms today. This gap is perpetuated by the basal reading series that dominate reading instruction in roughly 90 percent of the elementary classrooms in the United States. Such textbook series are often viewed as complete systems for teaching reading, for they include not only a graded series of books for the students to read but teachers' manuals telling teachers what and how to teach, workbooks and dittos for the students to complete, sets of tests to assess reading skills, and often various supplementary aids. Because of their comprehensiveness, basal reading systems leave very little for other kinds of reading activities in the schools where they have been adopted. This is all the more unfortunate because current theory and research strongly support such conclusions as the following:

- Basal reading series typically reflect and promote the misconception that reading is necessarily learned from smaller to larger parts.

◻ The sequencing of skills in a basal reading series exists not because this is how children learn to read but simply because of the logistics of developing a series of lessons that can be taught sequentially, day after day, week after week, year after year.

◻ Students are typically tested for ability to master the bits and pieces of reading, such as phonics and other word-identification skills, and even comprehension skills. However, there is no evidence that mastering such skills in isolation guarantees the ability to comprehend connected text, or that students who cannot give evidence of such skills in isolation are necessarily unable to comprehend connected text.

◻ Thus for many if not most children, the typical basal reading series may actually make learning to read more difficult than it needs to be.

◻ So much time is typically taken up by "instructional" activities (including activities with workbooks and skill sheets) that only a very slight amount of time is spent in actual reading—despite the overwhelming evidence that extensive reading and writing are crucial to the development of literacy.

◻ Basal reading series typically reflect and promote the widespread misconception that the ability to verbalize and answer, orally or in writing, is evidence of understanding and learning. Thus even students who appear to be learning from a basal reading series are being severely shortchanged, for they are being systematically encouraged not to think.

◻ Basal reading series typically tell teachers exactly what they should do and say while teaching a lesson, thus depriving teachers of the responsibility and authority to make informed professional judgments.

◻ "Going through the paces" thus becomes the measure of both teaching and learning. The teachers are assumed to have taught well if and only if they have taught the lesson. Students are assumed to have learned if and only if they have given "right" answers.

◻ *The result of such misconceptions about learning and such rigid control of teacher and student activities is to discourage both teachers and students from thinking, and particularly to discourage students from developing and exercising critical literacy and thinking skills needed to participate fully in a technologically advanced democratic society.*

Recommended Action for Local Administrators and for Policymakers

For Local Administrators:

◻ Provide continual district inservice for teachers to help them develop a solid understanding of how people read and how children learn to read and how reading is related to writing and learning to write.

◻ Provide time and opportunities for teachers to mentor with peers who are trying innovative materials and strategies.

◻ Support teachers in attending local, regional, state, and national conferences to improve their knowledge base, and support continued college coursework for teachers in reading and writing.

◻ Allow/encourage teachers to use alternatives to basal readers or to use basal readers flexibly, eliminating whatever their professional judgment deems unnecessary or inappropriate; for example,

—encourage innovation at a school level, offering teachers a choice of basals, portions of basals, or no basal, using assessment measures that match their choice

—discuss at a school level which portions of the basal need not be used, and use the time saved for reading and discussion of real literature

—provide time for teachers to work with one another to set up innovative programs.

□ Give teachers the opportunity to demonstrate that standardized test scores will generally not be adversely affected by using alternatives to basal readers, and may in fact be enhanced.

□ Provide incentives for teachers to develop and use alternative methods of reading assessment, based upon their understanding of reading and learning to read.

□ Allow/encourage teachers to take charge of their own reading instruction, according to their informed professional judgment.

For Policymakers:

□ Change laws and regulations that favor or require use of basals, so that

—state funds may be used for non-basal materials

—schools may use programs that do not have traditional basal components

—teachers cannot be forced to use material they find professionally objectionable.

□ Provide incentives to local districts to experiment with alternatives to basals, by

—developing state-level policies that permit districts to use alternatives to basals

—changing teacher education and certification requirements so as to require teachers to demonstrate an understanding of how people read, of how children learn to read, and of ways of developing a reading curriculum without as well as with basals

—mandating periodic curriculum review and revision based upon current theory and research as to how people read and how children learn to read

—developing, or encouraging local districts to develop, alternative means of testing and assessment that are supported by current theory and research in how people read and how children learn to read

—funding experimental programs, research, and methods of assessment based upon current theory and research on reading and learning to read.

Prepared for the Commission on Reading of the National Council of Teachers of English by the present and immediate past directors of the Commission, Connie Weaver and Dorothy Watson, and based on the *Report Card on Basal Readers,* written by Kenneth S. Goodman, Patrick Shannon, Yvonne Freeman, and Sharon Murphy and published by Richard C. Owen, Publishers, 1988. See also the Commission on Reading's Position Statement "Report on Basal Readers"; one copy is free upon request from the National Council of Teachers of English if a self-addressed and stamped envelope is sent with the request. Write NCTE, 1111 Kenyon Road, Urbana, IL 61801.

Major Contributions to the Whole Language Movement, 1880s to 1990s

1887	*John A. Comenius* produced the first picture book for children. He wrote about "whole world . . . whole language," in talking about his view of children's learning. He believed that in order to learn children had to enjoy learning.
1890s	*John Dewey* wrote about the issues of relevancy in education and authenticity in learning.
1908	*Edmund Burke Huey* suggested that we won't really know how to teach reading until we study what children do when they are learning how to read, that is, what happens naturally.
1923	*Walter Lippmann* wrote about the importance of visual imagery to the understanding of vicarious experience.
1930s	*John Dewey* said we should place the learner at the center of the classroom curriculum; we are teaching children, not subjects.
1930s	*Louise Rosenblatt* described the learner's transactions with good literature as exploration and experience; the reader creates a new text in the mind, one that is different from that of other readers and the author as well.
1930s	*Alvina T. Burrows* advocated children's expressing themselves in writing from the very beginning of schooling.

1940s	*John Dewey* suggested that the best learning was really the act of inquiry. He also wrote about what education should be like for a democratic society.
1940s	*Jean Piaget* described children as active constructors of their own categories of thought while organizing their understanding of the wrold.
1940s	*Leland Jacobs* wrote about the power of good literature to enrich and shape human lives.
1950s	*Lev Vygotsky* described human learning as social. He pointed out that most of what we learn we learn as we interact with others. He also talked about learning in terms of the "zone of proximal development," that we learn best when we are challenged, when we have to stretch our minds.
1950s	*Noam Chomsky* discovered that language is made up of underlying rules and patterns, and that it is through these rules and patterns that we learn language and are able to communicate.
1960s	*Hilda Taba* wrote about the importance of social interaction and child-centered learning.
1960s	*Eric Lenneberg* wrote that the human brain was built in part for language learning—that there is a biological foundation for human language learning.
1960s	*Alexander Luria* described research that demonstrated the specificity of brain area to function; the human brain is much more complex than a general information-processing organ.
1960s	*Roger Brown* and *Ursula Bellugi* demonstrated that child language learning is highly patterned and consistent. They concluded that during language development children try to figure out the rules and how they work.
1960s	*Sylvia Ashton-Warner* wrote about encouraging children to be responsible for their own learning.
1960s	*Jean Piaget* said that child development research had shown that children were sophisticated learners and information processors, and their higher mental functions and operations so complex that behavioral theory could not account for it.
1960s	*Albert Maslow, Carl Rogers,* and others wrote about the need for schools to use collaborative learning for students to be self-actualized.
1960s	*Kenneth Goodman* conducted his first major research project and discovered that children read about one-third more words correctly in context than they do from a list. He concluded that when we read, we must be using cues other than sound-letter associations alone. He also found that

nearly half of the repetitions children make when reading in context are attempts to self-correct.

1960s	*Kenneth Goodman* wrote an article called "Reading Is a Psycholinguistic Guessing Game."
1960s	*Charlotte Huck* helped teachers know children's literature and how to use it effectively in classrooms.
1960s	*Doris Lee* and *Roach Van Allen* promoted the importance of language experiences for children with language they already used in meaningful ways.
1960s	*Jeanette Veatch* helped popularize the use of trade books and children's choice in school reading programs.
1970s	*Frank Smith* began a series of books that synthesize research findings from various fields. He described what was being discovered about how we learn, comprehend, and perceive.
1970s	*Michael A. K. Halliday* described language learning as learning how to make meaning with language. He suggested that schools must reflect the processes human beings naturally employ to make sense of the world. Halliday also talked about learning as *scaffolding*.
1970s	*Ulrich Neisser* and *David Ausubel* described human learning in terms of the creation of cognitive schema. Their research suggested that human beings categorize and interrelate sensory data in the brain and then use those categories of meaning to make sense of new data.
1970s	*Harold Rosen, Arthur Applebee, Gordon Wells,* and *Nancy Stein* researched and wrote about the effects of being read to and of storytelling on children's language development, on their sense of story, and on their learning to read.
1970s	*The Bullock Report* suggested that schools must concern themselves more with writing and that clearly the writer's intention is of primary importance.
1970s	*Donald Graves* and *Donald Murray* described what good writers do when they write. From their work came our understanding of the writing process.
1972	*Marie Clay* developed big books so groups of children could really "see" the print.
1975	*James Britton* cautioned that writing does not consist of discrete, hierarchical, and measurable steps.
1977	*Jerry Harste* and *Carolyn Burke* wrote that teachers teach from a theoretical base, one of which is whole language.

1978   *Dorothy Watson* established the first teacher support group for whole language teachers (TAWL).

1970s   *Charles Read* found that children's misspellings are patterned and consistent. He concluded that children are trying to figure out the underlying rules of spelling and coined the term *invented spelling*.

1970s   *Frank Smith* told us that research shows that learners acquire knowledge and skills as they do things—just as they learn language by using the language—not by studying about language. Learners must be engaged in active learning, in actively making sense for themselves.

1970s   *Martha King* advocated child-centered, literature-based classrooms.

1970s   *Bill Martin, Jr.,* advocated using high-quality children's literature in school reading programs.

1970s   *Yetta Goodman, Carolyn Burke,* and *Dorothy Watson* developed the Reading Miscue Inventory to research reading and help educators explore the nature of children's reading.

1970s   *Kenneth Goodman* conducted his second and third major research studies. First, he examined readers at grades 2, 4, 6, 8, and 10 and found that children at every grade and age attempt to do the same things when they read. He began to describe the components of the reading process. He also concluded that there must be no hierarchy of skills that all learners go through. Second, he examined the reading of several different linguistic groups and concluded that there is one reading process and that it is the same for all languages and dialects.

1979   *Donald Holdaway* described his lap-reading approach to shared book.

1982   *Emelia Ferreiro* and *Anna Teberosky* confirmed that indeed children play active roles in their own language learning and that they learn both reading and writing in similar ways.

1980s   *Courtney Cazden* found that young children develop considerably more language in enriched or elaborated environments than in restricted or corrected environments.

1980s   *Ulrich Neisser* discovered that worldwide the status of children's cultural group is the primary determinant of school achievement.

1980s   *Paulo Freire* wrote that literacy development is based on oral language and prior knowledge—knowledge about the world—and one can be used to enhance the other.

1980s   *Carole Edelsky* and *Karen Smith* wrote about the roles teachers assume in whole language classrooms.

1980s	*Carole Edelsky* wrote about the importance of authenticity in reading and writing events for children.
1980s	*Brian Cambourne* synthesized and described the natural conditions that best promote learning.
1980s	*Frank Smith* wrote about the importance of engagement with demonstrations as the foundation of literacy development and that learners must come to want to "join the literacy club."
1980s	*Gordon Wells* and others described language learning in terms of collaboration and negotiation of meaning between young language learners (novices) and older more expert language learners.
1980s	*Shirley Brice Heath* wrote that how we use language and how we expect language to mean is culturally determined and differs from one cultural group to another.
1980s	*Ann Brown* contributed her insights about meta-awareness. She told us that the more aware the learner is of the processes involved and the processes he or she is employing, the better the learning tends to be.
1980s	*Dorothy Watson, Yetta Goodman, Jerry Harste, Carole Edelsky, Judith Newman, Lucy Calkins, Lynn Rhodes,* and many others have devoted much effort to helping teachers apply theory to practice and evaluate their practice as they observe children's responses.
1980s and 1990s	*P. David Pearson, Marie Clay, Donald Graves, Rob Tierney, Roger Farr, Peter Johnston,* and others explored process-based evaluation and developed alternatives to standardized tests.
1980s and 1990s	*Yetta Goodman* wrote about the teacher as researcher—whole language teachers as reflective observers and informed decision makers—they learn how to teach because they are "kidwatchers."
1990s	*John Willinsky* wrote about the promise of the new approach to literacy and school learning.
1990s	*Frank Smith* synthesized most current perspectives on how human beings learn and think. He also wrote about the bureaucratic takeover of classrooms.
1990s	*The National Education Association* called for a move toward whole language instruction across the United States.
1990s	*Patrick Shannon, Jonathan Kozol, Michael Apple, Elliot Eisner, John Goodlad, Albert Shanker,* and others wrote about the need for restructuring schools because of the failure of reform to improve education significantly.

REFERENCES

Goodman, K. (1989, November). Whole language research: Foundations and development. *Elementary School Journal, 90*(2), 113–128.

Goodman, Y. (1989, November). Roots of the whole language movement. *Elementary School Journal, 90*(2), 207–221.

Watson, D. (1989, November). Defining and describing whole language. *Elementary School Journal, 90*(2), 129–142.

Index of Authors Cited

Subject Index